The Military in Politics

CHANGING PATTERNS IN BRAZIL

The Military in Politics

CHANGING PATTERNS IN BRAZIL

By Alfred Stepan

PRINCETON UNIVERSITY PRESS

PRINCETON, NEW JERSEY

This book has been composed in Linotype Times Roman
Printed in the United States of America
by Princeton University Press,
Princeton, New Jersey

First Princeton Paperback Edition, 1974
Second Hardcover Printing, 1974

To Nancy

Contents

List of Tables and Figures

TABLES

FIGURES

Acknowledgments

IN THE SIX YEARS since I first became interested in the problem of civil–military relations in Brazil and the writing of this book, many individuals and institutions have helped me. Perhaps my most fundamental obligation is to the over one hundred Brazilian men of public affairs, both civilian and military, who in interviews and conversations provided criticism, commentary, and guidance that gave this book a living dimension.

I am grateful to Professor Cândido Mendes, Director of the *Instituto Universitário de Pesquisas do Rio de Janeiro*, for his comments over the last five years, and for the research assistance Ana Lúcia Malan at the Institute kindly extended me in Brazil. Fernando Pedreira, author of the best analysis of the background to the 1964 Brazilian crisis, *Março 31, Civis e Militares no Processo da Crise Brasileira*, spent literally hundreds of hours talking and arguing Brazilian politics. Without these conversations, many of the nuances and emotions of the key incidents would have remained foreign to me. Brazilian social scientists Alberto Guerreiro-Ramos and Alexandre de Barros made invaluable comments on an earlier draft.

Professor Morris Janowitz read the manuscript and gave me the benefit of his comprehensive knowledge of military institutions. Professor John J. Johnson was generous with advice in the formative stage of the project. From the academic profession also, Albert Fishlow, Robert Packenham, and Thomas Skidmore offered their insights at various stages in the writing.

U.S. army attachés in the U.S. embassy in Rio, General Vernon Walters and Colonel Arthur Moura, through their wide knowledge of Brazil and their willingness to engage in debate and to arrange occasional introductions, aided the study in many ways. From government, Harry Weiner, Elizabeth Hyman, and Everett Burlando made useful comments on previous drafts. It goes without saying, of course, that none of them necessarily agrees with or endorses the views expressed in this book.

An earlier version of the book was submitted as a doctoral dissertation at Columbia University. Professor Juan L. Linz, first as a stimulating teacher at Columbia and now as a valued colleague at Yale, has been of great help in many discussions of comparative politics. Columbia University Professors Douglas Chalmers, Ronald M. Schneider, and Charles Wagley extended intellectual assistance far beyond any formal responsibility and contributed invaluable criticisms.

I am very grateful to The RAND Corporation which, out of its own funds, supported my field research in Brazil and its subsequent development and evolution into a book. The views expressed in this study, however, are mine and do not reflect the opinion or policy of The RAND Corporation or its government, foundation, or private sponsors.

To my great friend, colleague, and occasional coauthor, Dr. Luigi Einaudi, of The RAND Corporation, I owe a very special debt. Much of the intellectual excitement of the last three years has come from his enthusiasm and support. In the initial stages of my research he was most generous not only in sharing data but in discussing research strategies drawn from his own field work on a similar project in Peru. In the final stages of writing, my continuing dialogue with him was a source of intellectual stimulation and an influence for clarity of expression. Other former RAND colleagues, Steven Canby, Alexander George, Herbert Goldhamer, Paul Hammond, Richard Maullin, Guy Pauker, William Quandt, Robert Slighton, and William Stewart, made useful contributions when my forays led me into their specialties. I am indebted also to Joseph Goldsen, who as former head of the social science department had faith in the project in its initial problematical stages, and to Fred Iklé, his successor, who encouraged me to complete it. Also at RAND, Geraldine Petty helped with research and production, Thomas Cockrell with editing, and many with the typing, in particular Susan Turner who typed the first formal draft. Joanna Hitchcock of Princeton University Press was of great assistance in overseeing the transition of the manuscript into a book.

My greatest debt is to my wife, Nancy, who though extremely busy with her own scholarly work, still had the energy and disposition to urge me past the worst moments, discuss ideas at all hours, and be my best editor and critic. I also want to thank my parents, whose warm interest in people and ideas started me on so many journeys.

Undoubtedly all the above institutions, colleagues, and friends will quarrel with part of the work. The final responsibility for the analysis and any factual errors is mine alone.

New Haven, Connecticut
January 1970

The Military in Politics

CHANGING PATTERNS IN BRAZIL

Introduction

CIVILIAN GOVERNMENT broke down in Brazil in 1964, and a military government came to power for the first time in the twentieth century.

In the period just before the military assumed power, I was in Brazil writing a series of articles on Latin America for the *Economist*. The experience of watching a country struggle with great problems and seeing the political system break down provoked many questions: What had been the old pattern of government, and of civil–military relations? Why had the old pattern come to an end? What would be the governing capability of the military and, specifically, what new political problems did the control of government present for the military as an institution?

Six years (and three field trips) later, writing now as a political scientist interested in comparative politics, I have placed these questions at the core of this work. In looking at the Brazilian experience, however, I have attempted to formulate and test some of the implicit and explicit models, propositions, and middle-range hypotheses found in the literature on civil–military relations. The most important areas of investigation have been the following: How do our present models of civil–military relations describe actual patterns? Are there important lacunae in our typologies? If so, what supplementary models are needed? Can we move toward probabilistic propositions concerning the conditions under which the propensity and ability of the military to execute a coup d'etat are increased or decreased? If the military assumes power after a long time in which they have not actually held power, what have been the macro-systemic and micro-political processes by which the political system passes from civilian to military dominance? Once the military has assumed overt control of the political system, what are the capacities and limits of the military to perform the much hypothesized "nation-building" function?

These questions are analyzed in four parts. Part I presents data on the organizational and institutional features of the Brazilian military in a comparative framework, and argues that while such

3

factors are relevant to any analysis of the role of the military in politics, they are almost never determinant. The approach with the most explanatory power is to analyze the military as a subsystem of the overall political system.

Based on these considerations, Part II illustrates the fact that the role of the military as a "moderator" of politics in the Brazilian system before 1964 had roots in civilian perceptions concerning the proper function of the military in society. In this moderating pattern of civil–military relations as it existed until 1964, the military frequently overthrew the executive without, however, actually assuming political power themselves. Comparative analysis of five coups and attempted coups in the period between 1945 and 1964 illustrates the informal rules, underlying assumptions, and the boundaries of the moderating pattern of civil–military relations. Electoral and editorial analysis is used to show that both the propensity of the military to initiate coups against the president and the success of such coups were intimately related to civilian attitudes concerning the appropriateness of such actions at the time.

Part III examines the political processes by which, from 1961 to 1964, during an atmosphere of growing political and economic crisis, the basic assumptions and attitudes supportive of the moderating pattern of civil–military relations were eroded. Components of a new pattern of civil–military relations began to emerge. In this section, general systemic changes, such as increasing socioeconomic mobilization, radicalization of the style of politics, and emergence of groups hitherto at the fringes of the political process, are related to changing attitudes within the officer corps about their proper role in Brazilian society and their function in furthering development. The actual mechanism of the 1964 "revolution" and the decision by the military to assume power are examined as a major boundary change in the political system, in which one pattern of civil–military relations was replaced by another.[1]

Part IV looks at the additional political requirements that are

---

[1] The military describes the coup of 1964 as a "revolution," and I have at times followed their usage in order to distinguish the coup of 1964 from earlier coups because the movement of 1964 resulted in a boundary change. It is clear, however, that the military movement of 1964 did not result in a social revolution. Philippe Schmitter argues, correctly I think, that the 1964 coup was in part a restoration movement endeavoring to reestablish Brazil's semicorporatist structure that had been breaking down in the years leading up to 1964.

4

made upon the military institution in its new role as director of the political system in Brazil. By closely observing a military organization in power, I have tried to assess the theoretical and empirical validity of often-heard arguments that the military's "monopoly of force," "stability," and "organizational strength" make it particularly well suited to resolve problems of development. The Brazilian experience indicates that these hypotheses must be severely qualified, and that the pattern of civil–military relations which the military attempted to impose after 1964 has left the military internally divided, increasingly isolated from civilians, reliant upon torture as a mechanism of political control, and without a creative program of social development.

The focus of this study is broad political change over time. Thus the theme of the study is large in *scope*—the relationship of a sub-system, the military, to the overall political system—and large also in the time period covered, as special attention is given to the events from 1945 to 1968. In the effort to focus on the functioning, change, and capacities of various civil–military models, no attempt has been made to provide a complete narrative of the political history of Brazil in the period, nor a full-bodied study of all facets of the military as an institution in Brazil.[2] My purpose has rather been to examine one country over a fairly long period of time, in

[2] The luxury of being able to focus on basic analytic problems concerning the role of the military in Brazilian society has been made possible by the great progress of scholarly studies, both Brazilian and foreign, of Brazil's recent social and political history. All who study Brazil owe an intellectual debt to them.

These studies have also relieved me of the task of providing a continuous narrative framework for this book. For the non-Portuguese reader, this framework is provided by the following books: Charles Wagley's *An Introduction to Brazil* (New York: Columbia University Press, 1963), an excellent, sensitive guide to the problems, nuances, and literature of contemporary Brazilian social structure; Thomas Skidmore's *Politics in Brazil, 1930–1964* (New York: Oxford University Press, 1967), which performs the invaluable task of presenting recent politics in a coherent framework, while his nearly one hundred pages of bibliographic notes direct the reader to the widely scattered primary and secondary source materials; and John J. Johnson's *The Military and Society in Latin America* (Stanford: Stanford University Press, 1964), which contains a rich and pioneering overview of the role of the Brazilian military in the nineteenth and twentieth centuries. A forthcoming book by Ronald M. Schneider will provide, in exhaustive detail, an analysis of many aspects of the Brazilian military which, because I have developed different themes, I have dealt with only sketchily in this work.

order to analyze the political and economic conditions that either support or erode different patterns of civil–military relations.

Scholars who are especially interested in how I proceeded with such research might turn first to the Appendix, "Researching a Semiclosed Institution—A Note on Sources and Field Techniques."

PART I

The Military in Politics:
The Institutional Background

PART I PRESENTS some factual information about the institutional, organizational, and social background of the Brazilian and other selected military bodies. It is appropriate to begin this study with presentation of such information. It provides institutional perspective for assessing the military's role in politics. Given the relative absence of such hard data in the literature concerning the military in developing countries, analysts all too frequently generalize from scarce or erroneous information, or fall back on drawing deductions from the "ideal type" of military organization. I hope to some extent to fill the lacunae in the case of Brazil and to suggest relevant questions and approaches for other countries as well.

An additional reason for this preliminary discussion of the particular features of the military is to provide background for my later discussion of the military as an integral part of the political system. Concerning military political behavior, it is my opinion that no one factor, whether institutional or otherwise, will have satisfactory explanatory or predictive power when taken alone. A basic argument throughout this work is that, precisely because the military is not isolated from politics but in fact performs diverse political functions, simple descriptions of "ideal" military institutions which may emphasize such features as military unity or national orientation often conceal more than they reveal about the interactions between the military and the political system.

It is necessary to stress the fact that the military is an integral part of the political system because two important schools of military analysis tend to argue implicitly the opposite case. In his astute review of the literature, Lyle McAlister states that the traditional antimilitary school of analysts has viewed the military as "an alien and demonic force which does not interact with other social groups but simply acts against them."[1] The newer, developmental school argues on the other hand that precisely because the military is an isolated institution not afflicted by the divisive allegiances of society in general, it is especially suited to act as a nation-building, modernizing bureaucratic force.[2] Both approaches tend to evaluate military behavior in terms of the military's institutional characteristics.

I feel it is more empirically accurate and theoretically useful to recast the analysis of the role of the military in politics in terms of the military as a political institution, subject to many of the pressures experienced in the polity at large. At the same time, I have used institutional information to try to determine how the military's special institutional characteristics help shape the style, range, and capabilities of its political response to these pressures.

[1] See his "Changing Concepts of the Role of the Military in Latin America," *Annals of the American Academy of Political and Social Science,* ccclx (July 1965), 87.

[2] A comprehensive review of the literature is Lyle N. McAlister, "Recent Research and Writings on the Role of the Military in Latin America," *Latin American Research Review,* xi (Fall 1966), 5–36. He outlines the major opposing propositions found in the literature in "The Military," in *Continuity and Change in Latin America,* ed. John J. Johnson (Stanford: Stanford University Press, 1964), pp. 136–160. I have reviewed the works of John J. Johnson, Edwin Lieuwen, and Robert Gilmore in "The Military's Role in Latin American Political Systems," *Review of Politics,* xxvii (October 1965), 564–568.

Chapter 1

*Military Organizational
Unity and National Orientation:
Hypotheses and Qualifications*

COMPARATIVE ANALYSIS

A classic criticism of the military has been that its codes, hierarchy, uniforms, and barracks set it dangerously apart physically and psychologically from civilian life. Recently, however, a new school of analysts, worried by the problems of national unity and nation-building in developing countries, has emphasized that the military can perform a constructive role in these areas precisely because its training, organization, and national recruitment mission help isolate it from subnational tribal, regional, or political pressures in the polity.

Guy Pauker, in his influential analysis of Southeast Asia, commented on the "habits of discipline, hierarchical organization, and responsible command" of the military. He urged that: "Ways must be found to utilize the organizational strength of the national armies and the leadership potential of their officer corps as temporary kernels of national integration."[1]

An influential exponent of this "neorealist" position in the area of Latin American politics is John J. Johnson. He argued:

> Until responsible civil services emerge, the armed forces as coherent groups of men often will be as competent as any other group concerned with national policy. Furthermore, for the next decade or more, they will on occasion be the most reliable institution to ensure political continuity in their countries. They will, in certain instances, stand as a bulwark of order and security in otherwise anarchical societies.[2]

[1] "Southeast Asia as a Problem Area in the Next Decade," *World Politics*, XI (April 1959), 342.

[2] John J. Johnson, *The Military and Society in Latin America* (Stanford: Stanford University Press, 1964), p. 261.

9

As a group, this school of analysts has helped make political observers sensitive to the fact that under some circumstances the military can make a contribution to development. Clearly, in a country such as Turkey the army has played an important role in nation-building and modernization.[3] In comparison to other elites, the military is often less parochial and more national in orientation.

While recognizing this, I nevertheless feel that both the traditional liberal critics of the military and the modern "neorealists" often overestimate the unitary, self-encapsulated aspects of the military institution, and underemphasize the degree to which a military organization is permeated and shaped by outside political pressures. Obviously the situation will vary from country to country. However, if we examine the question of the military's contribution to national unity, much evidence exists that in many developing countries not only is the military not isolated from the tensions experienced by the general population and therefore not able to act as an integrating force, but the military is itself an element in the polity that may transform latent tensions into overt crises.

The armies of many of the new nations were originally created as instruments of imperial control. As such they were often deliberately constructed with extreme tribal, racial, and religious imbalances.[4] This policy, coupled with the normal differential rates of recruitment based on education and inclination, makes these armies all too often both unrepresentative and explosive. Contrary to the national orientation and national integration hypotheses, the power to "socialize to national identity" of these armies has often been very weak. Primordial sentiments and loyalties frequently express themselves in violence. Three of the most costly civil wars in the newly independent nations had their immediate origins within the military.

In Nigeria a mix of tribal loyalties and intertribal animosities permeated the whole society.[5] As in most new nations the initial

[3] For Turkey, see Dankwart A. Rustow's chapter on the military in *Political Modernization in Japan and Turkey*, ed. Robert E. Ward and Dankwart A. Rustow (Princeton: Princeton University Press, 1964), pp. 352–388.

[4] A listing of some of the more important cases is found in Morris Janowitz, *The Military in the Political Development of New Nations* (Chicago: The University of Chicago Press, 1964), pp. 51–59.

[5] See, e.g., the extremely perceptive article written before the outbreak

10

stages of modernization tended to exacerbate traditional conflicts and intensify primordial sentiments.[6] But they were felt in the army even more strongly because the requirements of cooperation, obedience, and command were more intense within the military than in society at large, and antagonisms were amplified. In addition, the existing tribal imbalances within the officer corps were inherently unstabilizing both because political actors were constantly tempted to interfere with the military hierarchy to shift the military balance of power, and because the dominant tribal group within the military was tempted to use its military power base to change the national political balance. The Ibo tribe of Eastern Nigeria, partly because of its Christianization and superior education, dominated the officer corps after Nigeria attained independence. In 1961, of the 81 Nigerian officers, nearly 60 were Ibos. Most were from the small Ibo heartland of Onitsha.[7] However, the more traditional Muslim tribes in Northern Nigeria dominated the federal political structure. Tensions between the two major groups finally culminated in a wholesale assassination of northern political leaders in a military coup led by Ibo officers.[8] Their action eventually resulted in the secession of Biafra, a civil war, and tremendous loss of life.

Another case where the army has been a major force of instability is Sudan. The Sudanese army has been called the "one African . . . modern military establishment" at the time of independence.[9] Upon independence, however, the officer corps was

---

of actual civil war by Richard L. Sklar, "Contradictions in the Nigerian Political System," *Journal of Modern African Studies*, III, no. 2 (August 1965), 201–213.

[6] A very useful theoretical analysis and empirical description of this general phenomenon is Clifford Geertz, "The Integrative Revolution: Primordial Sentiments and Civil Politics in the New States," in *Old Societies and New States: The Quest for Modernity in Asia and Africa*, ed. Clifford Geertz (New York: The Free Press of Glencoe, 1963), pp. 105–157.

[7] See William Gutteridge, "Military Elites in Ghana and Nigeria," *African Forum*, XI (Summer 1966), 31–41, and his *Military Institutions and Power in the New States* (New York: Praeger, 1965), pp. 105–108.

[8] A detailed account of the tribal aspects of the coup is contained in Martin Kilson, "Behind Nigeria's Revolt: Tribal Power Struggle," *New Leader*, January 31, 1966, pp. 9–12.

[9] James S. Coleman and Belmont Price, Jr., "The Role of the Military in Sub-Saharan Africa," in *The Role of the Military in Underdeveloped Countries*, ed. John J. Johnson (Princeton: Princeton University Press, 1962), p. 366.

almost exclusively composed of Arabs from the north, while the
sergeants and enlisted men were largely non-Arab blacks from the
south. Racial tensions first broke out in a mutiny of black sergeants against their Arab officers in 1955 and later in continuing
guerrilla warfare that had cost an estimated 500,000 lives by
1968.[10]

Indonesia from 1958 to 1961 was also torn by a civil war led
by army elements stationed in Sumatra and the Celebes. In assessing causes for the civil war, one expert observer wrote, "The most
obvious explanation would be that all these senior officers, and their
junior commanders in Sumatra and the Celebes, were fighting for
the 'states rights' of their respective provinces."[11]

As these examples illustrate, one cannot confuse the "ideal type"
of military organization and its presumed unity and insulation
from local politics and sentiments with empirical reality.[12]

BRAZILIAN MILITARY: RECRUITMENT STRUCTURE

The Brazilian military outwardly appears to conform to a national and therefore integrating institution. Indeed, a motto is
stamped on many of the army publications: "The Army—Agent
of National Integration." Its proudest claim is that the army is, in
the words of a minister of war:

> . . . unquestionably a part of the people, perhaps the most rep-
> resentative of the people, because within its ranks the classes
> mix, the social standards become the same, the creeds and
> political parties are ignored, differentiation and inequality among

[10] See Lawrence Fellows, "The Unknown War for the Sudan," *New York
Times*, September 22, 1968.

[11] Guy J. Pauker, "The Military in Indonesia," in Johnson, *Role of the
Military*, p. 212.

[12] A subject needing further study is to what extent the unbalanced tribal
or regional composition of many military institutions creates difficulties for
the military in regard to their capacity to govern effectively. In Pakistan,
for example, the fact that nearly 95 percent of both officers and enlisted
men in the early 1960s came from West Pakistan was a source of weakness
in regard to the military's ability to apply martial law in East Pakistan. (The
above datum comes from an unpublished MS on the political role of the
Pakistan military by Richard Sisson, Professor of Political Science, University of California at Los Angeles.) In Brazil in São Paulo, hostility to
the young military modernizers (*tenentes*) in the early 1930s was based
partly on the fact that virtually none of the *tenentes* were natives of São
Paulo.

12

men are forgotten. . . . The Army . . . has been since the beginning of the Nation the great armor which sustained the unity of the Homeland, preserving it from threats of fragmentation, assuring the cohesion of that archipelago of provinces that tended to become isolated, each with its own peculiarities.[13]

Undoubtedly, the army and the navy played a major role in suppressing the regional revolts that rocked Brazil between 1824 and 1848.[14] Other undeniable contributions were the army's roles in linking the country by road-building and in establishing settlements in the previously almost unpopulated areas of the vast hinterland.[15] But today how strong is the army's ability to inculcate a sense of national identification in its members? Is it exclusively a nationally oriented institution, or is it also strongly influenced by local factors? Does the ideal-type image obscure important aspects of the political behavior of the military?

To attempt to answer the question for Brazil, I have first analyzed the military draft structure. Evidence indicates that the claim to be a "melting pot," in which distinct regional and social characteristics disappear, is a gross oversimplification. The recruitment policy of the Brazilian army has traditionally been that of drafting men from an area *as close as possible to each garrison*, the vast majority of which are located in urban areas. In practice, this means that most of the draftees are urban and they serve in a unit less than ten miles from their homes and families. Additional factors inhibiting socialization to a national perspective or to army standards are that draftees are normally released after serving nine months of their year of obligated service and, while on active duty, normally return to their homes every weekend. Quite often, indeed, recruits eat lunch and spend their nights at their family's home during their period of service in the army.[16]

[13] General A. de Lyra Taveres, *The Brazilian Army* (Guanabara, Brazil: EGGCF, 1967), pp. 3, 6.

[14] An excellent bibliographic guide to these regional revolts can be found in Stanley L. Stein, "The Historiography of Brazil, 1808–1889," *Hispanic American Historical Review*, XL (May 1960), 234–278.

[15] Characteristic contemporary assessments by the army of its role in national integration are: Brasil, Ministério da Guerra, Coronel Octávio Costa, *Exército: Fator de Integração Nacional* (Rio de Janeiro: Imprensa do Exército, 1967); and Tavares, *The Brazilian Army*. Numerous references to the Brazilian military's contribution to national integration can be found in Johnson, *The Military and Society in Latin America*, pp. 177–243.

[16] This assessment is based on personal observation and on conversations

13

These recruitment policies are formalized in army regulations. The major reason for local recruitment seems to be a desire to eliminate the considerable cost of transportation involved in taking a recruit from his home for a short stay in a different geographical area. Because Brazil has no organized reserve, local recruitment also increases the likelihood that a recruit will reside near the unit in which he formerly served, making it easy for the unit to call him up in an emergency. A third reason for the recruitment policy is a deliberate attempt to slow the rural exodus by not drafting rural recruits to serve in urban garrisons and thus risking the possibility that they would not return to the countryside upon completion of their military service.[17]

What of the career-enlisted men and officers? Do they conform more closely to the image of the professional military man as encapsulated in a national institution without real links to his region of origin in what S. E. Finer termed the military's "systematized nomadism moving from one garrison town to another"?[18]

On the whole, one must answer in the negative. Family ties are still very important in Brazil. In addition, military pay scales are low. In order to avoid high costs for transportation to visit families and for other personal reasons, many officers, if they are not attending service schools or serving in army headquarters in Rio, prefer to be stationed close to their families. For example, Brazil's strongest army, the Third Army, headquartered in the state of Rio Grande do Sul, is predominantly made up of natives of the state. It is estimated that in the Third Army units in Rio Grande do Sul all the draftees, 95 percent of the career corporals, 70 to 80 percent of the sergeants, and 50 to 60 percent of the officers are from the state of Rio Grande do Sul.[19] Thus the national army of Brazil

---

with garrison commanders and draftees during visits to numerous garrisons. Eating at home is encouraged because it saves the local garrison money on food rations.

[17] Some aspects of the policy are discussed in Brasil, Ministério da Guerra, Coronel Hygino de Barros Lemos, *O Exército e o Êxodo Rural* (Rio de Janeiro: Biblioteca do Exército, 1959). The reasons behind the recruitment policy were explained to me by the then chief of the Brazilian army schools, General Idalio Sardenberg, Rio de Janeiro, September 11, 1967.

[18] *The Man on Horseback: The Role of the Military in Politics* (London: Pall Mall Press, 1962), p. 9.

[19] These rough estimates were given to me by the Chief of Army Schools, General Idalio Sardenberg, in Rio de Janeiro, September 11, 1967, and by the Public Relations Officer of the Third Army in Pôrto Alegre, Rio Grande

has some of the recruitment characteristics of a state militia, since it is largely manned by soldiers from the immediate area. Another feature of the federal army also reduces its nation-building potential. Brazil, with a population of 90 million, has far more draftable men than it needs. Indeed, as in many developing countries, the problem quite often becomes one of establishing criteria for selecting draftees.[20] As a result of excess supply, the army can afford to be very selective in recruiting draftees. Their choice lies between either emphasizing the nation-building role of the army by deliberately drafting a cross section of the population or satisfying army requirements for skilled and literate draftees who can rapidly develop some degree of technical military competence.

Official Brazilian publications often make allusions to massive numbers of illiterates who enter the army each year and are released only when they have become literate. The barracks are said to be "huge classrooms" within which the men of the countryside are given their first exposure to modernity.[21] This is rarely the case. Analysis shows that faced with the choice between educating rural illiterates and drafting already trained men, the Brazilian army chooses the latter alternative. This is acknowledged in an official but little-known publication which explains and documents that the army prefers to select

> youths from urban centers, since they are better able by their occupations and self-confidence to adapt themselves to the needs of military life; city youths have a higher literacy rate and provide an economic saving on transportation. . . . The armed organizations are not interested [in drafting] men from the rural areas because they are in general illiterate and unskilled. The

---

do Sul, September 23, 1968. The state of Rio Grande do Sul is overrepresented in the officer corps as a whole, and I doubt that the other armies are so heavily staffed with locally born officers. The Second Army, headquartered in São Paulo, is the least heavily staffed with locally born officers because São Paulo has historically had a low rate of officer recruitment and a high rate of resignations.

[20] William Gutteridge says that recruit squads in Ghana often have 40 applicants for every place. He cites similar problems of excess supply and the necessity of constructing criteria for admission in Malaya, Nigeria, and Sierra Leone. See Gutteridge, *Military Institutions*, pp. 74–79.

[21] See, e.g., Brasil, Ministério da Guerra, General Aurélio de Lyra Tavares, *O Serviço Militar Como Elemento de Uma Política de Valorização do Brasileiro* (Rio de Janeiro: Imprensa do Exército, 1961), and Brasil, *Exército: Fator de Integração Nacional*.

15

short duration of military service and the requirements of the military necessitate that those who are selected are already literate and have some technical training.[22]

My own visits to numerous garrisons generally confirm this picture. In Brazil, there is no centralized mechanism of recruitment. Each unit, in conjunction with a few local government officials, drafts its own recruits from its immediate geographical area. Whether to choose illiterates or not becomes a matter of the personal preference and professional needs of unit commanders. As one officer said to me: "We don't have to take any illiterates because sufficient literates are of draft age. We accept illiterates as our quota of sacrifice." How high is the normal quota? The commandant of the First Battalion of Light Combat Cars in Santa Angelo, Rio Grande do Sul, said that while his immediate area of recruitment was 40 percent illiterate, his unit was only 4 percent illiterate because he needed literate recruits to handle the technical equipment.[23] Similarly, in the Third Infantry Division, a staff officer stated that, in an artillery regiment of 220 men, there were only three illiterates. The infantry, which was less technical, could afford more illiterates and had about 10 percent.[24] The commander of a coastal artillery battery in Rio de Janeiro, in an informal conversation, commented that almost all the recruits he selected were high school graduates, both because they were better trained, and, as the group of young men most hostile to the military, he felt it would be useful if they were exposed to the military institution and had an opportunity to realize that the army was identified with the interests of the people.[25]

The chief of schools for the Brazilian army was equally candid in an interview:

We draft only a small percentage of draft-age people. We try

[22] Brasil, *O Exército e o Êxodo Rural*, pp. 8, 10. The Director of the Brazilian Naval Academy, Admiral Alvaro de Rezende Rocha, said that only literates were accepted as enlisted men in the navy. Interview during visit to *Escola Naval*, Rio de Janeiro, September 19, 1968.

This translation is the author's, as are all other translations in this book, unless otherwise noted.

[23] Interview, Santa Angelo, Rio Grande do Sul, September 25, 1968.

[24] Interview, Santa Maria, Rio Grande do Sul, September 24, 1968.

[25] Informal conversation, September 18, 1968, Rio de Janeiro. It should be noted that in this area there is an especially high concentration of high school graduates. Nonetheless, there are also many slum-dwellers.

16

to select draftees who are the best of the group. I believe illiterates form less than 5 percent of the total.[26]

THE POLITICAL SIGNIFICANCE OF THE BRAZILIAN RECRUITMENT STRUCTURE

It is clear that an army organized on a local basis, with an exclusive system of recruitment that favors the literate over the illiterate, the urban over the rural, cannot bring ordinary soldiers from different geographical and educational sectors of Brazil into face-to-face cooperation in a nationally oriented institution. The hypothesis, therefore, that the recruitment structure of the military makes a major contribution to nation-building needs to be seriously qualified.

In fact, a locally recruited army in a federal system of politics has some serious political implications. Brazil has many political disputes which involve conflicts between individual states and the central government. In addition, many of the individual states have strong state military police forces, normally called militias even though they are full time. São Paulo, for example, had a French military mission for most of the 1906–1924 period and in the late 1920s was building a strong air arm. In the classic period of the "Old Republic," between 1894 and 1930, its state militia normally outnumbered federal troops garrisoned in the state by ten to one. In 1965 the size of the state militia in São Paulo was over 30,000 men. This state militia still has light armored personnel carriers with machine guns. It continues to outnumber federal troops stationed in the state, although the ratio has diminished. In 1965 it was estimated that the state militia of Rio Grande do Sul had a force of 15,000 men, Minas Gerais over 13,000, and Guanabara 13,000.[27]

[26] Interview, General Idalio Sardenberg, Rio de Janeiro, September 11, 1967. I feel this figure is too low, and that the actual percentage of illiterates among the draftees is probably closer to 10. At any rate even the figure of 10 percent significantly underrepresents the probable 35 to 45 percent of the draft-age males who are illiterate. For estimates on Brazilian literacy rates see, UNESCO, *Statistical Yearbook: 1965*, p. 40.

[27] The political history of the state militias is one of the major gaps in the social science literature on Brazil. A very short journalistic treatment is "Polícia: Tradição é o seu traço comum," *Visão*, November 5, 1965, pp. 57–58. A flat official institutional history of the São Paulo militia is Capitão Luiz Sebastião Malvasio, *História da Fôrça Pública* (São Paulo: Fôrça Pública do Estado de São Paulo, 1967). The official history of the militia

17

Since 1964, the successive military governments have attempted to tighten army control over the militias. Before 1964, these militias were largely commanded by the governors of the states.[28] Equipment routinely includes rifles, machine guns, trucks, occasional armored personnel carriers and some light mortars. Judged by fire power alone, the state militias have not been a match for the federal army since the 1930 revolution curtailed their equipment and autonomy. But since they were often the armed representatives of powerful state governors, at least until 1964, and since the federal army itself had a territorial recruitment base, the state militias nonetheless presented a periodic *political* and psychological threat to the national army. The local base of the national army, together with the fact that state politicians have been armed through state militias, has several times precipitated a crisis of loyalty that fragmented entire sections of the national army. In the conflicts of 1930, 1932, and 1961, armed civil war either occurred or seemed imminent.

In each case, a strong governor or state leader was initially in conflict with the national army. The state leaders were all backed by their state militias. In all three cases there was sustained "psychological warfare" in which appeals were made to local loyalties of federal troops, as against national loyalty to the federal army.

In 1930, when Getúlio Vargas, the governor of Rio Grande do Sul, was defeated in a disputed presidential election, his partisans began to organize for civil war. Local newspapers began a campaign aimed at neutralizing the federal army in the state. Various

---

of Minas Gerais is quite informative about its role in political crises; see Coronel Geraldo Tito Silveira, *Crônica da Política Militar de Minas* (Belo Horizonte: Imprensa Oficial do Estado de Minas Gerais, 1966). Coronel Aldo Ladiera Ribeiro of the militia of Rio Grande do Sul is writing a multivolume, *Esbôço Histórico da Brigada Militar*. Budgetary information on the state militias is contained in the state budgets. Many of the militias publish magazines on a regular basis.

Comparative figures on the size of the state militias and the size of the federal troops garrisoned in each state during the "Old Republic" are found in Brasil, Ministère de l'Agriculture, Industrie et Commerce, Direction Genérale de Statistique, *Annuaire Statistique du Brasil*, première année (1908–1912), I, 228–248.

[28] In the periods of authoritarian and centralizing rule from 1937 to 1945 and from 1964 to the time of writing the central government took a series of steps aimed at reducing state control of the military. It remains to be seen how lasting the current measures will be if Brazil returns to open democratic politics.

state slogans were used, such as "gauchos do not fight against gauchos." When the uprising began, the Third Army fell apart. Large sections of it eventually joined the rebels. A federal commander acknowledged that appeals made by the families of the soldiers "without doubt contributed to the conversion of many."[29]

Similiarly, in the counterrevolution of 1932 led by the state of São Paulo, federal garrisons near the city capitulated to the rebels and militia forces without a shot being fired. Months of discussion among the ranks had made it clear that the soldiers were reluctant to fight against their fellow *Paulistas* in the state militias, especially to defend a cause about which they had doubts.[30]

In 1961, after the resignation of President Jânio Quadros, the three military ministers attempted to block Vice-President João Goulart's assumption of the presidency. Goulart was a native of Rio Grande do Sul. His fiery brother-in-law, Brizola, was the governor of the state. Brizola, with strong support from the state militia and the people, declared the state in complete opposition to the ministers of the federal armed forces. The commander of the Third Army in the state had not originally taken a position in the conflict, but as civilian resistance grew, the loyalty of his troops wavered. He sent a telegram to the military ministers, declaring he would not follow their orders because it would precipitate a civil war.[31] The military ministers capitulated because the rest of the army refused to march against the Third Army on the grounds that public opinion was strongly against the military ministers.[32]

Contrary to the suggestion that the national army is relatively immune to regional and local influences, these three cases reveal that in times of great political crisis, especially in a crisis involving regional claims, state leaders have been most successful in using state militias and the rhetoric of regionalism to win over or effectively neutralize whole segments of the national army. Clearly,

[29] See General Gil de Almeida, *Homens e Factos de Uma Revolução* (Rio de Janeiro: Calvino Filho, 1934), p. 188 and *passim*. Also see Jordan Young, "Military Aspects of the 1930 Brazilian Revolution," *Hispanic American Review*, XLIV, (May 1964), 180–196.

[30] See the account by a major military leader of the rebels, Euclides Figueiredo, *Contribução para a História da Revolução Constitucionalista de 1932* (São Paulo: Livraria Martins, 1954), *passim*.

[31] See the excerpts from the Command Diary of the Third Army reproduced in the Rio weekly, *O Cruzeiro*, December 2, 1961.

[32] Interview with a key military figure of the 1961 crisis, Marshal Oswaldo Cordeiro de Farias, Rio de Janeiro, September 27, 1968.

19

the examples illustrate that to study the role of the Brazilian or any other army adequately, one cannot proceed from the proposition that the army, because of its mission and organization, is exclusively a nationally oriented and unified institution. Instead, as this and the following chapter show, there is a constant need to evaluate military institutional characteristics within the larger framework of the overall political system.

Chapter 2

The Size of the Military:
Its Relevance
for Political Behavior

No SINGLE FACTOR, institutional or otherwise, taken in isolation can explain or predict the political behavior of the military. To illustrate the pitfalls of any such single factor analysis, and the need for a broader and more functional approach to the study of the military, I examine briefly, in a comparative perspective, the presumed influence of the size of the military in determining its role in society.

The numerical size of the military establishment in relation to the size of the civilian population in a country has often been treated as an independent variable that directly affects civilian–military relations. A classic formulation of this thesis is de Tocqueville's:

> In spite of all precautions, a large army amidst a democratic people will always be a source of great danger; the most effectual means of diminishing that danger would be to reduce the army.[1]

Reasoning of this sort is the basis of the often-heard statement that if the countries of Latin America and other developing countries had smaller armies, they would have a greater chance of stable democracy. This assumption—that military rule is a function of size—was likewise at the heart of many predictions about the military's role in Africa. Edward Shils, for example, asserted that while circumstances might incline the new states of sub-Saharan Africa toward oligarchy, "they are not threatened, however, by military usurpation because they scarcely have any military forces. They certainly have no indigenous military elite."[2] Yet one of the

[1] Alexis de Tocqueville, *Democracy in America* (New York: Schocken Books, 1961), II, 324.
[2] "The Military in the Political Development of the New States," in *The Role of the Military in the Underdeveloped Countries*, ed. John J. Johnson (Princeton: Princeton University Press, 1962), p. 54.

21

first coups in sub-Saharan Africa was in the Togo Republic, the country with the smallest army (200 men) of any new nation.[3] Another commentator, W. F. Gutteridge, the author of the standard account of the African armies, also made size a key variable.

While the armed forces of Africa remain small in proportion to the total populations and to the areas of the countries . . . they are unlikely to be able to consolidate their positions and establish military regimes. . . . This is almost certainly the answer to those who pose the question of the possibility of military coups in Nigeria or more particularly in Ghana. . . .[4]

He was sharply disproved in his expectations when Ghana and Nigeria experienced military coups in 1966.

In Latin America especially, it is heard that size of the armies is a basic cause of instability. However, the African examples suggest that where the overall political system is weak, or lacks legitimacy in the eyes of major participants, the military, no matter how small, will be able to overthrow the government. Indeed, several Latin American instances indicate that even if virtually no army exists, civilian dissension can create governmental instability. Venezuela, for example, is often referred to as the classic case of "militarism." No elected president finished his term until 1964. Yet in fact, in the nineteenth century, the military institution was extremely weak and often numbered less than a thousand. The entire army was dismissed in 1872 and 1876. The weakness of the national polity was so severe, however, that armed civilian bands led by provincial *caudillos* often assumed the central governing power of the state.[5]

[3] For a chart giving basic data on the armed forces of the new nations shortly after independence, see Morris Janowitz, *The Military in the Political Development of New Nations* (Chicago: The University of Chicago Press, 1964), pp. 20–21.

[4] *Military Institutions and Power in the New States* (New York: Praeger, 1965), pp. 143–144. The above two quotes are also cited in the excellent article by David C. Rapoport, "The Political Dimensions of Military Usurpation," *Political Science Quarterly*, LXXXIII (December 1968), 556.

[5] An excellent study of civilian armed behavior is Robert L. Gilmore, *Caudillism and Militarism in Venezuela, 1810–1910* (Athens, Ohio: Ohio University Press, 1964), esp. pp. 49–159. One of the most famous Latin American formulations of the argument that, because civilian anarchy is always imminent due to conflicts in the society, "democratic Caesarism" is the most viable form of government was written by a Venezuelan, Laureano Vallenilla Lanz, *Cesarismo democrático. Estudios sobre las bases*

Another interesting case in point is Bolivia. In 1952 Bolivia had one of the few fundamental social revolutions in Latin American history. Many of the officers were dismissed, and the size of the army was greatly reduced.[6] As revolutionary unity declined, presidents rebuilt the military as a counterweight to the still armed tin miners who had been part of the original revolutionary coalition. In 1964, after a period of growing political strife, this army overthrew the man most responsible for rebuilding it, President Paz Estenssoro.[7] The point is that governmental instability was more responsible for the size of the military than the size of the military was responsible for governmental instability.

Indeed, the persistence of governmental instability in Latin America has helped create the impression that the military itself is relatively large. This is erroneous. A recent comparison ranking the size of 88 military establishments in relation to total population includes 19 of the 20 Latin American countries. No Latin American country ranked in the top quarter, and only three were in the second quarter.[8]

Turning to an analysis of the Latin American countries themselves, what, if any, relationships exist between the size of the military and military intervention, if we attempt to test the hypothesis quantitatively?

Joseph E. Loftus, in his study of the size and expenditures of the Latin American armies, estimated the size of the military establishment in each country in 1955, 1960, and 1965. If the average for each country is divided by the total population for

---

sociológicas de la constitución efectiva de Venezuela, 3rd ed. (Caracas: Garrido, 1952).

[6] Because the military academy was temporarily closed down, numerous references are found which allude to the "disbanding" of the military after the revolution. Actually less than half of the entire officer corps was dismissed. Also, those officers who had been dismissed previously for cooperating with the Villarroel regime were reincorporated. (Informal conversation with Victor Paz Estenssoro, president of Bolivia, 1952–1956, 1960–1964, in Los Angeles, April 18, 1969.)

[7] See William H. Brill, Military Intervention in Bolivia: The Overthrow of Paz Estenssoro and the MNR, Political Studies, no. 3 (Washington: Institute for the Comparative Study of Political Systems, 1967).

[8] See Bruce M. Russett, et al., World Handbook of Political and Social Indicators (New Haven: Yale University Press, 1964), pp. 74–76. The same book also reveals that, in regard to expenditure on defense as a percentage of GNP, no Latin American country ranked in the top 30 of the 83 countries listed, pp. 79–80.

23

these years, it is possible to rank-order the variable of military personnel per capita for each of the 20 countries.[9]

Measurement of military intervention is intrinsically more difficult and any result will at best be impressionistic. With this important caveat in mind, we will use Robert D. Putnam's "military intervention index" for Latin America, which rates each country on a scale from zero to three each year according to the degree of military intervention in the political system. By totalling the sums for each country between 1951 and 1965, we can get a military intervention score.[10] Construction of these variables makes it possible to do a Spearman rank correlation to determine what relationship, if any, exists between the size of the military as a percentage of the population and military intervention. The coefficient of correlation between the two variables is a very low 0.153, indicating no significant detectable relationship.[11] The scattergram displaying metric rather than ranked values confirms an essentially random pattern (see Fig. 2.1). The most striking "anomaly" is that of Chile. It has the second largest military establishment in relation to its population yet one of the lowest military intervention scores. In that case, factors stemming from the political system itself are dominant and the correlation between size and activism is the exact reverse of that often hypothesized. Conversely, a country such as El Salvador has the eighth smallest army in pro-

[9] *Latin American Defense Expenditures, 1938–1965* (Santa Monica, Calif.: The RAND Corporation, RM-5310-PR/ISA, January 1968), Appendix D, pp. 86–99. Latin American population estimates for these years are from the *Statistical Abstract of Latin America: 1965* (Los Angeles: University of California, Latin American Center, 1966), pp. 10–11.

[10] See his "Toward Explaining Military Intervention in Latin America," *World Politics*, xx (October 1967), 83–110. This is an interesting and suggestive article but taken as a whole it probably places too much faith on the reliability and significance of exclusively quantitative indicators. For an attempt to construct a constitutionality index from 1935 to 1964 see Martin C. Needler, *Political Development in Latin America: Instability, Violence, and Evolutionary Change* (New York: Random House, 1968), pp. 81–86.

[11] Using a somewhat different time-frame and different population datum Putnam arrived at an even lower figure of 0.07. I prefer my figure because he uses only one year for his estimate of size of military and size of population. Also, he uses the estimate contained in Russet, *et al., Political and Social Indicators*, pp. 74–76, that Mexico has the highest ratio of military personnel to total population in Latin America. All other reliable sources that I have checked place it near the bottom of the 20 Latin American countries. Since Mexico has one of the lowest military intervention scores, this has skewed Putnam's figure downward.

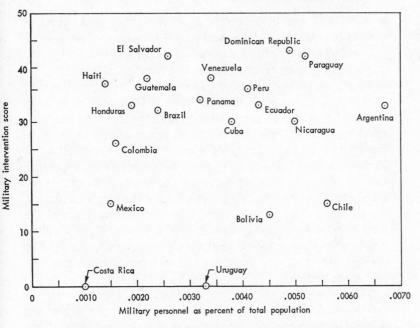

FIG. 2.1 SCATTERGRAM OF RELATIONSHIP BETWEEN MILITARY PERSONNEL AS PERCENTAGE OF TOTAL POPULATION AND MILITARY INTERVENTION FOR ALL LATIN AMERICAN COUNTRIES, 1951–1965

SOURCES: See footnotes 8, 9, and 10 of this chapter.

portion to its population in the whole of Latin America. Yet only the Dominican Republic had a higher score on military intervention.

In Brazil a longitudinal approach to the question of army size and military intervention does not add any further support to the general hypothesis that military intervention is a function of the large size of the military but rather indicates the importance of political factors such as legitimacy. From independence in 1822 until 1889, Brazil was almost unique among Latin American countries in that there were no military governments, largely because the monarchy provided a legitimacy formula that was compatible with and acceptable to dominant social and economic groups within the country.[12] The army represented 0.72 percent of the popula-

[12] For a perceptive, more detailed discussion of the sources of stability during the monarchy see Richard M. Morse, "Some Themes of Brazilian History," *South Atlantic Quarterly*, LXI (Spring 1962), 159–182. Also see

tion in 1824 and 0.30 percent in 1851, during those years of civilian control; but it represented only 0.17 percent of the population in 1894, as it finished a period of military government.

Moving to the immediate present, in 1968 the total military force in Brazil, which included the air force and the navy, was approximately 234,000 men. Of these roughly 39,000 were in the navy and 28,000 in the air force, with 167,000 in the army. Roughly speaking, there exists a total of 20,000 career officers in the three branches of service in Brazil, of whom 13,373 are army officers.[13] In this recent period of sharp dispute over an acceptable legitimacy formula in Brazil, of rising economic and social loads on the political system, and of the first military rule in the twentieth century, the Brazilian army in 1968 represented only 0.18 percent of the total population in Brazil, estimated in that year at 89,376,000. This contrasts with the substantially higher percentage of 0.72 in the first half of the nineteenth century, in a period of civilian control of the country.

The argument in this chapter has been that political variables are frequently far more important for determining the role of the military in society than the absolute size of the armed forces. Even if we discuss merely the numbers of military men, it is extremely important to disaggregate this figure and examine such questions as the dispersion of the military, which units are strategically located in terms of internal political power, which units are best equipped and therefore have a comparative advantage over other units, and what is the command and control relationship between different units. I propose to touch briefly on these factors in the case of Brazil, for they are all important for later discussions.

Because of its institutionalized participation in political events

---

Alfred Stepan, "The Continuing Problem of Brazilian Integration: The Monarchical and Republican Periods," in *Latin American History: Select Problems—Identity, Integration, and Nationhood*, ed. Frederick B. Pike (New York: Harcourt, Brace & World, 1969), pp. 259–296.

[13] The figures for the air force and navy are necessarily approximate since official figures on the size of these two branches of the armed force in Brazil have not been released. The figures here are the estimates most often cited publicly by knowledgeable Brazilians. The army figures come from the official army publication, Brasil, Ministério do Exército, *Efetivos do Exército: Exposição do Ministro do Exército ao Senado Federal* (Rio de Janeiro: Imprensa do Exército, 1968). A detailed discussion of the sources for estimating the size of all Latin American armed forces is contained in Loftus, *Latin American Defense Expenditures, 1938–1965*.

and its geographical dispersion throughout the country, as well as because of its comparatively greater size, the Brazilian army has been the most politically powerful of the three services in the twentieth century. Its activity, rather than the navy's or air force's, has been decisive in the civil–military crises of 1930, 1945, 1954, 1955, 1961, and 1964. Different branches of the army also have different political weight in Brazil. The army is divided into four major territorial commands, with the First Army headquartered in Rio de Janeiro, the Second Army in São Paulo, the Third in Pôrto Alegre, and the Fourth in Recife in the northeast. Historically, the First and Third Armies have been the most important. The importance of the First Army is due to its location in the political center of Rio. For internal, political reasons many of the best equipped elite forces have traditionally been stationed in the *Vila Militar* just outside Rio. The Third Army, in Pôrto Alegre, owes its importance to the fact that it is situated near the border of two of Brazil's historic enemies, Paraguay and Argentina. As a result, the Third Army is larger and better equipped than either the Fourth Army in the northeast or the Second Army in São Paulo. The recruitment base of the Third Army is largely from Rio Grande do Sul, and Rio Grande do Sul's central role in national politics since the late 1920s also places the Third Army in a position of prominence.

In 1968, the great bulk of the Brazilian armed forces were located in the Rio area and in Rio Grande do Sul. As the military government's concern over counterinsurgency has grown, the army has initiated a policy called "operation presence," in which military units are to be spread out more evenly across the entire nation, especially into potential insurgent areas, so that a military presence is established everywhere. By this policy, the military hopes to discourage by its mere presence any revolutionary activity that may exist, or suppress it if necessary. This policy has been strongly encouraged by the United States.[14]

In fact, although "operation presence" is new, the geographical dispersion of the army has always been important in Brazil and has always reflected political as much as strategic considerations. Unlike in the United States, where tactical units such as the di-

[14] Interviews with various senior officers. References to this policy are found in General A. de Lyra Tavares, *A Ação do Exército no Programa do Governo* (Rio de Janeiro: Imprensa do Exército, 1968), pp. 18–31.

vision are kept together for training purposes, a division in Brazil is often subdivided into regiments and battalions which are scattered over a hundred mile radius or more. One of the historical reasons for this splitting up of units is that it extends the capability of the armed forces to control the population. Given the wide physical separation of units, however, the loyalty of local units is often open to question during times of great national political conflict, since the geographical scatter weakens the command links of the army. Senior commanders of divisions or whole armies often have very few troops under their operational command. This means that middle-level officers commanding the regiments and battalions are often extremely important politically. For example, in the 1964 movement that overthrew President Goulart, the decision of the colonel commanding the Fourth Infantry Regiment in Osasco was considered by some key military and political activists to be just as important as the decision of the general in charge of the entire Second Army in determining the military balance of power in the São Paulo region. This was because the regiment of less than 1,300 men was the largest single body of combat troops in the area that could be mobilized at any one time.[15]

The wide distribution of units and consequent dispersion of effective decision-making power in the Brazilian army also explains why there is a need for broad political consensus within the army before the army can initiate decisive political action against an elected president. Because of the virtual operational autonomy of many regiments, divisional and army commanders run the very real risk of having their orders disobeyed unless they have first sounded out opinion among middle-level officers. As we see in later chapters, in the explosive situations during the 1961 and 1964 civil–military crises, this factor was crucial. In the internal military crises of 1965 and 1968, this command structure facilitated the imposition of authoritarian (hard-line) demands by captains, majors, and colonels on the generals in charge of the military government.

This digression into the effect of the geographical and power distribution of the Brazilian armed forces on the political activity of military officers has been made to illustrate once again the importance of multi-factor analyses of the military and its role in politics. This is not to argue, of course, that size is not one factor,

[15] Interview with Colonel Antonio Lepiane, Commander of the Fourth Infantry Regiment, Second Army, Osasco, São Paulo, September 2, 1968.

among many, that plays a part in determining political roles. The existence of a large aggregation of 20,000 military officers in Brazil, with a common occupational speciality, mode of organization, and pay scale does, of course, make the officers a political force that at the very minimum acts as a pressure group, although never a totally united one. How this officer group is formed and how it has responded to Brazilian politics is the subject of the next chapter.

Chapter 3

*Social Origins and Internal
Organization of the Officer Corps:
Their Political Significance*

THE DATA

Who are the Brazilian army officers? How much can be learned about their political behavior by studying the social origins and internal organization of the officer corps?

In Latin America there has been much discussion about such questions, yet virtually no hard aggregate data exist on the socioeconomic origins of the officers.[1] Only after these have been established for particular countries can we attempt to evaluate their significance.[2] Fortunately I was able to obtain limited access to the files of the Brazilian Army Academy (*Academia Militar das Agulhas Negras*, AMAN), which contain information on the socioeconomic status of the fathers of incoming cadets.[3] Unlike in the

---

[1] The most notable exception is José Luis de Imaz's data on senior officers in Argentina in his *Los Que Mandan* (Buenos Aires: Editorial Universitaria de Buenos Aires, 1964), pp. 45–84. Luigi Einaudi's research on the Peruvian military will provide useful data for Peru. The fathers' occupations for one class at the Mexican military academy is given in Javier Romero, *Aspectos psicobiométricos y sociales de una muestra de la juventud mexicana* (Mexico City: Dirección de Investigaciones Antropológicas, 1, 1956), pp. 13–15, 45–51, cited in Lyle N. McAlister, "The Military," in *Continuity and Change in Latin America*, ed. John J. Johnson (Stanford: Stanford University Press, 1964), pp. 145, 264.

[2] Socioeconomic origins as a determinant of political behavior are central to José Nun's argument in "The Middle-Class Military Coup," in *The Politics of Conformity in Latin America*, ed. Claudio Véliz (New York: Oxford University Press, 1967), pp. 66–118, and to John J. Johnson's *The Military and Society in Latin America* (Stanford: Stanford University Press, 1964), esp. pp. 105–107, 250–251.

[3] After various unsuccessful attempts to piece together data from sources such as academy graduation year-books and Brazil's *Who's Who*, and to gain more direct access to military personnel files, I was introduced to the commandant of the military academy by the commandant of the army General Staff School (ECEME). I was especially fortunate in that the com-

United States, there are no lateral sources of nonacademy entrance for regular line officers, and thus the data from the files present a complete profile of all incoming regular officers (except for nonline officers like doctors and some engineering specialists).

Table 3.1 gives the fathers' occupations for *all* cadets entering the Brazilian Army Academy in 1941, 1942, and 1943. Table 3.2 provides the same information for the five-year period between 1962 and 1966. Exact categorization of social class on the basis of job title is impossible. The academy files contain only broad categories such as "military" and "civil servant." The upper ranks of these undoubtedly have a traditional upper-class life style and the lower ranks that of the skilled lower class. Nonetheless in the tables I have attempted to indicate rough trends.

These tables should dispel any lingering image that Brazilian military officers are recruited from the upper socioeconomic strata. In the 1941–1943 period, 19.8 percent of the cadets listed their fathers' occupations as belonging to the category I have classified as traditional upper class, but by 1962–1964 this had been reduced to 6.0 percent. Especially notable is the paucity of military officers who are sons of *fazendeiros* ("large landowners"). In 1941–1943 they accounted for 3.8 percent of cadets, and by 1962–1966 for only 0.5 percent.

Concerning lower-class recruitment, the army is often considered a major source of upward mobility in Brazil. Belief is widespread that the Latin American officer corps is increasingly being drawn from the lower social and economic classes and that this has implications for political behavior. The Brazilian data indicate, however, that this conjecture needs to be partially qualified. As an aggregate, lower-class representation among cadets increased from 3.8 percent in the 1941–1943 period to 9.0 percent in the 1962–1966 period (or 16 percent if "orphans" are included in this category). However, if the data are disaggregated, we see that repre-

mandant became interested in sociological research on the military. He and some members of his staff had recently read the Portuguese version of Morris Janowitz's *The Professional Soldier*. They felt similar research into the socioeconomic origins of the cadets and the professional training of the Brazilian military would be useful; so my request for permission to research the files was granted. I gratefully acknowledge this permission and the hospitality extended me as a guest of the academy in July and September 1968.

31

sentation from the unskilled lower classes has actually declined from 2.3 percent in the first period to 0.4 percent in the second.

Two factors were at work in Brazil to account for the relatively slow overall increase in lower-class representation and the actual decline in recruitment from unskilled groups. First, there were steps taken to professionalize the officer corps. One part of this process involved raising the educational standards of the military academy. The entrance examination has become progressively more difficult and narrowly technical. The 1966 entrance examination consists of five parts—physics, chemistry, draftsmanship, mathe-

TABLE 3.1

FATHER'S OCCUPATION OF THE 1,031 CADETS ENTERING
BRAZILIAN ARMY ACADEMY, 1941–1943

Traditional Upper Class	No.	Middle Class	No.	Skilled Lower Class	No.	Unskilled Lower Class	No
Landowner	39	Business executive	32	Electrician	1	Domestic help	13
Ambassador	1			Craftsman	8	Worker	7
		Military	219				
Doctor	44			Seaman	4	Peasant	4
		Merchant &	265				
Lawyer	42	tradesman		Machinist	2		
Engineer	41	Civil servant	163				
Dentist	23	Accountant	23				
Magistrate	7	Bank Clerk	19				
Rentier	7	Teacher	26				
		Druggist	19				
		Small farmer	15				
		Miscellaneous	7				
Total	204 (19.8%)		788 (76.4%)		15 (1.5%)		24 (2.3%)

SOURCE: Tables 3.1 and 3.2 were compiled by the author from the files of the Brazilian Military Academy.

32

TABLE 3.2

FATHER'S OCCUPATION OF THE 1,176 CADETS ENTERING BRAZILIAN ARMY ACADEMY, 1962–1966

Traditional Upper Class	No.	Middle Class	No.	Skilled Lower Class	No.	Unskilled Lower Class	No.
Landowner	6	Business executive	45	Electrician	9	Worker	2
Doctor	14			Craftsman	32	Peasant	2
		Military	410				
Lawyer	30			Machinist	12	Fisherman	1
		Merchant	140				
Engineer	10			Railman & longshoreman	29	Total	5
		Civil servant	152				(0.4%)
Dentist	7						
		Accountant & notary	31	Cab & truck driver	11	Unknown (Orphans)*	79
Magistrate	3						(6.7%)
		Bank clerk	21	Miscellaneous	8		
Rentier	1						
		Teacher	5				
		Journalist	3				
		Druggist	7				
		Tradesman & clerk	75				
		Pensioner	5				
		Small Farmer	8				
		Miscellaneous	18				
Total	71 (6.0%)		920 (78.2%)		101 (8.6%)		

SOURCE: See Table 3.1.

* No information existed in the files on the background of the orphans. Some undoubtedly are sons of deceased military men and as orphans are entitled to free education at the military high schools. The majority, however, probably come from lower-class backgrounds.

matics, and Portuguese.[4] To gain entry to the academy, it is necessary to have completed high school and, normally, to have specialized in the sciences. This leads directly to the second reason for the very slow expansion of lower-class recruitment. While the military academy has been raising its standards, the rest of the Brazilian educational system has barely managed to keep ahead of the population explosion. Brazil remains a country of nearly fifty percent illiteracy. Many children do not go to school. Of those that do, poverty and poor schooling itself cause a massive attrition rate in attendance. While 4,701,627 school children entered the first grade in 1963, only 2,248,684 passed on to the second grade. In the same year, only 646,521 children were graduated from the fourth grade.[5] Until the national educational system is significantly expanded and improved, the lower classes will continue to be underrepresented in the officer corps. As Table 3.3 shows, only 4 percent of the adults in Brazil had completed high school in 1950, yet graduation is a prerequisite for entrance to the military academy.

Data contained in Tables 3.1 and 3.2 show that the Brazilian army officer corps is still drawn overwhelmingly from the middle classes. In 1941–1943, 76.4 percent of the cadets had fathers with middle-class occupations. In 1962–1966, the figures were virtually the same (78.2 percent).

There are various problems with the data. The category "military man," for example, can mean anything from general to sergeant. "Civil servant" refers to anyone from the highest level technocrat to a maintenance man in a public building. Given the aggregate nature of the data, there is no way of resolving the question of relative weightings within these large all-inclusive categories. If more detailed information had been available in the cadet service record books, this figure would undoubtedly have shown a shift from the middle to the lower-middle class. It should be noted, however, that even lower-level military men and civil servants are covered by minimum-wage laws, operate within a bureaucratic hierarchy, and are recipients of numerous fringe welfare and hospital privileges. They are also literate and urban. With such a life

---

[4] The entrance examination for 1966 is contained in Brasil, Academia Militar das Agulhas Negras, *Concurso de Admissão: Questões Propostas* (1966). The legal, medical, and academic requirements for admission are printed in Brasil, Ministério da Guerra, *Instruções para o Concurso de Admissão e Matricula: AMAN* (1967?).

[5] Brasil, *Anuário Estatístico do Brasil: 1966*, pp. 406–410.

style most of them would, at a minimum, qualify as lower-middle class.

Because of the gross nature of the data concerning the occupational level of the cadets' fathers, I attempted to construct other indicators of the socioeconomic origins of cadets to see if they confirm the picture derived from the data on fathers' occupations. Table 3.3 shows the fathers' educational level, rather than occupation, and roughly comparable data for the nation as a whole. Given this breakdown, we can see that entrance to the military academy is a source of upward mobility for the 61 percent of cadets whose fathers attended only eight or fewer years of school. This

TABLE 3.3

EDUCATION LEVEL OF FATHERS OF CADETS AT THE BRAZILIAN ARMY
ACADEMY, 1963–1965, AND NATIONAL ADULT SAMPLE, 1950

	Cadets' Fathers %	National Adult Sample %
Illiterate	0.0	(50.6)*
Some elementary school attendance or less, first to fourth years	30.0	79.8
Completed elementary school		16.2
Some junior high school attendance, fifth to eighth years	30.9	
Some high school attendance	9.5	
Completed high school		3.2
Some university attendance	29.6	
Completed university		0.8
	100.0 (N=713)	100.0*

SOURCES: Data for the cadets' fathers were obtained from the files of the *Academia Militar das Agulhas Negras*. The National Adult Sample is based on the 1950 census estimates and reproduced in UNESCO, *Statistical Yearbook: 1965*, pp. 40, 70–71.

* Many people have attended an elementary school but are still classifiable as illiterate. Since these categories are not mutually exclusive the total is more than 100 percent. When one excludes the category "Illiterate" because it is subsumed under the category "Some elementary school attendance or less," the percentage becomes 100.

35

indicates that the center of gravity of recruitment is lower-middle class. However, it is also clear that for the almost fifty percent of Brazilians whose parents are illiterate, entrance to the academy in this period was virtually precluded as a source of mobility because none of the cadets were reported to be sons of illiterates (although the data on occupation make it probable that some parents were in fact illiterate).

Although no hard data exist, conversations with older officers and scattered references in the literature on the Brazilian military suggest that in the late nineteenth and early twentieth centuries, lower academic qualifications for entrance to the academy meant that the officer corps probably had a higher percentage of sons of illiterates than today. This may indicate that professionalization of the officer corps and raising standards has had the effect of decreasing the role of the military as an avenue of social mobility. One further measure of the socioeconomic origins of Brazilian officers is the assessment by cadets themselves of their families' economic status. The figures show quite strikingly that the cadets' self-image is that they do not come from wealthy families, although some undoubtedly do (see Table 3.4). However, even though most of the cadets come from average income families, many also come from such large families that entrance to the academy may be a

TABLE 3.4

SELF-ASSESSMENT BY BRAZILIAN ARMY ACADEMY CADETS
OF FAMILIES' ECONOMIC STATUS

	1962	1963	1964	1965	1966
Rich	0%	0%	0%	0%	0%
Above average	21	34	26	27	8
Average	70	56	66	66	82
Below average	} 9	} 10	} 8	} 7	8
Poor					2
Total	100%	100%	100%	100%	100%
Number	280	248	244	218	186

SOURCE: Files of the *Academia Militar das Agulhas Negras*.

36

major avenue of upward mobility, even a means to prevent downward mobility. Of the 1967 class of cadets, 43 percent came from families with six or more children.[6]

Where do the officers come from? A general hypothesis for developed and developing countries is that they come from the rural or less-developed areas of the country.[7] From this hypothesis, it is often inferred that they will be especially sympathetic to modernizing these areas and that this plays a role in the political behavior of military men. What does Brazilian evidence tell us about where army officers were born, and do the data support the hypothesis?

The most underdeveloped area of Brazil is the northeast. The area was lagging so far behind economically dynamic areas of the center south that in 1959 a special regional development agency, SUDENE, was established to stimulate its growth. The nine states in SUDENE made up 35 percent of Brazil's population in 1940 (the census year closest to the birth year of most of the 1960s' cadets) and 33.2 percent in 1960. However, Table 3.5 shows that only 14 percent of the Brazilian Military Academy cadets in the period 1964–1966 were natives of SUDENE states.[8] The reason undoubtedly is poor primary and secondary school systems in the region. Educational requirements for entrance to the academy are probably too high for these states to be competitive.

At the other end of the scale, the most industrialized and educationally developed state of Brazil, São Paulo, is also underrepresented in the officer corps. São Paulo sent only 8.3 percent of the total cadets to the military academy in the period 1964–1966, though the state represented 17.4 percent of the population in 1940 (18.3 percent in 1960). A major reason for this underrepresentation is that the state provides numerous and usually much better-

---

[6] Files of *Academia Militar das Agulhas Negras*.

[7] Morris Janowitz gives an empirical demonstration and a theoretical discussion of why this is so for the United States in his *The Professional Soldier: A Social and Political Portrait* (New York: The Free Press of Glencoe, 1960), pp. 85–89. He argues this is also so for most of the new nations in *The Military in the Political Development of New Nations* (Chicago: The University of Chicago Press, 1964), pp. 55–58.

[8] This is not a new phenomenon. Analysis of the academy files shows that of the cadets from the classes of 1941 to 1943, 11.4 percent came from what are now the SUDENE states. Nonetheless it remains a historic fact that a disproportionate number of prominent military figures in the twentieth century have come from the northeast.

TABLE 3.5

Birthplace of Army Cadets, 1964–1966

State	Total Cadets	State % All Cadets	State Population as % of National Total	Rough Ratio of Represen- tation
Acre	1	.18	0.2	9/10
Alagoas**	6	1.08	1.8	6/10
Amazonas	1	.18	1.2	2/10
Bahia**	22	3.95	8.4	5/10
Ceará**	20	3.59	4.7	8/10
Espírito Santo	3	.54	1.7	3/10
Goiás	—	—	2.8	—
Guanabara	233	41.83	4.6	90/10
Maranhão**	7	1.26	3.5	4/10
Mato Grosso	10	1.80	1.3	14/10
Minas Gerais	57	10.23	13.8	7/10
Pará	6	1.08	2.2	5/10
Paraíba**	2	.36	2.8	1/10
Paraná	13	2.33	6.0	4/10
Pernambuco**	3	.54	5.8	1/10
Piauí**	6	1.08	1.8	6/10
Rio de Janeiro	19	3.41	4.8	7/10
Rio Grande do Norte	4	.72	1.6	5/10
Rio Grande do Sul	80	14.36	7.7	19/10
Santa Caterina	9	1.62	3.0	5/10
São Paulo	46	8.26	18.3	5/10
Sergipe**	9	1.62	1.0	16/10
(All SUDENE states)	(79)	(14.01)	(33.2)	(4/10)
Total	557	100.0	99.0*	

SOURCES: The data on the birthplace of the cadets are drawn from the files of AMAN. The state populations are from the 1960 census, *Anuário Estatístico do Brasil: 1966*, p. 37.

* The total is only 99% because Brazilian territories are not included.
** Signifies member of SUDENE.

paying career opportunities due to the industrial and commercial dynamism of São Paulo. In addition, the tradition of tension between São Paulo and the federal government (most pronounced in the 1932 São Paulo counterrevolution with secessionist overtones), and the state's maintenance of an excellent well-armed state militia have contributed to low applications to the military academy. These reasons also explain the high rate of officers from São Paulo who leave the army early in their career. All these factors combined have meant that São Paulo, while it is the industrial heart of Brazil, has traditionally been extremely underrepresented at the general officer level.[9] In 1935, for example, none of the 36 generals on active duty came from São Paulo. In 1964, of the 89 line generals on active duty for whom data on the state of birth were available (out of a total of 102) only three were from São Paulo and all three were junior ranking.[10]

The most overrepresented state is Guanabara, the metropolitan area of Rio de Janeiro and the bureaucratic and military headquarters of Brazil. Guanabara is almost a hundred percent urban. Although its population accounted for only 4.3 percent of Brazil's total population in 1940 (4.6 percent in 1960), 233 out of the 557 cadets entering the academy, or 40 percent of the entire cadet student body in the 1964–1966 period, were born in what is now Guanabara.[11] Part of the high percentage is due to the fact that almost 48 percent of the cadets are sons of civil servants or military men. The vast bulk of Brazil's civil servants work in Rio. The largest and best equipped military units have traditionally been located in the *Vila Militar* on the outskirts of Rio, undoubtedly as a means of political control. The General Staffs and most of the important schools of the three military services are also located in Rio de Janeiro.

The next most overrepresented state is Rio Grande do Sul. This state is the horse-riding and ranching capital of Brazil. In addition, after Rio, the largest garrisons of the Brazilian army have traditionally been located in this state because it borders Uruguay and

[9] Barcelona in Spain, like São Paulo in Brazil, is the industrial but not the bureaucratic center of the country. It also has a history of conflict with the central government and is analogous to São Paulo in being sharply underrepresented in the officer corps. See Julio Busquets Bragulat, *El Militar de Carrera en España: Estudio de Sociología Militar* (Barcelona: Ediciones Ariel, 1967), pp. 89–99.

[10] The 1935 datum is from the *Almanaque do Ministério da Guerra: 1935.* The low figure for this year may have been the result of purges of officers following the 1932 *Paulista* revolt. Unfortunately, the Almanaques for years earlier than 1935 do not give data on officers' birthplace. The 1964 datum is based upon Army Ministry biographical press releases and interviews.

[11] This percentage has grown a bit over time, but it clearly is not a new phenomenon. In 1941–1943, the area that is now Guanabara sent 36.4 percent of all cadets.

39

Argentina. Both these factors have contributed to its traditional overrepresentation. This overrepresentation in the officer corps sheds light on the awareness and sympathy that national army garrisons located in Rio Grande do Sul have shown to popular feeling in the state expressed during the crises of 1930 and 1961.[12]

Another significant trend in recruitment has been that sons of military families have increased. In 1941–1943 they represented 21.2 percent of all cadets admitted. In 1962–1966 this had increased to 34.9 percent.[13] There are a number of reasons for this. The great industrial growth and diversification of job opportunities have meant that the sons of the upper and upper-middle classes increasingly have gone into the much better-paying jobs in industry and commerce. On the other hand, constant upgrading of academic and especially scientific qualifications for entry to the military academy, in conjunction with the grossly deficient and excessively classical educational system of the country as a whole, has meant that the vast majority of lower-class and middle-class Brazilians do not meet the academic standards the military desires. There has thus been a growing shortage of qualified officer applicants. My examination of academy files showed that from 1950 to 1965 there were fewer than two applicants for every place in the academy. Since many of these were unfit for physical or health reasons, the number of candidates qualifying for the academic examination was even lower. This demonstrates more than anything else that for a high school graduate a career as a Brazilian army officer is not an elite career in the sense of being much sought after and difficult to attain. The Brazilian situation contrasts very sharply with the situation in the new nations where the scarcity of alternative ca-

[12] Rio Grande do Sul's overrepresentation in the army is not as strong as in the past. A study of the *Almanaque do Ministério da Guerra: 1935* indicates that 36 percent of all generals on active duty were from Rio Grande do Sul. Of the 89 active duty line army generals in 1964 for whom data were available, 17 (19.1 percent) had been born in Rio Grande do Sul.

[13] Research in France and Spain shows a similar trend toward an increasing percentage of officer candidates coming from military family backgrounds. The bulk of officer cadets also come from the nonindustrial middle and lower-middle classes. Madrid, like Rio de Janeiro, is greatly overrepresented. Bragulat, *El Militar de Carrera en España*, pp. 51–165, gives the Spanish data and discusses Western European trends. The French data are excellently presented in Raoul Girardet and Jean-Pierre H. Thomas, "Problèmes de Recrutement," in *La Crise Militaire Française: 1945–1962*, ed. Raoul Girardet (Paris: Librairie Armand Colin, 1964), pp. 11–72.

reers makes the military career very much sought after. In Pakistan, for example, Manfred Halpern noted there were over three thousand applicants for the 80 vacancies at the Pakistan military academy (or over 37 candidates per vacancy).[14]

This gave rise in 1950 and early 1960 to an increasing growth and dependence upon the military-supported and military-directed high school system as the source of cadets. Sons of career military personnel are given free tuition. Only if there are extra places can sons of civilians go, and then they must pay.[15]

The combination of all these factors meant that the Brazilian army became even more inbred in the 1950s and 1960s than the figures on "sons of military" indicate. In 1939, 61.6 percent of the cadets at the military academy entered directly from civilian high schools. From 1962 to 1966, however, only 7.6 percent of all cadets had attended civilian high schools. The shortage of candidates forced a new recruitment policy in 1966 to reverse this trend. The fact still remains that probably up to 90 percent of the present post-war generation of army officers in Brazil entered the military academic system around the age of twelve.

The increasing self-recruitment of the Brazilian military coupled with the intensification of the military educational program undoubtedly were factors in the growing corporate consciousness of the military and their loosening of links with civilians in the period leading up to and after their seizure of power in 1964.[16]

[14] The Brazilian problem of shortage of applicants is discussed in Colonel Everaldo de Oliveira Reis. "O Problema de Falta de Subalternos," *A Defesa Nacional: Revista de Assuntos Militares e Estudos Brasileiros*, no. 608 (July–August 1966), pp. 99–102. The Pakistan data are from Manfred Halpern, *The Politics of Social Change in the Middle East and North Africa* (Princeton: Princeton University Press, 1963), p. 269.

[15] These regulations are formally listed in the brochures for these high schools. See, e.g., Brasil, Ministério do Exército, Diretorio Geral do Ensino, *Guia do Candidato ao Colégio Militar* (1966), p. 4. This rule that the military high schools are meant for sons of career military and that others must pay contrasts with the situation in Turkey where anyone who passes the examination is given free education at the military high schools. See Kemal H. Karpat, *Turkey's Politics: The Transition to a Multi-Party System* (Princeton: Princeton University Press, 1959), p. 341.

[16] This latter theme is developed in Part III. The shortage of qualified cadets became so acute in 1966 that military recruitment from sons of military reached over 40 percent. In 1966, to compensate for the shortage of applicants, a law was passed that allows the top three male students in the graduation class of any accredited civilian high school to enter the academy without taking the examination. Also, for the first time, there was

SOCIAL ORIGINS AND THEIR MEANING FOR POLITICAL BEHAVIOR

What general conclusions can be drawn from the data concerning the social origins and composition of the Brazilian officer corps?

Clearly, very few officers are sons of traditional landowners. Neither are they recruited from the major industrial state of Brazil, São Paulo. The officers do not, therefore, have kinship or personal ties with either of the two major sources of economic wealth and power in the country.

This fact is very important in terms of the military's own self-image. From interviews and other sources, two aspects about the bearing of social class on military behavior emerged. Military officers feel that they do not come from the upper classes or the elite. While admitting that they come from the middle class, they see themselves as a nonclass group, with no special *class* interests.[17]

Brazilian military officers see the traditional elites as having narrow and personal interests that are not in harmony with what the military considers broader national concerns. The same idea is expressed by officers concerning the lower classes, especially the urban trade union workers, whom the military view as championing narrow sectarian goals often opposed to national well-being. Military men regard themselves as a social and organizational group whose interests coincide with or contribute to national development in general. This self-image supplements the normal tendency of the military to view themselves as an organization with a mission to

---

an aggressive sales campaign to increase applicants for the academy. The result was that in the classes of 1967 and 1968 almost *half* of the cadets had gone to civilian schools. These new civilian cadets had a slightly greater percentage of lower class backgrounds. Four percent of this new category were sons of illiterates. Though no hard data exist, there are scattered indications that the percentage of cadets who are sons of enlisted men is increasing. The above comments are based on interviews with the staff of AMAN and a study of the files.

[17] Karl Mannheim has characterized "intellectuals" as an "unanchored, relatively classless stratum." This stratum is free from specific class interests and "subsumes in itself all those interests with which social life is permeated." Brazilian officers in conversation often described their own social position in strikingly similar terms. Quotes from *Ideology and Utopia* (New York: Harcourt, Brace & World, 1966), pp. 155–157.

Unfortunately, we do not have hard data on how other Brazilians perceive the status of the military as an occupation in comparison with other occupations. Bertram Hutchinson's "The Social Grading of Occupations in Brazil," *British Journal of Sociology* (June 1957), pp. 176–189, does not include any military job categories.

defend the nation. It has contributed to their perception of the legitimacy of their arbitration of political events in moments of crisis. A typical statement is that of former army officer Juracy Magalhães, foreign minister in the military-dominated government of 1964–1966:

> It is necessary to understand that the Brazilian armed forces, in comparison with the armed forces in some other countries, are far from constituting a privileged caste, but represents one of the most important and well-defined sectors of our middle class. . . . The armed forces, identified, as I mentioned above, with popular aspirations and loyal to them, exercise in practice a form of moderating power whenever there is manifested a strong and legitimate movement of public opinion. The armed forces intervene in the political scene supporting that manifestation and acting as instruments of transformation.[18]

Belief by the military that the officer corps has no special class affiliations has even been turned into a major rationale for the extension of military power. A general, advocating the case that the military should not yield power in 1968 but remain for five or ten years if necessary, argued that the military was the sole institution with no links to special elite groups within the nation. Precisely because of this, he felt it was the only institution without vested interest in the status quo. This, he felt, freed it to act solely in the interests of the national good.[19]

The classic theory of military professionalism has emphasized the unique organizational features that separate a military man from the civilian. In Brazil, however, the "popular" origins of the military, in comparison to other elites, has helped foster the belief that the military is merely *o povo fardado* ("the people in uniform"). This concept of identity between the people and the army has given some psychological legitimacy to appeals to the military from civilians to intervene in politics in their defense at times of crisis. Conversely, it has given sanction to the belief that it is the

[18] Brasil, Ministério das Relações Exteriores, Discurso do Embaixador, Juracy Magalhães em Washington, 16 de Fevereiro de 1965, *Textos e Declarações Sobre Política Externa: Primeiro Aniversário de Revolução de 31 de Março de 1964* (1965), p. 135.

[19] See various speeches to this effect by General Affonso Albuquerque Lima cited in *Jornal do Brasil* in November and December 1968.

43

duty of the military to come to the defense of civilians if called.[20] One source of psychological tension within the military since 1964 has been the conflict between the growing isolation, authoritarianism and unpopularity of the military among the people on the one hand, and this traditional image of the military as *o povo fardado* on the other. Military men cherished this image.

Since the army officers were viewed as "the people in uniform," officers have traditionally been allowed to vote and to hold elective and appointive public office. As a citizen in uniform, an officer is expected to care about political issues. Furthermore, while the army officer is not supposed to speak in the name of the army, the army has in fact institutionalized military debate over public and political issues. What do these debates reveal about officer corps opinion?

The most important forum for this institutionalized political debate within the military is the Military Club in Rio de Janeiro.[21] Biennial elections of the Military Club have traditionally been fought over broad public issues roughly similar to those being debated throughout the country. Election results show how far the Brazilian officer corps is from being a monolith. In 1950 the nationalist slate, sympathetic to the creation of the national oil monopoly, *Petrobrás*, and the return of Vargas to politics, won 3,879 to 2,708 in a bitterly contested election.[22] After an intense

[20] For references to the image of the army as "the people in uniform" and for a discussion of some political implications, see Murilo Carvalho, "On the Belief System of the Brazilian Military" (MS, March 1968). The paper is on file at the International Data Library and Reference Service, Survey Research Center, University of California at Berkeley, no. 29/68.

[21] Article 1, subparagraph 3, of the bylaws of the Military Club states that one of the objectives of the club is to facilitate the expression of civic and patriotic sentiment over issues that could wound or advance national honor. However, article 2 states that these civic manifestations should not be associated with any particular political party; *Estatuto do Clube Militar* (Rio de Janeiro: Imprensa do Exército, 1968), pp. 3–4.

[22] In the election of 1948, no fundamental issues were being debated in the country at large, and the election in the Military Club was routine. Only 820 members voted, and the winner received 793 votes. In the politically heated national presidential election year of 1950, the number of officers who voted jumped to 6,805. General Newton Estillac Leal won the presidency of the club, and when Vargas won the national election, Leal was appointed Vargas' minister of war. Leal was opposed by the commandant of the Superior War College, General Oswaldo Cordeiro de Farias.

In that same year, Major Nelson Werneck Sodré, the most distinguished Marxist intellectual in the army, defeated one of the major intellectuals of the Superior War College, Lt. Col. Jurandyr de Bizarria Mamede, for the

campaign the more anti-Communist "Cruzada Democrática" mobilized votes to win the 1952 election 8,289 to 4,489.[23]

In the 1962 election a general who had sharply defended Vice-President Goulart's right to assume the presidency in the crisis of 1961, and who had publicly applauded the nationalization of a foreign utility company and urged land reform, was narrowly defeated by 4,884 votes to 4,312.[24] This fact illustrates that the momentary unity of the army during their overthrow of President Goulart in 1964 was not a result of permanent ideological unity but rather of their interaction with the political system in a time of crisis.

Let us turn now to the question of what effect the middle-class origins of the Brazilian officer corps have on the behavior of the military as an *institution*. One of the most interesting writers on this subject has been José Nun. Nun sees the middle-class origin of the military as crucial to their political role in society. He argues that since the middle classes in general are extremely heterogeneous and lack a clear class perspective, their internal divisions make them incapable of ruling. At the same time they fear the rise of the lower classes. Since the military are themselves middle class in social composition, the middle sectors find themselves "allied to a sector with a remarkable degree of institutional cohesion and articulateness. In other words the armed forces become one of the few important institutions controlled by the middle class."[25] The middle classes look to the military to resolve political crises. Seen

---

post of director of the cultural department of the military club. Fourteen years later, these two men were among the intellectual leaders of the two opposing camps in the 1964 revolution.

[23] All of the above election figures were obtained from the military club archives, vol. 24, entitled *Livro de Atas das Assembleas Geraes*, with the permission of the acting president, General Leontino.

[24] For good reporting on this election, see the *Diário de Notícias* from May 22 to 31, 1962. Two caveats should be borne in mind when interpreting the results of the elections. Any officer who holds a commission in any of the three armed services is allowed to be a member of the *Clube Militar*. Thus the electorate includes a number of ex-enlisted men from the navy and air force (who cannot join their own services more socially restrictive clubs) and a good number of relatively uninfluential elderly retired officers.

[25] Nun, "The Middle-Class Military Coup," p. 76. Nun's ideas were presented in an earlier form in "A Latin American Phenomenon: The Middle Class Military Coup," in *Trends in Social Science Research in Latin American Studies* (Berkeley: University of California, Institute of International Studies, March 1965), pp. 55–99.

in these terms, military intervention is not threatening to the middle classes. Nun argues that the military "tends to represent" middle-class interests and to compensate for the middle classes' inability to establish themselves as a well-integrated group. The armed forces "assume the responsibility of protecting the middle class."[26]

Nun's hypothesis is valuable in that it points out that the middle classes often urge the military to intervene in the political process. I argue later, in fact, that at different times all political groups do this, whether lower or upper class in origin or from the right or left in political affiliation. The Nun thesis has serious shortcomings, however, for explaining the political behavior of the military. As Nun himself admits, the political disorganization of the middle classes in Latin America to a great extent arises from their complete disunity, which, while it may be a stimulus to a military coup, can never be a guideline for a military government. How can a military government "represent" middle class policies over which the middle classes themselves are deeply split?[27]

A further note of caution must be raised about Nun's thesis. Are "middle-class military governments" strongly supported by civilian middle classes whom the military are supposed to have assumed the "responsibility of protecting"? Analysis of military regimes in power suggests that the military often acts primarily to

[26] Nun, "The Middle-Class Military Coup," pp. 103–112.

[27] As a recent study of middle-class Argentine voting in Buenos Aires indicates, the middle class does not represent any one political viewpoint, but is extremely divided right across the entire political spectrum (see Table 3.6). Instead, what one often has is a number of middle-class groups competing *against* each other *for* the attention of different groups within the military.

TABLE 3.6

MIDDLE-CLASS VOTING PATTERNS: BUENOS AIRES, 1957

	Com.	Soc.	Perón	UCRI	UCRP	PDC	Con.	PCI	Other
Upper-middle	2.4	11.2	13.2	15.8	28.5	8.7	2.8	8.7	8.9
Lower-middle	4.0	16.2	21.3	19.4	25.2	4.4	0.9	1.1	7.5

SOURCE: Peter G. Snow, "The Class Basis of Argentine Political Parties," *American Political Science Review*, LXIII (March 1969), Table 6, p. 166. The above figures are percentages.

defend itself as an institution from articulate criticism coming from middle class sectors. For example, in Argentina the military executed a coup in 1966. In order to consolidate power and to stifle opposition, the military government invaded the state universities. Since in Argentina the upper classes tend to go to private or Catholic universities and the lower classes do not attend universities at all, the state universities are generally attended by people of middle-class origin. After the intervention, a public opinion poll showed that while the upper and lower classes supported the government, the most outspoken groups in opposition were in the "middle class."[28]

To take a further example, in Brazil in 1964 the military overthrew João Goulart with considerable backing from the middle and upper classes. Trade unions and peasant leagues were suppressed or destroyed, and the lower classes bore the brunt of the stabilization policy from 1964 to 1967. It thus seemed to fit Nun's description of a middle-class military coup. Nonetheless, the military's subsequent attack on political parties, civil liberties, civil service tenure, and the universities (all privileges and activities which the middle and upper-middle classes use and enjoy much more than the lower classes) meant that middle-class support had decreased by the time the military had been in power for a year.

Indeed, a plausible hypothesis would be that a strong military regime that does not respect traditional civil liberties and rules of the game of politics will be perceived as most threatening to those who have enjoyed some of the fruits of the old system (i.e., the middle and upper classes). The lower classes, precisely because they are excluded from the political game of democracy will tend to be more tolerant of the antipolitical "clean out the thieves" posture of the military.

An attitude study taken in Brazil eleven months after the military had assumed power in April 1964 tends to support such a hypothesis. It illustrates that when a military regime was actually in power, attitudes favorable to the extension of military influence varied inversely with wealth: the wealthier a person, the more he wanted military influence to be *decreased*. Conversely, the poorer a person, the more he favored *increasing* military influence (see

[28] See "Popularidad," *Primera Plana*, no. 235, June 27, 1967, p. 13.

47

Table 3.7).[29] Despite these qualifications, it is probably true to say that the continuing middle-class fears of the lower class remains a source of their support for the military's antimobilization policies.

BUREAUCRATIC NORMS IN THE MILITARY AND THEIR EFFECT ON POLITICAL ACTIVISM

There are other features of the Brazilian military structure that also tend to lessen the significance of socioeconomic origins as determinates of political behavior. Although I have argued in preceding pages that it is a dangerous oversimplification to see the Brazilian military as an encapsulated, unified, professional body completely dominated by its bureaucratic and organizational structure, nonetheless it is important to note that certain rational and bureaucratic norms do exist within the military and that these

[29] There are other polls that speak to the general question. James C. Davies, in a questionnaire administered in Brazil a few months after the 1964 coup, made the statement: "A few strong leaders could make this country better than all the laws and talk." Only 4 percent of the respondents with a low socioeconomic status disagreed with the statement, while 90 percent agreed. This was in strong contrast to higher socioeconomic status respondents, 44 percent of whom disagreed and 54 percent of whom agreed. While the interpretation of the specific political significance of these responses is open to question, it is clear that higher socioeconomic status groups are much more reluctant than the lower classes to see civil liberties violated by a strong-man government. It is precisely this reluctance that often brings the civilian middle classes into conflict with the military middle classes when an authoritarian military regime is in power. See Davies, "Political Stability and Instability: Some Manifestations and Causes," *Journal of Conflict Resolution*, XIII (March 1969), pp. 5–6.

The available published opinion polls in Brazil likewise do not show middle class support for the military government. In November 1967, in answer to the question, "Whom would you vote for if a direct election were held for the presidency today?" the incumbent military president received an identical low 11 percent from both the middle-class respondents and the lower-class respondents. See the survey analysis for 1966 and 1967 in the *Jornal do Brasil*, November 15, 1967, p. 14.

None of the above three surveys mentioned meets the standards one would like for ideal survey evidence: the USIS survey, because it was sponsored by a foreign government, the United States; the James Davies survey, because the sample is too small ($N = 153$); and the Marplan survey, printed in the *Jornal do Brasil*, because of uncertain methodology. The point is that this is the only available evidence, and none of it supports the hypothesis of the congruence of civilian middle class opinion and military middle class opinion. While this evidence cannot be used to refute the hypothesis totally, it at least indicates that much more survey work is needed before the hypothesis can be accepted.

48

TABLE 3.7

PERCENTAGES EXPRESSING SPECIFIED ATTITUDES TOWARD MILITARY
INFLUENCE, BY ECONOMIC STATUS, FEBRUARY 1965
SÃO PAULO, RIO, AND RECIFE

Attitude	Economic Status			
	Better off	Modest	Poor	Favelas of Rio Separately
Military should have:				
less influence	56	38	23	16
more influence	21	25	37	42
same influence	18	21	12	10
No opinion	5	16	28	32
Total %	100	100	100	100
N	57	411	1017	136

SOURCE: USIS, *Latin American Attitudes Toward Social Reform*, R-212-65.
Released January 17, 1969. Poll available for analysis from the
Roper Center for Public Opinion Research.

give the military officer corps some capacity to socialize its members to its own norms. The norms also influence how the military acts as a political institution.

A common stereotype describes Latin American armies as top-heavy with colonels and generals. It contributes to a general belief that rational professional procedures are foreign to the Latin American military.

However, unlike most of the Central American armies, many major armies in Latin America, such as those of Chile, Brazil, and Peru, conform closely to bureaucratic norms such as rank structure. For example, Table 3.8 shows that the distribution of ranks in the armies of Brazil and the United States is fairly similar. In both armies, the largest single group is the captains. Nor is the Brazilian army top-heavy in comparison to the United States. In 1964 only 14.9 percent of all Brazilian officers were colonels or generals, compared to 16.4 percent for the United States in the same year.[30] (This contrasts sharply with Guatemala, where a com-

[30] Until new regulations were passed in 1966, the vast majority of Brazilian officers received a double promotion upon retirement. Thus while

TABLE 3.8

DISTRIBUTION OF OFFICERS ON ACTIVE DUTY BY RANK
IN THE ARMIES OF BRAZIL AND THE UNITED STATES

	Year	Gen.	Col.	Lt. Col.	Maj.	Capt.	1st Lt.	2nd Lt.	% Total
U.S. {	1920	.4	4.1	4.7	14.9	35.9	32.6	7.4	100.0
	1950	.8	9.4	11.5	20.7	34.9	13.9	8.8	100.0
	1964	.4	4.7	11.3	17.4	32.9	18.4	14.9	100.0
Brazil	1964	1.0	4.2	9.7	15.7	29.9	23.1	16.4	100.0

SOURCE: The U.S. data for 1920 and 1950 came from Janowitz, *The Professional Soldier*, p. 67. The 1964 U.S. data were provided by Steven Canby, based upon U.S. Department of Defense records. The Brazilian data were tabulated from Brasil, Ministério da Guerra, *Almanaque do Exército: 1964*. Einaudi's data on the Peruvian military are roughly similar.

bination of automatic promotions every three or four years and slack compulsory retirement procedures has resulted traditionally in an army with from 35 to 50 percent of all active duty officers in the highest rank of full colonel!)[31]

An even more important area of officer corps professional norms exists in their educational and promotion structure. Bureaucratic norms are closely adhered to in regard to educational standards in the officer corps in Brazil. Each major step in an officer's career requires attendance at a specified military school. This makes for a strong corporate imprint on officers. In the army, all officers who have command responsibility must attend the four-year military academy (*Academia Militar das Agulhas Negras*, AMAN). To be promoted to captain, all officers are obliged to attend for one year the junior officers' school (*Escola de Aperfeiçoamento de Oficiais*, EsAO). To be eligible for promotion to general, or for appointment to the general staff of any of the four armies or service schools, an officer must also pass the difficult entrance examination

the active duty rank structure was normal, the retired rank structure was completely inflated. Lieutenant colonels became "pajama generals" and Brazil has over a hundred retired officers holding the rank of marshal.

[31] Reforms begun in 1967 are slowly changing this situation. The Guatemalan data are from a forthcoming dissertation on the Guatemalan military by Caesar Sereseres of the University of California at Riverside.

to the General Staff School (*Escola de Comando e Estado Maior do Exército*, ECEME) and then attend a course of three years' duration.[32] (The comparable training period in the General Staff School in the United States is only nine months long.) Normally, less than 25 percent of the applicants pass this entrance examination.[33] Thus, any real success in the Brazilian army is dependent upon academic achievement.

In addition, there are many specialized technical schools and opportunities for study abroad (mostly in the United States or France). Increasingly, a year's study at the Superior War College (*Escola Superior de Guerra*, ESG) is becoming the norm for senior colonels and junior generals.

Since most Latin American armies have very little or no recent combat experience, academic achievement is extremely important for subsequent promotion. In Brazil, for example, 40 of the 102 army line generals on active duty in 1964 had graduated first in their class at one of the three major army service schools.[34] In an army with extensive combat experience such as that of the United States, officers like Eisenhower, with poor academic records at the military academy, or officers with deviant bureaucratic performance, such as Patton, have opportunities in war to demonstrate other talents. Academic achievement becomes relatively less important. Morris Janowitz shows that in a sample of top United States Army leaders, only 36.4 percent had even graduated in the top quarter of their class at West Point.[35] In Peru, on the other hand, 80 percent of the division generals in Einaudi's sample had graduated in the top quarter of the class at the military academy.[36]

[32] Interview with General Reynaldo Mello de Almeida, commandant of ECEME, Rio de Janeiro, August 2, 1968.

[33] Interview with the officer in charge of administering the entrance examination to ECEME, Rio de Janeiro, July 19, 1968.

[34] Based on analysis of *Almanaque do Exército: 1964*.

[35] See *The Professional Soldier*, pp. 134–135.

[36] This figure is contained in Einaudi's forthcoming study of the Peruvian military. It was Einaudi who first brought this aspect of the more developed Latin American armies to my attention. He makes a strong argument that far from being insufficiently bureaucratic in promotion standards, the Peruvian military has been too academic and bureaucratic.

It is tempting to argue that the permanent prestige achieved by graduating at the top of an academic class is an example of "achieved-ascription" and once again illustrates the danger of perceiving Parsons' pattern variables as polar pairs at the opposite ends of a traditional to modern continuum; see Talcott Parsons, *The Social System* (Glencoe, Ill.: The Free Press of Glencoe, 1964), pp. 66–67.

Enough has been said to show that the mere fact of middle-class composition of a military establishment cannot in itself explain political behavior or political intervention, although at any one historical moment it may be one of several factors influencing this course of events.

Furthermore, work done on social class and politics in other countries leads one to be extremely cautious in drawing direct behavioral inferences from the social background of members of organizations or their political leaders. With regard to *individuals*, and the effect of social origins on their political behavior, it is clear from numerous historical examples that aristocrats have often led populist movements, and that lower-class leaders or caudillos have headed or been the bulwarks of traditional higher-class governments. For example, in Cuba a lower class ex-sergeant, Batista, and his cronies were the representatives of the traditional order, while the predominantly middle-class leaders of Castro's guerrilla force revolutionized the country and destroyed the largely middle-class regular army.[37]

In regard to middle-class background, the picture is especially unclear because most contemporary political leaders, whether they are democratic, Communist, facist, or anarchic, are normally middle class. Indeed, elite analysis of politically antagonistic movements often reveals the *similarity* of the opposing movements at the aggregate level of broad socioeconomic origin of their leaders. R. C. North and I. D. Pool's analysis of modern China is typical:

> For the greater part of three decades the Kuomintang and the Communist Party have fought each other with all the bitterness of a class war. On the surface the rival interests involved in this conflict seem clear, for here are all the superficial characteristics of a struggle between masses on the one hand and classes on the other. . . . But an examination of membership data raises the question: how far does the character of the Kuomintang and Communist leadership support or contradict these preconceptions? . . . Despite all the detailed differences, *we find ourselves forced to concede that a major portion of the elite of both movements came from quite similar high social strata.*[38]

[37] On the middle-class background of Castro and his guerrilla leaders, see Theodore Draper, *Castroism, Theory and Practice* (New York: Praeger, 1965), pp. 60–81.

[38] "Kuomintang and Chinese Communist Elites," in *World Revolutionary*

This is not to argue that class origin is irrelevant in determining political behavior, but rather to suggest that *by itself* it is almost never determinant of the political behavior of elites. Other factors, such as the historical development of the country and the perception of which groups are threatening and which groups are allies in the face of any particular crisis, are equally, if not more, important. In Egypt, for example, Nasser and seven of the eleven men who founded the Free Officers group in 1949 had in 1936 entered the first military academy class open to all Egyptians. Most of them were of a more humble social origin than the cadets previously admitted, but this factor was reinforced by the "cohort" experience of sharing classes together, and, in addition, experiencing as a group Egypt's first humiliating defeat by Israel. Combination of all these events, rather than shared socioeconomic origins, is what gave the Egyptian officers around Nasser their group unity and shared values, although even then many of their operational policy orientations were shaped only after they had come to power.[39] However, this example serves to show that all three analytical approaches—socioeconomic origins, cohort or experiential analysis, and contextual historical analysis—are necessary in discussing the role of the military in politics.[40]

The foregoing analysis has not completely resolved the question of the political significance of the socioeconomic origins of the Brazilian officer corps. However, enough logical and empirical questions were raised to indicate that socioeconomic features are in themselves indeterminant of political behavior.

While no attitude study exists for the Brazilian military, a plausible hypothesis is that for most individual military officers so many life experience and career pattern variables intervene between their entry into the military school system at ages 14 to 18

Elites: Studies in Coercive Ideological Movements, ed. Harold D. Lasswell and Daniel Lerner (Cambridge: The M.I.T. Press, 1966), p. 376. Emphasis added. The same book also documents that both German Nazi and the Soviet Communist leadership elites were basically middle class.

[39] See P. J. Vatikiotis, *The Egyptian Army in Politics* (Bloomington, Indiana: University of Indiana Press, 1961), pp. 44–68.

[40] All these dimensions prove to be involved in the surprisingly similar South Korean coup of 1961. See C. I. Eugene Kim, "The South Korean Military Coup of May, 1961: Its Causes and the Social Characteristics of Its Leaders," in *Armed Forces and Society: Sociological Essays*, ed. Jacques Van Doorn (The Hague: Mouton, 1968), pp. 298–316.

and their promotion to colonel or general 25 or 35 years later, that the direct impact of socioeconomic origin has been considerably weakened. Recent political experience, job position, and current life style will have much more predictive value in regard to present attitudes.[41]

CONCLUSION

What have been some of the politically relevant implications to emerge from this initial study of the military as an institution?

At the most general level, I think it is apparent that the ideal type of military institution—a highly unified organization with a private code and values, isolated from the general pressures of the political system at large—often simply does not exist. Consequently political deductions drawn from the ideal type can be basically misleading. Through a series of political interactions, the military subsystem normally is both shaped by and shapes the political system. Later analysis will clearly illustrate that the military institution in Brazil is also a political institution that, like political parties, pressure groups, or parliaments, often performs, in one way or another, a variety of political functions. These can include articulating specific demands, ordering power relationships between groups, formulating and implementing policy, and even selecting or removing the executive.

It is necessary to analyze the behavior of a military institution in the total context of its political environment for two reasons. First, at the most basic level, the political roles any military establishment performs are to a great extent derived from the position

[41] The one major elite attitude study in Latin America tends to strengthen this line of reasoning. In Venezuela an elite opinion survey attempted to establish the strength of 38 background variables in predicting political attitudes. Among the background variables were respondents' present income, region of birth, age, present occupation, fathers' occupation, and fathers' level of education. The background variable of "present occupation" had much the strongest predictive power of the 38 variables. It predicted 84 percent of all attitudes. Parents' primary occupations ranked seventeenth and only predicted 31 percent of attitudes, while parents' levels of education ranked thirty-fifth and only predicted 10 percent of attitudes.

See Donald D. Searing, "The Comparative Study of Elite Socialization," *Comparative Political Studies*, I (January 1969), 471–500. The Venezuelan figures are secondary analysis of the primary data collected by the CENDES-M.I.T. group and first reported in *A Strategy for Research on Social Policy*, ed. Frank Bonilla and José A. Silva Michelena (Cambridge, Mass.: The M.I.T. Press, 1967).

54

of the military subsystem within the political system itself, rather than from features of the military institution alone. This is so whether we are speaking of the Napoleonic French Revolutionary army, Communist politically controlled people's armies, the relatively noninterventionist Chilean army, or a primitive army such as that of Venezuela in the nineteenth century. In each case the structure and function of the army is closely related to the structure of politics at the time. Second, at a less basic level, it is logically and empirically evident that the ideology, social composition, and structure of a particular army do not totally predetermine its political behavior in specific crises. Various courses of action are usually open at any one time to a military, and the choice of a course is to a great extent related to events within the political system itself.

Institutional characteristics of military establishments are by no means politically irrelevant, however. A central task of the political sociology of the military is to look at both the military institution and the political system and to determine how the special institutional characteristics of a particular military establishment shape its response to influences coming from the political system. At times the institutional variable is extremely important. For example, as we have seen, where subnational conflicts are central issues in politics, the regional, tribal, or federal recruitment structure of the military institution is often crucial in determining the political sympathies or the ruling capability of the military.

The presence or absence of bureaucratic norms for promotion and assignment within the military organization is also another instance of the possible importance of institutional factors in political events. If bureaucratic norms are only weakly established, then a president has greater freedom to promote or assign military personnel according to his own political criteria. If, on the other hand, the army has routinized bureaucratic criteria for promotion and assignments, then the president's freedom to manipulate promotions for his own political ends is much more constrained. In Brazil, as I show later, the fact that such norms existed in the early 1960s meant that President Goulart's attempt to go beyond established institutional norms of promotion and discipline in order to build political support became sharply counterproductive.

Another politically significant institutional variable is the level and content of military education. In many Latin American countries where it appears on the surface that the military institution controls large areas of politics, in reality, given the low level of military economic and political education as well as confidence, the military is often manipulated and co-opted by civilian elites. However, as I show in detail in Part III, where there are highly developed military schooling systems, such as in Brazil and Peru, the military tends to develop its own doctrines of development and its own cadres of *tecnicos*, so that if the military establishment assumes executive power it is more likely to abandon its traditional *caretaker* role and become the central policy maker and *director* of the political system.

Within this context, once political power has been assumed by the military, the degree of ideological unity obviously also becomes a politically important variable. The less unified a military institution, the greater is the potential for policy discontinuity and even coups. The political significance of ideological splits within a single military institution, once in a position of power, is one of the central questions discussed in Part IV.

Finally, analysis of the particular mix of pressures within military institutions sheds light on some of the inherently nonmilitary aspects of military coups.[42] We have seen that the military is not a monolithic institution, psychologically or politically isolated from civilian life. Given the fact that a reasonably highly developed bureaucratic military, such as the Brazilian, places a high value on maintaining its command and disciplinary structure, its *political heterogeneity*, when coupled with the desire to maintain *institutional unity*, often inhibits the military from initiating coups against the state for fear of splitting its own organization. Thus institutional organization of the military acts to a certain extent as a restraint against political activism. In these circumstances, as will be seen in the "moderator model" of civil–military relations presented in Part II, much of the stimulus creating the necessary cohesion among military officers sufficient to initiate the bold act of removing a president comes from outside the military institution itself.

[42] For a similar argument see David C. Rapoport, "The Political Dimensions of Military Usurpation," *Political Science Quarterly*, LXXXIII, (December 1968), 551–573.

PART II

The "Moderating Pattern"
of Civil–Military Relations:
Brazil, 1945–1964

A BASIC ASPECT of civil–military relations is the potential tension that exists between the civilian political rulers' need to maintain an armed force as an instrument of foreign policy and internal order, and their need to ensure that military power does not usurp political power. This tension has been resolved in a variety of ways in different countries. One can briefly summarize much of the literature on these problems as containing four different models or ideal types of civil–military relations. These could be called the aristocratic, the Communist, the liberal, and the professional models.[1] To oversimplify, we can say that in each of these different models, the two key variables are value congruence and/or control mechanisms.

The aristocratic model presents the simplest resolution of potential tension between civilian and military power, and historically has been the most successful. Its essence lies in the fact that in an aristocratic society the social values and material interests of the political and military elites are naturally congruent. Military officers are drawn mainly from the aristocracy and define themselves as aristocrats and not as officers. As aristocrats, they maintain their prestige and wealth by supporting the aristocratic form of government. The military has a low level of internal differentiation so that little special training is needed to qualify as an officer. In the absence of a professional military, the classic tension between

[1] Of course, other models exist. These are presented as the four that speak most significantly to the question of how the civilian rulers can control the military rather than be controlled by them.

57

the professional class of officers seeking primarily military goals and the political elite is absent.

This model begins to break down when the aristocratic society itself begins to break down. With industrialization, the technical aspects of military strategy require a more specialized officer corps. With expanded educational opportunity, the way is open for the admission to officer rank of men outside the aristocracy. These processes in turn create a potential source of civil–military tension, since the officers come increasingly to define themselves first as professional military men and only secondarily as aristocrats. At some point self-conscious control devices may be introduced, such as restricting entry to the officer corps to aristocrats in an artificial attempt to maintain value congruence.[2]

In the liberal model of civil–military relations, the political elite are intensely aware of the potential conflict between themselves and the military, and deliberately seek to ensure that the military has no legitimacy to act in the political sphere. Ideally, the military is to be kept apolitical. Since value conflict is recognized as a potential threat, great emphasis is laid on neutralizing devices. The standing army is kept small. After a war, the army is rapidly demobilized. Countervailing military forces are created in the form of militias, as a check against the regular army. Some attempt at value congruence may be made by drafting citizens into the army rather than relying on professional career soldiers and by providing multiple avenues of entry into the officer corps. This pattern of civil–military relations has the best chance of success in a society with strongly developed civilian institutions and without constant external security threats. Classic examples are provided by Switzerland, and by the United States in the nineteenth century.

Unlike the aristocratic or liberal models, in both the Communist and professional models of civil–military relations there is a high value placed on military strength and expertise. In both, how-

[2] For a thoughtful analysis of some of the components of the aristocratic model, see Gaetano Mosca, *The Ruling Class*, trans. H. D. Kahn (New York: McGraw–Hill Book Company, 1939) pp. 222–243. A general analysis, as well as an interesting description of one aspect of the model, the purchase system of commission as a means of tying rank to wealth, is found in Samuel Huntington, *The Soldier and the State: The Theory and Politics of Civil–Military Relations* (New York: Random House, 1964), pp. 19–30, 470–473.

ever, civilian control of the military is an essential element. In the Communist model, the liberal ideal of an apolitical military is rejected. The Polish Communist theoretician Wiatr writes: "The rejection of the concept of an army man as an apolitical expert becomes, in the socialist countries, one of the elements of integration of the army and society."[3] This integration is achieved by constant political indoctrination and by ensuring that the vast majority of higher army officers are Communist party members. Thus the integration of values that marked the aristocratic model of civil–military relations is also a part of the Communist model. In the latter case it is achieved "by the *politicization* of the professional soldier, who no longer is treated as an expert only, but acts also as a member of the Communist Party and through the Party participates in the political decision-making not as a soldier but as a politically active citizen."[4] The Communist countries also show extensive use of control devices, such as the presence of political commissars in military units, political intelligence surveillance, and ideological purges.

In the Communist model of civil–military relations, two areas of weakness exist. When external security threats are great, the military officers may strive for professional autonomy, or the military may begin to dominate the Communist party if it weakens, as in China during the cultural revolution.[5]

In the professional model, as in the Communist, the goal of the civilian politicians is to maintain a strong military force under civilian government control. The major theoretician of the model,

[3] Jerzy Wiatr, "Expert and Politician—The Divergent Aspects of the Social Role of the Army Man," *Polish Sociological Review*, no. 1 (1964), p. 53.

[4] Jerzy Wiatr, "Military Professionalism and Transformations of Class Structure in Poland," in *Armed Forces and Society: Sociological Essays*, ed. Jacques van Doorn (Paris: Mouton, 1968), p. 238. Emphasis added.

[5] The most complete study of civil–military relations in the Soviet Union is by Roman Kolkowicz in *The Soviet Military and the Communist Party* (Princeton: Princeton University Press, 1967); for a description of the party's military control mechanism, see pp. 81–98. For China, see Ellis Joffe, *Party and Army: Professionalism and Political Control in the Chinese Officer Corps, 1949–1964*, Harvard East Asian Monographs, no. 19 (Cambridge, Mass.: Harvard University Press, 1965). For the dramatic increase of army political power in China during the Cultural Revolution, see Stephen A. Sims, "The New Role of the Military," *Problems of Communism* (November–December, 1969), pp. 26–32, and Ralph L. Powell, "The Party, The Government and the Gun," *Asian Survey*, x (June 1970), 441–471.

Samuel Huntington, suggests that civilian control is ensured not through value congruence or extensive control devices, but by civilian toleration of the autonomous development of military influence within the military sphere. Huntington argues that the pursuit of professional military goals by military men in itself tends to restrict military energy to its proper, nonpolitical sphere. "The essence of objective civilian control is the recognition of autonomous military professionalism."[6] In his view, civilian control is achieved "not because the military groups share in the social values and political ideologies of society, but because they are indifferent to such values and ideologies. The military leaders obey the government not because they agree with its policies but simply because it is their duty to obey."[7]

These four models of civil–military relations are the classic ones used to describe how the military is controlled by civilian politicians. Other models exist, of course, such as that of military dictatorship or the modernizing military, where civilian control is absent and the military controls the entire political system. Formulating them in succinct form here allows us to ask the following questions: How closely do civil–military relations in Latin American countries approximate these models? Do the civilian political elites consistently strive to attain the goals described in any of the four models?

It is safe to say that in twentieth-century Latin America not one country meets the conditions of the aristocratic model of civil–military relations. The officer corps is predominantly middle class in social composition, rather than aristocratic or upper class. In addition, while Latin American society is only semimobilized, it cannot be characterized as aristocratic in overall organization. Finally, the officer corps in most countries is at least partially professionalized, so that there is a certain degree of tension between military elites and civilian elites.

The applicability of the Communist model is also limited: only Cuba and to some extent Mexico with its one dominant political party seem to fit this model of civil–military relations. This leaves

---

[6] Samuel Huntington, *The Soldier and the State*, p. 83. Huntington calls this model one of "objective control."

[7] Samuel Huntington, "Civilian Control of the Military: A Theoretical Statement," in *Political Behavior: A Reader in Theory and Research*, ed. Heinz Eulau, Samuel J. Eldersveld, and Morris Janowitz (Glencoe, Ill.: The Free Press, 1956), p. 381.

us with the liberal and professional models, and consciously or not, most writers on civil–military relations have tended to analyze the Latin American experience in terms of one or another of these two models. This is understandable, since superficial elements of both these models are found in many Latin American countries. The military is to a certain extent professionalized in its institutional structure, its education, and technical training in many countries, including Peru and Brazil. Elements of the liberal model are found in the widespread belief that military government is illegitimate.

However, in most cases it strains the political reality of civil–military relations in Latin America to attempt to force them into the boxes provided by the two models. For the liberal model to be appropriate as a description of civil–military relations, strong civilian institutions are necessary, and there must be a systematic effort by the major political actors to keep the military out of politics. As I show later, however, the very absence of strong political institutions in a country such as Brazil has meant that all major actors attempt to co-opt the military as an additional supportive force in the pursuit of their political goals. With regard to the professional model, as Huntington recognized, the success of the model is dependent upon a political system that is stable enough for politicians to refrain from interfering with purely internal military affairs or using the military for partisan political purposes. "The antithesis of objective civilian control is military participation in politics." "Objective control" is impossible as long as civilian groups are "unwilling simply to accept a politically neutral officer corps" and as long as there are "multifarious civilian groups anxious to maximize their power in military affairs."[8] Such civilian groups often exist in abundance in Latin American countries.

The four models sketched above are necessarily highly abstract, and no political system represents a pure type. Twentieth-century United States, for example, is a combination of the liberal and the professional models. Late nineteenth-century Germany and Austria combined the aristocratic and professional models. Nonetheless, the very difficulty of fitting the Latin American patterns of civil–military relations satisfactorily into any of the four models found in the literature suggests that it might be useful to formulate other models to aid in the recognition of recurrent patterns of civil–

[8] Huntington, *The Soldier and the State*, pp. 83–84.

military relations. Part II of this work is devoted to the analysis of such a model, which I have called the "moderator" model.

THE MODERATOR MODEL OF CIVIL–MILITARY RELATIONS

Before describing the specific characteristics of the model, it is useful to sketch out some of the broad characteristics of the political culture within which this pattern of civil–military relations develops. Most Latin American countries are semielitist, semimobilized, and semideveloped. Characteristically, no group or political party has effectively harnessed political and economic power to meet the demands of development. Political demands are high, but political capacity to convert these demands into effective outputs is low. The society is "praetorian" in the sense that all institutions— the church, labor, students—are highly politicized. But at the same time, the political institutions are weak.[9]

In such a society the military is also politicized, and all groups attempt to co-opt the military to augment their political power. This constant co-option rules out professionalization in Huntington's sense, even though formal indicators of professionalism may appear to be increasing. Thus in the case of Peru, Brazil, and Argentina, hierarchical structure, internal differentiation, and promotion patterns all indicate a fairly professional military, yet at the same time the military is highly politicized in each of these countries.[10] This pattern of civil–military relations, in which all political actors routinely attempt to involve the military in politics, differentiates it from the liberal model where the goal is an apolitical military.

These facts of military politicization are often obscured, however, because Latin American social and political elites see themselves as part of Western European culture. Part of their heritage is to view the parliamentary form of government as an inherent

[9] A systematic attempt to define the "praetorian" society is found in David Rapoport, "A Comparative Theory of Military and Political Types," in *Changing Patterns of Military Politics*, ed. Samuel Huntington (New York: The Free Press, 1963), pp. 71–101. An analysis close to my conception is Samuel Huntington, *Political Order in Changing Societies* (New Haven: Yale University Press, 1968), pp. 192–263.

[10] For a criticism of the use of formal indicators of development as a measure of political development in themselves, see my article, "Political Development Theory: The Latin American Experience," *Journal of International Affairs*, XX, no. 2 (1966), pp. 223–234.

part of a civilized and developed polity. In this view, military rule is thus ruled out as a legitimate solution to the problem of development. These aspirations coexist with a praetorian society. This uneasy coexistence is probably the key component of the moderator model of civil–military relations. It also sheds light on the nature and limits of the military's role in that society.

Typically, the parliamentary processes sought as an ideal form of government provide an ineffective mechanism for resolving political conflicts in a praetorian society. Political parties are often fragmented. Given the desire by the political elites to maintain internal order, to check the executive, and to control the political mobilization of new groups, and given also the absence of other institutions to carry out these tasks efficiently, political elites often find it expedient to grant the military a limited degree of legitimacy to perform these specific tasks under certain conditions. However, only a low legitimacy is given to the idea of government by the military itself.

In such a pattern of civil–military relations, the military is repeatedly called into politics to be the moderator of political activity, but is denied the right systematically to attempt to direct changes within the political system. Unlike the "nation-building" or "reform" military seen in some of the new nations, the military task in the moderator model is essentially the conservative task of systems maintenance. Military activity is usually restricted to the removal of the chief executive and the transference of political power to alternative civilian groups. Military acceptance of this role is contingent upon military acceptance of the legitimacy and feasibility of parliamentary political forms, and upon their assessment that in comparison to civilians they possess a relatively low capacity for ruling.

Like the aristocratic and professional models of civil–military relations, the moderator model does not rest upon a set of controls imposed by civilians, but on a set of norms both within and without the military. The norms encourage a highly political military whose political acts are nonetheless limited to certain boundaries. In this sense, the model assumes a military that is both controlled and yet highly politicized, and the nature of the control is very different from that found in the other models.

The key components in this pattern of civil–military relations may be summarized as follows:

63

1. All major political actors attempt to co-opt the military. A politicized military is the norm.
2. The military is politically heterogeneous but also seeks to maintain a degree of institutional unity.
3. The relevant political actors grant legitimacy to the military under certain circumstances to act as moderators of the political process and to check or overthrow the executive or to avoid the breakdown of the system, especially one involving massive mobilization of new groups previously excluded from participation in the political process.
4. Approval given by civilian elites to the politically heterogeneous military to overthrow the executive greatly facilitates the construction of a winning coup coalition. Denial by civilians that the overthrow of the executive by the military is a legitimate act conversely hinders the formation of a winning coup coalition.
5. There is a strong belief among civilian elites and military officers that while it is legitimate for the military to intervene in the political process and exercise temporary political power, it is illegitimate for the military to assume the direction of the political system for long periods of time.
6. This rough value congruence is the result of civilian and military socialization via schools and literature. The military doctrine of development is also roughly congruent with that of parliamentary groups. The military officers' social and intellectual deference facilitates military co-option and continued civilian leadership.

Given the perspective of this pattern of civil–military relations, many somewhat paradoxical characteristics of Latin American politics fall into place. Whereas military intervention has traditionally been seen as representing the *decomposition* of the political system, in terms of the moderator model it may be seen as the normal method of *composition* in political life. What before have been viewed as rapid, secret, or unilateral coups d'etat by the military against civilian governments are now seen as slowly evolved, open, and dual responses of civilian and military elites to particular political crises, in which both cilivians and the military look to the military for the resolution of the crisis. What has been called "pathological interventionism" in terms of the liberal model becomes the normal functioning of the political system in the mod-erator model, whereby civilians look to the military to perform a moderating role at certain times.

Part II examines Brazilian politics and civil–military relations as a paradigm case of the moderating pattern. The analysis deals with the period between 1945 and 1964, during which this pattern of civil–military relations was dominant and before it broke down in the revolution of 1964. Undoubtedly the parameters of the model were better established, the rules of the game more widely understood, and communications more sophisticated in Brazil than in other Latin American countries. Nonetheless, I believe that de-tailed research would reveal that some of the behavioral patterns and supportive attitudes that characterized the moderating pattern of civil–military relations in Brazil from 1945 to 1964 have been prominent at various times in many other countries of Latin America.[11]

The questions raised by the model and which I attempt to answer in Part II are these: Which civilians have wanted the military to play a political role, and why? What influences did civilian attitudes have on the propensity and capacity of the military institution to perform the highly political act of deposing a president? Under what conditions were coups likely to fail? Chapter 4 examines the political reasons, historical development, and internal logic of this pattern of civil–military relations. In Chapter 5 some of the major hypotheses of the model are tested by comparing the military coups and coup attempts in Brazil in 1945, 1954, 1955, 1961, and 1964.

Two further introductory points can be raised at this point, one concerning the choice of the word "moderator" to describe the model, and the other concerning the definition of military legiti-macy. According to the model described in the following chapters, the military in Brazil enjoyed the power to moderate the political system at times of crisis. The term "moderating power" does have a sense specific to Brazil, where, during the monarchy, the em-peror had the constitutional function of intervening to resolve the political crisis at times of institutional deadlock on political con-flict. This function was called *o poder moderador* ("the moderating power"). Many Brazilians have noted that since the fall of the

[11] Though the moderator model broke down in Brazil in 1964, throughout this book I often use the present tense to describe the model in order to emphasize its general characteristics.

65

monarchy in 1889, the military has both assumed and been delegated the traditional "moderating power" originally exercised by the emperor.

I have retained the Brazilian terminology to describe this model of civil–military relations, but I intend to use it in a broader generic sense to combine the meanings of the terms "arbiter" and "moderator." I prefer these to "guardian" because I do not mean to imply that the Brazilian military always exercised a benevolent, parental authority. The term "umpire" implies more formal rules than in fact existed, and does not carry the necessary connotation that the exercise of the arbiter-moderator function required a degree of *invitation* and *acceptance* to be effective. No analogy for the moderating function is perfect, however, and the full sense of the term will only emerge in my analysis of the dynamics of civil–military relations and military coups as they occurred in Brazil between 1945 and 1964.

The second point I wish to make concerns the legitimacy of the political role for the military. When we discuss the legitimacy of a government or the legitimacy of a political role for the military, we are largely concerned with what the participant civilian political groups considered appropriate political processes, given all the circumstances. My analysis indicates that the military was often felt to be the only available structure that could perform certain functions the participant elite felt had to be performed. Military performance of these functions—whether checking the executive or maintaining internal order—was thus granted some degree of legitimacy, even by many groups who on cultural grounds were deeply antimilitarist.

Thus when I argue in the following chapters that civilian groups "sanctioned" military intervention at certain times, my point is not to argue that I think such action was morally legitimate, just, or correct, but rather to illustrate how deeply embedded such activity was in the political system itself. I have thus attempted to develop systematically John J. Johnson's interesting insight that the phenomenon that exists in many countries of Latin America and that needs analysis is not "militarism" but "civil-militarism."[12]

[12] John J. Johnson, *The Military and Society in Latin America* (Stanford: Stanford University Press, 1964), pp. 119–125.

Chapter 4

Civilian Aspects of the "Moderating Pattern"

Introduction

Historically, civilians who form the politically relevant strata of Brazilian society have always attempted to use the military to further their own political goals. Coupled with the diversity and openness of the Brazilian military institution, this has meant that military officers have always been highly politicized. A further consequence of the internal diversity of the military and persistent attempts by civilian groups to co-opt military officers into politics is that the military is never unified in its political beliefs and ideology, but is normally reflective to some degree of the broad range of civilian opinion.

To understand how this situation has arisen in Brazil, one can divide politically relevant civilians into three main groups, and examine each in turn. These elite groups are:

1. The president and his chief advisors, i.e., the government.
2. The antiregime civilians who oppose not only the government but the regime itself, and who wish to change the basic rules and authority structure.
3. The proregime civilians who, while supporting the basic rules of the regime, frequently disagree with the government and desire to check the executive by other than legislative or electoral methods.

Historically, proregime civilians were the most important group for determining the role of the military in the political system and the course of military coups in Brazil. Nonetheless, the other two groups have also played an important role.

Politicization of the Military: The Executive

Brazilian presidents, for several reasons, have always tried to use the military officers as personal instruments of their govern-

67

ment. In Brazil, as in many other developing countries, the relatively weak capacity to mobilize economic resources is matched by the government's relatively weak regulative, extractive, and distributive capability. The president often finds his reform proposals blocked by Congress, by powerful, entrenched elites, or by conflicting demands from his constituency.

In these circumstances, a classic maneuver has been for the president to attempt to gain military support for his proposals directly or indirectly, as a club against his opponents. Since the three military ministers and the commanders of the major territorial armies are appointed by him, the president can and has used these appointments as a means of gaining military support.

Examples of presidential co-option of the military exist in nearly every Brazilian government between 1937 and 1964 except Kubitschek's, whether they involve strong, semiauthoritarian presidents like Getúlio Vargas, or weak populist presidents, such as João Goulart.

In 1937, for example, a key element in Vargas' successful institution of the *Estado Nôvo* was the active support of the military; the *Estado Nôvo* granted him increased powers which allowed him to introduce many social and economic reforms and to prolong his stay in office.[1]

Similarly, President Jânio Quadros attempted to use the military as a major element in his strategy to gain more adequate political support for his programs. Quadros resigned in 1961 after occupying the presidency for less than seven months. As he wrote later, his resignation was a political maneuver designed to increase his political power by mobilizing popular and military support.[2] From

[1] For Vargas' explanation to a military audience of why the *Estado Nôvo* was necessary, and for his praise of the military for their support, see his *A Nova Política do Brasil* (Rio de Janeiro: Livraria José Olympio Editôra, 1938), v, 242–243. For an English language analysis of the *Estado Nôvo*, there is John W. F. Dulles, *Vargas of Brazil: A Political Biography* (Austin: University of Texas Press, 1967), pp. 162–274.

[2] Originally it was widely assumed that Quadros resigned because he lacked military support or because he wanted to prevent an impending coup. See, e.g., Hélio Jaguaribe, "A renúncia do Presidente Quadros e a crise política brasileira," *Revista Brasiliera de Ciências Sociais,* i (November 1961), 272–311. However, no solid evidence has been unearthed to date to prove this. Norris Lyle, a doctoral candidate in history at the University of California at Los Angeles who has done extensive field research on Quadros' career, argues that on the basis of his data the military definitely did not pressure Quadros into resigning.

the presidential viewpoint, he felt the necessary structural reforms were blocked by a Congress "pulverized" by regional, state, municipal, and personalistic differences.

Quadros asserts that the military ministers also became convinced of the need to change the political structure and participated in the search for "formulas or solutions attempting to strengthen governmental authority without sacrificing the fundamental aspects of democratic process." His eventual plan to modify the political system along Gaullist lines failed, Quadros commented bitterly, because of the "vacillation of the military."[3]

João Goulart, when president, was able to use elements of the military very effectively in many crisis situations. Despite the fact that there was considerable military resistance to his assumption of presidential office in 1961, and despite the fact that he was finally overthrown by the military in April 1964, at no time did Goulart want an apolitical military. In fact in most of the major problems his government faced, Goulart actively used the military as one of his major policy instruments.

In the succession crisis of 1961, Goulart assumed the presidency only after a compromise had been reached with elements of the military, in which the office of the president was weakened by creation of the new office of prime minister. The compromise called for a plebiscite to be held in 1965 to decide whether Brazil should maintain a prime-ministerial form of government or return to full presidential powers.

Goulart was naturally unhappy with this compromise. He began to campaign for an earlier plebiscite. Statements and manifestos by Goulart-appointed generals in key positions were a vital part of this campaign. On August 10, 1962, the military ministers issued a statement urging an early plebiscite. Congress accepted April 1963. Goulart pressed Congress harder for an October 1962 plebiscite to be held in conjunction with the scheduled congressional and gubernatorial elections. His brother-in-law, Governor Leonel Brizola of Rio Grande do Sul, threatened to use force if Congress did not comply with this request. Congress was nonetheless hesitant and stalling.

[3] Jânio Quadros and Afonso Arinos de Mello Franco, "O Porquê da Renúncia," *Realidade* (November 1967), pp. 31–34. Quadros, both as a politician and a personality, is so complex and ambiguous that not even this explanation can be taken as the last word on the resignation.

General Jair Dantas Ribeiro, the commanding officer of Brazil's largest army, the Third Army headquartered in Rio Grande do Sul, then implicitly threatened Congress by sending a telegram to the minister of war. By releasing the telegram to the press, he gave the move the coloration of a manifesto or ultimatum:

> In the face of the intransigence of Congress . . . and in view of the first manifestations of discontent which are foreshadowed in the territory of the states occupied by the Third Army, it is incumbent upon me, as the officer responsible for guaranteeing law, order . . . and private property of this territory, to inform you that I find myself without the proper conditions to assume with security and success the responsibility of carrying out such a mission if the people revolt because the Congress refused the plebiscite before or, at the latest, together with the October elections.[4]

President Goulart at the time in no way condemned the obvious political threat made by the general. The plebiscite, largely as a result of these pressures, was moved up to January 1963. In June of that year Goulart appointed General Dantas Ribeiro minister of war, the senior post in the army.

A resident French correspondent, writing on Goulart's successful drive for the plebiscite, commented that the generals Goulart appointed to command the First, Second, and Third Armies were for Goulart "the most effective instruments of pressure against Congress in the battle for the return to presidentialism."[5]

Another example of Goulart's use of the military was his request to Congress on October 5, 1963, for a state of siege. In the next two days the major governors on the left, center, and right, the trade unions, and representatives of the political parties all protested. Goulart withdrew his request on October 7, 1963.[6] In this case, it was probably Goulart's military allies, the three military ministers, who urged him to make the initial request. The relevant point, however, is that Goulart, on the basis of his presumed mili-

[4] Entire statement printed in *O Estado de São Paulo*, September 13, 1962.

[5] J. J. Faust, *A Revolução Devora Seus Presidentes* (Rio de Janeiro: Editôra Saga, 1965), p. 39.

[6] For a description of the protests, especially from the left, see the account of Goulart's minister of justice, Abelardo Jurema, *Sexta-Feira, 13: Os Últimos Dias do Govêrno João Goulart* (Rio de Janeiro: Edições O Cruzeiro, 1964), pp. 129–131.

tary backing, made a major overture to change the rules of the national political game without prior political coordination or soundings with civilian groups. He was willing to rely upon and utilize the military as his major policy instrument.

Brazil is not unique in Latin America in having presidents requiring active partnership from the armed forces, instead of professional neutrality or passivity. In Chile, the major period of military activism in politics between 1924 and 1931 was in part the result of President Alessandri's deliberate attempt to politicize the officers so that they would pressure a recalcitrant Congress to pass his reform legislation.[7]

Another classic use of the military by presidents is as an extra-legal force to repress political opponents. One of the first uses to which President Roca put the greatly strengthened federal army of Argentina in the 1880s, for example, was to curtail the powers of provincial governors.[8] Later, after the first middle-class radical government came to power in 1916, the new president, Hipólito Yrigoyen, systematically attempted to transform the professional army into a personal political force to control provincial elections.[9] In Brazil, the federal army was also often used in the period of the "Old Republic" for similar purposes. In the modern Brazilian period one of the more celebrated attempts by a president to use the army to eliminate a political opponent was President João Goulart's attempt to abduct his most vociferous critic, Governor Carlos Lacerda of Guanabara, using a paratrooper unit.[10]

These examples indicate that presidential utilization of the military in politics occurs frequently in Brazil and Latin America, especially in cases where the president is faced with dissension

[7] Liisa North, *Civil–Military Relations in Argentina, Chile, and Peru*, Politics of Modernization Series, no. 2 (Berkeley: University of California, Institute of International Studies, 1966), pp. 26–31.

[8] Marvin Goldwert, "The Rise of Modern Militarism in Argentina," *Hispanic American Historical Review*, XLVIII (May 1968), 189–191.

[9] *Ibid.*, pp. 191–200; and Robert A. Potash, *The Army and Politics in Argentina, 1928–1945* (Stanford: Stanford University Press, 1969), pp. 29–54.

[10] See Fernando Pedreira, *Março 31, Civis e Militares no Processo da Crise Brasileira* (Rio de Janeiro: José Alvaro, 1964), pp. 17–22; and Thomas Skidmore, *Politics in Brazil* (New York: Oxford University Press, 1967), pp. 263–265. Congressional discussion of the incident is well reported in the *Jornal do Brasil*, November 23–25, 1963. Much mystery still surrounds this episode and it is uncertain what Goulart planned to do with Lacerda.

71

among politically relevant groups. In this circumstance, presidents have traditionally attempted to increase their own power resources by using the armed forces as an instrument of political power.

POLITICIZATION OF THE MILITARY: ANTIREGIME FORCES

The same situation exists with antiregime civilians in Brazil. By antiregime civilians I mean those political actors attempting to change the basic rules of the entire political system and to alter the principles of authority and legitimacy. The most important groups who fall within this definition have also traditionally used the armed forces as an instrument of their political strategy, and have attempted to co-opt them ideologically.

This process began with the birth of the Brazilian Republic, when the Republicans systematically recruited military support in the overthrow of the monarchy.[11] Similarly, the "Old Republic" came to an end in 1930 not so much because of the efforts of the young rebellious lieutenants within the army (the *tenentes*), but because of movements in the two major states of Minas Gerais and Rio Grande do Sul. Political leaders of these states waged a major campaign to win support or at least passivity from the army before the revolt. Several senior army officers were informed ahead of time that civilians would launch a revolution against the established regime. It was argued that given the nation's need to establish a new political order, it was the duty and obligation of the military not to resist.[12] Officers and enlisted men of Rio Grande do Sul were bombarded with these and regional arguments long before the revolution was launched in the state.[13]

[11] Detailed documentation of this process is presented by June E. Hahner, *Brazilian Civilian–Military Relations, 1889–1898*, Latin American Studies Program Dissertation Series, no. 2 (Ithaca, N.Y.: Cornell University, 1967), pp. 28–46. A good account of the Republican party's attempt to exploit and exacerbate tensions between the military and the monarchy, and the efforts to win military officers over to the side of the revolution, is found in George C. A. Boehrer's chapter, "O Partido Republicano, O Exército e a Revolução de 1889," in his *Da Monarquia à República* (Rio de Janeiro: Ministério da Educação e Cultura, 1954), pp. 275–286.

[12] See e.g., General Tasso Fragoso's account of his solicitation by Lindolfo Color, a key civilian leader of the revolutionary movement, in General Tristão de Alencar Araripe, *Tasso Fragoso: Um Pouco de História do Nosso Exército* (Rio de Janeiro: Biblioteca do Exército, 1960), pp. 541–548.

[13] The commanding officer of the federal military region in Rio Grande do Sul gives details of this campaign and its corrosive effect on the soldiers'

Again in 1945 when the *Estado Nôvo* regime was overthrown, and in 1964, when democratic, competitive politics broke down, there were similar, systematic efforts by civilians and military men to co-opt the military to change the political regime.[14] No more, indeed, than the presidents, have the antiregime forces in Brazil wanted a professional and apolitical military. Rather, antiregime groups have constantly employed the rhetoric that the military's special responsibility for the destiny of Brazil requires that they become active participants in creating a new political order. A study of other antiregime groups in Latin American countries reveals a similar process at work. In Argentina, for example, the middle class Radical party systematically attempted to use the military to gain power between 1890 and 1905. These attempts played a prominent part in the revolts of 1890, 1893, and 1905.[15]

While not important in Brazil to date, the one major antiregime movement in Latin America that has not depended on co-opting the military is the Castroite guerrilla movement, which aimed to destroy the regular military in the process of winning power. However, even this movement has wanted a political military; in the view of the Venezuelan and Guatemalan guerrilla ideologists, revolutionary success would be easier to attain under a military than under a civilian regime because a repressive military regime forces the left to recognize revolution as the only viable strategy.

THE MILITARY AND THE PROREGIME STRATA

The most interesting elite group within the political system in Brazil in terms of its attitude toward the military is what I have called the proregime civilians. In this group I include congressmen, governors, political party leaders, newspaper editors, and voters who generally accept the constitutional framework and support the existing regime, but who may or may not support the government at specific times.

---

will to resist; see General Gil de Almedia, *Hômens e Factos de Uma Revolução* (Rio de Janeiro: Calvino Filho, 1934), pp. 179–221.

[14] Both of these cases are discussed in detail in Chapter 5. The strategy of the two other major antiregime movements in Brazilian history, the 1935 Communist rebellion, and the 1938 Brazilian fascist (*Integralista*) uprising were also both predicated not so much on popular mass civilian support as on military support which had been strenuously cultivated.

[15] Ricardo Caballero, *Yrigoyen: La Conspiración Civil y Militar del 4 de Febrero de 1905* (Buenos Aires: Editorial Raigal, 1951), and North, *Civil–Military Relations*, pp. 26–30.

It is this large group of people that have historically expected the military to play the key political role of checking the actions of the executive. In most political systems that have evolved beyond tribal chieftainships, or primitive, one-man dictatorships, one of the traditional goals of these civilians has been to control the executive within an accepted sphere of action. In strong party systems, whether of the British parliamentary type, or of the Communist type, the party itself performs this function. In a political system such as that of the United States, where the party system is relatively weak, there are other strong institutions, such as the legislature, which can perform the functions of veto or in extremes those of impeachment. The judiciary can also implement constraints on presidential authority by determining the constitutionality of executive decrees. In addition, and very importantly, elections themselves act as an important method of restraint by periodically subjecting the executive mandate to renewal.

In Brazil, however, as in many of the developing areas, the political institutions of the legislature and the judiciary are at times subject to complete executive control. Elections are often uncertain affairs or they are controlled outright by the executive. Many members of the polity have for these reasons felt little confidence in the efficacy of these institutions to check executive activity. Informally or formally, proregime civilian groups outside the government often tend to assign this task to the military.

The process leading to this state of affairs is clearly seen in congressional debates over the political role of the military in Brazilian society at the time of framing new constitutions. Congress is an important index of the opinion of proregime civilians in Brazil's federal system, since it is here that many of the most powerful groups within the political system publicly articulate their demands. The Brazilian Congress has been one of the strongest in Latin America in this century, and local and regional groups have traditionally received much of their financing via congressional legislation.[16] Congress also passes or blocks such basic reforms as enfranchisement of illiterates or agrarian reform. It normally plays a part in the careers of the major national political leaders, who

[16] The Chilean Congress is probably the most powerful. The Brazilian Congress has been eclipsed by the executive in the two periods of authoritarian rule, 1937–1945 and 1964 to the time of writing. In Chapter 6 the policy-making weaknesses of the Brazilian Congress are discussed.

74

often move from the mayoralty of a large city to the Congress as a deputy, back to the state as a governor, and finally back to Congress as a senator, or on to the presidency.

The proregime civilians met collectively in 1892, 1934, and 1946 to draft new constitutions for Brazil. At these assemblies they expressed their ideas and opinions as to what they felt was the necessary and appropriate function of the military in the Brazilian political system. Their opinions, as expressed in the constituent assemblies, are an index of the *de facto* legitimacy accorded the military to perform a political role in checking the powers of the presidency and as such are extremely important in that legitimacy flows from operative attitudes. In addition, the final product of the constituent assemblies, the constitutions themselves, while not able to create a power that did not exist, could ratify an existing power and furnish it with the language and rationale necessary for its communication to the military and to other political actors.

The constitutions adopted in 1891, 1934, and 1946 were virtually identical in their two major conclusions in regard to the role of the military in Brazilian politics. This role was described in two key clauses.[17] The first stated that the military was a permanent, national institution specifically charged with the task of maintaining law and order in the country and of guaranteeing the continued normal functioning of the three constitutional powers: the executive, the legislature, and the judiciary. The second clause made the military obedient to the executive, but significantly stated that they should only be obedient "within the limits of the law" (*dentro dos limites da lei*). This in effect authorized the military to give only discretionary obedience to the president, since obedience was dependent upon their decision regarding the legality of the presidential order.

The constitutional obligation of the military to ensure the proper functioning of and balance between the executive, legislature, and the judiciary has meant that in any clash between the president and the legislature, appeals have been made by civilians to the military to fulfill their constitutional obligation to defend the prerogatives of the Congress.

These constitutional provisions would be less significant if it

[17] 1891 Constitution, art. 14. 1934 Constitution, art. 162. 1946 Constitution, art. 176–178.

could be shown that they were either unconsciously included in the constitutions, habitually so included, or were included due to imposition by the military themselves. But the evidence suggests that they were none of these. On the contrary, the role imposed constitutionally on the military, as expressed by the two clauses above, was consciously adopted in spite of the fact that certain members of the constituent assemblies brought forward specific amendments to abolish the two clauses because they gave too much power to the military within the political system.[18]

That this conception of the role of the military is a conscious choice on the part of the participant political strata and not just habitual is demonstrated by the fact that neither of the two centralized constitutions that were drafted without using a constituent assembly—the imperial constitution of 1824, which lasted until the fall of the empire in 1889, and the Vargas *Estado Nôvo* authoritarian constitution of 1937—mentions the clause specifying military support of the president *dentro dos limites da lei*.[19] The *Estado Nôvo* constitution clearly shows, in fact, that a strong government would not accept the implied check upon its own powers given by the *dentro dos limites da lei* clause, because the constitution without qualification states that the military shall be "obedient to the authority of the president"; it also gives the military no such missions as guaranteeing the various branches of the government or maintaining internal order.

Finally, while all three constituent assemblies were held in periods after changes of regime and thus in periods of high military strength, the evidence does not support the thesis that the *dentro dos limites da lei* clause is in the constitutions of Brazil because of military pressure. Deodoro da Fonseca, president of Brazil during the 1891 constituent assembly, was himself the military general who overthrew the Empire, and he specifically objected to the clause and fought vigorously against it. He felt it would be bad for military

[18] For opposing amendments and arguments in 1891, see Câmara dos Deputados, *Annais de Constituinte de 1891*, I, 180–181, and III, 33. For 1946, the various arguments against this provision in the special committees, and in the Chamber of Deputies, are summarized in José Duarte, *A Constituição Brasileira de 1946: Exegese dos Textos a Luz dos Trabalhos da Assembléia Constituinte* (Rio de Janeiro: Imprensa Nacional, 1947), III, 292–303.

[19] See *Constituição Política do Império* (25 de Março de 1824), art. 147, and *Constituição de 10 de Novembro de 1937*, art. 161.

discipline.[20] The drafter of the constitution, Ruy Barbosa, a civilian, has also written that many military men opposed the article on the grounds that it would divide the military and involve them in politics and that the military viewed the clause with "profound apprehension and decided antipathy."[21]

In the drafting of the 1946 constitution, the military had very good links with the subcommission on national security that drew up the draft copy of the constitution. Of the three members, one had been an officer in the army from 1904 to 1945 and another, Silvestre Pericles de Góis Monteiro, was the brother of General Góis Monteiro, one of the most influential military officers in Brazil at that time. It is fair to assume that if strong military pressure had been applied, it would have been applied on this subcommission on national security via the two of its three members with the strongest military connections. Nonetheless, it was this subcommittee that drafted the constitutional clause in regard to obedience, which unqualifiedly asserted that the military was "under the supreme authority of the president of the Republic."[22] It was the larger constitutional commission that argued for and reinstated the clause that military obedience should be discretionary and contingent upon presidential orders being "within the limits of the law."

What were the arguments that were advanced and, after discussion, accepted by the majority of the proregime, politically relevant, strata over the years? The framer and principal advocate of the first constitution of the Republic, Ruy Barbosa, was known as a major spokesman against an overlarge role for the military in society. The theme of his presidential candidacy in 1910 was the need to contain military influence and ensure civilian control. Nonetheless, he still argued in 1892, and reiterated later, that the clause "within the limits of the law" was necessary because real obedience can only come if the superior of the military (i.e., the

[20] See the speech by Deputado João Mangabeira of May 19, 1923 in the Chamber of Deputies, reproduced in full in *O Tempo*, Ano III, Número XIII (January 15, 1924), pp. 185–190. Also, see M. Seabra Fagundes, *As Fôrças Armadas na Constituição* (Rio de Janeiro: Biblioteca do Exército, 1955), pp. 28–38.

[21] Ruy Barbosa, *Comentários à Constituição Federal Brasileira* (São Paulo: Saraiva, 1932), I, 403.

[22] See Duarte, *A Constituição Brasileira de 1946*, pp. 293–296. For membership of the subcommittee and the draft proposal, see *Diário da Assembléia Constituinte*, March 28, 1946, pp. 642–643.

president) is obedient to the law.[23] Thus, despite his antimilitarism, he expressed uncertainty in regard to the capacity of the civilian political system to produce and maintain presidents who would operate "within the law" without any military check.

In the 1946 debates it is clear that civilians desired to give the military legitimate grounds to refuse to obey any president acting beyond what they considered the established legal framework. A labor party representative on the constitutional commission wanted to assure civilian control but did not want it to be absolute: "I am of the opinion that we ought to give to the military the moral force necessary so that they can react against orders which are contrary to the national interest."[24] One congressman specifically argued that the clause "within the limits of the law" was necessary, because "there ought to be a check on particular governments which would oblige officers . . . to carry out orders which are not within the law."[25] Most of the commentary on the constitution, while recognizing the ambiguity of the constitutional provision, did not criticize the general sense.

It is clear that many major actors in Brazilian politics have felt anxiety about the ability of civilian institutions to check the chief executive. They felt the need for a checking device, and before 1964 they consistently expressed the belief that the military was the appropriate institution for carrying out this role. In their informal attitudes they accorded legitimacy to the concept that the military was an integral part of the political system and they constitutionally sanctioned the view that the military had under certain conditions the obligation to intervene in the political process. To ensure that the military had the necessary autonomy to implement this function, they consistently made military obedience to the president not automatic, but discretionary. Thus *de facto* attitudinal legitimacy was supported and routinized by *de jure* constitutional legitimacy.

The fact that these attitudes had been incorporated in the Brazilian constitutions meant that an acceptable political formula existed, as well as a subtle but nonetheless widely understood language, for the politician and the public to use in appealing to the military to intervene in politics to check or even depose a presi-

---

[23] Ruy Barbosa, *Comentários à Constituição Federal Brasileira*, I, 400.
[24] *Diário de Assembléia Constituinte*, May 8, 1946, p. 1548.
[25] *Ibid*., pp. 1548, 1549.

dent. As we shall see this was repeatedly used in the 1945–1964 period.[26]

While Brazil is the paradigm case of this "moderating pattern" of civil–military relations, other Latin American countries have also given *de jure* legitimacy to the military performance of the role of checking the executive or guaranteeing the constitution. For example, the 1965 constitution of Honduras states that the "armed forces are instituted in order to . . . maintain peace, the public order, and the rule of this constitution; and above all to see that the principles of free suffrage and noncontinuity of the presidency of the Republic are not violated."[27] Thirteen other Latin American countries specifically charge the military with the role of protecting or guaranteeing the constitution.[28]

The picture that emerges of the goals and strategies of major political actors in Brazil is one in which elite groups who are generally favorable to the regime ascribe legitimacy to the military for what one might call a "moderator role" in the political society. Neither of the two other political groups—the executive and his supporters, and the antiregime forces—consistently articulate the feeling that the military should be apolitical. As a result, the military has played a crucial role in politics in Brazil, with all groups trying to co-opt the military in times of political conflict, and with actual coups against the executive representing the *combined* efforts of both civilian and military groups.

THE MODERATING PATTERN OF CIVIL–MILITARY RELATIONS: TWO HYPOTHESES CONCERNING MILITARY COUPS

A consideration of the ways in which civilians attempt to co-opt the military into politics in Brazil (and of the normal institutional inhibitions working against military intromission in politics in the form of an actual coup against the government) suggests the possi-

[26] See Chap. 5.　　　　　　　　　　[27] Article 319.

[28] These figures first came to my attention in an unpublished manuscript on the military and development by Luigi Einaudi. After the presidential election in Chile in 1970, the anti-Allende parliamentary majority predictably adopted the "moderator model" when they implicitly gave the military the role of maintaining the constitutional status quo, thus checking the executive.

An interesting project for further research would be to construct a typology of constitutions in Latin America and Western Europe according to the position they designate to the military in regard to the internal legality of the state and to see if different provisions correlate with different rates or styles of coups.

79

bility that civilian attitudes toward the military may be as or even more important in determining the dynamics of coups than military ideology or military goals. This in turn suggests two hypotheses of civil–military relations, in which the normal picture of unilateral intervention is reversed and the military becomes more a dependent than an independent variable.

The first hypothesis correlates the propensity of the military to intervene with the cohesion of the relevant political strata, and argues that this propensity is high when civilian cohesion is low, and low when civilian cohesion is high. The second hypothesis relates the success of coups to the degree of public legitimacy ascribed to the executive and to the military. Military coups tend to be successful when, before the coup attempt, executive legitimacy is low and the legitimacy given by the relevant political strata to the military to intervene is high. According to this hypothesis, coups tend to be unsuccessful when executive legitimacy is high and the legitimacy given to the military to intervene is low.

I propose to examine the first of the hypotheses in this chapter, and the second in the next. The first of the hypotheses raises the question of the conditions that tend to increase or decrease the propensity of the military to attempt to intervene in the political process. What is suggested is that the propensity of the military to intervene in central political issues is increased when the executive and the proregime strata are sharply divided over political goals. At such times, a president tends to attempt to increase his own power resources by using the military as an instrument. Conversely, significant elements of the proregime civilians tend to become antigovernment and to make appeals to the military to perform the moderating role of checking the executive. The stronger the proregime civilians' rejection of a president, the greater is the possibility of the formation of a strong coalition of civilians to encourage the military to exercise its traditional moderating role of checking the executive. Likewise, antiregime groups become most effective when major groups that were previously part of the proregime force join their ranks. Until some proregime groups join the antiregime group, the antiregime group remains relatively isolated and cannot make convincing appeals to the military to overthrow the regime.

This analysis suggests that, even if we assume (as I do) that at all times there are some military officers anxious to overthrow the government for personal reasons, either selfish or ideological, the attitudes of the proregime civilians are likely to be determining. My previous discussion of the bureaucratic norms of obedience and command, and of the normal internal differences over politics that exist within the military suggests that it is difficult for the military to put together a winning coalition for a coup unless there is a major split between the executive and the proregime strata and the latter begin to articulate the belief that in these circumstances the military should perform the moderating function.

, The absence of such a split means that the president is less likely to risk tampering with the promotion or disciplinary structure of the military, the two acts most likely to create a temporary military consensus against the president on grounds that the military as an institution is threatened. In addition, without splits among civilians, military activists are also likely to be isolated, without strong civilian allies. This also makes it easier for the president to discipline minority elements within the military plotting to overthrow him.

This analysis of political activities of civilians and military officers under normal political conditions strengthens the hypothesis that attempts by the military to intervene in the exercise of its moderating function will correlate inversely with the degree of cohesion between the proregime strata and the executive.

To assess the hypothesis, one can examine the entire period from the consolidation of the "Old Republic" in 1898 until its fall in 1930. In this thirty-two-year period, the military as an institution became involved three times in the resolution of political questions or in coup attempts. The first was during and after the election of 1910 when, after a split among the politicians, the major civilian faction opposed to the president, Afonso Pena, "began putting pressure on the War Minister to permit himself to be announced as a candidate."[29] They were successful in their attempt to co-opt him (and many other military officers), and military-political activism, never too far beneath the surface, increased sharply in this period of bitter political conflict.[30]

In the second case, in 1922, there was again a major split among the participant political strata. The minority faction involved the

---

[29] José Maria Bello, *A History of Modern Brazil, 1889–1964*, trans. J. L. Taylor (Stanford: Stanford University Press, 1966), p. 205.

[30] Even in this period, however, a civilian caudillo politician, Pinheiro Machado, was probably more powerful than the military.

military in a crisis revolving around the institutional honor of the military. The minority faction's efforts to involve the military were facilitated by existing military animosity due to the appointment of a civilian as minister of war and President Epitácio Pessoa's veto of the military budget. This, in conjunction with widespread dissatisfaction among younger officers, set the stage for a young lieutenants' revolt (the *tenentes* revolt) which continued on and off until a new president was inaugurated who was more acceptable to the civilian groups involved.[31]

The third case of military involvement was in 1930. In this year, two of the three big states, Minas Gerais and Rio Grande do Sul, refused to recognize the president's choice for his successor. After the election, in which the president's choice won, a civil war broke out. The military eventually stepped in and ended the war by deposing the incumbent president, and handing over power to Getúlio Vargas, the defeated candidate.[32]

The three cases of military intervention in the resolution of political crises all revolved around elections. In each there were deep

[31] The revolt itself was almost exclusively military in origin and precisely because it was so isolated from civilians it failed. (Interview with former *tenente* Marshal Oswaldo Cordeiro de Farias, Rio de Janeiro, September 11, 1968.)

Many accounts emphasize the military origins of *tenentismo*. However, the growth of military-political activism in 1921–1922 was intricately related to the deep split of the ruling elite over the presidential campaign of 1922 between the official candidate, Arthur Bernardes, and the candidate of the "Republican reaction," Nilo Peçanha. By 1921, as José Maria Bello observed, "political peace . . . had been shattered. . . . Once more the small group of men who ruled Brazil by controlling the large states was split. . . . Exploited by clever demagogues, the partisan campaign soon agitated even the military" (*History of Modern Brazil*, p. 243). A good discussion linking the political crisis with the military crisis is contained in Nelson Werneck Sodré, *História Militar do Brasil* (Rio de Janeiro: Editôra Civilização Brasileira, 1965), pp. 198–214. Documents relating to the 1922 revolt and the forged letter that presidential candidate Bernardes was supposed to have written criticizing the military are in Hélio Silva, *1922: Sangue na Areia de Copacabana* (Rio de Janeiro: Editôra Civilização Brasileira, 1964).

[32] The bibliography of the 1930 revolution is vast but no definitive account exists. Thomas Skidmore, *Politics in Brazil*, pp. 332–336, gives a brief review of the literature in his valuable footnotes.

My treatment of 1910, 1922, and 1930 is of course highly schematic and abstract. At a more detailed level each case is distinct and extremely complex. A full treatment of each of these civil–military crises will be contained in a forthcoming book by Ronald M. Schneider.

divisions among civilians.[33] In 1910 the military was co-opted; in 1922 the military acted unsuccessfully; and in 1930 they acted successfully. These three cases tend therefore to confirm the hypothesis that military involvement is high when cohesion among the relevant political elites is low. The hypothesis would be further strengthened if we could demonstrate the opposite, i.e., that in those cases where military political involvement was low, elite cohesion was in fact high. Fairly strong support for this aspect of the hypothesis is provided by an examination of election results in the same period. Between 1898 and 1930, Brazil was ruled by decentralized state oligarchies that cooperated at the national level in a single party, the *Partido Republicano*. It was a period of low and static political mobilization as measured by the percentage of the population participating in national elections. In the four elections from 1894 to 1906, for example, only 2.45 percent of the population voted, and in the four elections between 1918 and 1926, only 2.04 percent.[34]

In such a low-mobility party system, the percentage of votes for the winning candidates is a good indicator of cohesion among the relevant civilian political strata because a significant opposition candidate ran in the election only if the political elites failed to agree to a compromise candidate. The hypothesis relating military action and elite cohesion can thus be tested by looking at the election results in this period.

In the three elections where military officers played a major role in the electoral process, as they did in 1910, 1922, and 1930, the winning candidates received only 57.7 percent, 56.03 percent, and 57 percent of the votes, respectively. In the elections where there was no major military activism, the winners' average percentage of votes was 91.6. The figures therefore give strong support to the

[33] Some would argue that the participation by the cadets of the military academy in the rioting and rebellion against compulsory vaccination in November 1904 should be included. I do not include it because it involved only a small portion of the army and was put down by the army itself. In any case the cadets' revolt started only after the civilians had done extensive rioting and the civilian insurrection continued after their military allies had capitulated. See Bello, *History of Modern Brazil*, pp. 180–183. The two brief enlisted men's mutinies aboard ship in 1910 have also not been included because of their short and isolated character.

[34] For a useful summary of the statistics of the presidential elections, see Alberto Guerreiro Ramos, *A Crise do Poder no Brasil* (Rio de Janeiro: Zahar Editôres, 1961), p. 32.

hypothesis that low military-political activism is a function of the high cohesion of the civilian elites (see Table 4.1).

TABLE 4.1

WINNING PRESIDENTIAL CANDIDATES' PERCENTAGE OF VOTES
AND MILITARY ACTIVISM: 1898–1930*

Election Year	Percentage of Total Vote Received by Winning Candidate	Major Involvement of Military as Institution before or after Election
1898	90.93	No
1902	91.71	No
1906	97.92	No
1910	57.07	Yes
1914	91.59	No
1918	99.06	No
1919	71.00	No
1922	56.03	Yes
1926	97.99	No
1930	57.74	Yes

* SOURCE: For the electoral figures, see n. 34, this chapter.

The second hypothesis of the moderating model of civil–military relations correlates the *success* and *failure* of military intervention in politics with the degree of legitimacy (*before* coups were attempted) ascribed by important civilians to the executive to exercise his office and to the military to perform its traditional moderating role. From 1945 to 1964, the period in which this model of civil–military relations particularly applies, every change of presidential power in fact raised fundamental questions among major civilian groups about the legitimacy of the new president, with the exception of the election of 1960. We would expect the propensity for military activism to be high throughout the period and, in fact, in every case except that of 1960, the military attempted to play a major role in the ratification or allocation of political power.

The systemic conditions underlying this military involvement, and the precise nature of the correlations between successful or unsuccessful military intervention and presidential and military legitimacy are explored in the following chapter.

84

Chapter 5

The Functioning of the "Moderating Pattern"—
A Comparative Analysis of Five Coups, 1945–1964

INTRODUCTION

Despite the fact that Brazil by 1964 was still politically semi-elitist, the entire period from 1945 to 1964 (especially from 1961 to 1964) was one of rapid mobilization. The size of the electorate more than doubled. Great, though sporadic, economic growth took place. This growth was accompanied by massive population shifts and chronic inflation, which became acute by 1963.

The pace of military activism also increased in this period. There were military coups in 1945, 1954, 1964, a frustrated coup attempt in 1961, and a movement toward a coup in 1955 that precipitated a countercoup in defense of constitutional authorities. The years 1945 to 1964 mark the period of Brazil's first experience with open, democratic, competitive politics. The military's role in arbitrating or moderating the political system increased as political conflict increased. Some reasons for this were suggested in the previous chapter. It was seen that all the major actors in the polity utilized the military to further their own political ends, and that coups could be considered not merely as a unilateral response of an arbitrary and independent military institution acting on behalf of its own institutional needs and ideology, but as a dual response of both military officers and civilians to political divisions in the society.

This chapter aims to examine the *dynamics* of these military coups in Brazil as they occurred between 1945 and 1964, and to draw out the rules of the game in the moderating pattern of civil–military relations.[1] I also propose to test some hypotheses that relate

[1] No attempt will be made to provide a complete narrative of each coup. A convenient summary of all the coups can be found in Glauco Carneiro, *História das Revoluções Brasileiras*, II (Rio de Janiero, Edições O Cruzeiro, 1965), 459–666. Thomas Skidmore, *Politics in Brazil, 1930–1964: An Experiment in Democracy* (New York: Oxford University Press, 1967),

the success and failure of military coups to the degree of prior civilian sanction for military performance of the moderating function.[2]

EXECUTIVE LEGITIMACY AND THE SUCCESS OR FAILURE OF COUPS

The most striking feature of the five military coups and coup attempts between 1945 and 1964 is that, with one exception, they all occurred only after a long period during which doubt had been openly expressed by the political elites concerning the right or legitimacy of the executive to retain or assume office.[3]

This fact, that military coups occurred when political elites were deeply divided, is in keeping with the argument earlier advanced, that the propensity for military involvement in politics increases in direct relation to the doubts that exist among the political elite over the question of who should rule the country.

In the period after 1945 these doubts were in each case expressed publicly as well as privately. Except for 1961 the debate was lengthy, often lasting several months. It was during this debate that military opinion, usually as divided as opinion in the polity at large, was formed. Military officers sought and were sought by civilian allies. Debate was a necessary preliminary step in any successful military coup. Wherever a fairly widespread debate did not occur, coups plotted or planned by the military failed.

---

is an excellent guide to literature surrounding the coups. Ronald M. Schneider's forthcoming work on the Brazilian military since the nineteenth century will discuss each coup in detail. See also John W. F. Dulles, *Unrest in Brazil: Political-Military Crises 1955–64* (Austin: University of Texas Press, 1970).

[2] By successful coups I mean the coups of 1945, 1954, and 1964, where the main goal of the military, the deposing of the chief executive, was achieved. In the unsuccessful coup of 1961, the military officers attempting the coup failed in their stated goal of blocking the vice-president from assuming the presidency. The case of 1955 is more complicated because it involved an unsuccessful civil–military movement to block the inauguration of President-elect Kubitscheck and Vice-President-elect Goulart. Though no actual coup was attempted, it can be called an unsuccessful coup movement. Because there was a fear that a minority might attempt this coup, the majority of the army officers executed a successful preventive constitutional coup to ensure the inauguration.

[3] The exception was in 1961 when President Quadros unexpectedly resigned after less than seven months in office. This produced a coup attempt by the military ministers in anticipation of what they incorrectly thought would be public support or at least acquiescence.

86

An examination of the coups between 1945 and 1964 illustrates this point. In 1945 the *Estado Nôvo* of Vargas was ended by a military coup that removed Vargas from office. Executive power was given to the chief Supreme Court justice, who supervised elections for the presidency the following month. The semifascist regime Vargas installed with the support of military officers in 1937 had originally derived a fair measure of its support from the fact that at the time authoritarian regimes seemed to presage the pattern of politics of the future. By late 1944, however, not only was it becoming increasingly apparent that the authoritarian governments of Germany and Italy would lose the war, but many in Brazil had begun to doubt the appropriateness or efficiency of authoritarianism. Especially important were the reactions of the officers in the Brazilian combat division in Italy (FEB), fighting with the Allies against Hitler's forces and Mussolini's fascist diehards. These officers were impressed with the organizational ability of the United States, in comparison to the weakness of fascist Italy.[4]

Opinions of the FEB officers were matched by growing doubts among civilians about Vargas' government. Vargas himself realized the need for change. He proposed a national presidential election, the first since 1930. But many civilians and military officers continued to doubt his sincerity. While his popular support among the masses actually increased between 1944 and 1945, mainly because of his favorable labor legislation, attacks by important civilian politicians mounted. They were reflected in newspapers and in the political activity of civilians. By mid-1944, an opposition group formed, threatening to go to any lengths if Vargas did not hold elections as promised. This group included some key civilian leaders of the 1930 Revolution, as well as several military officers.[5]

Doubts about the legitimacy of Vargas' rule reached the level of newspaper editorials months before the coup of 1945. The *Jornal*

[4] See chap. 12 for a discussion of the FEB experience and its contribution to officer opinion.

[5] The best source detailing the changed mood in the country and its impact on the military is the informative autobiography of General Góes Monteiro, as told to Lourival Coutinho, *O General Góes Depõe* (Rio de Janeiro: Livraria Editôra Coelho Branco, 1955), pp. 395–469.
General Góes was probably the most influential general of the 1930–1945 Vargas era and he was the war minister who supervised the deposition of Vargas in 1945. A review of the events leading to Vargas' overthrow is contained in John W. F. Dulles, *Vargas of Brazil: A Political Biography* (Austin: University of Texas Press, 1967), pp. 251–274.

do Brasil commented simply, "While Senhor Vargas is in Catete [the presidential palace] the country will have no confidence or tranquility."[6] After Vargas altered the elections, *The Diário Carioca* editorialized:

> The dictatorship of Senhor Getúlio Vargas struck against the people of Brazil one more liberty-taking, treasonous blow. . . . The Brazilian people now do not trust in its government. . . . The government cannot preside honestly over the election.[7]

Especially important were attitudes of those supporting the government. Juan Linz ably discusses the relation of this group to governmental stability in his analysis of the breakdown of democratic regimes:

> Beliefs in legitimacy of authority are decisive in crisis situations, particularly important for those having a share in the authority structure and most to those required to use force to implement decisions of those in power. Ultimately, legitimacy is involved in decisions about the state of emergency and in those that may involve the loss of life for those challenging or defending authority.[8]

In the case of the 1945 coup, debate about presidential legitimacy created doubts within the core group of civilian and military supporters of Vargas. From the civilian side, an important loss to Vargas occurred when his foreign minister, Oswaldo Aranha, long one of Vargas' most powerful allies, resigned and later joined the opposition. The declining viability of authoritarian ideology between 1944 and 1945 among powerful civilian politicians was also measured by the fact that by November 1944 the author of the *Estado Nôvo* constitution, Francisco Campos, privately urged Vargas to espouse the cause of democratic government. He later publicly broke with Vargas's government.[9]

In the crisis of 1954 the same debate about the authority of the president occurred at private and public levels, involving both civilian and military actors. In this case, presidential legitimacy was questioned at the moral level.

[6] October 11, 1945.   [7] October 13, 1945.

[8] "The Breakdown of Democratic Regimes," paper prepared for the Seventh World Congress of Sociology, Varna, Bulgaria, September 1970.

[9] The details of this slow disassociation from Vargas by many of his key staff members can be found in Dulles, *Vargas of Brazil*, pp. 251–274.

Vargas was elected to the presidency in an open contest in 1950, five years after the *Estado Nôvo* had been ended by a military coup. By early 1954 his government faced a series of problems including a balance of payments deficit, difficulties in resolving conflicts between the pay demands of trade unions and army officers, charges about secret collaboration with Perón, and apparently even a decline in personal vigor. Nonetheless, his government was still legitimate enough easily to defeat an attempted impeachment proceeding.[10]

However, pressure against his government quickly reached crisis proportions when an air force major was killed in an assassination attempt against Vargas' outspoken critic, Carlos Lacerda. A sensational investigation followed. Responsibility for the assassination attempt was traced to President Vargas' personal bodyguard, and numerous cases of corruption involving the president's closest associates were brought to light. Although Vargas himself was never implicated, the legitimacy of the president to continue in office and as commander-in-chief of the armed forces was seriously questioned.[11]

Legitimacy concerns more than the quantity of people in favor of an institution or a man. In crisis situations, the quality and intensity of the support, or opposition, is often crucial. In the crisis of 1954, the assassination attempt and subsequent revelations of financial scandal demoralized and immobilized many of Vargas' supporters. Aggressive active support for the president among his own inner circle waned. Indeed, early in the crisis, his finance minister and his minister of transport discussed the feasibility of Vargas' temporarily stepping down.[12] When the leader of the lower

[10] For an overview of the political and economic strains on the Vargas government in this period see Skidmore, *Politics in Brazil*, pp. 100–142. For accounts of Vargas' occasional depression and talk of resignation even before the assassination crisis, see the account of his daughter in chap. 11 of "A Vida de Getúlio Contada por Sua Filha, Alzira Vargas, ao Journalista Raul Guidicelli," in *Fatos & Fatos*, September 21, 1963. Francisco Campos gave a similar account; see Dulles, *Vargas of Brazil*, p. 314.

[11] For a good description of the intense emotional atmosphere surrounding these investigations and their erosive effect on support for Vargas, see J.V.D. Saunders, "A Revolution of Agreement Among Friends: The End of the Vargas Era," *Hispanic American Historical Review*, XLIV (May 1964), 197–213.

[12] See the autobiography of the then vice-president, who became president upon Vargas's death, Café Filho, *Do Sindicato ao Catete: Memórias Poli-*

house of Congress, a Vargas supporter, was asked about his ability to rally congressional support for the beleaguered president, his response was characteristic of the lowered intensity of support among those closest to Vargas, "I do not have the parliamentary force for a political counteroffensive. The distaste [for resistance] is complete. The opposition campaign in the Congress, in the press and radio has weakened it too much."[13]

Weeks before the military finally acted on August 24 to remove Vargas from office, many newspapers devoted editorials to demands for Vargas' resignation. The prestigious and normally progressive *Correio da Manhã* asserted on August 10 that Vargas lacked the force of government and the principle of authority and concluded that the only solution was for Vargas to resign. Two days later, still twelve days before the military demanded Vargas' renunciation of office, the *Diário Carioca* was equally insistent: "There is no longer any doubt that the continuation of democratic institutions in Brazil is dependent upon the removal of Senhor Getúlio Vargas from power."[14]

The issue of the legitimacy of the executive plays a key role in determining how coup activists formulate arguments addressed to still loyal presidential defenders, both civilian and military. A recurrent theme in Brazilian military coups is the need to avoid bloodshed and military disunity. Activists often argue that, because a president's legitimacy is being seriously questioned by large numbers of the politically powerful civilians, the activists are forced to take action against a president in order to prevent chaos or anarchy from developing. Thus their own threat of action against him is usually couched as a defensive rather than an offensive move. In this way, responsibility for any possible loss of life or bloodshed is subtly shifted from the activists to the military defenders of the president. The implication is that public and military sentiment against the president is so strong that only if the military as a *whole* refrains from defending him can bloodshed be avoided.[15]

---

ticas e Confissões Humanas, I (Rio de Janeiro: Libraria José Olympio Editôra, 1966), 301–303.

[13] *Ibid.*, p. 319.   [14] Editorial, August 12, 1954.

[15] This bargaining strategy is essentially what Thomas Schelling has called a "threat." "The distinctive character of a threat is that one asserts that he will do, in a contingency, what he would manifestly prefer not to do . . . the contingency being governed by the second party's behavior. Like the ordinary commitment, the threat is a surrender of choice, a renunciation

For example, in the 1954 coup against Vargas, the war minister had been a passionate defender of the president. Yet once the coup decision was announced, the activists argued to the presidential defenders that they had been forced to act by public opinion and that now their bridges were burned, and their only option was removal of the president. The onus of avoiding a military split and possible civil war effectively paralyzed the war minister. The intensity of his support declined. A fellow cabinet minister described the demoralized minister of war as saying that "if he received the order he would imprison the generals and put the troops into the street, but—he did not tire of repeating—there would be bloodshed."[16]

The successful coup of 1964 involved even more complex issues than the coups of 1945 or 1954. In 1964 military officers did not restrict themselves to the overthrow of the president, but after the coup they actually assumed governing power for the first time in the twentieth century. However, in this coup, as in the preceding ones, the legitimacy of the president was widely debated well before military intervention occurred.

A major question concerning Goulart's legitimacy in late 1963 and early 1964 related to whether he would abide by the democratic constitution laid down in 1946 concerning his right to succeed himself, or whether he would attempt to alter the constitutional limits and rule in a *Peronista* fashion, or with Communist support. Most fearful were the center and right, but even the left had some apprehensions.[17]

For example, in September 1963, when Goulart asked Congress for emergency powers to rule by a state of siege, his actions were greeted with widespread shock. Goulart's own minister of justice, Abelardo Jurema, later wrote that "from the owners to the workers' union, the response was the same—protest against the measure. From the students to the intellectuals, press or radio, no one understood the situation and no one trusted the president to rule by decree."[18]

---

of alternatives." See the chapter, "Enforcement, Communication, and Strategic Moves," in his *The Strategy of Conflict* (New York: Oxford University Press, 1963), p. 123.

[16] José Américo de Almeida, *Ocasos de Sangue* (Rio de Janeiro: José Olympio Editôra, 1954), p. 30.

[17] This will be discussed in greater detail in Part III.

[18] Abelardo Jurema, *Sexta-Feira, 13: Os Últimos Dias do Govêrno, João Goulart* (Rio de Janeiro: Edições O Cruzeiro, 1964), p. 130.

The governor of the state of Minas Gerais, Magalhães Pinto, supported Goulart in the 1961 struggle over Goulart's assumption of the presidency, but by late 1963 he was disquieted enough about the possibility of "revolution from above" that in November he made tentative arrangements with ex-Foreign Minister Alfonso Arinos for the state of Minas to attempt to resist any coup by Goulart by shutting off all major points of entry into the state and by winning the adherence of other states of the union to the cause of opposition to Goulart.[19]

The unsuccessful coup movement of 1955 and the aborted coup attempt of 1961 were different in many respects from the successful coups of 1945, 1954, and 1964. In both 1955 and 1961, coup movements were directed not against a president already in office, but against men who were about to assume the office. In each case, therefore, coup plans were predicated on possible *future* misdeeds rather than on allegedly unconstitutional acts already committed. In the circumstances, military officers behind the coup plans found themselves unable to build support, either among important civilian groups or among their fellow officers.

Indeed, in the crisis of 1955, some of the most important and influential opponents of the president-elect refused to countenance the demands of their own political party to annul the elections. The defeated presidential and vice-presidential candidates issued statements rejecting the use of armed force in the resolution of the crisis.[20] Furthermore, military opinion on the whole sided with the civilians. Marshal Juarez Távora, the defeated presidential candidate, later assessed military feeling about the legitimacy of a military coup in 1955 in the following terms: "I think the majority of the army officers felt that Kubitschek would have a bad government, and would allow Communism to grow. But they did not feel that they had the right to block his inauguration by violence."[21]

[19] Alfonso Arinos is quoted as saying, "I was to be the foreign minister charged with obtaining recognition of a state of belligerency, which would facilitate our purchase of arms, procurement of aid, and international recognition for our position"; see Pedro Gomes, "Minas: Do Diálogo ao 'Front,' " in *Os Idos de Março: e a Queda em Abril*, by Alberto Dines, *et al.* (Rio de Janeiro: José Alvaro, 1964), pp. 73–74.

[20] For their statement and the impact it had on denying legitimacy to any armed attempt to block the inauguration, see various stories in the *Jornal do Brasil*, November 8, 1955.

[21] Interview with the author, Rio de Janeiro, October 8, 1968.

The coup of 1961 was similar in the strong backing given by civilians to presidential claims to office. When Quadros resigned unexpectedly, the three military ministers unilaterally announced their intention to block constitutional succession of João Goulart. In a joint note issued to the public, they declared their decision to exercise what they considered their rightful and constitutional moderating role.[22] Certainly the strong resistance of Goulart's home state of Rio Grande do Sul was crucial. But support for Goulart's claims to office was also strong in many other parts of the country, even among a number of governors who were members of the UDN (União Democrática Nacional) party, the traditional enemy of both Vargas and Goulart. Juracy Magalhães, the UDN governor of the state of Bahia, for example, on hearing of President Quadros' resignation, said flatly, "João Goulart is president."[23]

In the city of Rio de Janeiro, the political nerve center of the country, a public opinion poll taken the day after the military ministers attempted a veto showed that 91 percent of those questioned wanted Goulart to assume the presidency.[24] As in 1955, leaders of the coup did not have the authority to reverse the legitimacy accrued by an election. In both cases presidential legitimacy was strong enough to rally important numbers of civilians.

CIVILIAN SANCTION FOR MILITARY INTERVENTION

Usually, civilian opinion is sufficiently fragmented and presidential legitimacy sufficiently strong to preclude formation of a civil–military coup coalition. It is only at times of tension and crisis concerning executive legitimacy that different political groups

[22] Their manifesto was reproduced in most of the major newspapers of Rio on August 30 and 31, 1961. It is also contained in Gileno dé Carli, *JQ, Brasília e a Grande Crise* (Rio de Janeiro: Irmãos Pongetti Editôres, 1961), pp. 61–63.

[23] *Última Hora*, Rio de Janeiro, August 26, 1961. For a statement of Goulart's right to the presidency by the UDN governor of the state of Pernambuco, Governor Sid Sampaio, see *A Tarde* (Salvador), August 28, 1961.
Brazil in this period elected presidents and vice-presidents separately. In the 1960 elections the vice-presidential victor, João Goulart, had run on a slate opposing the presidential victor, Jânio Quadros. When Quadros resigned, some people argued that Goulart was not an acceptable successor to Quadros. Legally, however, the question was quite clear: the vice-president was the constitutional successor of the president.

[24] See *O Jornal*, September 2, 1961.

seek allies among other civilians with whom they do not normally cooperate, and seek renewed contacts with military officers in order to build a resistance against the executive. The actual decision by the military to initiate a coup and take the bold action of removing a president from office is the consequence of a twofold process: civilian solicitation to act, and effective construction of a civil–military coup coalition. In the moderating pattern these are closely related in successful coups. How is this civilian opinion communicated, what effect does it have on the success or failure of coups, and, specifically, what role does it play in the internal military process of building a coup coalition?

Communication by civilians of their desire for military intervention in politics and military gauging of civilian receptivity or opposition to a possible coup is facilitated by the numerous communication channels that exist between civilians and military officers.[25] An exceedingly important channel is provided by the structure and function of the military bases. Provincial base commanders normally carry protocol rankings higher than most civilian authorities. The task of maintaining internal order routinely brings the military officers into intercourse with civilian authorities. Many commanding officers, for example, spend much of their time receiving civilian groups at the army base or attending civilian gatherings. Castello Branco's command diary, written while he was commander of the

---

[25] An important area of civil–military communication within the government is the National Security Council, which is normally half military and half civilian and is concerned almost exclusively with internal politics. The staff members of the president's *Casa Militar* (Military Household) are essentially political liaison men from the president to the military and politicians. The hundreds of military men serving in key posts in such government institutions as the National Steel Company act as two way communicators between the military and the bureaucracy. An important link with the governors is provided by the governors' traditional practice of appointing an active duty army officer as the secretary of security to their state government.

The Superior War College has a nine-month program devoted to national development and internal security and many of the students and staff are civilians. This relationship is maintained by probably the most active alumni association in Brazil.

The newspapers, as we have seen, constantly send messages to the military, but by giving wide coverage to debates in the *Clube Militar*, manifestos, and "off the record" political complaints by powerful military officers they also provide a national forum for military-political opinions. All the main newspapers have a full-time correspondent whose only job is to cover military politics.

Fourth Army at Recife, has almost daily references to his involvement in local political and social issues.[26] In general, access of dominant socio-economic groups to garrison commanders is greater than for most of the lower classes: in the course of travel and duty in the interior, however, army officers also become aware of the poverty of rural Brazil. These continuing contacts contrast sharply with Janowitz' description of the relative social and political isolation of the commander of a military base in the United States.[27]

These normal channels of communication are particularly important during times of acute political crisis. In 1945, 1954, and 1964, when the military successfully carried out coups against the president of the country, civilian pressure to intervene in the political process mounted and was conveyed to military officers through the medium of personal contacts, public manifestos, and newspaper editorials. Civilian demands for military intervention were couched in terms of presidential illegitimacy and the constitutional obligations of the military to guarantee the effective functioning of the three traditional powers of the government and internal order. Demands to intervene usually stated that the president was acting illegally, and that under these conditions the "obedience within the limits of the law" clause relieved the military of their duty to obey the president.

By mid-1945, for example, War Minister General Góes noted that he was "sought after incessantly" by politicians as well as military men who were trying to convince the military to take a position.[28] The civilian opposition specifically drew Góes into making a guarantee that the army would ensure free elections, as promised by Vargas, and this guarantee was given wide publicity.[29] By

[26] This command diary was written by his aide and is contained in Castello Branco's archives, which are located in the library of the General Staff School (ECEME) in Rio de Janeiro. My visits and discussions with other commanders confirmed that this is a routine pattern of civil–military interaction. See bibliography for a discussion of the *Arquivo do Marechal H. A. Castello Branco.*

[27] See Morris Janowitz, *The Professional Soldier, A Social and Political Portrait* (Glencoe, Illinois: The Free Press of Glencoe, 1960), pp. 204–207.

[28] Coutinho, *O General Góes Depõe*, pp. 404–409.

[29] See the biography of one of the major civilians active in the campaign against Vargas, by Carolina Nabuco, *A Vida de Virgílio de Melo Franco* (Rio de Janeiro: Livraria José Olympio, 1962), p. 180. Virgílio de Melo Franco's own book, *A Campanha da U.D.N.* (Rio de Janeiro: Livraria

July 1945, the question of military intervention was being raised in newspapers such as the *Jornal do Brasil*. The task specified for the military was that already informally agreed upon between civilians and military men, namely, the guaranteeing of free elections.

In the crisis of 1954, weeks before the military actually demanded Vargas' resignation most of the newspapers had openly urged the military to do so. Similarly in 1964, governors, women's groups, and business groups systematically lobbied the military to take political action to check President Goulart.

In contrast to the successful coups of 1945, 1954, and 1964, the unsuccessful coup movement of 1955 and the abortive coup attempt of 1961 occurred at times when civilians were making fewer appeals to the military to intervene in the political process.

In 1955, although appeals were made to the military to intervene, they came from one political party alone, unaccompanied by any widespread civilian movement against the president-elect. The appeals were therefore too narrowly partisan to create the necessary winning coalition of civilians and military officers for the execution of a coup.

In the case of the 1961 coup attempt, where the military ministers reacted hurriedly and unilaterally to the unexpected resignation of President Quadros by announcing their intention to block the assumption of presidential power by Vice-President Goulart, there was no time for the development of the kind of long-term public debate that characterized the successful coups, nor for the informal sounding out of civilian attitudes toward such a move. Following their decision to attempt a political veto, it became apparent that the military ministers had misjudged the extent of civilian support, and that Goulart in fact enjoyed a high degree of legitimacy. Faced with strong civilian opposition and the refusal of the Third Army to back the decision to block Goulart, the military ministers had to reverse themselves.

Interviews with coup activists within the Brazilian military underscore the crucial role that prior civilian sanctioning plays in the internal military process of building a winning coup coalition.

Editôra Zelio Valverde, 1964) has a wealth of material on the politicians' appeals for military help against Vargas.

General Golbery do Couto e Silva, a key actor in the coup activities of 1961 and 1964, made the following interesting comment:

> Military activists for or against the government are always a minority. If a military group wants to overthrow a government, they need to convince the great majority of officers who are either strict legalists or simply nonactivists. Activists do not wish to risk bloodshed or military splits, so they wait until a consensus has developed. *Thus movements to overthrow a president need public opinion to help convince the military itself. This was so in 1945, 1954, and 1964. In 1961 the military chiefs acted against public opinion and had to back down.*[30]

A senior general in the army made a similar point in relation to the coup of 1964:

> Many military activists were ready to overthrow Goulart in 1963 but they waited until public opinion pushed them further and created unity so there was no risk of civil war. By late March the journals were asking the military to solve the problem. This and events like the São Paulo march in favor of legality[31] pushed the military into activity. Military unity is extremely important. Only if the military is split will there be a civil war. The optimum is if we have unity and are on the right course. But the most fundamental thing is to stay unified.[32]

Marshal Cordeiro de Farias, who played a central role in the revolts of 1922, 1924, and 1930 and the coups of 1945, 1954, 1961, and 1964, and can therefore be considered the archetypal military activist, made a similar argument concerning the role of civilian attitudes and opinions:

[30] Interview, Brasília, September 18, 1967. Emphasis added. Vilfredo Pareto places a similar stress on the central role the normally passive majority plays in the resolution of conflict between the small group of strong defenders of the government and the small group of activists committed to overthrowing the government. See his *The Mind and Society*, ed. Arthur Livingston, 4 vols. (New York: Harcourt, Brace & World, 1935), IV:1453–1454 (number 2096).

[31] The general was referring to a march in São Paulo by approximately a quarter of a million people demonstrating against the policies of the Goulart government.

[32] Interview in Rio de Janeiro, October 11, 1968, with a senior general in the army who asked not to be cited by name.

The only purely military revolts were the *tenentes'* revolts of 1922 and 1924, and we failed. The successful movements of 1930, 1945, 1954, and 1964 were highly political and civilian in formation and execution.[33]

He specifically contrasted the unsuccessful coup of 1961 and the successful coup of 1964 in terms of the civilian support for the coup of 1964.

Significantly, a general who was a strong supporter of Goulart and who opposed the coup and was later expelled from the army for it, explained the inability of Goulart's army defenders to rally support as a function of the civilian desire for the coup to succeed.

Public opinion in the country had been convinced by propaganda that Brazil was moving toward chaos and Communism; thus the people were for the coup and we had no force of resistance.[34]

I do not mean to imply that the military action can be explained solely in terms of civilian support and urging. In all cases of intervention being examined, an element of institutional self-interest was involved and in some cases even the personal self-interest of the coup leaders. Often, in fact, the threat to institutional self-interest or survival is the key factor in *finally* creating officer consensus, for whenever the traditional areas of military institutional authority are upset, such as its disciplinary and hierarchical structure, even nonactivists and legalists within the officer corps are provoked into action.[35] However, the point still holds that before the military actually intervened successfully in 1945, 1954, and 1964, there was in each case a rough congruence between the opinion of the civilian and military elites. There exists the logical possibility of course that this congruence was the result of the civilians knowing

[33] Interview, Rio de Janeiro, September 11, 1968.

[34] Interview with General Luiz Tavares da Cunha Mello, Rio de Janeiro, October 10, 1968.

[35] This point was reached in the 1964 crisis, for instance, when President Goulart tolerated a naval mutiny in late March 1964 and refused to allow military punishment of the mutineers. This proved the turning point for many military officers and made many of them for the first time active supporters of the plot to remove Goulart from office. Edwin Lieuwen in his *Generals vs. Presidents* (New York: Frederick A. Praeger, 1964), pp. 107–109, emphasizes that corporate self-interest is a major component of coups.

the military were going to act and therefore simply getting on the "bandwagon." Empirically, however, the analysis of the actual civil–military crises has underscored the fact that while a bandwagon effect may have been at work in some stages of the crises, at other stages elite civilian opinion was pushing, not following, the military.

SUCCESSFUL VERSUS UNSUCCESSFUL COUPS: COMPARATIVE EDITORIAL ANALYSIS

It is clear from the analysis of the coups of 1945, 1954, 1955, 1961, and 1964 that the Brazilian military has historically not viewed itself as isolated from the political system, but rather as inextricably bound up with politics and often sensitive to, though not exclusively dependent upon, civilian opinion. Its traditional view of itself as the people in uniform (*o povo fardado*) is in keeping with its highly political role.

In an attempt to give greater precision to the general argument that military activism is roughly *congruent* with civilian political elite attitudes, I formulated two hypotheses and attempted to evaluate them systematically and quantitatively. These hypotheses, a logical result of the pattern of civil–military relations already described, are:

Successful military coups against the executive correlate with a prior low legitimacy accorded to the executive by the civilian participant political elites and a prior high legitimacy accorded by these same civilians to the military to perform their moderating role by removing the executive.

From this hypothesis, the converse hypothesis follows: unsuccessful military attempts to remove the executive correlate with prior high legitimacy accorded by the civilian political elites to the executive, and prior low legitimacy to the military to perform their moderating role by removing the executive.

To evaluate these hypotheses, I turned to the editorials which appeared in the major Brazilian newspapers before the coups between 1945 and 1964 for a measure of the legitimacy ascribed to both the executive and the military. If the hypotheses are correct, an analysis of editorial opinion should show that before the successful coups of 1945, 1954, and 1964, a majority of the newspapers openly expressed doubts about the legitimacy of the presi-

99

dent, and openly expressed the opinion that in the circumstances it would be appropriate for the military to intervene in the political system in fulfillment of its traditional and constitutional duty to guarantee the constitution and check the executive. Editorial opinion for the unsuccessful coups of 1955 and 1961 should be the reverse.

Analysis of editorials is feasible[36] and meaningful in Brazil. Brazil has one of the highest standards of journalism of any developing country. Rio de Janeiro, like Paris, has a much wider range of politically relevant newspapers than any city in the United States. Many of the major newspapers are family-owned, and their history goes back to the nineteenth century. The tradition of independence is reasonably strong,[37] and my analysis, supported by editorial writers, indicates that in the months before the five coups being analyzed the newspapers were neither censored nor effectively pressured, with the exception of the *Estado do São Paulo* in 1945.[38] The newspapers are thus a relatively useful indicator of middle- and upper-class opinion.

Nine newspapers were selected as the most politically important for the participating elites.[39] Of these, I have classified five as rela-

[36] Almost all issues of the major newspapers (going back to the late nineteenth century) are on file at the *Biblioteca Nacional* in Rio de Janeiro. The editorial offices of the newspapers in most cases also have a complete file.

[37] The two major periods of censorship in twentieth-century Brazil were from the start of the *Estado Nôvo* in November 1937 until it was relaxed in February 1945, and from December 13, 1968 (the Fifth Institutional Act) until the time of writing. Brief, sporadic censorship occurred *after* the coups of 1955 and 1964 and during the coup attempt of 1961. Thus, for the purposes of our analysis, the press was never effectively censored in the period under examination, namely, *before* the coups or coup attempts of 1945, 1954, 1955, 1961, and 1964.

[38] None of the editors or editorial writers I interviewed said there had been censorship before the coups. I discussed this point with Oswaldo Peralva (a stout critic of the post-1964 government), a director of the *Correio da Manhã*, Odylo Costa Filho, who had been with *Diário de Notícias* for the 1945 and 1954 coups, Alberto Dines, editor-in-chief of the *Jornal do Brasil* (he was briefly jailed for attacking the military in December 1968), and Wilson Figueiredo, who between 1945 and 1964 worked with the *Estado de Minas*, *Fôlha de Minas*, *Diário Carioca*, and the *Jornal do Brasil*. These discussions were held in Rio in September and October 1968.

[39] In my original selection I included the major regional newspapers, *Estado de Minas* (Belo Horizonte), *Correio do Povo* (Pôrto Alegre), *A Tarde* (Salvador), *Jornal do Comércio* (Recife). In regard to their final

tively nonideological newspapers: *Correio da Manhã, Jornal do Brasil, Diário Carioca, O Jornal* and *Diário de Notícias*. Of course, all newspapers have some ideology. Nonetheless, these five papers are less obviously partisan and less systematically predictable as to their position on any particular crisis than the other newspapers in the sample. Four newspapers have been classified as ideological newspapers: *O Estado de São Paulo, Tribuna da Imprensa,* and *O Globo* on the whole speak for the conservatives and those on the right, while *Última Hora* represents the left.[40] The major bias of the analysis is that it underrepresents the left, and overrepresents middle- and upper-class opinion. In fact *Última Hora* is the only nontabloid, consistently left-wing newspaper in Brazil. While recognizing this limitation, analysis of these newspapers reveals much about the roles upper-status civilians expect the military to play in the political system.

The editorials have been explored in some detail, not only to test the hypotheses relating executive legitimacy to military intervention, but also because they so richly illustrate the complexity and sublety of the moderator model of civil–military relations during times of crisis and the preparation of coups in Brazil. Several interesting points are worth noting.[41] First, debate reached the level of editorial concern several weeks if not months before the actual military coup. Coups in Brazil before 1964 were highly

---

editorial opinion they were similar to the major national newspapers. They were not included in this analysis however, because in almost all cases they clearly followed trends that were first set in Rio de Janeiro and São Paulo. The major exceptions were the *Correio do Povo*, which because of the Rio Grande do Sul regionalism and the explosive pro-Goulart movement centered in Pôrto Alegre was one of the strongest backers of native son Goulart's right to be president in 1961, and the *Jornal do Comércio*, which because of elite fears in the northeast of Brazil, took an early strong stand against Goulart in 1964. Another reason for not including them in this analysis is methodological; their editorial opinion was normally expressed in much more obscure language and therefore would have been much more difficult to classify rigorously.

[40] This selection was made after discussing the question of the most important and influential newspapers with both civilian and military political activists. All nine papers appeal to at least one major sector of opinion, so they are thus all politically relevant. No one paper is clearly the most important.

[41] In all, well over a thousand editorials were read. The following generalizations are based on a reading of all the editorials in fourteen newspapers for each of the precrisis periods.

public affairs, heralded through the newspapers and therefore not unilateral or unexpected. Second, all the newspapers examined were involved. Third, a highly consistent, symbolic language of legality, constitutionality, and military obligation to the country was employed throughout to urge the military to take political action. Finally, while sanctioning military intervention, civilians rarely gave the military *carte blanche* to decide by themselves what action to take. Demands were often quite specific as to the limits and purposes of military intervention in politics. The military task during a crisis period varied from informing the president that the military was unprepared to enforce a particular presidential decision, to actual removal of the president from office.

If we begin with the coup of 1945, the general thrust of editorial comment at the time when there were signs that Vargas might tamper with the electoral rules or postpone the presidential elections was that it was the military's obligation to do everything necessary to supervise free elections. On August 10, 1945, two and a half weeks before the military coup removed Vargas from office, *O Jornal* stated in its major editorial of the day:

> The Brazilian armed forces are deeply conscious of their responsibilities in the present political situation. . . . It is incumbent on them to maintain the constitutional powers and laws of the Republic.
>
> Nothing is more right and legitimate than that the political parties should ask the army, navy, and air force to intervene in the sense of guaranteeing the election laws already designated, and to impede them from being modified.

The *Diário Carioca*, another nonideological newspaper, editorialized:

> It is absolutely logical . . . that the decisive role in this hour of transition falls to the armed forces.
>
> What should we do?
>
> Cross our arms and wait?
>
> Or call upon the armed forces in a country whose government is flagrantly illegal and is not based on the least fraction of legality. On the army falls the responsibility of respecting the simple concepts of juridical order, without which our lives in

society are impossible. We appeal to the armed forces because they are the only organized force capable of imposing order on the chaos instilled by the government itself.[42]

Prior to the 1954 coup, after the assassination attempt and subsequent unearthing of the "sea of mud" corruption and financial scandals, many civilians representing the participating political elite felt that it was time for Vargas to resign. The message communicated to the military and civilian newspaper readers was that the circumstances warranted military exercise of the moderating role to "supervise" the transfer to power from President Vargas to Vice-President Café Filho. The *Diário de Notícias* stated simply on August 20, 1954, four days before the coup: "The armed forces are invited to mediate as the sentinels of law and the guardians of the constitution, of tranquility and of the progress of the country." Eight days previously, on August 12, the same newspaper had indicated precisely the task they expected the armed forces to perform: "From the conduct of the supreme directors and leaders of the land, sea, and air forces ought to result clearly the road to follow, within the limits of a strictly constitutional solution. This is the transference of the government to the vice-president of the Republic."

The ideologically conservative papers at the time did not merely request military intervention, but stridently condemned the military for allowing the president to continue in office and for showing reluctance or hesitancy in exercising their constitutional obligations. The *Estado de São Paulo*, traditionally a powerful foe of Vargas, commented:

There continues in São Paulo and Rio and in other places a civilian movement urging the armed forces to convince the chief of the nation to vacate his office. The armed forces however are unfortunately not unanimous in this respect. If the armed forces believe they are serving Brazil and respecting the constitution by maintaining in the presidential office a completely discredited

[42] August 13, 1945. In 1945, no left-wing newspaper existed. It was the mobilization of politics from 1949 on that created the ideological newspapers such as the *Última Hora* and the *Tribuna da Imprensa*. The militantly anti-Vargas paper, *Estado de São Paulo*, which would have supported the opinions of the papers already quoted, was under government control until Vargas was overthrown and so wrote no editorials during this entire period.

103

citizen, they will in fact be giving *carte blanche* to new immorality and even to new crimes.[43]

The *Tribuna da Imprensa* concurred in an editorial on August 13, when the coup was still two weeks away:

Do the military chiefs think that the crisis of authority in the country can last longer than the fifteen minutes it takes to bring the minister of war to Catete by car to transmit the appeal of the chiefs of the armed forces?

The military is sworn to defend the country, to guarantee its institutions, and it is this oath that it must fulfill.

The one newspaper from the left taking an opposing position was *Última Hora*, commenting the day before the coup:

Vargas resists a wave of provocation and subversion which aims to envelop him and has declared, incisively and categorically, that he does not and will not yield to the imposition of violence or to any *golpe* or extralegal solution.

In the 1964 crisis, President Goulart attempted to mobilize support to force the Congress to pass a series of reforms. Civilian elites feared that Goulart would close Congress and rule by decree. In these circumstances, many participants in the political system argued that it would be illegal for the military to continue to obey the president. They emphasized the military's duty to maintain the three constitutional powers of the legislature, judiciary, and executive, to maintain internal order, and to obey the president only if he were acting legally. The *Diário de Notícias*, on March 23, over a week before the coup of 1964, editorialized:

If the highest executive is opposed to the constitution, condemns the regime and does not comply with the laws, he automatically loses the right to be obeyed. . . . The armed forces are charged by article 177 of the constitution to defend the country and to guarantee the constitutional powers, law and order.

O Globo, on March 18, referred to Goulart's attempt to use his key military officers to pressure Congress and urged the military to refuse to cooperate with Goulart:

[43] August 24, 1954.

The armed forces that some maliciously seek to associate with the attempt to intimidate Congress will not fail [the country]. Under the supreme authority of the president, but within the limits of the law (article 176 of the constitution), they will defend the constitutional powers, law and order (article 177). They will thus not allow sectarian or subversive groups, be they intimates or not of the chief executive, to pronounce against the Congress and attempt to move against it, because they cannot endorse illegal acts and processes against the constitution.

Two of the most respected newspapers, *Correio da Manhã* and *Jornal do Brasil*, both of which strongly backed Goulart's right to assume the presidency in 1961 after Quadros resigned, urged the army to control Goulart. They argued that military discipline itself was being destroyed by Goulart's actions. This quote from the editorial in the *Correio da Manhã* appeared on March 31, a few days after a naval mutiny in Rio de Janeiro which Goulart had tolerated:

Enough of this farce! Enough of this psychological warfare unleashed by the government with the object of convulsing the country and advancing his *continuista* politics. . . . Up to what point does he want to fragment the armed forces by means of indiscipline, which each day is becoming more uncontrollable? The legislature, the judiciary, the armed forces, the democratic forces ought to be alert and vigilant, ready to combat all those who attempt to overthrow the regime.

Brazil has already endured too much with the present government. Basta!

The *Jornal do Brasil* similarly referred to the mutiny and the threat to military discipline, traditionally an area of great sensitivity on the part of the armed forces:

The state of law has submerged in Brazil. . . . Only those who retain the power of acting to reestablish the state of law remain effectively legitimate. . . .

The armed forces were all—we repeat, *all*—wounded in what is most essential to them, the fundamentals of authority, hierarchy and discipline. . . .

This is not the hour for indifference, especially on the part

105

of the army, which has the power to prevent worse ills. . . .
The hour of resistance by all has now arrived.[44]

The tone of editorial opinion was very different in the case of
the unsuccessful coup movement of 1955 and the unsuccessful coup
of 1961.

In 1955, the movement to block the inauguration of President
Kubitschek was led by a civilian, Carlos Lacerda, editor of the
vitriolic *Tribuna da Imprensa*.[45] A number of military officers were
sympathetic to Lacerda's moralistic criticism of Kubitschek and
also to his anti-Communist attack on Vice-President-elect Goulart.
However, throughout the crisis period from the October election
to November 11, 1955, the general support for a coup was far
less strong than in the previous cases examined. Only the *Tribuna
da Imprensa* and the *Estado de São Paulo*, both ideologically on the
right, openly advocated military intervention.[46] In comparison with
the editorials of the *Tribuna da Imprensa* (which at times wrote
as though a military coup were imminent, although no such consensus for the coup existed in the army at the time), those of the
prestigious *Correio da Manhã*, which had generally supported the
coups of 1945, 1954, and 1964, strongly urged the inauguration
of Kubitschek and talked only of the military duty to refrain from
a *golpe*:

> The military conscience that illuminated the birth of the Re-
> public will not bury the regime. . . . Soldiers and military leaders
> of the stripe of General Lott, whose democratic fidelity is sym-
> bolic of the thinking that rules from top to bottom, will not act
> as centurions of a *golpe*.[47]

[44] March 29, 1964.

[45] Lacerda was an extremely effective right-wing demagogue who later
became the governor of Guanabara, and later still one of the most acid
critics from 1966 to 1968 of the military government.

[46] The *Tribuna da Imprensa* had editorialized: "The inauguration of
these two irresponsible adventurers can only be avoided by an act of force.
The hour of action depends on the armed forces. The people have only
three arms now—they are called the army, the navy, and the air force.

"The option is between a 'legal' dictatorship which corrupts and degrades
everyone, and a regime of emergency which will prepare for the effective
conquest of democracy" (November 4, 1955). Five days later, their tone
was even more hysterical: "Kubitschek and Goulart . . . cannot take office,
should not take office, will not take office" (November 9, 1955).

[47] November 5, 1955.

The nonideological newspaper *O Jornal* concurred with the *Correio da Manhã* that circumstances did not call for military intervention and the exercise of the traditional moderating function:

We are certain that in no circumstances would the army, air force, or navy consent to serve as instruments of ambitions that do not stem from the popular political vote.[48]

The situation was the same in 1961. When the military ministers unilaterally decided to block the inauguration of Goulart as Quadros's successor, even the traditionally promilitary newspaper *Diário de Notícias* failed to support the military, stating rather that the military's claim of implementing their moderating function was illegitimate:

In the name of preserving order it is proposed to perpetrate a fatal attack on the constitution, mortally wounding the regime. . . . The decision of the military chiefs, on the pretext of preventing disorder, could on the contrary precipitate the country into chaos, into an armed civil war, into economic and financial bankruptcy, into the total subversion of the social, political, and even ideological order. . . . The dangers which allegedly could result to the institutions with the presence of Senhor João Goulart in the presidency would be, by any hypothesis, incomparably less grave than those flowing from the repudiation of the representative system.[49]

The *Correio da Manhã*, which sharply attacked Goulart in late March 1964, in 1961 strongly urged that he be installed as president. The editorials illustrate clearly that a sharp distinction was drawn between the feeling of uncertainty about a president's capacities and belief in his legitimacy to rule: "We have always expressed reservations about the personal character of the new president, but the fact is that he is the new President and that Senhor Goulart must be inaugurated as soon as he arrives in the country."[50] Four days later, after a manifesto was issued by the military ministers declaring their intention to prevent Goulart from returning to Brazil in the interests of national security, the paper expressed severe disapproval:

[48] November 5, 1961.   [49] August 27, 1961.
[50] August 27, 1961.

TABLE 5.1

CLASSIFICATION OF EDITORIAL OPINION IN REGARD TO LEGITIMACY OF PRESIDENT BEFORE COUPS OR COUP ATTEMPTS; 1945, 1954, 1955, 1961, 1964

	+2	+1	0	−1	−2
	President, president-elect, or vice-president with presidency vacant should be strongly supported. His blockage or removal would be illegitimate.	President, president-elect, or vice-president with presidency vacant is legal.	Ambiguous or neutral in regard to question of legitimacy of president, president-elect, or vice-president with presidency vacant.	President, president-elect, or vice-president with presidency vacant is acting illegally, or president-elect was illegally elected or vice-president with presidency vacant does not have authoritative claim to presidency.	President, president-elect, or vice-president with presidency vacant should not hold the presidency. He should resign, be impeached, not inaugurated, or forced from office.
Successful Coups					
1945 Coup*				Correio da Manhã Jornal do Brasil Diário Carioca Diário de Notícias O Jornal	
1954 Coup	Última Hora			Jornal do Brasil O Globo O Jornal	Correio da Manhã Diário Carioca Diário de Notícias O Estado de São Paulo Tribuna da Imprensa

(*Successful Coup Movements continued*)

1964 Coup	*Diário Carioca*	*Última Hora*	*Correio da Manhã* *Jornal do Brasil* *O Globo* *Diário de Notícias*	*O Jornal* *O Estado de São Paulo* *Tribuna da Imprensa*

Unsuccessful Coup Movements

1955 Coup	*Diário Carioca* *O Jornal* *Correio da Manhã*	*Última Hora*	*O Globo* *Jornal do Brasil*	*O Estado de São Paulo* *Diário de Notícias*	*Tribuna da Imprensa*
1961 Coup	*Correio da Manhã* *Jornal do Brasil* *Diário Carioca* *Diário de Notícias* *O Globo* *Última Hora*	*O Jornal*			*Tribuna da Imprensa* *O Estado de São Paulo*

* In 1945 only five of the nine papers examined for other coups are included. *O Estado de São Paulo* was under government censorship. *O Globo* ran no editorials, and *Última Hora* and *Tribuna da Imprensa* had not yet been founded.

TABLE 5.2

CLASSIFICATION OF EDITORIAL OPINION IN REGARD TO LEGITIMACY OF MILITARY'S EXERCISE OF MODERATING POWER BEFORE COUPS OR COUP ATTEMPTS; 1945, 1954, 1955, 1961, 1964

	+2	+1	0	−1	−2
	Military has duty to remove president or block president-elect or vice-president with the presidency vacant from assuming office.	Military should play a major role in re-solving the crisis and should not obey president if he is acting illegally. Military should not help put in power a president-elect or vice-president who is a threat to security and order of country.	Ambiguous or neutral in regard to role of military support of president, president-elect, or vice-president when presidency is vacant.	Military should support the president, president-elect, or vice-president when the presidency is vacant.	Military has no right whatsoever to remove president or block the president-elect or vice-president with presidency vacant. The executive needs the aggressive support of the military.
Successful Coups					
1945 Coup*		O Jornal Diário de Notícias Correio da Manhã Jornal do Brasil Diário Carioca			
1954 Coup	Diário Carioca Diário de Notícias O Estado de São Paulo Tribuna da Imprensa	Correio da Manhã Jornal do Brasil O Globo	O Jornal		Última Hora

(*Successful Coup Movements continued*)

1964 Coup	Correio da Manhã Jornal do Brasil O Globo •Diário de Notícias O Jornal O Estado de São Paulo Tribuna da Imprensa			Diário Carioca	Ultima Hora

Unsuccessful Coup Movements

1955 Coup	Tribuna da Imprensa	O Estado de São Paulo	Jornal do Brasil O Globo Diário de Notícias	O Jornal	Correio da Manhã Diário Carioca Ultima Hora
1961 Coup	O Estado de São Paulo Tribuna da Imprensa		O Globo O Jornal	Jornal do Brasil Ultima Hora	Correio da Manhã Diário Carioca Diário de Notícias

* In 1945 only five of the nine papers examined for other coups are included. *O Estado de São Paulo* was under government censorship. *O Globo* ran no editorials, and *Ultima Hora* and *Tribuna da Imprensa* had not yet been founded.

We read the manifesto of the military ministers. It is a *golpe* abolishing the Republican regime in Brazil. It is military dictatorship.[51]

After the state of Rio Grande do Sul and its state militia resisted the *golpe*, the military ministers capitulated. General Golbery, one of the most important military officers involved in the 1961 coup attempt, who later resigned from active duty to organize civil–military opinion against Goulart, has remarked: "1961 was a disaster for the army. We decided that we would attempt to overthrow Goulart (in 1964) only when public opinion was clearly in our favor.[52]

In an attempt to evaluate further the hypotheses relating the success of military coups to the degree of legitimacy ascribed to the executive and to the military, I have attempted to construct a rough measure of legitimacy by formulating five broad categories indicating the degree to which editorials gave support to the executive to continue in office, and another indicating the degree of support for military intervention. The last firm position that a newspaper assumed in the two- to six-week period before the crises of 1945, 1954, 1961, and 1964 is placed in one of the five categories.[53]

The five-category classification passes from the top category representing great legitimacy for the president, to the lowest category indicating no support for the president. Similarly, with the degree of legitimacy ascribed to the military, the top category indicates high legitimacy for the military to intervene and the lowest category none, with other categories falling between the two extremes. The results of this classification are presented in Tables 5.1 and 5.2.

While recognizing an irreducibly subjective and qualitative element in the original selection and subsequent classification of the editorials, the classification of the newspapers in Tables 5.1 and 5.2 has been used to give quantitative weight to the range of sup-

[51] August 31, 1961.

[52] Interview, Brasília, September 18, 1967.

[53] In a project devoted only to content analysis a more rigorous *Q* sort approach should be used with multiple coders. An interesting endeavor would be to construct the comparative legitimacy weights for each day in the crisis. Unfortunately, given the lack of reproducing facilities in the *Biblioteca Nacional* and the relative difficulty of obtaining access to all the editorials, this was beyond the time and financial resources of the author who in the circumstances was the only coder.

port for the president and the military in each of the coups. By assigning values to each category ranging from + 2 for the top category down to − 2 for the lowest category, I have given a quantitative weight to the full range of supports for the president and the military, and have correlated these supports with the success or failure of the coups.

TABLE 5.3

MILITARY MODERATING POWER LEGITIMACY SCORES: EDITORIAL
ANALYSIS OF SUCCESSFUL AND UNSUCCESSFUL COUPS

Successful Coups	Average Score for Nonideological Papers*	Average Score for all Papers
1945	+1.0	+1.0
1954	+1.2	+1.0
1964	+0.6	+0.4
Average	+0.93	+0.8
Unsuccessful Coups		
1955	−1.0	−0.4
1961	−1.4	−0.4
Average	−1.2	−0.4

TABLE 5.4

PRESIDENTIAL LEGITIMACY SCORES: EDITORIAL ANALYSIS
OF SUCCESSFUL AND UNSUCCESSFUL COUPS

Successful Coups	Average Score for Nonideological Papers*	Average Score for all Papers
1945	−1.0	−1.0
1954	−1.6	−1.2
1964	−0.8	−0.8
Average	−1.1	−1.0
Unsuccessful Coups		
1955	+1.0	+0.3
1961	+0.8	+0.2
Average	+0.9	+0.25

* The newspapers I have classified as nonideological are: *Correio da Manhã, Jornal do Brasil, Diário Carioca, O Jornal,* and *Diário de Notícias.*

113

On the basis of these weights, it is clear from Table 5.3 that the general hypothesis is borne out that in the moderator model the successful performance of a coup by the military correlates highly with the prior legitimacy given to the military by civilian elite opinion to perform this task. Similarly, Table 5.3 shows that in the case of unsuccessful coups, the degree of legitimacy for the military was far lower. Conversely, in the case of presidential legitimacy, Table 5.4 shows that successful coups were preceded by a *low* legitimacy being ascribed by this segment of public opinion to the president, whereas unsuccessful coups occurred in times when presidential legitimacy was high.

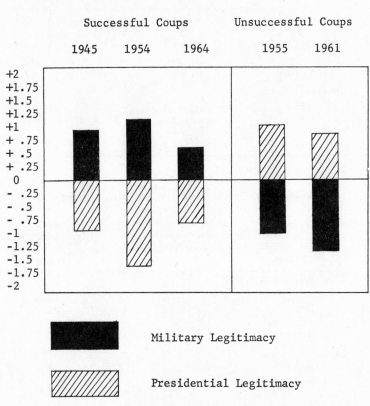

FIG. 5.1 EDITORIAL ANALYSIS OF NONIDEOLOGICAL NEWSPAPERS: RELATIONSHIP OF MILITARY LEGITIMACY AND PRESIDENTIAL LEGITIMACY IN SUCCESSFUL AND UNSUCCESSFUL COUPS

114

Finally, the material is presented in visual form in Figure 5.1, where the correlations are most strikingly seen. Here it is clear that the hypotheses correlating successful and unsuccessful coups with the degree of presidential and military legitimacy is strongly supported.

THE BOUNDARIES TO MILITARY COUPS PRIOR TO 1964

Although the Brazilian 'military has repeatedly intervened in politics in the twentieth century and on occasion removed a president from office, at no time before 1964 did the military assume the highest office of the nation. Nor did they receive much encouragement from civilians for such an act. Indeed, the extent of military involvement in Brazil always differed enough in comparison to involvement in other republics of Latin America for the Brazilian military to have been characterized as more "constitutional" than the military of other Latin American nations. Military men in Brazil generally perceived themselves in these terms.

In each of the coups before that of 1964, a crucial element of the coup itself, of the creation of the coalition between civilians and military officers, and of the consensus among military officers has been the understanding that a permanent restriction existed on the extent of military intervention in politics. This restriction, a central characteristic of the moderator model, effectively placed a boundary to military intervention at the removal of the executive, ruling out any assumption of governmental power by the military officers involved.

This understanding had two components: civilian attitudes to the military role in politics; military attitudes toward their legitimacy and capacities to form a government.

The distinction between the legitimacy of military intervention and the illegitimacy of military rule may appear almost too subtle to be communicated. In fact, however, the distinction has been clearly made and understood by all the major actors in the Brazilian political system. For example, no editorial I examined in the weeks before the coups of 1945, 1954, or 1964, or before the coup attempts of 1955 and 1961, ever explicitly asked the military to assume power,[54] although dozens of the editorials demanded that the

---

[54] The closest was Carlos Lacerda's demand for a "regime of exception" in *Tribuna da Imprensa* in 1955. This, however, could have been a regime led by civilians and backed by the military. In 1964 the owner of the

115

military intervene to remove or check the executive. From the civilian viewpoint, the argument was often made in this period that military action against the president could be trusted exactly *because* the military knew and respected the traditional limitations on military intervention that prevented them from assuming the powers of the government.

In the following characteristic editorial, the conservative newspaper *O Globo* attempted to overcome any civilian doubts about the outcome if the military forced Vargas to resign in 1954. Arguing that in the past the military had refrained from usurping the power of government from civilian hands, it promised that in this case too the military would continue to guarantee a judicial, constitutional state. *O Globo* therefore sanctioned military intervention to remove the president, but underscored in its editorial that the rules of the game prohibited the assumption of political power by the military:

> The great test of the political maturity reached by our military classes was that of the October 29, 1945 overthrow of Vargas, in which they gave the world a rare example of the respect for civilian political institutions and lack of self interest by giving power to the judicial organs. Today we can be certain that the appearance of a military condottiere would not be possible. . . . If tomorrow the president of the Republic were to leave the presidential palace by his own free will, as most Brazilians would prefer, or if he were to leave through coercion, as may in fact happen, nonetheless Brazil would continue to enjoy a judicial, constitutional state.[55]

Another feature of the successful coups in this period was that in each case there was consensus among the military not only that armed intervention would occur, but also as to which civilian groups would receive political power following the removal of the chief executive.

In 1945 and 1954, this agreement was worked out by the top military leaders of the coup in concert with civilian groups. The war minister, Góes Monteiro, talked with the presidential candidates

---

Estado de São Paulo wanted a military regime to assume power but this was never stated in an editorial.

[55] August 23, 1954.

of the two major parties before deposing President Vargas in 1945. All agreed that Vargas should be deposed and temporary power should be transferred to the judiciary, which would then supervise open elections so that the winning candidates could be inaugurated on schedule.[56] The final negotiation for the resignation of Vargas was carried out by General Cordeiro de Farias, and illustrates military concern that channels of communication be kept open between all actors. General Cordeiro de Farias was chosen for the task because he had been one of the leading members of the Brazilian Expeditionary Force (FEB) and had good relations with the three major figures involved in the crisis. These were the presidential candidate of the opposition party, Brigadier Gomes; the government's presidential candidate, General Dutra; and President Vargas himself. As Cordeiro de Farias commented:

> I went because I was extremely close to them all. Gomes was my brother from the days of the *tenente* revolt of 1922, and Dutra and I had cooperated on many army measures in the 1930s and 1940s. I had worked with Vargas since the Revolution of 1930. I liked and respected Vargas and that is why I went.[57]

In 1954, the parameters of military action were again clearly spelled out in private conversations and in public statements such as editorials. The military, it was clearly implied, should supervise the transfer of power from President Vargas to the vice-president, Café Filho. In a traumatic meeting at the Military Club in Rio de Janeiro on August 14, the question of what the military should do in the crisis was debated for hours. Finally, an emotional resolution was passed, backed largely by the junior officers, demanding the immediate resignation of the president. In a famous address, Juarez Távora, vice-president of the Military Club and comman-. dant of the Superior War College, successfully reversed this resolution, by arguing that all the legal steps open to the military had first to be taken, and that junior officers had to leave the handling of the crisis to their seniors in the army. He emphasized that the military should only act slowly and unanimously. Recognizing that

[56] For details of this agreement see Coutinho, *O General Góes Depõe*, pp. 441–469, José Caó, *Dutra* (São Paulo: Instituto Progresso Editorial, 1949), pp. 240–245, and Nabuco, *A Vida de Virgílio de Melo Franco*, pp. 192–195.
[57] Interview, Rio de Janeiro, September 14, 1968.

117

the president still had some powerful backers within the military, Távora told the packed audience that one of the most important things was to avoid "brothers in arms being slain by each other."[58]

Only after eight more days of continuous meetings between military leaders and civilians, did 27 key army generals issue a formal manifesto detailing the background to the crisis and announcing their intention to act:

> The undersigned . . . aware of their duties and responsibilities to the nation . . . declare in all conscience that they judge the best road to pacify the people and maintain the unity of the armed forces is through the resignation of the present president of the Republic, and his substitution in accordance with constitutional norms.[59]

Numerous observers have attempted to contrast the 1954 coup against Vargas with the constitutional countercoup of 1955, and have talked of the different groups of officers involved in each case. This creates an image of polarization among the officers that was not present. The military in 1954 acted only after the danger of polarization had passed. In fact, many of the leading members of the groups supposedly or actually opposed to the overthrow of Vargas by the military in 1954 nonetheless signed the manifesto announcing the intention of the military to depose the president in order to maintain military unity. Signers of the manifesto, later viewed as opposed to the coup that followed, were General Lott, the titular leader of the countercoup of 1955, General José Machado Lopes and Pery Constant Bevilacqua, two of the most important generals supporting Goulart's right to the presidency in 1961, and General Jair Dantas Ribeiro, President Goulart's minister of war in 1964.[60] These officers were sufficiently committed to constitutionalism, or to nationalist politics, that undoubtedly they would not have signed the manifesto against Vargas if specific boundaries to military action had not been acknowledged, namely,

[58] Typescript of speech in the personal archives of Marshal Juarez Távora. The speech was shown to me by the marshal in the course of an interview on October 8, 1968 in Rio de Janeiro.

[59] A photocopy of the manifesto with all signatures is contained in Bento Munhoz da Rocha Netto, *Radiografia de Novembro* (Rio de Janeiro: Editôra Civilização Brasileira, 1961), pp. 118–119.

[60] *Ibid.*

118

limiting military intervention to the transfer of political power to the vice-president, according to the constitutional ruling.

The 1955 countercoup, implemented to thwart any attempts to block the inauguration of the victors of the presidential elections, was also the result of careful planning. The military plan had been tentatively formulated five months before it was actually put into operation. Minister of War General Lott and the commander of the *Vila Militar,* General Odílio Denys, had developed a winning coalition among those higher officers who were convinced of their duty to execute a prevention coup against any civil–military attempt to prevent the inauguration of the victors of the election.[61] When the countercoup was decided upon, it had the support of the key troop commanders in Rio de Janeiro and São Paulo.[62] Immediately after the first steps of the coup were initiated, General Lott demonstrated his awareness of the need for agreement on limits to intervention when he called in the presidents of the Senate, the House of Deputies, and the Supreme Court, and asked them to "provide for the legal substitution of President Carlos Luz strictly in accord with the constitution because we are not about to assume control of civil power. This is not our objective."[63]

This strict limiting of the moderating role of the army to removing the president from office and the Congress's rapid validation of the act made any resistance on the part of the air force or the navy less feasible. Acceptance of this boundary thus was crucial in 1955 both to the building of a winning coup coalition, and to the prevention of effective resistance by officers in the navy or air force.

Another rule of the game of the moderating pattern was that defenders of the overthrown president were not purged from the military. After the successful coups of 1945, 1954, and 1955, the

[61] For a description of how the coalition was organized and for parts of the operations order, see the biography of Lott by Major Joffre Gomes da Costa, *Marechal Henrique Lott* (Rio de Janeiro: no publisher, 1960), pp. 279–313.

[62] For a participating general's description of the decision to make the countercoup and a list of all army unit commanders present at the decision, see General Joaquim Justino Alves Bastos, *Encontro com o Tempo* (Pôrto Alegre: Editôra Globo, 1965), pp. 294–300.

[63] Interview by Lott given to the Rio de Janeiro weekly, *Manchete,* November 19, 1955, reproduced in Joffe Gomes da Costa, *Marechal Henrique Lott,* p. 301.

119

opponents of the coup were usually transferred to distant posts and their promotion slowed. For reasons which will be analyzed in Part IV, this norm was broken after the 1964 coup. Lack of purges made the negotiation of coups easier. The "defenders" could agree not to resist in the knowledge that their position as an officer or their life was never in danger for having been on the losing side. Absence of such rules of the game in Nigeria or Indonesia made coups there bloody total conflicts in which the losers were killed.

An extremely important element of the maintenance of a boundary at the point of removal of the executive in all the successful coups in Brazil between 1945 and before 1964 had been the low belief of the military officers in their qualifications to rule. In essence, until the 1960s, the military institution in Brazil prided itself on its constitutionality. This belief in constitutional forms of government itself was based on military confidence that the crises could be effectively resolved by returning the government to civilian control and bringing a new president into office, and the belief that the military had a low legitimacy to rule in comparison to civilians.

Indeed, a major reason why the movement to prevent the inauguration of Kubitschek and Goulart in 1955 failed was that, in the event of the rejection of the results of the election, a civil–military government would have had to come into being and many military officers doubted the legitimacy of such a regime. An important spokesman for this view was General Castello Branco. In an address to the Superior War College on September 19, 1955, he strongly questioned the capacity or legitimacy of the military to form such a "regime of exception":

> There are those who argue that the best way for the military to participate in the recuperation of the country is to intervene and take control of the government. The most sincere argue that this is necessary in face of the incapacity of the political institutions to resolve the problems of the nation.
>
> Do the armed forces really have the political capacity to learn the solutions to the political and administrative problems of the nation? . . . The armed forces cannot, if they are true to their tradition, make Brazil into another South American *Republi-*

queta. If we adopt this regime, it will enter by force, will only be maintained by force, and will go out by force.[64]

Yet by 1964, the military had in fact decided to inaugurate a "regime of exception," making it the first military government of the twentieth century in Brazil. Why did this reversal of all that President Castello Branco had argued for in 1955 occur, and why did he emerge as the leader of the kind of military government he had so effectively denounced in 1955?

Obviously, for such a marked change in the pattern of civil–military relations that had existed between 1945 and 1964 to occur, the beliefs on which it rested, such as the belief in the capacity of civilians to ultimately find solutions to political problems and military self-doubt as to their own capacity to govern effectively, must have been severely questioned.

[64] The typescript of the address, "Os Meios Militares na Recuperação Moral do Pais," is in the *Arquivo do Marechal H. A. Castello Branco.*

PART III

The Breakdown of the "Moderating Pattern" of Civil–Military Relations and the Emergence of Military Rule

NINE DAYS after the revolution of March 31, 1964, the Supreme Revolutionary Command, composed of the commanders-in-chief of the three military services, unilaterally issued the First Institutional Act. This act baldly stated that the revolutionary movement had "deposed the previous government and had the capacity to form a new government." It said that the revolution did not seek to legitimatize itself through Congress because "the revolution legitimatizes itself."[1] Under the authority it had decreed itself by this Institutional Act, the Supreme Revolutionary Command took the first of what were to be many steps to purge the political system. On April 10, it issued a list cancelling the mandates of 40 congressmen and suspending for ten years the political rights of 100 politicians, trade union officials, intellectuals, and other political actors.[2] The next day the Supreme Revolutionary Command forced 122 officers out of active duty in the military.[3]

Clearly, unlike the military coups of 1930, 1945, 1954, and 1955, the military in 1964 had not merely removed a chief executive; they had assumed political power in the nation. By assuming power the military went beyond the parameters of the moderating pattern of civil–military relations that had dominated in the period after 1945; the political system as a whole had undergone a "boundary change." Underlying this change was a major change in ideol-

---

[1] Excepts from the *ATO Institucional* of April 9, 1964, in the *Diário Oficial*.

[2] See the *Diário Oficial*, April 10, for the list of the hundred "cassados" (cassar = to annul; to cancel).

[3] *Diário Oficial*, April 11, 1964.

ogy: the military were going to be the directors not the moderators of politics.

Any analysis of the political and military context in which a major boundary change occurs must take into consideration international as well as domestic forces. Because of the immense controversy over the role of the United States in the overthrow of Goulart, the international context must be discussed before an analysis is made of all the other aspects that played a role in the boundary change. Two important views on the United States role are diametrically opposed. The first holds that the United States was the major force behind the military coup. This position is summed up in the title of a widely read book in Brazil, *O Golpe Começou em Washington* (The Coup Began in Washington.)[4]

The opposite opinion is epitomized in the congressional testimony of the former ambassador to Brazil, Lincoln Gordon:

> The movement which overthrew President Goulart was a purely 100 percent—not 99.44—but 100 percent . . . Brazilian movement. Neither the American Embassy nor I personally played any part in the process whatsoever.[5]

Both these positions distort the reality, and oversimplify the complexity, of events. The United States *did* play a supportive role in the boundary change, but U.S. pressures were rendered more influential in Brazil than they might have been because, to a significant extent, unlike in Cuba after 1959 and Peru in 1968, U.S. policies were congruent with and found reinforcement in some powerful conservative domestic political and military trends.

Turning first to United States policies toward Brazil, although probably no definitive account can ever be given of the U.S. role (the accounts of key U.S. participants are only just beginning to be published), the record is already clear that the United States official policy—economic, political, and military—was to weaken the Goulart government, especially in its last nine months, and to strengthen the military government of General Castello Branco

[4] Edmar Morel, *O Golpe Começou em Washington* (Rio de Janeiro: Editôra Civilização Brasileira, 1965).

[5] See his testimony in *The Nomination of Lincoln Gordon to be Assistant Secretary for Inter-American Affairs*, Hearing Before the Committee on Foreign Relations, Senate, 89th Cong., 2nd sess., February 7, 1966, pp. 44–45.

124

that succeeded Goulart.[6] By mid-1963, the U.S. government, afraid of the growing radicalization of the Goulart government, moved from a position of mild support to one of opposition. Almost no new grants of aid were made to the central government, while political opponents of the president, such as Carlos Lacerda, governor of Guanabara, received preferential treatment. This policy of aiding the opposition forces was known by State Department officials as one of strengthening "islands of sanity" in Brazil. In May of 1964, the assistant secretary of state for inter-American affairs, Mr. Thomas C. Mann, candidly described this policy to Congress.

We were aware in January by the time I got there—I do not know how much earlier—that the erosion toward Communism in Brazil was very rapid. We had, even before I got here, devised a policy to help certain state governments. We did not give any money in balance of payments support, budgetary support, things of that kind, which benefit directly the central government of Brazil. That was cut back under Goulart."[7]

On the purely military level, the U.S. military attachés—men such as General Vernon Walters—had long experience in Brazilian politics and close personal ties to Brazilian military officers, ties dating back to the time when they fought together as allies in World War II. The United States was certainly aware of the broad outlines of impending coup movements. Indeed, some speculations had appeared in the Brazilian press about coup plans, and most knowledgeable Brazilians knew more than was to be found in the newspaper reports. In turn, the coup organizers were undoubtedly aware that the United States would be generally sympathetic to their plans. The president of the United States sent his congratulations to the coup victors even before President Goulart had fled the country. The U.S. ambassador to Brazil, Lincoln Gordon, became a forceful proponent of massive aid increases to the new military government

[6] The history of U.S.-Brazilian relations in this period needs to be the subject of a full-length book.

[7] Reproduced in *Unnecessary Dollar Costs Incurred in Financing Purchases of Commodities Produced in Brazil*, by the controller general of the United States, B-146820, March 19, 1965, Appendix II, p. 21. Cited in Carlos F. Díaz-Alejandro, "Some Aspects of the Brazilian Experience with Foreign Aid," Center discussion paper no. 77 (New Haven: Yale University, Economic Growth Center, October 1969), p. 11.

following the coup, and was optimistic enough about the Brazilian revolution to call it "one of the critical points of inflection in mid-twentieth century world history."[8]

Under the military government, the USAID mission soared until it became the third largest U.S. program in the world.

What of the less obvious but equally important question of the U.S. government's attempt to export anti-Communist counterinsurgency ideology. The evidence is reasonably clear on this point. The United States government had, with the exception of Cuba and Mexico, a virtual monopoly of the foreign military missions in Latin America until the late 1960s. The U.S. Latin American military policy involved military arms assistance, technical assistance, and extensive educational programs. Latin American military officers and enlisted men were trained in schools run by the United States in Panama, Fort Leavenworth, and elsewhere, and were heavily exposed to U.S. doctrines at the Inter-American Defense College in Washington.

With the rise of Fidel Castro and the start of the Vietnam war, the Kennedy government shifted the rationale of the U.S. military AID policy to Latin America away from that of hemispheric security to that of internal security.[9] To combat "Communist-inspired" in ternal warfare, the United States campaigned throughout Latin America for the idea that the Latin American armies should divert their energies toward counterinsurgency and civic action.[10] Given the privileged U.S. access to an important Latin American elite— the military—it is important to examine the ideological content of U.S. military doctrines for the possible light they throw on changing attitudes within the Latin American military.

A review of U.S. military journals shows a very sharp increase in U.S. concern for internal warfare after 1961. The *Air University Library Index to Military Periodicals* does not contain categories for counterinsurgency or civic action in its 1959–1961 volume. In

[8] See Lincoln Gordon's letter to the editor in *Commonweal*, XCII (Aug. 7, 1970), p. 379.

[9] For a guide to the administration's arguments for this shift, see Michael J. Francis, "Military Aid to Latin America in the United States Congress," *Journal of Inter-American Studies*, VI (July 1964), pp. 389–401.

[10] See Willard F. Barber and C. Neale Ronning, *Internal Security and Military Power: Counterinsurgency and Civic Action in Latin America* (Columbus, Ohio: Ohio State University Press, 1966) for a detailed listing and documentation of U.S. government aid and military schooling programs, as well as formal military treaties in Latin America.

EMERGENCE OF MILITARY RULE

the volume covering 1962–1964, there are 160 entries for counter-insurgency and 42 more entries for counterinsurgency study and training. There are 33 entries on civic action.[11] A listing of some of the titles in the main U.S. military journals—all widely distrib-uted to the Latin American military—reveals the militant cold war tone and proselytizing nature of much of the military writing in the United States in this period:[12]

MATA (military assistance training advisor) Army Conditioning Course Puts Cold War Warriors on the Spot

Counterinsurgent Allied Soldiers—By the Hundreds

Damn the *Insurrectos*

Counterinsurgency Courses Conducted Army-wide

Counterinsurgency: Global Termite Control

The Search for and Development of Soldier-Statesmen

Civic-action—A Counter and Cure for Insurgency

A central aspect of U.S. counterinsurgency doctrine was the belief that to be effective necessitated military concern with and study of all areas of society. A faculty member of the U.S. Army War College, writing in the confident period of 1964, stated: "Counterinsurgency is by definition geared to military, political, economic and civic action. . . . The major problem before us is to learn to orchestrate the magnificent counterinsurgency resources we have into a single symphony and to *persuade the governments we help to apply their energies and resources against threats that confront them.*"[13]

United States policy urging the Latin American military to be-come more deeply involved in all stages of society in order to wage an effective campaign against internal war implicitly encouraged a deeper involvement of the military in politics, and to this extent

[11] The *Air University Library Index to Military Periodicals* indexes 72 military publications by topic and is the starting point for any study of con-temporary U.S. military thought. The 1962–1964 volume is xv, no. 4.

[12] Starting from the top these articles appeared in *Army Information Digest* (October 1963), *U.S. Naval Institute Proceedings* (September 1962), *Military Review* (January 1964), *Army Information Digest* (July 1962), *Marine Corps Gazette* (June 1962), *Army* (April 1963), and *Military Review* (August 1962).

[13] Lt. Col. Jonathan F. Ladd, "Some Reflections on Counterinsurgency," *Military Review* (October 1964), pp. 76 and 78. Emphasis added.

can be considered a contributing factor in the creation of military regimes. In a policy paper by Einaudi, Maullin, and Stepan, we argued that "the United States' attention to threats from the Left has meant that the U.S. had ignored, and inadvertently even contributed to, problems on the Right. . . . United States' perceptions about the seriousness of the Communist threat and about the subsequent need for counterinsurgency and civic action for the Latin American military are producing undesired results."[14]

While profound internal changes that were only marginally related to U.S. influence were occurring in Brazil in the years leading up to assumption of power by the military, it is also important to note that many special conditions were present in Brazil that were not present in other Latin American countries, and that these made for unusually close personal relationships and policy perspectives between important groups in Brazil and the U.S. military establishment.

One of the most important facts bringing about a close similarity in aims and outlook between elements of the Brazilian military and the U.S. military mission was the participation of Brazil in World War II. Brazil was the only country in Latin America to send ground combat troops to fight in the war, and a Brazilian Expeditionary Force (FEB) of divisional strength fought in Italy as part of the U.S.-commanded Fourth Corps. The result of this participation was an integration of Brazilian material, organization, procedures, and tactics with those of the United States that has no parallel in the rest of Latin America. Just as important, from this experience arose a whole set of close personal friendships that persist even to this day. An especially close tie existed between the operations officer for the Brazilian force, Castello Branco, later the first president of the military government in Brazil, and the liaison officer between the U.S. Fourth Corps and Brazilian force, Vernon Walters, who was to become the U.S. military attaché to Brazil between 1962 and 1967.[15]

Another legacy of the Brazilian participation in World War II was a special relationship between the allies incorporated in the

[14] Luigi Einaudi, Richard Maullin, Alfred Stepan, *Latin American Security Issues* (Santa Monica, Calif.: The RAND Corporation, P-4109, April 1969), p. v.

[15] The significance of the Brazilian Expeditionary Force is discussed at length in Chapters 8 and 11.

agreement setting up the Joint Brazil–United States Defense Commission and still in active existence. The agreement institutionalized a program of high-level exchange on security issues that is not found in other bilateral treaties in Latin America.[16]

The great size and future world-power potential of Brazil also had special implications for U.S.–Brazilian relations. Because Brazil viewed itself as an apprentice world power, the Brazilian military has participated in overseas military operations to a degree unmatched by any other Latin American military. In addition to participation in World War II, Brazil for many years manned the U.N. peacekeeping force in Suez. A Brazilian general was also the first commander of the U.N. air force in the Congo.[17] The great-power aspirations also helped to account for Brazil's especially close attention to the cold-war ideology of the great powers, containing such doctrines as those of total and limited nuclear warfare and later that of internal warfare.[18]

For the United States, the great size of Brazil contributed to an intense "attraction-fear" relationship. The fear, especially pronounced and frequently voiced between 1961 and 1964, was that since Brazil has borders with every country in South America except Chile and Ecuador, a "pro-Communist" Brazil could serve as a sanctuary and training ground for guerrilla operations throughout South America. The same strategic position of Brazil was later a point in favor of massive assistance to the military government in Brazil, because Brazil could in essence perform an anti-Communist hegemonic role for the United States in South America.

The ally relationship between the U.S. and Brazil, and both countries' perceptions concerning Brazil's potential big-power status, contributed to other special features in U.S.–Brazilian relations. A U.S. advisory mission helped in the establishment of the Brazilian Superior War College and the mission remained at the school until 1960. The United States is still (1970) the only foreign country with a liaison officer with faculty status at the Brazilian Superior War College. Students from the college also make tours

[16] For a copy of the public version of the agreement, see Barber and Ronning, *Internal Security and Military Power*, 285–287.

[17] See R. Reynolds, "Brazil's Overseas Military Operations," *Military Review*, XLVI (November, 1966), 85–91.

[18] It is symptomatic that Brazil stations two full-time officers at the U.S. Army Command and General Staff College in Fort Leavenworth for the task of translating into Portuguese that school's publication, *Military Review*.

of U.S. military establishments and often pay a special visit to the U.S. president.[19]

The evidence clearly indicates, therefore, that there has been an unusually close relationship between the U.S. and the Brazilian military. However, it does not support the frequently heard argument that the Brazilian military's concern with internal warfare and counterinsurgency was solely the result of U.S. doctrine or training. A close study of the published work of the most important strategic thinker at the Brazilian Superior War College (ESG), General Golbery do Couto e Silva, reveals that in the mid-1950s, well before the basic U.S. concern with counterinsurgency, Golbery's own interest in revolutionary warfare was already being clearly articulated.[20]

Golbery argued in an interview that in the 1950s United States military thinkers were essentially preoccupied with nuclear warfare, and that the Brazilian Superior War College "was concerned with local warfare and revolutionary warfare before the United States, because nuclear warfare for us was technically impossible and politically less probable. Our actual problems in Brazil made fear of revolutionary warfare much more relevant than it was for the United States."[21]

Another assumption that must be qualified is that, owing to the special relationship existing between the Brazilian and the U.S. military, Brazil, more than any other Latin American country, must have chosen to send its officers and troops to U.S. schools, and that this also largely accounts for Brazil's adoption of the counterinsurgency ideology. However, if one examines the lists of foreign graduates of two of the most important U.S. schools devoted to disseminating doctrines and tactics of counterinsurgency, the United States Special Warfare Center and School at Fort Bragg, North Carolina, and the United States Army School of the Americas in the Canal Zone in Panama, one finds that Brazil was the most underrepresented of the Latin American nations. By 1963, of the 112 Latin American officers graduated from Fort Bragg, only two were Brazilians; of the

[19] See Chapter 8 for a detailed discussion of the Brazilian Superior War College and its role in the breakdown of the democratic regime in 1964.

[20] See his two major works which are based upon his lectures at the Escola Superior de Guerra in the 1950s: *Planejamento Estratégico* (Rio de Janeiro: Biblioteca do Exército, 1955), and *Geopolítica do Brasil* (Rio de Janeiro: Livraria José Olympio, 1967).

[21] Interview, August 29, 1968, Rio de Janeiro.

16,343 Latin Americans graduated from the Army School in Panama, only 165 were Brazilians.[22] These somewhat surprising figures are probably due to the fact that, since many of the courses are taught in Spanish, language has proved a barrier for the Portuguese-speaking Brazilians. Secondly, Brazilians, for reasons indicated in the discussion of the interview with Golbery, felt they had developed adequate counterinsurgency doctrines of their own and that their schools were as good as those of the United States.

This latter point should not be overstressed, for many Brazilian officers do attend U.S. military schools; my data show that about one-third of the Brazilian army line generals on active duty in January of 1964 had received some U.S. schooling.[23]

This brief survey of U.S. attempts to influence the course of Brazil's development in the 1960s shows that on economic, political, and military grounds the United States was supportive of the events that led to the overthrow of Goulart and the establishment of military government in Brazil. Despite this, however, it would not do intellectual justice to the complexities of the situation in Brazil and the internal dynamics of Brazilian politics, nor to the entire question of the breakdown of democratic regimes, to put all the explanatory weight on external factors such as the role of the United States. Even though, for example, there existed an influential group of Brazilian military officers with close links to the United States, the fact remains that in 1950–1952, 1955, and 1961 the Brazilian officer corps was profoundly divided over such issues as nationalism, the Korean war, and anti-Communism. The groups within the military who later emerged as most clearly associated with the United States cold-war policies in 1964 *lost* in the internal military struggles of 1955 and 1961. The assumption of power by the pro-U.S., militant anti-Communist generals in 1964 was thus far from foreordained.

It is very important therefore to study some of the internal factors that played a part in shifting the ideological center of gravity within the Brazilian military and many civilian groups. Why did a minority opinion become a majority opinion? Why did ideas of internal warfare come to seem so relevant to numerous Brazilians,

[22] For tables breaking down all graduates from Latin America by country, see Barber and Ronning, *Internal Security and Military Power*, pp. 145 and 149.

[23] See Table 11.1, p. 240.

131

both military men and civilians, by early 1964. These questions can only be answered within the wider context of a whole series of changes that were occurring in Brazil in the late 1950s and early 1960s, changes that tended to strengthen opposition to the traditional parliamentary system of politics and even to the democratic framework of politics. This growing opposition was found among both military officers and civilian groups. The slowing of the Brazilian economy and soaring inflation led to middle-class fears of erosion of status and an actual decline in lower-class wages. The growing awareness of the magnitude of economic and social problems facing the government, and the seeming inability of successive civilian governments to implement solutions to these problems, produced a suspended belief in the efficacy of democratic formulas both on the right and the left. Widespread fears among military officers of mutinies by enlisted men created a temporary coalition between military officers who were deeply divided on other issues.

This analysis does not ignore, nor does it attempt to condone, the role of the United States, but it does try to place this role in the wider perspective of changes occurring within the Brazilian polity, for it would be simplistic to ignore the fact that massive changes and fears within Brazil itself, fears felt by both civilians and military officers, contributed to an atmosphere in which a military coup was actively sought by a large number of civilians. Here the experience of the Dominican Republic was qualitatively different from that of Brazil, because in the Dominican Republic United States armed forces invaded the country to reverse the existing trend of politics. In Brazil, some existing trends found reinforcement in United States policy. These and many other factors form a central part of the analysis in Part III of the events leading up to the coup against President Goulart and the coming to power of the military.

Two intellectual orientations guide the inquiry into the events leading to the boundary change in Brazilian politics in 1964. The first is that, in general, regimes fall more from internal weaknesses than because of the strength of the opposition.[24] Thus, while not ignoring the civil–military coalition that attempted to overthrow

[24] Juan Linz develops this point theoretically and empirically in "The Breakdown of Democratic Regimes" (paper prepared for the Seventh World Congress of Sociology, Varna, Bulgaria, September 14–19, 1970). This work and Linz's lectures on the breakdown of democratic regimes in Germany, Spain, and Italy provide an analytic framework for much of Part III.

Goulart as early as 1962, I also study the "loads" on the political system and attempt to analyze the strengths and weaknesses of the governmental strategy in coping with these loads.[25]

The second working hypothesis is that while powerful economic and political structural strains normally contribute to the breakdown of a regime, these macro-sociological factors do not in themselves lead inevitably to its fall. The diffuse, generalized factors that are placing strains on the system have to be brought to a crisis by the interaction of key actors and issues at the micro-political level. Thus, in addition to studying the wider, structural factors that contributed to the breakdown in 1964, it is necessary to reconstruct the actual resolution of specific crises occurring in the period of the revolution itself. This allows us to get closer to such crucial variables as the quality of individual political leadership, problem-solving behavior, and the decisive impact of specific highly symbolic incidents. The essence of much politics is precisely what goes on at this level—and what is often overlooked in an exclusively macro-analysis.

[25] Since in Brazil the three military ministers were defeated handily in their 1961 attempt to block President Goulart from assuming the presidency, the hypothesis that it was not the inherent strength of the anti-government forces that accounted for the fall of Goulart seems reasonably strong. I discuss leadership factors in somewhat greater detail in my "Political Leadership and Regime Breakdown: Brazil, 1964" (paper prepared for the Seventh World Congress of Sociology, Varna, Bulgaria, September 14–19, 1970).

Chapter 6

*The Growing Sense of Crisis
in the Regime, 1961–1964:
Its Impact on the "Moderating Pattern"*

INTRODUCTION

The assumption by the military of governmental power in 1964 represented a breakdown of the old pattern of civil–military relations and the emergence of a new role for the military in Brazilian society. The argument throughout this work has been that the military is not an autonomous actor but should be thought of as a subsystem that responds to changes in the overall political system. Accordingly, in this chapter I attempt to illustrate how the military's change of role was basically related to major changes in the political system. A growing sense of crisis developed in Brazil between 1961 and 1964 as increasing economic loads and social mobilization led many politicians of the right and the left to argue that the regime itself was unworkable. The widespread belief in impending crisis played a major role in eroding the limits of military activism which had hitherto prevented the military from assuming control of the government.

A central aspect of the moderator role is that it maintains the general rules of the political game. But when the rules of politics are themselves widely questioned by many political actors, the role of moderator or arbitrator becomes less relevant or feasible. If politicians, for example, believe that the regime is unworkable, the question of who should receive political power following the removal of the president becomes much more difficult. The way clearly opens for the military to assume a new political role in society: that of *director* instead of *moderator* of the political system. If the military themselves feel that a new set of measures must be implemented, the military role may shift from that of system-maintenance to system-change.

The very processes of deepening economic, social, and ideological

134

conflicts in the period between 1961 and 1964 generated within significant numbers of officers a feeling of institutional insecurity, authoritarian attitudes, and desires for system-transformation that were increasingly out of harmony with the major premises of the moderating pattern of civil relations. Before examining the response of the military to this changing political environment, it is first necessary to examine in some detail these changes themselves. At the broadest level we can categorize the changes in the Brazilian political system between 1961 and 1964 in the following manner: (1) an increasing rate of political and economic demands made on the government, (2) a decreasing extractive capability due to the decline in the growth of the economy, (3) a decreasing political capacity to convert demands into concrete policy because of fragmentation of support, and (4) the increasing withdrawal of commitment to the political regime itself.[1]

Some of these trends may in fact have been "cyclical" rather than "secular." Politically, however, the important factor is that in the atmosphere of crisis that dominated Brazil from 1962 to 1964 they were perceived by much of the political elite as evidence of a structural crisis.

THE INCREASING RATE OF DEMANDS

An important ingredient of the legitimacy of a political regime is the belief among politicians that the regime provides an appropriate formula for handling the major demands of society as a whole. Widespread socioeconomic mobilization tends to generate new demands on the government, and the continued appropriateness of the political regime will depend upon its ability to adapt and maintain its capacity to deal with these demands.[2]

What changes were occurring in Brazil's social structure in the 1950s and early 1960s, and what was the relationship between these

[1] This framework owes much to the suggestive analysis of the capabilities of political systems in Gabriel A. Almond and G. Bingham Powell, Jr., *Comparative Politics: A Developmental Approach* (Boston: Little, Brown & Co., 1966), esp. pp. 190–212; and in Gabriel A. Almond, "Political Development: Analytical and Normative Perspectives," *Comparative Political Studies*, I (January 1969), 447–470.

[2] The major formulation of this point is Karl Deutsch's "Social Mobilization and Political Development," *American Political Science Review*, LV (September 1961), 493–514. For a similar discussion of the relationship between capability and legitimacy see David Easton, *A Systems Analysis of Political Life* (New York: John Wiley & Sons, 1965), p. 57.

135

changes and the demands being placed upon the economic and political system?

One steady change was the population growth. Brazil had an average annual population increase of 3.0 percent, one of the highest in the world. In terms of comparative loads on the different economic systems, it compared with 2.4 percent for India, 1.2 percent for France and West Germany, 1.0 percent for Japan and less than 1.0 percent for Bulgaria, Denmark, and England.[3]

A high rate of urbanization also put new demands on the economic and political system. Economically, much of the rural population in Brazil had lived near the subsistence-farming level, making few demands on the production and marketing capabilities of the economy as a whole. Politically, much of this population was "parochial" in Almond and Verba's sense of the term: "the parochial orientation . . . implies the comparative absence of expectation of change initiated by the political system."[4] The parochial makes few demands on the output functions of government such as public services, social welfare, or secondary education.

In the decade 1950 to 1960, Brazil's rural population grew from 33 million to only 39 million, while the urban population grew much more rapidly from 19 million to 32 million.[5] This new, rapidly expanding urban population created a whole series of increased requirements for transportation, jobs, distribution of food and housing.[6] With regard to the political system, the rapid urbanization decreased the number of "parochials" and increased the

[3] All growth rates are for the years 1958–1966, cited in United Nations, *Demographic Yearbook 1966*, pp. 104–111.

[4] Gabriel A. Almond and Sidney Verba, *The Civic Culture* (Princeton: Princeton University Press, 1963), p. 18.

[5] Brasil, *Anuário Estatístico do Brasil—1962*, p. 27. Figures rounded off to the nearest million.

[6] For example, at the aggregative level, agricultural production for domestic consumption grew at an annual rate of 3.3 percent from 1957 to 1961 and thus stayed ahead of the 3 percent annual population increase. However, at the disaggregative level of specific types of foods being supplied to urban areas, new loads were put upon the production and marketing capacity of the economic system. These resulted in a shortage of the types of foods consumed by the urban sectors, such as meat and dairy products, as indicated by the rise of the wholesale price index of foods of animal origin from a base of 100 in 1953 to 1,815 in 1963—an increase which was 308 points above the overall increase in the cost-of-living index for Rio de Janeiro. See Werner Baer, *Industrialization and Economic Development in Brazil* (Homewood, Illinois: Richard D. Irwin, 1965), pp. 150–153.

136

number of "subjects," that is, "people oriented toward the output, administrative, or 'downward flow' side of the political system."[7]

The output load of the government was also increased by populist executives who attempted to co-opt the new social groups by initiating extensive social welfare legislation. Numerous politicians attempted to win political followings by articulating and championing the just, latent demands of the new social groups.

In this atmosphere of increasing social mobilization and inflation, growing demands were made on the regulative and distributive capabilities of the government. The government became more and more involved in strike arbitration and in setting minimum wages.[8] The demands on the distributive capability led the government increasingly to subsidize bread prices and bus fares, which contributed to enlarged budget deficits. In addition, since domestic supplies of wheat (for the bread) and oil (for the enlarged bus services) were low, the government had to increase imports of these consumption items.[9]

In addition to this rapid growth of demands originating from the urban sector of the political system, significant elements of the rural population itself shifted in the early 1950s from "parochial" status to "subject" status, or even to "participant" status. In March 1963, rural workers were granted the right to form rural unions, and for the first time came under the protection of the

[7] For this definition of the "subject political culture," see Almond and Verba, *The Civic Culture*, pp. 19–26.

[8] In Brazil, as in most of Latin America, effective wage levels are normally determined not by collective bargaining at the factory or industry level at numerous decentralized points within the economy, but by the action of the national government in setting minimum-wage levels. In Brazil, therefore, strikes are not only economic demands, but also direct demands on the political capacity of the government to regulate disputes and real wages within the society. The degree to which labor demands were increasingly articulated and the government's regulative capacity strained is illustrated by strike arbitration figures. In 1959, for example, government labor tribunals were involved in 524 labor conflicts; by 1963 this figure had risen to 1,069. See the section on "Conflitos do Trabalho" in Brasil, *Anuário Estatístico do Brasil—1962*, p. 271, and the 1966 edition, p. 339. While a four-year time-span is too short to assert that this was a secular trend, the dominant impression in Brazil was clearly one of spiraling labor conflict.

[9] For a description and bibliographic guide to unsuccessful attempts by presidents to eliminate price subsidies, see Thomas Skidmore, *Politics in Brazil, 1930-1964* (New York: Oxford University Press, 1967), pp. 174–178, 193–197, 268–270.

137

minimum-wage law.[10] This law hastened the competition between individual political leaders, the church, and the government's highly political land reform agency (SUPRA) to organize the peasants into cooperatives, peasant leagues, and rural unions. It is true that the revolutionary nature and class consciousness of Julião and the peasant leagues were overrated and overpublicized.[11] Nonetheless, viewed historically, a major change was occurring in the quality and quantity of political demands that the peasants and their political mentors were making on the political system.[12]

A final indicator of increasing social mobilization is the electoral system. With regard to actual participation in the political process via voting, the total number of voters increased sharply from 6,200,805 in the 1945 presidential election to 14,747,221 in the 1962 congressional and gubernatorial elections.[13] More importantly, political intensity and ideological polarization in the 1962 elections were much greater than in previous elections, as numerous nationalist leftists staged vigorous campaigns and were opposed by militant free-enterprise, anti-Communist business groups.[14] This increasing electoral competition both reflected and created a rising level of demands upon the political system.

THE DECREASING EXTRACTIVE CAPABILITY: ECONOMIC DECLINE

How well were the Brazilian economic and political systems able to respond to this growth of demands resulting from rapid social mobilization?

[10] For a discussion of the law, see Caio Prado Junior, "O Estatuto do Trabalhador Rural," *Revista Brasiliense* (May–June 1963), pp. 1–13.

[11] For an analysis of the nonrevolutionary aspects of Julião, see Anthony Leeds, "Brazil and the Myth of Francisco Julião," in *Politics of Change in Latin America*, ed. Joseph Maier and Richard W. Weatherhead (New York: Praeger, 1964), pp. 190–204; Benno Galjart, in "Class and 'Following' in Rural Brazil," *América Latina*, VII (July–September 1964), 3–24, emphasizes the traditional and mutually competitive aspects of the peasant leagues.

[12] The most extensive treatment of the overall growth of rural activism is Neale Pearson, *Small Farmer and Rural Worker Pressure Groups in Brazil* (Ph.D. thesis, University of Florida, 1967).

[13] *Anuário Estatística do Brasil—1966*, p. 535.

[14] Two collections of articles concerning the 1962 elections at the local, state, and national levels are the issue of *Revista Brasileira de Estudos Políticos*, no. 16 (January 1964), and Themistocles Cavalcanti and Reisky Dubnic, eds., *Comportamento Eleitoral no Brasil* (Rio de Janeiro: Fundação Getúlio Vargas, January 1964).

Many of the demands were satisfied by the rate of growth in the per capita gross national product (GNP), which for most of the 1950s was one of the highest in the world. In 1962, however, the growth rate began to decline sharply, and in 1963 there was an actual decline in the per capita GNP (see Fig. 6.1).

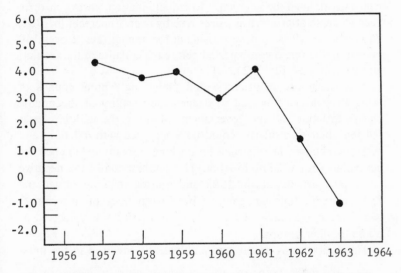

FIG. 6.1. PERCENTAGE CHANGE IN REAL PER CAPITA GNP, 1957–1963

SOURCE: International Monetary Fund, *International Financial Statistics: Supplement to 1966/67 Issues*, p. 28.

In terms of political capability, the increased social mobilization and later the downturn in economic growth increased the demands made upon the distributive capability of the government in regard to goods, services, and payments.

In response to these demands and in a populist effort to generate greater support, the Goulart government increased government expenditure. The percent of gross domestic product (GDP) allocated to current account expenditure of the federal government—operational costs of the bureaucracy, subsidies and transfers—rose from 10.9 in 1959 to 14.4 in 1963.

At the same time, however, government tax receipts, which had risen from 17 to 23 percent of the GDP from 1955 to 1959 fell to

139

20 percent by 1963.[15] Thus in Almond and Powell's vocabulary of governmental capability we can characterize the Brazilian situation in 1962–1964 as one in which the government's capability to "extract" resources such as revenue was declining while the loads on its "distributive capability" were increasing.[16]

One result was a rapid increase in the government's budget deficit which accelerated the inflation.[17] Brazilian inflation, always chronic, became acute after 1961 as prices rose by over 50 percent in 1962, 75 percent in 1963, and were rising at the annual rate of over 140 percent in the three-month period before the collapse of the Goulart government (see Fig. 6.2).

This sharp rise in prices set off increasingly bitter rounds of wage struggles and tended to deepen the hostility of the middle classes to labor and the government. Many in the middle classes felt that their own salaries could not keep pace with inflation, and they often blamed labor strikes for pushing costs up and blamed the government for yielding to labor. The combination of the negative per capita growth rate in 1963 and soaring inflation turned the Kubitschek multiple-sum game of Brazilian politics into a zero-sum game where each major labor gain from a strike was perceived as a loss to other groups.

The military was deeply and ambivalently involved in the infla-

[15] See Joel Bergsman, *Brazil's Industrialization and Trade Politics* (Berkeley: University of California, Brazil Development Assistance Program, preliminary version, February 1969), pp. 73–74. Bergsman's figures are from EPEA, *Diagnóstico Preliminar, Finanças Públicas*, ministry of planning, Rio de Janeiro, December 1965 (mimeo) and the Fundação Getúlio Vargas.

[16] For their definitions of "extractive capability" and "distributive capability" see Almond and Powell, *Comparative Politics*, pp. 195–198.

[17] This is not to argue that the inflation in Brazil was completely "monetary" in origin, as opposed to "structural." For example, wheat yield per hectare fell from 816 kilograms in 1950 to only 625 kilograms in 1960, inducing the government to feel it politically necessary to assume the subsidization of wheat imports. This was done to prevent the price of bread from rising sharply. Clearly this was a structural source of inflation that essentially had its origin in the agricultural sector of Brazil. Nonetheless, the point that the government was distributing more than it was able to finance is still valid. Government figures also show a decline in this period in the productivity per hectare of the two staples of the lower-class diet: rice and black beans. See Baer, *Industrialization*, Table 7-3, p. 154.

For a survey of the literature concerning the causes and effects of inflation in Latin America, see Werner Baer, "The Inflation Controversy in Latin America: A Survey," *Latin American Research Review*, XI (Spring 1967), 3–25.

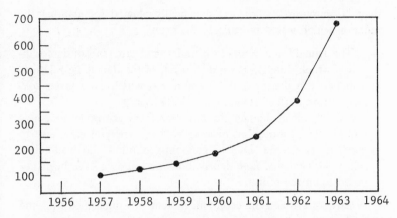

FIG. 6.2. COST OF LIVING PRICE INDEX, 1957–1963

SOURCE: International Monetary Fund, *International Financial Statistics: Supplement to 1966/67 Issues*, p. 27.

tion–strike–inflation syndrome. The strikes engendered increasing violence and the military was often invoked to protect strikers against hostile state governments or employers and in some cases to prohibit the strike. The belief grew among military officers that the government's encouragement of strikes and the granting of large pay increases contributed to inflation, violence, and the erosion of their own status and salaries. Increasingly, military journals complained about inflation and the threat it presented.[18] Characteristically, their articles attempted to document the decline in military real take-home pay in relation to other groups, especially labor unions.[19]

The political significance of the military reaction to inflation was particularly important because the military began to identify the labor unions and mobilization politics as being the most culpable factor. An example of this changing mentality is found in one of the more important documents of the military revolution of April 1964, *Documento LEEX*.[20] In it the militant trade unions, with

[18] See, e.g., "Inflação e Salários," *Revista do Clube Militar*, no. 163 (1963), pp. 10–11, and "O 'Affaire' Vencimentos," in the same issue, pp. 8–9.

[19] See the detailed article by Capitão de Corveta, José Augusto Didier Barbosa Vianna, "Vencimentos dos Militares," *Boletim do Clube Naval*, no. 176 (4° Trimestre, 1963), pp. 121–134.

[20] Significantly, *LEEX* stands for *Lealdade ao Exército* ("loyalty to the

their "Communist" allies, are specifically blamed for creating the inflation which was demoralizing the army:

> The armed forces lament the underhand processes of demoralization which threaten them as a result of the damaging relationship between unions and Communists—which even some government authorities refer to as a Fifth Army.
>
> As a result of demagogic and anarchic wage policies, a new and privileged group has been created in society at great cost to many other people. Due to galloping inflation and insufficient salary adjustments, new deprivations and abuses have been imposed upon the military.[21]

A sense of crisis in the economic system was intensified by some indications that the industrialization process was not merely temporarily slowing but was actually facing possible secular decline. The argument was raised that the import substitution which had been a vital ingredient of Brazil's rapid industrialization in the 1950s was approaching the "exhaustion" point by the early 1960s.[22] Also, Brazil's export stagnation contributed to serious foreign exchange difficulties and an import constraint.[23]

The pressure on Brazil's economy was intensified because it coincided with a declining capacity to extract resources from the international environment: for both private[24] and public[25] resources

---

army"). The document was clandestinely issued in late January or early February 1964. Copy in possession of the author.

[21] *Documento LEEX.*

[22] An influential article advancing this thesis was Maria Conceição Tavares, *et al.*, "The Growth and Decline of Import Substitution in Brazil," *Economic Bulletin for Latin America*, IX (March 1964), 1–59.

[23] This decline was partly due to a deterioration in the terms of trade. Nathaniel Leff argues that it was also due to a *de facto* discrimination against exports because of the acceptance by Brazilian policymakers of an "export surplus" theory of trade. See his "Export Stagnation and Autarkic Development in Brazil, 1947–1962," *Quarterly Journal of Economics*, LXXXI (May 1967), 286–301, and his "Import Constraints and Development: Causes of Recent Decline of Brazilian Economic Growth," *Review of Economics and Statistics*, XLIX (November 1967), 494–501.

[24] Private capital also reacted negatively to the 1962 profit remittance law. Werner Baer estimates that the inflow of private foreign capital declined from 108 million U.S. dollars in 1961 to 71 million in 1962, and to 31 million in 1963. See Baer, *Industrialization and Economic Development in Brazil*, p. 200.

[25] A major loan negotiation begun with the IMF broke down in June 1963. An account of the 1963 U.S.–Brazilian negotiations for aid is given

were drying up, through concern at (and in reprisals for) Brazil's inflation, economic nationalism, and political radicalization. By mid-1963, the U.S. government began to curtail new development-aid contracts with the Brazilian central government. In 1963, debt-repayment obligations were so staggering that the finance minister reported to the cabinet that amortization and interest payments already scheduled for the years 1963–1965 would amount to $1.8 billion, or about 43 percent of the expected export revenues for that period.[26]

The Decreasing Capacity to Convert Demands into Policy: Fragmenting Patterns of Support

In the early 1960s, Brazilian politicians spoke increasingly of the systemic crisis facing the country because of the increased level of demands and the decreased capacity of the economic system to satisfy them. Awareness of the crisis and the need for corrective action could have resulted in generation of new political inputs of support for a government attempting to implement a development policy.[27] In Brazil, however, the political system was characterized by a relatively weak aggregation of support; that is, there was a relatively low conversion of demands into powerfully supported programs.

In practice this meant that the executive was faced with a variety of well-articulated raw demands, but it could not convert these demands into a developmental program backed by a power combination that could be relied upon for the minimal support necessary to implement the program. Illustrative of the weakness of aggregation of support was the response to the cluster of problems related to inflation and balance-of-payments difficulties. There was widespread desire among major political groups and actors for a pro-

---

by the then Brazilian ambassador to the United States, Roberto Campos, in Alberto Dines et al., O Mundo Depois de Kennedy (Rio de Janeiro: José Alvaro, 1965), pp. 114–121. An insight into the U.S. government's basic distrust of President Goulart is found in Lincoln Gordon's testimony, U.S. Congress, Senate, The Nomination of Lincoln Gordon to be Assistant Secretary for Inter-American Affairs, Hearings before the Committee on Foreign Relations, Senate, 89th Cong., 2nd sess., February 7, 1966.

[26] The finance minister's report is reprinted in Correio da Manhã, July 5, 1963, cited in Skidmore, Politics in Brazil, p. 257.

[27] See Easton, Systems Analysis, chap. 10, "Support as an Input of Systems," for an elaboration of this point.

gram to curtail the inflation and alleviate the foreign-exchange shortage. However, there was very little conversion of this demand into a set of strongly supported policy programs. From the early 1950s, each presidential term had seen the formulation of a stabilization program. The "Aranha Plan" under Vargas in 1953–1954, the "Lopes–Campos Plan" in 1958–1959 under Kubitschek, a plan under Quadros, and finally the "Dantas–Furtado Plan" in 1963 under Goulart all attempted to implement stabilization policies. Each was abandoned when the president was unable to get support to implement the plans. As a consequence, the presidents bowed to interest groups and sectoral demands that destroyed any coherent stabilization program.[28] Robert Daland, in his comparative study of Brazilian development plans, commented:

> Brazil does not have political institutions which can efficiently perform the function of aggregating diverse interests. . . . A consequence of this basic political situation is an inability of the "system" to produce dominant political support behind any one national policy or leader through the mechanisms of the democratic process of elections and related behaviors as envisaged in the Brazilian Constitution.[29]

To gain insight into the roots of such weak institutions of aggregation, let us consider briefly a major potential source of aggregation of interests—the party system. Before the 1964 revolution, the two strongest congresses in Latin America were the Brazilian and Chilean. The Brazilian Congress had important veto power over key structural issues, such as land reform, tax reform, constitutional reform, and the granting of votes to illiterates. In addition, its capacity to appropriate a larger amount of funds than the executive requested made it a central organ in any attempt to establish priorities for development planning or for implementing a program of fiscal stabilization. Thus, if significant aggregation of interests and support for a reform program were to take place in

[28] For a description of each plan and a bibliographic introduction, see Robert T. Daland, *Brazilian Planning: Development Politics and Administration* (Chapel Hill: University of North Carolina Press, 1967). He gives a particularly good analysis of the raw articulation of demands and the total failure to aggregate support that led to the collapse of the "Dantas–Furtado Plan"; see pp. 157–170.

[29] *Ibid.*, p. 197.

Brazil, the political party system, especially in its congressional aspect, would be a key component in this support.

The party system since 1945 had never been very effective in this function,[30] however, and there were signs that it was becoming less so in the crisis period of the 1960s. No single major party since 1945 had significantly increased its percentage of nonalliance votes. In fact, the percentage of party alliance votes had been growing at every congressional election (see Table 6.1). The growth of short-

TABLE 6.1

Growth of Electoral Alliances in Congressional Elections, Percentage of Major Party Vote; 1945–1962

	PSD	UDN	PTB	Party Alliances
1945	42.3	26.3	10.1	—*
1950	22.2	14.0	13.6	16.7
1954	22.0	13.6	14.9	25.7
1958	18.4	13.2	14.7	33.3
1962	15.6	11.2	12.1	41.0

SOURCE: Ronald Schneider, "Election Analysis," in *Brazil Election Factbook: Number 2, September 1965*, by Charles Daugherty, James Rowe, Ronald Schneider (Washington: Institute for the Comparative Study of Political Systems, 1965), p. 60.

* In 1945, no party alliances were allowed.

term alliances had a disaggregating effect on any program the parties may have stood for at the national level because the alliances were normally local or state alliances entered into only for the purposes of winning a seat. Parties standing for different policies at the national level formed temporary alliances at the local level. These alliances "were so varied that almost every possible combination of parties could be found in one state or another. . . . For example, [in 1962] the PSD and the UDN were allied for congressional elections in three states, the PSD and the PTB in two others, and the UDN and the PTB in still two others."[31]

The alliances normally disappeared after the election and were unrelated to sustained aggregated support for any program. For

[30] The most complete analysis of the structures and functions of the parties is Phyllis Peterson, *Brazilian Political Parties: Formation, Organization, Leadership, 1945–1959* (Ph.D. diss., University of Michigan, 1962).

[31] Schneider, "Election Analysis," p. 64.

145

example, none of the 26 alliances made for the 1958 elections endured. None was among the 32 alliances made for the 1962 elections.[32] This steady growth of temporary election alliances made it increasingly difficult to make the representatives responsible either to the party or to the wishes of the electorate, and has been characterized as a process of "progressive inauthentication."[33]

Within the party system the major source of aggregation in the 1950s under the Vargas and Kubitschek governments was an uneasy coalition between the rural bosses and nationalist entrepreneurs of the PSD and the urban labor leaders of the PTB. The Brazilian political scientist, Hélio Jaguaribe, in his formulation of various possible models of Brazilian growth, termed this coalition "a party of development" and implied that it was an intrinsic part of the success of the pragmatic "neo-Bismarckian model" that he considered the most appropriate for Brazil's development.[34] The growing radicalization (both left and right) within the Brazilian polity and the differential attitudes of the PTB and PSD toward industrial strikes and especially agrarian reform (with its emotional side issues such as rural unionization, land invasion, and constitutional change allowing for expropriation of land without prior payment of cash), increasingly fragmented this major source of aggregation. In 1960, these two parties had allied in eight of the eleven states in which gubernatorial elections were held. In 1962, they were not allied in any of the eleven gubernatorial races.[35]

Not only were the existing patterns of aggregation and support weak in Brazil, but many of the major structural changes that were occurring, such as urbanized industrialization in São Paulo[36] and

[32] Pompeu de Souza, "Eleições de 1962: Decomposição Partidária e Caminhos da Reforma," *Revista Brasileira de Estudos Políticos*, no. 16 (January 1964), 10–11.

[33] *Ibid.*, p. 7.

[34] Hélio Jaguaribe, *Desenvolvimento Econômico e Desenvolvimento Político* (Rio de Janeiro: Editôra Fundo de Cultura, 1962), pp. 83–84, 101.

[35] Ronald Schneider, "Election Analysis," p. 66. See also Skidmore, *Politics in Brazil*, pp. 229–233.

[36] In São Paulo, rapid industrialization was negatively correlated with programmatic party aggregation. São Paulo has been the breeding-ground of the most important populist, personalist party in post-1945 Brazil, the PSP (*Partido Social Progressista*). The state also presents an extreme case of party proliferation. In 1962, for example, the delegation of deputies to the Federal Congress was fragmented; for the 59 deputy seats, 11 parties

the rural peasant leagues,[37] were politically highly fragmented and personalist, and thus could not provide a solid base of support for a government program.

THE INCREASING WITHDRAWAL OF CIVILIAN COMMITMENT TO THE POLITICAL REGIME

Although great loads existed on the political system by early 1964, what made the crisis a total one in which the constitutional, democratic framework of government was called into question was the widespread belief and argumentation by politicians on the left and the right that the system was unworkable.[38] In the collapse of any democratic regime, the attitudes and beliefs of the loyal opposition and the defenders of the regime are usually more critical for its survival than the beliefs and actions of the disloyal opposi-

---

sent representatives, the *largest* party sending only 9 deputies, while even the sixth largest party sent 5. This trend toward fragmentation had been growing steadily since 1954. See Oliveiros S. Ferreira, "A Crise de Poder do 'Sistema' e as Eleições Paulistas de 1962," *Revista Brasileira de Estudos Políticos,* no. 16 (January 1964), 179–226, esp. p. 221.

[37] The leagues were often in direct competition for such distributionist outputs of the government as the one medical station to be installed in the area, or the one agriculture extension station. In addition, under the terms of the labor law, the government could grant official recognition to only one of the unions in each geographical sector, thus setting up fierce competition within the movement as a whole. Viewed in these terms, the peasant leagues were not a new unified class movement giving their support to coherent patterns of reform. Rather, they were congruent with the over-all systemic pattern of high articulation but low aggregation of demands. One UNESCO observer stressed this point and concluded that the peasant leagues were the functional equivalent of the nineteenth-century rural "followings" of the traditional rural leaders, the *coroneis.* See Galjart, "Class and 'Following' in Rural Brazil"; see also Alfred C. Stepan, "Discussion: The Middle Classes in Latin America," *New Politics,* IV (Spring 1965), pp. 87–90.

[38] Uruguay from 1964 to 1968 experienced worse economic difficulties, but the much greater belief in the political system enabled it to survive. For example, for the year June 30, 1966, to June 30, 1967, prices rose 64.5 percent. In the next twelve-month period prices rose 182.6 percent. Then from June 30, 1968, to June 30, 1969, the existing regime mustered all its resources and reduced the rate to an amazingly low 7.8 percent. (Even Uruguay's "political capital" may soon be exhausted, however, if the economy is not basically reconstructed.) See, "Uruguay: Un éxito a medias," *Economist para América Latina* (August 6, 1969), p. 30.

tion.[39] Significantly, those most empowered to defend the regime, the last two presidents in power before the breakdown in 1964, Quadros and Goulart, were both pessimistic about the chances of the political system's working effectively, and a case could be made that they both worked harder at attempting to change the regime than at achieving more limited goals within the existing framework.[40] Quadros in fact resigned in hopes of being given a Gaullist mandate to implement major structural reforms. His successor, Goulart, frequently talked of his powerlessness to govern the country and indeed appeared to allow some problems to worsen so as to strengthen his claim that the system required basic change.[41]

In addition to presidential ambiguity over the effectiveness of the political system, the near civil war that occurred after President Quadros' resignation in 1961 and Goulart's assumption of the presidency greatly increased the mobilization of forces within Brazil on both the left and the right. In both groups the episode of Quadros' resignation strengthened the feeling that Brazil was entering a revolutionary stage that called for a new political order. Politicians from the left and right made attempts to resolve the political crisis by extraparliamentary means. The curtailment of the powers of the office of the president before Vice-President Goulart was allowed to assume the presidency was in essence an attack on the regime by centrist and conservative civilians and military officers. Many frustrated democratic leftist reformers who had been proregime became antiregime and argued that reform could only come through massive pressure and plebiscitary democracy, or even revolution. President Goulart's advisor, Leonel Brizola, spoke of the need to form clandestine armed groups of men (the *grupos de onze*). Conservatives prepared to defend themselves by force. In the countryside landowners armed themselves in prepara-

[39] This point is elaborated in Juan Linz, "The Breakdown of Democratic Regimes" (paper prepared for the Seventh World Congress of Sociology, Varna, Bulgaria, September 14–19, 1970).

[40] The almost universal reaction of Quadros' close advisors to his sudden resignation was a bitter fury that measures they felt could have been taken within the limits of the existing political framework were aborted. Discussions with Cândido Mendes, New York, Spring 1965. Cândido Mendes had been an advisor to President Quadros. Likewise, Goulart abandoned the Furtado Plan of development and various other policies by not attempting to implement them systematically.

[41] For a particularly striking case of Goulart's emphasizing his helplessness, see the interview he gave to *Manchete*, issue of November 30, 1963.

148

tion for civil war.[42] In the cities, especially São Paulo, right-wing vigilante units proliferated.[43]

This sense that the regime was doomed and that Brazil was at the threshold of revolution dominated much of the political dialogue in the period 1961 to 1964. The right-wing authoritarian nationalist, Oliveiros S. Ferreira, a leading columnist for the *Estado de São Paulo*, a few months before the coup of 1964 argued characteristically:

> With the renunciation of President Jânio Quadros there opened a crisis of regime—perhaps the most grave in the entire history of the Republic—a power vacuum which must be filled or we will be plunged into the chaos of a civil war. The question that was placed before all lucid men after the renunciation was how to surmount the crisis; that is, what conception of historical process, which types of organizations, and what form of popular associations should replace the conceptions, parties, and regime which have demonstrated themselves incapable of resolving ... the great national problems.[44]

Celso Furtado, a prominent member of the reformist democratic left, the first director of SUDENE, and the chief designer of the Three-Year Development Plan formulated in 1963 for Goulart, writing before the revolution, also described the situation as a crisis of regime:

> The country's economy, at the mercy of a series of structural constrictions, is by the very nature of its problems in an unstable situation. The primary forces of development—population growth, urbanization, desire for improved living conditions ... are piling up like political energy in the waters of a river that

[42] For an interesting article on the evolution of the belief in the need for violent revolutionary change among the Catholic university left, see Thomas G. Sanders, "Catholicism and Development: The Catholic Left in Brazil," in *Church and States: The Religious Institution and Modernization*, ed. Kalman Silvert (New York: American Universities Field Staff, 1967), pp. 81–99.

[43] In an interview with former officials of a São Paulo vigilante unit, they asserted that as early as June 1963 they held massive private meetings and were arming themselves.

[44] Oliveiros S. Ferreira, *As Fôrças Armadas e o Desafio da Revolução* (Rio de Janeiro: Edições GRD, 1964), pp. 13–14. Ferreira himself was active in a civil–military group attempting to overthrow Goulart and impose an authoritarian nationalist solution to the Brazilian impasse.

has been dammed. The disturbing action of these pressing forces tends to increase with the reduction in the economy's rate of growth. We have seen that this reduction led to an aggravation of the inflationary process, which indicates that these forces are seeking an outlet through an effort that is becoming increasingly sterile. However, the tension created by these dammed-up forces has led to the awakening of a wide number of groups who have become aware that development is threatened by structural obstacles that are beyond the capacity for action by the present ruling groups. . . . Situations of this kind lead, almost inevitably, to the disruption of the existing balance of forces and the abandonment of conventional political methods.[45]

An analysis of newspaper editorials in the period preceding the coup of 1964 reveals that the crisis was essentially one of regime, in comparison to the preceding crises of 1945, 1954, 1955, and 1961, all essentially crises concerning individual governments. Before these latter coups, the major theme of editorials was the illegitimacy of the chief executive. This element was of course present in the crisis of 1964. But the editorials even more emphatically voiced fear of social disintegration and political "subversion." There was an overtone of panic absent in other years.

The *Jornal do Brasil*, for example, shrilled, "the state of law has submerged in Brazil," and stressed that it was in such situations that "revolutions like that of Russia in 1917" emerged.[46] The *Diário de Pernambuco* ran an editorial entitled, "Fruits of Generalized Madness," and warned that Brazil faced an hour of "desolation" unless the situation were basically altered.[47] Even the normally moderate *Correio da Manhã* feared that with each incident "indiscipline was getting more uncontrollable" and apocalyptically warned that it was impossible "to continue in this chaos in all areas."[48]

A number of other indicators reveal the atmosphere of regime crisis. The level of civilian arming on the right and left was unquestionably much higher than that preceding the other coups between 1945 and 1964. (The only comparable civilian arming was that preceding the crisis of regime at the end of the "Old

[45] Celso Furtado, *Dialéctica do Desenvolvimento* (Rio de Janeiro: Editôra Fundo de Cultura, 1964), p. 134.
[46] Front page editorial in large type, March 29, 1964.
[47] Editorial, March 31, 1964.   [48] Editorial, March 31, 1964.

Republic" in 1930.) As I explain in greater detail later, the coup of 1964 was also preceded by unprecedented crises of authority within the army, and mutinies among enlisted men.

Another symptom was the quickened pace of elections, plebiscites, and extraparliamentary attempts to change political rules of the game.[49] Normally in Brazil the presidential election, held once every five years, is the only political contest in which national power is perceived to be in the balance. In the three and a half years between October 1960 and March 1964, however, the country experienced the turmoil of six such major political contests, all relatively inconclusive. These contests began with the presidential election in October 1960, followed by the resignation of Quadros in August 1961 and the near civil war which was resolved only when Goulart accepted the presidency under a new prime-ministerial form of government. Then came the fiercely contested congressional and gubernatorial elections of 1962, President Goulart's long bitter campaign to hold a plebiscite to regain former presidential powers, and the plebiscite itself in January of 1963. President Goulart requested Congress to rule by state of siege in October of that year. Finally there was the March 1964 drive for "basic reforms," with the implicit threat to close Congress and hold a new plebiscite.

The atmosphere leading up to the civil–military crisis of 1964 was in a fundamental way unlike that preceding the crises of 1945, 1954, and 1955. One of the key aspects of civil–military relations as they existed before 1964 was that influential civilians and military officers believed that civilian political groups as a whole could rule within the parliamentary constitutional framework, and that the political demands emerging from social and economic changes could be transformed into acceptable outputs by the political system. This was an essential element in the return of executive power to civilians following the military coups of 1945, 1954, and 1955, and the maintenance of a boundary to military activity.

The civil–military crisis of 1964, however, was a crisis over the appropriateness, effectiveness, and legitimacy of the political system in meeting the challenge of development. It was the belief in the appropriateness and effectiveness of existing civilian institu-

[49] Juan Linz, in his paper, "The Breakdown of Democracy in Spain," discusses such increased political activity as a characteristic feature associated with the breakdown of democratic regimes.

151

tions that was eroded in the years before 1964, especially after 1961. The feeling that the political system was incapable of meeting the demands upon it, and that the legitimacy of the constitutional regime was declining undermined a basic element of the pattern of civil–military relations as they had existed since 1945. The boundary change in civil–military relations was thus intrinsically related to changes in the wider political system of which the military forms a part.

Chapter 7

The Impact of Political and Economic
Crises on the Military:
Growth of Institutional Fears, 1961–1964

INTRODUCTION

The sense of growing political and economic crises and the mobilization of groups hitherto at the fringes or unrepresented in politics had profoundly divisive effects on politics in Brazil between 1961 and 1964. It also had profoundly divisive effects on the military as an institution. The economic crisis, new tactics of co-opting the military, the awakening political consciousness of enlisted men within the military, and the development of new ideologies following the success of the Cuban revolution, all contributed to making the military a more insecure, authoritarian institution. Increasing numbers of military officers developed attitudes that were no longer in harmony with the moderating pattern of civil–military relations.

Many of the processes at work in Brazil from 1961 to 1964, such as the adult literacy campaigns (the most important being MEB [*Movimento de Educação de Base*]), the political awakening and organization of the peasants, and the evolution of the trade unions from their co-opted status in the corporate state structure established by Vargas to one of greater political autonomy, were exciting and basically healthy aspects of political development. It was not inconceivable that these changes could have been accepted by the military. Another major and essentially cautious institution, the church, starting from a position to the right of the military in the late 1950s, embraced and championed many of these trends and moved consistently to the left.[1] The military as an

[1] It goes without saying that the church, like the army, is not a monolithic institution. I am speaking here only of shifts in the center of gravity of each institution. The church today continues to have some very active right-wing and reactionary members. Luigi Einaudi, Michael Fleet, Richard Maullin and I analyze the recent evolution of the Latin American church

institution, however, felt itself threatened and grew hostile to the entire style of mobilization politics. After the coup of 1964, the military governments used their new powers to repress all the trends mentioned above. As a consequence, the military has moved substantially to the right of its position in the late 1950s. Why did the military respond to change in this way?

Consistent with traditional politics, the crises between 1961 and 1964 set in motion attempts by all major actors to bring the military, or groups within the military, onto their side to resolve problems and strengthen their power bases. Both the left and the right attempted to penetrate the military more deeply and systematically than in previous times. On the right, for example, the anti-Communist business groups, such as IBAD (*Instituto Brasileiro de Ação Democrática*) and the more intellectual IPÊS (*Instituto de Pesquisas e Estudos Sociais*), hired ex-military officers in an attempt to influence active duty officers. IPÊS from 1962 to 1964 paid ex-officers to establish an intelligence system to monitor "Communist" influence on the government and to distribute their findings clandestinely on a regular basis to key military officers throughout Brazil. By their own estimate, IPÊS spent between $200,000 and $300,000 a year in this intelligence gathering and distribution network.[2] The left similarly looked to the military to increase their own political position and power base.

This process of politicization was consistent with the rules of politics as they had traditionally existed in Brazil. However, what made these attempts to politicize the military in the long run destructive of old patterns of civil–military relations was that the military perceived the process for the first time as threatening to their own institutional integrity. Especially significant was the development of the fear that politics was at such a radicalized stage and the existing political parties and groups so fragmented that no group within the polity had the competence to rule the country. The rhetoric of mobilization and radicalization, coming in the wake of the Cuban revolution, was feared by many officers as the prelude to destruction of the traditional army. The increasing politicization

---

in our *Latin American Institutional Development: The Changing Catholic Church* (Santa Monica, Calif.: The RAND Corporation, RM-6136-DOS, October 1969).

[2] Interview with Glycon de Paiva, Rio de Janeiro, September 6, 1968. He was a director of IPÊS from 1962 to 1964, and at the time of the interview was a vice-president of IPÊS.

of the enlisted ranks, especially sergeants, intensified this fear among officers, and was seen to threaten military discipline. Finally, the growing use of political criteria for promotions in the army in order to create an armed force loyal to the president, always a factor in the Brazilian military, was feared by many officers to have reached alarming proportions. Many felt it endangered not only the hierarchical structure of the military and the personal career-expectations of the officers, but also tended to destroy the non-partisan role of the military itself.

All these factors contributed to the development of attitudes within the officer corps that were no longer consistent with the traditional moderating role of the military. The belief that no political group had the competence to rule, the fear of mobilization politics and the conviction that they threatened the institutional survival of the military, eroded many of the basic premises of the moderating pattern. At the Superior War College, indeed, an ideology developed that both questioned basic structural features of the political system and implicitly envisioned a new political role for the military. The content of this ideology and its implications for civil–military relations are discussed in the following chapter. In this chapter, some aspects of the institutional fears that developed among the military between 1961 and 1964 are analyzed.

FEAR OF DESTRUCTION OF THE OFFICER CORPS: THE IMPACT OF CUBA

A key feature of the Cuban revolution for civil–military relations in Brazil, and indeed for other Latin American countries, lay in the fact that the revolutionary leaders destroyed the regular army and replaced it with a popular militia.[3] While fear of Castroist influence had made armies more sensitive to the need for reforms they saw as necessary to inoculate society against the Castro "virus,"

[3] The military did not greatly fear Communism as such. Many military regimes in Latin America, such as those of General Pérez Jiménez in Venezuela, Odría in Peru, and General Rojas Pinilla in Colombia, had co-existed with the Communists in the past, and in fact had used Communist support as a weapon against the democratic trade-union movement, which the military considered a greater threat than the Communists. The Communist party often emerged even stronger at the end of military rule than before. See Robert J. Alexander, *Communism in Latin America*, 3rd ed. (New Brunswick: Rutgers University Press, 1963), pp. ix–xix.

it also made the military more fearful of the radical left, which encourages mass action, both rural and urban.[4]

In the already turbulent Brazilian situation, the effect of the Cuban revolution on the civilian left was to increase their belief in the efficacy of the tactics of violence. At the least, it helped sweep up the radical nationalists in the rhetoric of a Cuban-style revolution. Catholic student activists (*Ação Popular*) entered into electoral coalitions with Communist students after 1959, and looked to Cuba as a revolutionary model. Peasant leagues invaded the land in the northeast, and President Goulart's brother-in-law, Leonel Brizola, urged the formation of revolutionary cells of eleven armed men (the *grupos de onze*). These groups were not Communistic but they frequently used the language and symbols of a Castro-style attack on the existing power structure.

Castro's victory in Cuba had a very different effect on the Brazilian military. While few military men believed that Goulart himself was a Communist, many feared he was a weak man who would rely on the support of Communists to effect a coup, and then be powerless to control them.[5] The fear of Castro-style Communism created a new factor in civil–military relations in Brazil—the possibility that one of the major actors in the political system might depart from the accepted rules of the game, in which traditionally everyone used the military for political ends but no single group threatened to destroy the military or their role of moderator of the political system. Here the *perception* that a threat was being made was as politically significant as the reality of any such threat.[6]

[4] Here the Latin American military's response to Castro had much in common with that of United States foreign policy—a desire for rapid defensive modernization such as that which inspired the Alliance for Progress, and simultaneously the tendency to adopt a more repressive stand against radical movements, witness, U.S. action in the Dominican Republic.

[5] General Golbery, one of the leading theoreticians of the Superior War College, of the 1964 revolution, and of the Castello Branco government, commented to the author that "Jango was never a leftist. He was an opportunistic *fazendeiro* ("landowner"). He was not even a *caudillo* such as Vargas, who was a smooth *caudillo*, or Brizola, who was a bravado *caudillo*. Jango was trying to use the unions for his own purposes, but the Communists were also infiltrating the movement and Jango was trying to use them." Brasília, September 18, 1967.

The Spanish military in 1936 had a similar image of minority government leader Casares Quirogo. He was seen as the "señorito who was blind to the threat of a Maximalist-Socialist revolution."

[6] After the 1964 revolution, the military conducted extensive investigations to unearth Communist influence. Their published evidence to date has

This perceived threat weakened the coalition between nationalist civilians and nationalist military officers sympathetic to left-wing reform. The existence of this coalition had been an important factor in the maintenance of the moderating power pattern in that it inhibited right-wing military men from assuming a governing role, or from systematically suppressing the civilian left. It also kept up a dialogue between the civilian and military left.

The military's fear that their institution would first be divided by Communist subversion and then replaced by a popular militia became an increasingly dominant theme in Brazilian military publications after Goulart assumed office in 1961.[7] *Documento LEEX*, which succeeded in recruiting military moderates to the conspiracy to remove Goulart from the presidency, emphasized the Cuban example on the first page:

> We should remember that it was only after betrayal had been consummated in Cuba [by] the virtual extinction of any possibility of resistance, that the Cuban dictator proclaimed the Marxist-Leninist ideology of the revolution which he was leading.

Specific reference was made to the destruction of discipline as a prelude to the destruction of the regular army:

> The armed forces will not accept the game which is being played to split the component parts of the military, to undermine its discipline, to destroy its efficiency, and in the end, *to substitute for it a version of a red army or a Cuban militia.*[8]

One of the original mobilizers of the revolution, and also one of the first to actually move troops against Goulart, was General Carlos Luiz Guedes. He wrote that, in his 1963 attempts to forge

---

been slight; see, for instance, the four very theoretical but factually sparse volumes published on the subject by the *Military Police Inquiry*, no. 709, *O Comunismo no Brasil* (Rio de Janeiro: Biblioteca do Exército, 1966–1967.) Also President Castello Branco promised a "white paper" in Communist infiltration in the Goulart regime but never produced it.

[7] Until late 1961 the *Revista de Intendência* published no hard-hitting anti-Communist articles. From late 1961 until the revolution, almost every issue contained one or more articles on the threat of revolutionary warfare. The same trend is noticeable in the army General Staff's publication, *Boletim de Informações*.

[8] *Documento LEEX*, clandestinely issued in late 1963 or early 1964. Copy in possession of the author. Emphasis reproduced from the original. The quotes are from pp. 1 and 4.

157

unity between the federal army troops in the state of Minas Gerais and the state militia of Minas, his most effective argument in creating unity was both units' fear of institutional destruction if a Communist-dominated revolution was successful. He argued,

> The Communists have arrived at the conclusion that if they dominate Minas they will have the country at their disposal. . . . We [the Federal troops and militia of Minas] are both in the same boat. If the worst comes to pass, it will affect us all equally. For the higher ranks, the price will be life itself; for the others, the least that will happen is the loss of jobs. Because the Communists in order to impose their regime will have to destroy all that exists. There will emerge a "popular" militia. . . .[9]

POLITICAL ACTIVISM OF THE SERGEANTS AND THEIR LINKS WITH THE TRADE UNIONS

One of the major areas where Brazilian officers feared a breakdown of hierarchy was at the level of career sergeants. Traditionally, sergeants in the army had been professionally unskilled and politically inactive. They were not "politically available" in the civilian struggle to gain a power base within the military. As the result of a combination of structural and political factors, however, the sergeants in the late 1950s and early 1960s became increasingly influential and politically active within the military. Until after World War II, sergeants tended to have a low level of education. Professionally and socially they were not too different from the bulk of the enlisted men within the army. The officers, on the other hand, were in constant face-to-face contact with their troops in the carrying out of their military duties, and also handled the troops' family and personal problems, thus solidifying their authority over the enlisted men by both "professional" and "traditional-patronal" relationships.

Brazil's participation in World War II and later its military assistance treaty with the United States led to an injection of more sophisticated equipment and more advanced staff work into the Brazilian army. These trends tended to withdraw officers from the constant troop contact provided in an army where an infantry company or battalion is the basic unit. After World War II, the Ser-

[9] Fourteen-page signed statement by General Carlos Luiz Guedes, April 1965. Presented to the files of *O Estado de São Paulo*. Copy in possession of author. Quotation taken from p. 4.

geants' School (*Escola de Sargentos das Armas*) was greatly improved. It became the major source for the training and selection of sergeants. It involved a full year's course, in which many of the students were accepted directly from civilian life. They became sergeants upon completion of the course. Much of the training was technical, in order to prepare the sergeants to handle the increasingly sophisticated weaponry. Recruitment to the school was based largely on an entrance examination and the competition was fierce. In 1967, 9,261 candidates applied, of which only 453 were accepted.[10]

The result of this professionalization of the corps of sergeants was that the sergeants assumed much of the professional day-by-day instruction and discipline of the enlisted men. Just as important, because the sergeants were now sufficiently educated, they increasingly assumed the informal role of "patron" of the enlisted men in regard to financial, legal, personal, and family matters, a function that in the past was performed exclusively by officers.[11]

The rise in the educational and professional status of the sergeants was not accompanied by a corresponding rise in their social or political position: this created a situation of status incongruity. The focus of their resentment was over the sharply differentiated legal status of officers in comparison to sergeants and other enlisted men. Officers were allowed to vote and to hold a wide variety of electoral and appointive political offices without relinquishing their commissions; they merely took a leave of absence during which their promotion by seniority was not affected. Sergeants and enlisted men, on the other hand, were denied the right to vote by the constitution, and the constitution also specified that only those eligible to vote could run for elective office.[12] This denial of political rights increasingly became a source of discontent among sergeants, contributing to their growing political consciousness. It was an issue championed by political groups seeking the support of the sergeants.[13]

[10] Figures contained in the analysis of total applicants, successful and unsuccessful, by state of origin, in "Origem dos Candidatos por Estados da Federação," on file in the *Diretoria Geral do Ensino, Estado Maior do Exército, Ministério da Guerra.*

[11] This comment was made by General Golbery in an interview in Brasília, September 17, 1967.

[12] Articles 132 and 138 in the 1946 constitution.

[13] For a discussion of this growing politicization of the sergeants in the

159

The new status of the sergeants within the military structure meant that they represented a socially powerful and distinct group. They could be appealed to by groups attempting to influence military behavior within the political system. The first dramatic demonstration of the independent power of the sergeants and the enlisted men was in the near civil war that occurred over the attempt by the three service ministers to block Vice-President Goulart from assuming the presidency in 1961 after the resignation of President Quadros. At a number of air bases the sergeants seized strategic locations and inhibited air action against pro-Goulart forces.[14] In some army units ordered to march against the pro-Goulart Third Army headquartered in Rio Grande do Sul, many of the sergeants refused.[15] In many other army units, the fear that the enlisted men might not comply with army orders increased officer pressure for a compromise solution to the question of Goulart's assumption of the presidency.[16]

The fact that numerous officers also opposed any attempt to prevent Goulart from assuming office tended to blur this sergeant–officer cleavage. However, in the aftermath of the victorious struggle to install Goulart, the sergeants and other politicians were strongly aware of the new powers possessed by sergeants both within the military and in national politics.

One important politician who attempted to utilize the sergeants was Brizola. General George Rocha, a member of the army General Staff in 1963 and 1964, said of Brizola's attitude to the sergeants: "The position of Brizola was that the sergeants could be the key. The impact of 1961 was important. It convinced Brizola that if he

---

1961–1964 period, see Nelson Werneck Sodré, *História Militar do Brasil*, pp. 372–389.

Also see Glauco Carneiro, *História das Revoluções Brasileiras*, vol. 2, chap. xxiv, "A Revolta dos Sargentos" (Rio de Janeiro: Edições o Cruzeiro, 1965), pp. 533–550.

[14] See the interesting interview with the major leader of the pro-Goulart forces, Governor Brizola, in *O Cruzeiro* (Rio de Janeiro), December 2, 1961.

[15] One commander of a battalion said 99 of his men were arrested for refusing to march. Taped interview with José Stacchini, March 3, 1965, São Paulo.

[16] For a description, see Gileno dé Carli's chapter, "O Dispositivo Militar," *JQ, Brasília e a Grande Crise* (Rio de Janeiro: Edições O Cruzeiro, 1961), pp. 34–54.

could win the sergeants he could immobilize the generals."[17] As the crisis of 1961–1964 intensified, both Goulart and Brizola openly sought the sergeants' support in return for backing their demands for greater political rights. Sergeants received special housing and other benefits. The officer corps construed this as a threat to their chain of command.

Trade unions also made major attempts to politicize the sergeants. This was facilitated by the fact that both conscripts and sergeants in the Brazilian army usually remain in their geographical area of origin during their tour of military duty, and maintain close social contacts with civilians.

By May 1963, the political evolution was such that at a meeting of associations of sergeants and warrant officers of all three services in Rio de Janeiro, the chief speaker announced that the sergeants would defend law but not the existing laws, which defended the rights of only a few. They insisted that Congress pass agrarian reform measures by a constitutional amendment. They warned that if any coup attempt was made against Goulart by the right, the sergeants would take action themselves.[18]

In an atmosphere of growing institutional insecurity, various officer groups within the military set up what amounted to shadow national security councils. One of these groups researched and clandestinely circulated a special report on the "sergeants' movement." This document is an indication of the degree of fear that had penetrated elements of the officer corps almost a year before the 1964 revolution. The document alleged that the sergeants were closely linked with the more militant trade unions and, in some important cases, with the Communists. It also commented that in some cases the officers were personally arming to defend themselves against the sergeants, and had removed ammunition from the troops and the firing pins from machine guns, in fear of a revolt. The report added that the sergeants' movement was still a minority in the army but that it had, nonetheless, widespread strength throughout the country in all three services.[19]

[17] Interview, General George Rocha, Rio de Janeiro, October 5, 1968.
[18] Carneiro, *História das Revoluções Brasileiras,* p. 536. Robert T. Daland discusses the political impact of this meeting in his "Four Months of Political Strife in the Military," in *The Dynamics of Government and Administration in Brazil,* ed. Frank Sherwood (MS, School of Public Administration, University of Southern California).
[19] *Movimento dos Sargentos: Relatório,* Rio de Janeiro, May 5, 1963. Copy in possession of the author.

161

It was in this atmosphere of anxiety among the officers that the sergeants' rebellion in Brasília burst. On September 12, 1963, sergeants and corporals of the air force and marines rose up in protest against a Supreme Court ruling upholding the denial of the rights of enlisted men to hold public office. They forcibly occupied strategic centers in the capital, captured a Supreme Court judge, the acting president of Congress, and a number of military officers. Within twelve hours the revolt was crushed. During and after the revolt, President Goulart took an ambiguous position, arguing that the revolt was an emotional outburst with no real political basis.[20] Leonel Brizola, a leader of the radical left, strongly defended the justice of the revolt, as did much of the trade-union leadership.[21]

The officer corps, however, viewed the sergeants' revolt as a profoundly disturbing event.[22] Their strongly adverse reaction accelerated the erosion of one of the basic premises of the moderating pattern.[23] An underlying assumption of this pattern had been that almost all major civilian factions had a significant military counterpart (though not, of course, on an exact one-to-one basis). Thus it was assumed that the military would reflect all shades of political opinion. This rough congruence assured that almost all major civilian groups had a sympathetic faction in the officer corps to whom they had access and could make political appeals. However the moderating pattern began to break down when economic development, social mobilization, and political conflict reached the stage where the industrial labor leaders appealed to their military counterparts—the career sergeants.

The sergeants' revolt, and a series of less sensational, but for the

[20] *O Estado de São Paulo*, September 15, 1963, p. 5.

[21] The revolt is described in Carneiro, *História das Revoluções Brasileiras*, pp. 533–550, and Abelardo Jurema, *Sexta-feira, 13: Os Últimos Dias do Govêrno João Goulart* (Rio de Janeiro: Edições O Cruzeiro, 1964), pp. 107–121.

[22] The commandant of Brasília during the revolt was General Nicolau Fico, who after the revolution was purged from the military, presumably on the grounds that he had been a strong supporter of President Goulart's political position. Significantly, even he points out that the sergeants' revolt was not supported by a single officer in Brasília. Interview, October 10, 1968, Rio de Janeiro.

[23] Numerous accounts of the coalition-building process for the revolution to displace Goulart stress the sergeants' revolt as a decisive factor. See, e.g., Fernando Pedreira, *Março 31: Civis e Militares no Processo da Crise Brasileira* (Rio de Janeiro: José Alvaro, 1964), pp. 19–20.

military officers equally threatening, events which finally culminated in the naval mutiny in Rio de Janeiro a week before the revolution (and which Goulart tolerated by granting amnesty to the mutineers) eroded the rough congruence of civilian and military opinion.[24] The military officers became increasingly self-referential and were closing off access to certain power groups, such as labor. Their response to the Brasília sergeants' revolt was indicative of this.

To illustrate the effect of the revolt on even those military officers sympathetic to reform and to the left, we might take the case of General Pery Constant Bevilaqua.[25] Bevilaqua had been one of the key generals supporting Goulart's right to assume the presidency in 1961, and was in fact one of the three army generals specifically threatened with court martial because of this support.[26] In January 1962, Bevilaqua sent a congratulatory letter to Governor Brizola of Rio Grande do Sul for having expropriated an American utility company in that state.[27] Bevilaqua advocated a reform position on many key political issues, including land reform. In addition, he was the candidate of the nationalist wing of the military for the presidency of the influential Military Club (*Clube Militar*) in 1962. Thus Bevilaqua (despite a reputation for being erratic) was considered sympathetic to Goulart and to the reform left. Yet for this general, the son of a marshal, the limits of his nationalism and leftism were reached at the moment when the army as an institution was threatened with indiscipline. Further, his support for basic reforms stopped short at the possibility of using mass mobilization weapons such as general strikes. At the time of the sergeants' revolt, General Bevilaqua was commander of one of Brazil's four armies, the Second Army, with headquarters in São Paulo. Immediately after the revolt in Brasília, the General Labor Command (CGT) threatened to launch a general strike in support of the sergeants' demands. General Bevilaqua then issued a directive to all the troops in his command in which it was clear that the threat to military institutional integrity was unacceptable

[24] See Chap. 9 for a description of this mutiny.

[25] This is the official spelling of his name in military records. His name, however, is frequently spelled Bevilacqua.

[26] *Tribuna da Imprensa*, August 31, 1961.

[27] Note the praise he receives for this in the nationalist left publication of Osny Duarte Pereira, *Cadernos do Povo Brasileiro*, vol. 3: *Quem Faz as Leis no Brasil?* (Rio de Janeiro: Editôra Civilização Brasileira, 1963), p. 146.

to him as an officer. His action was symptomatic of how serious the erosion of reform-leftist military support had been. The outraged tone of the general's command makes his position clear. The troops were soldiers, given the constitutional duty to "defend the country and to guarantee the constitutional powers, law and order." In passionate language, he condemned large sections of the trade union movement as

> . . . illegal and fraudulent groups . . . enemies of democracy . . . revolutionary syndicalism threatens democratic institutions. The union between military men who have forgotten their oath before the flag and malefactors, the syndicalists, is humiliating. It is humiliating to see sergeants led to raise arms against the nation. The sergeants are manipulated in their innocence by enemy elements in the country, who are entrenched in the ditch of disastrous revolutionary syndicalism, and are stimulated to rebellion by unscrupulous politicians . . . eager to bury democracy.[28]

His directive proscribed any relationship between members of his command and the militant trade union movement.

A day after the sergeants' revolt erupted, General Castello Branco became chief of the army General Staff. At his inauguration ceremony, attended by all the generals in Rio, he alluded specifically to the dangers to the army of the new radical politics:

> There are opportunistic reformers who by means of steady antinational undermining attempt to replace it [the armed forces] and institute a popular army with an imitation militia, with a doubtful ideology, destined to agitate the country with rebel pronouncements and to perturb by subversion and mutiny the life of the people.[29]

Five days after the sergeants' revolt, an officer of the General Staff published a long article, entitled "The End of an Army," in which he argued that the Russian Revolution of 1917 was initially a moderate revolution which was taken over by extremists after the army had been destroyed through a series of political acts, "always approved by the government," which eroded its unity and integrity.

[28] The complete text of General Bevilaqua's directive to the Second Army can be found in *O Estado de São Paulo*, September 19, 1963, p. 60, and *Jornal do Brasil*, September 19, 1963.
[29] *O Estado de São Paulo*, September 14, 1963.

He commented, "The suffering of the Russian officers in that period was indescribable." The lesson for Brazil was clear.[30]

Military officers' perceptions that rising militant trade-union influence among enlisted men was destroying institutional cohesion broke down the image of the military as "above class"—an intrinsic part of its pre-1964 image as moderator.

POLITICIZATION OF PROMOTION PATTERNS

Since all presidents to some extent have used military assignments to key commands and promotions to general as a means of ensuring military loyalty, promotions within the military in Brazil have always had a political content. It is difficult for an outsider to assess changes in the political nature of these promotions, but there is little doubt that resentment was growing among many senior officers between 1961 and 1964 that President Goulart was using political criteria to an excessive degree for promotion to the rank of general.[31]

What was politically significant about this trend was the feeling, which became fairly widespread throughout the officer corps, that not only was the government under Goulart encouraging indiscipline among the sergeants, but it was also undermining the army's hierarchy at the top by sharply downgrading professional criteria for promotion. A study of the *Almanaque do Exército* for 1964 reveals that, of the line officers promoted to general grade during President Goulart's tenure, only 5 out of 29 (17.2 percent) had graduated first in their class in any of the three major service schools. This contrasts with the 34 out of 73 (46.5 percent) of those officers promoted to general before Goulart came to the presidency.[32] Since ranking in army schools has traditionally been closely correlated with promotion, the above data does seem to bear out the officers' complaint that criteria for promotion had changed under President Goulart.

[30] Lt. Col. Adyr Fiuza de Castro, "O Fim dum Exército," *O Estado de São Paulo*, September 17, 1963, p. 16.

[31] This charge was made to me by the vast majority of officers with whom I spoke and who were still on active duty by 1966. It should be noted that political criteria for promotion became even more decisive after the revolution of 1964.

[32] The *Almanaque do Exército* is issued annually and contains the names of all officers on active duty, and a wealth of information such as schools attended, dates of promotion, medals received. If an officer graduates first in one of the three major service schools, he receives a special academic medal, the *Medalha Marechal Hermes Aplicação e Estudo*.

165

Discreet manipulation of assignments and promotions can strengthen a president. But excessive reliance on this political tactic can become counterproductive because it tends to upset the career expectations of all those passed over for promotion and turn them into active opponents of the government. Likewise, promotion to high positions of officers who fail to satisfy the usual institutional criteria is not always effective in creating loyalty at large, because such men are often resented and therefore not influential within the military. To the extent that they are not representative of the feelings of the rank and file officers, the president runs the risk of cutting himself off from accurate information about opinion within the officer corps.

There is evidence that President Goulart's handling of senior army officers was counterproductive in just the ways described, and contributed both to his overthrow and to growing rejection by officers of their traditional moderating role. To attempt to assess the hypothesis that resentment over promotion was an instrumental factor in making officers active plotters in the coup against Goulart, I studied the promotion patterns of the 102 line generals on active duty in 1964. I divided the generals in each promotion grade according to seniority (time spent in grade) so that each grade was divided into first, second, third, and fourth quarters. Those who had been in a grade longest (and therefore in this case normally had not received a promotion under Goulart) were placed in the first quarter. Those recently promoted (therefore by Goulart) were placed in the fourth quarter. I then classified all those generals expelled after the 1964 revolution as "active defenders" of President Goulart,[33] and compared them with the anti-Goulart officers who had been "active plotters" in the 1964 revolution.[34]

If promotions were unrelated to coup activism, then one would expect to find coup activists scattered evenly in the four quarters representing seniority. In fact, however, 40 percent of the coup activists were in the first quarter, while only 6 percent were in the fourth quarter. Thus, it seems probable that many coup

[33] Twenty of the 102 generals were formally purged from the army in 1964. Their names were contained in lists published in the *Diário Oficial* on April 11, June 13, September 24, and October 8, 1964.

[34] I asked three of the most influential organizers of the revolution to list which generals they considered active in planning and mobilizing the revolution. I classify a general an "active plotter" if his name appears on at least two of the three lists.

activists were officers who had either been passed over for promotion or were worried that they would be passed over. When we compare the group of coup activists with the group of Goulart supporters, we find the situation roughly reversed. None of the purged officers were in the first quarter, that is, were men passed over for promotion, whereas 40 percent were in the bottom quarter, indicating they had been recently promoted by Goulart. It seems, therefore, reasonably clear from this analysis that personal anxiety over future promotions contributed to coup activism among the officers.

Another indication that military officers were worried about the survival of the military institution was the behavior of the sons of military officers in regard to the coup of 1964. A reasonable hypothesis is that sons of military officers conform more closely to the military code of obedience than officers who are not from military families, and as a group are less prone therefore to assume political positions. Kurt Lang, in his study of high-ranking German officers under Hitler, found that "most of those coming from soldiers' families tended to take the ritualistic attitude." By this he meant that they tended not to join the anti-Hitler conspiracy, but attempted to avoid political involvement and remain in the neutral and "militarily correct" position.[35]

Brazil, however, showed the opposite tendency. Of the 102 line generals on active duty in 1964, 23 definitely were sons of military officers.[36] Seven (30.4 percent) of these were active plotters against Goulart, while only one (4.3 percent) was an active defender of the president. Of the 79 officers who did not appear to come from military families, 17 (20.6 percent) were active plotters and 19 (24.1 percent) active defenders. Thus in 1964 we can say that sons of military officers were somewhat overrepresented among the

[35] Kurt Lang, "Bureaucracy in Crisis: A Role-Analysis of German Generals under Hitler" (master's diss., Department of Sociology, University of Chicago, 1952), p. 68.

[36] As each officer is promoted to general, the War Ministry gives biographical material to the press. These handouts usually say something to the effect that General X is the son of Mr., Doctor, or Engineer (or Major, Colonel, or General) X. I examined these releases in the archives of *O Estado de São Paulo* and the *Jornal do Brasil* and also received limited access from the War Ministry. I double-checked this information on fathers' occupations in my interviews where possible. The fact that I was not able to confirm that more than 23 were sons of officers does not rule out this possibility. Nonetheless, the figures are probably roughly accurate.

plotters and strongly underrepresented among the defenders of Goulart. A plausible hypothesis is that sons of military officers felt more identified with the military institution and reacted more strongly against what they felt to be an erosion of hierarchy. The above relationship gains increased political significance when we remember that the data (Chapter 3) showed that the percentage of cadets at the Military Academy who were sons of officers and the percentage who had attended military high schools had increased sharply from the early 1940s to the early 1960s.

The combination of the military's increasing institutional insecurity and their growing feeling that none of the existing civilian political parties or figures had the power to solve the economic crisis contributed to an intensification of the belief that the old boundaries to military activism were no longer appropriate.

GROWING REJECTION OF TRADITIONAL BOUNDARY TO MILITARY ACTION

The maintenance of a boundary to the military's role in the political system—limiting them to removing a president—had always meant that major participants in the political system were free to continue to operate after such a removal.

Among significant groupings of military officers, two distinct but mutually reinforcing sentiments emerged out of the structural crisis of 1961–1964. One was the belief that there were some key political actors, both civilian and military, who were either so corrupt or so sympathetic to Communism that they were *illegitimate* participants in the system and had to be removed from politics semipermanently. This could only be done if the military themselves had a strong role in the government and so could execute these purges.

An even more basic feeling was that the economic and political systems were so profoundly disturbed that radical changes were necessary. These changes, it was believed, could only be accomplished by a military rule in which many of the normal constitutional privileges were suspended long enough for restructuring to be completed.

One of the first groups of plotters in the 1964 revolution had as a core the three military ministers who had failed in their attempt to block Goulart from assuming the presidency in August 1961. In early 1962, the group drafted an Institutional Act that could

168

(and eventually did) serve as a broad guideline to the political system after the removal of Goulart. It is significant that this draft explicitly underlined the need not only for some politicians to be purged from active politics but also for the military to assume powers for a relatively long period in order to restructure the political system. The draft specifically called for the establishment of a military junta, the dissolution of the state and federal representative chambers, and the suspension of constitutional rights.[37]

Equally important was the fact that some key civilian groups accepted the necessity of military rule. The publisher of one of Brazil's most influential newspapers, the conservative *O Estado de São Paulo*, was shown the draft and argued that the military, if they removed Goulart, should not shrink from assuming responsibility for ruling, and should not return governmental power to civilians as they had in 1945 and 1954. He specifically criticized the idea that the military should limit their action to removal of the president:

> We cannot again commit the errors that resulted in the total failures of the beautiful movements that destroyed the dictatorship in October 1945, and caused the fall of Getúlio, again by the work of the army, in August 1954. The failure of these two movements can be summed up by the fact that the authors of these movements hastened the return of power to men who came from the past and who formed their attitudes in the atmosphere of the dictatorship, the source of all the wrongs that still plague us. The Brazilian armed forces wanted then to demonstrate the disinterestedness of their action. But this fear of responsibility, far from being of benefit to the nation, was a cause of a deception that once again was suffered by the public. It becomes indispensable this time that things go differently. We need to act with absolute certainty, defining, before the military units go into action, what we want and what we intend to do.[38]

He went on to comment that he felt that the court system was in need of "radical cleaning": "The purging of the ranks of the judiciary is absolutely necessary but it should be done by stages." He also

[37] The complete draft is reprinted in José Stacchini, *Março 64: Mobilização da Audácia* (São Paulo: Companhia Editôra Nacional, 1965), pp. 22–24.

[38] Júlio de Mesquito Filho, "Roteiro de Revolução," *O Estado de São Paulo*, April 12, 1964.

said that "things have reached a level of political, administrative, and social decomposition in Brazil of truly alarming proportions." He felt that a military rule of two or three years would be necessary, whereas elements of the military estimated that five years was essential.[39]

Other civil–military groups formed. They articulated a program that went far beyond the traditional moderator role. A group called the *Frente Patriótica Civil–Militar* ("Civil–Military Patriotic Front") had a program consisting of "ten commandments of the law of the people" with authoritarian nationalist and reformist overtones.[40]

Another group in the air force published its own manifesto. This document and others of its kind demonstrated a profound desire to expel certain groups from the political system, including military and student groups. Its first seven points were: (1) to revoke the mandate of the Communist deputies, (2) to revoke the commissions of Communist military officers, (3) to exclude, expel, or retire (depending on the circumstances) Communists in the military, (4) to ban professional students, (5) to limit repetition of failed courses at the university to one year, (6) to dismiss Communists or pro-Communists from the civilian sections of the federal government, the decentralized agencies, and the quasi-governmental corporations, and finally, (7) to deny the political rights of numerous politicians felt to be pro-Communist, such as Goulart, Brizola, Pinheiro Neto, Darcy Riberio, Neiva Moreira, and Dante Pellacani.[41]

Most of the documents just cited were written between 1962 and 1963. At that time, they represented a more militant view than that found in general within the military. But in the last months of the crisis of discipline in the military, numerous new recruits were won over to this point of view, and by the time of Goulart's re-

[39] *Ibid.*

[40] This group is discussed in greater detail in Chapter 11. The programmatic and emotional aspects of groups such as this were not important in the Castello Branco government but formed a key part of the makeup of the younger "hard line" officers. For the complete "ten commandments," see Stacchini, *Março 64*, pp. 20–22. To get a flavor of the ideas and emotional quality of the movement, see Oliveiros S. Ferreira, *As Fôrças Armadas e o Desafio da Revolução* (Rio de Janeiro: Edições GRD, 1964). Ferreira was a leading political columnist, a professor in São Paulo, and a key member of the movement.

[41] Stacchini, *Março 64*, pp. 19–20.

moval, the emotional desire of the military to purge whole groups went well beyond the boundaries of their traditional moderating role.

The events of 1961 and 1964 had contributed to a series of new attitudes in the bulk of the officer corps that were no longer in keeping with the exercise of this traditional role. By 1964, the winning coalition within the military felt that they were too institutionally threatened to relinquish power to civilians.

What increased the significance of such changes of attitude is that the military in this period was also developing its own ideology of national development and internal security at the *Escola Superior de Guerra*, which we shall now discuss.

Chapter 8

The Impact of Political
and Economic Crises on the Military:
The Escola Superior de Guerra
and the Development of a
New Military Ideology

A CRUCIAL SUPPORTIVE ATTITUDE for the moderator role of the Brazilian military, and especially for the maintenance of a limit to this role at the removal of the executive from office, was the widespread belief by the military officers that, in comparison to civilians, they had relatively low legitimacy to rule. In addition, as we have seen, the military officers did not have a high level of confidence that they were well endowed in terms of political or economic training to rule the nation. These two beliefs, that the military lacked both capacity and legitimacy, were central to Castello Branco's arguments against military assumption of political office in 1955.[1] They were instrumental in the return of power to civilians after the military had removed the presidents from office in 1945, 1954, and 1955. The crises of 1961–1964, however, in addition to eroding civilian confidence in the democratic framework of politics, also altered the military officers' previous image of their relative incapacity and illegitimacy to rule the country.

Brazil is the paradigm case of a military that felt it lacked the legitimacy to rule. However, such a belief has been an element in many military governments in Latin America, which, owing to their lack of political confidence, are only transitional or caretaker in form. Most cases of what appears to be long-term military rule turn

---

[1] On the purely negative side the military's perception of their relative illegitimacy and incapacity to rule was reduced by such events and experiences as increasing inflation, declining economic growth rate, the civilian inability to implement a plan for stabilization and development, the suicide of President Vargas in the aftermath of the assassination attempt by his bodyguard on Carlos Lacerda, and the renunciation by President Quadros after only six months in office.

out to be one-man, personalist dictatorships which manipulate and dominate rather than represent the military. Some military leaders in Latin America have, of course, experimented with directed social change with military support before the 1960s, such as General Ibáñez in Chile in the mid-1920s, General Cárdenas in Mexico in the 1930s, Colonels Toro and Busch and Major Villarroel in Bolivia in the late 1930s and mid-1940s, and Colonel Arbenz in Guatemala from 1950 to 1954.

The mid-1960s in Latin America, however, saw a change in the nature of military government; governments were more doctrinal, and initially more institutionally backed and self-confident in their attempts to direct and control social and economic change. Despite many dissimilarities, these characteristics were shared by the Brazilian military government that came to power in 1964, the Argentinian military government of 1966, and the Peruvian military government of 1968.

The emergence of this new pattern of military regimes was related to basic changes in the national and international environments of the late 1950s and early 1960s. The growth of doctrines of revolutionary warfare and, specifically, the rise of Castro engendered in military officers a complex set of responses: fear of Communism (especially because of its threat to the regular army), growth of counterinsurgency doctrines, and a conviction that basic change was necessary to avoid revolution. Because the strategy of revolutionary warfare was perceived to involve all phases of society, the military's concept of security began to encompass all aspects of social and political life. The military became concerned with civic action, with their role as a "nation-builder," and with global development plans. These responses involved a considerable expansion of the role of the military and a belief in the legitimacy of these new roles.[2] These were all ideas advocated by the United States and taught in its schools for Latin American military officers. However, as the case of the Peruvian military government illustrates, these ideas did not always result in harmonious relations

[2] A thorough and brilliant analysis of some psychological and political implications of this type of military ideology of total counterrevolutionary warfare (especially in the context of a weak political system) is Raoul Girardet's discussion of the French army; see his "Problèmes Idéologiques Et Moraux," and "Essai D'Interprétation," in *La Crise Militaire Française, 1945–1962: Aspects Sociologiques et Idéologiques*, ed. Raoul Girardet (Paris: Librairie Armand Colin, 1964), pp. 151–229.

173

with the United States. To a significant degree, the idea of a more active political role for the military took root because the military institutions felt it was relevant and adaptable to their own countries' problems. Brazil, Argentina, and Peru all reshaped the idea to fit their own perception of their country's development and security problems.

The institutions contributing most to the reshaping and dissemination of the new concepts of national security and development, including a deepening military involvement in politics, were the Superior War Colleges of each country. In Peru it was the *Centro de Altos Estudios Militares* (CAEM), in Argentina the *Escuela Nacional de Guerra*, and in Brazil the *Escola Superior de Guerra* (ESG).[3] It was largely because of the ESG that, as the general sense of crisis in Brazil deepened, significant numbers of officers began to feel that they had the most appropriate and realistic strategy to develop the country, and the most qualified technocrats to implement this strategy. The role of the ESG in the breakdown of the traditional pattern of civil–military relations in Brazil therefore deserves study. Because so little is known about it we must begin with the basic facts.

FOUNDING AND ORGANIZATION OF THE ESG

Brazil participated in World War II by sending a division, the *Fôrça Expedicionária Brasileira* (FEB) to fight in Italy.[4] Weak coordination among the branches of the military itself and weak coordination of national strategy in all its military, industrial, and bureaucratic components spurred the desire after the war to formalize both a Joint Service General Staff and a National Security Council. Later the key organizers of the FEB, such as General Cesar Obino and the artillery commander, General Cordeiro de Farias,

---

[3] For a brief description of the ideology of CAEM, see Victor Villanueva, *El Militarismo en el Peru* (Lima: Empresa Gráfica T. Scheuch, 1962), pp. 174–183.

In the early 1960s the Indonesian army's Staff and Command School formulated a development and security doctrine much of which was later implemented when the military assumed power in 1965. For the doctrine and an insightful analysis see Guy J. Pauker, *The Indonesian Doctrine of Territorial Warfare and Territorial Management* (Santa Monica, Calif.: The RAND Corporation, RM-3312-PR, November 1963).

[4] The members of this unit played a crucial role in civil–military affairs from 1945 on. The unit is henceforth referred to by its Brazilian initials, FEB.

developed the idea of a special school to formulate a new doctrine of national security and development. Because the United States had a national war college, and because the FEB had been integrated with a U.S. army corps in Italy, the Brazilians requested a U.S. advisory mission to help in the formation of the school. This U.S. mission remained in Brazil from 1948 until 1960.[5] Significantly, Peru's CAEM did not have U.S. officers of faculty rank, and unlike Brazil, Peru sent some of its military faculty to such civilian-run training programs on the problems of national development as those of the United Nations Economic Commission for Latin America and the Latin American Institute of Economic and Social Planning in Chile.

General Cordeiro de Farias was entrusted with the work of developing the subject matter and organization of the school in Brazil. After spending most of 1948 and part of 1949 on the task, he recommended a school patterned after the United States National War College, but different in two respects. The United States, he argued, was already a developed nation; so its main concern was the mobilization of existing resources for warfare. This task was carried out at the Industrial College of the Armed Forces. The main task of the United States National War College was that of foreign policy. General Cordeiro de Farias felt that in a developing country like Brazil, however, the question of a strong armed force could not be separated from the question of economic development, nor the question of national security from that of education, industry, or agriculture.[6] He advocated that in the new Brazilian War College the functions of the U.S. Industrial College of the Armed Forces and the National War College be combined, and in addition that emphasis on internal aspects of development and security be greater than in the U.S. National War College.

The other Brazilian innovation was to make civilian participation a key aspect of the War College. In the United States, the National War College was mainly military, and the only civilians were those coming from the government agencies concerned with foreign affairs. But precisely because the Brazilian school was to be concerned with all phases of development and security, it was felt it needed civilians from areas such as education, industry, com-

[5] Interview with Colonel Harvey, U.S. Army, the U.S. liaison officer to the ESG, Rio de Janeiro, March 17, 1967.
[6] Interview, Rio de Janeiro, September 16, 1968.

175

munications, and banking.[7] The decision to include civilians as a central part of the ESG proved to be crucial for the development of the school. It brought military officers into systematic close contact with civilian leaders.[8] This gave them civilian allies who shared many of their ideas on development and security, and also gave the military confidence to discuss problems on terms of equality with civilian specialists.

The military felt the participation of civilians in the ESG was so valuable that over time the ratio of civilian members to military increased. In the initial class of 1950, only 16 of the 62 graduates were drawn from civilian life, but 646 of the total 1,276 graduates in the overall period of 1950–1967 were civilians.[9] The second commandant of the ESG, Marshal Juarez Távora, explained his thinking: "As commandant I wanted to increase the representation of civilians. I felt that the aim of the school was not only to train military men but also all those who would influence the government."[10]

The *Escola Superior de Guerra* was formally established by presidential decree under Dutra on August 20, 1949. By 1963 its charter decreed its mission as preparing "civilians and military to perform executive and advisory functions especially in those organs responsible for the formulation, development, planning, and execution of the politics of national security."[11] That national security was considered to comprise a wide range of affairs is indicated by the names of the seven academic divisions: (1) Political Affairs, (2) Psychological-Social Affairs, (3) Economic Affairs, (4) Military Affairs, (5) Logistical and Mobilization Affairs, (6) Intelligence and Counterintelligence, and (7) Doctrine and Coordination.[12]

[7] The military members were to be drawn from all three services, the majority being colonels, then brigadier generals, and on exception, lieutenant colonels (or corresponding naval ranks).

[8] The civilians were supposed to have the equivalent of a university degree and to have already demonstrated marked qualities of leadership.

[9] Data contained in the heavily documented short history of the ESG written by General Augusto Fragoso while commandant of the school, "A Escola Superior de Guerra (Origen—Finalidade—Evolução)," *Segurança & Desenvolvimento: Revista da Associação dos Diplomados da Escola Superior de Guerra*, ano XVIII, no. 132 (1969), pp. 7–40.

[10] Interview, Rio de Janeiro, October 8, 1968.

[11] Decreto No. 53,080 de 4 de Dezembro, 1963, Capítulo II, Seção 4.

[12] *Ibid.*, Capítulo V, Seção 1.

176

By 1966, the ESG had graduates from many of the key sectors of the political and economic power-structure: 599 were military officers, 224 were private businessmen, there were 200 civil servants from the major ministries and 97 from decentralized government agencies, 39 were federal Congressmen, 23 were federal and state judges, and 107 were various professionals—such as professors, economists, writers, medical doctors, and Catholic clergy.[13] The requirement that civilians have the equivalent of a university education has meant virtually the total absence of representation from trade unions.[14]

The graduates of the ESG were members of a very active alumni association, which served as a focus for intellectual and social contact with other graduates, with the ESG itself, and with society as a whole.[15] Well-attended weekly luncheons with prominent speakers were held in Rio de Janeiro, and other major cities (especially São Paulo) had similar, although less frequent, meetings. There was an official liaison officer in each major government ministry.[16]

An important source of ideological as well as social information was the *Boletim da Associação dos Diplomados da Escola Superior de Guerra*.[17] Each year the alumni association, in conjunction with the ESG, formulated and researched a special project. The key researchers for these projects were civil and military graduates,

[13] Figures provided by the *Escola Superior de Guerra* and reprinted in Glauco Carneiro, "A Guerra de 'Sorbonne'," *O Cruzeiro*, June 24, 1967, p. 20. These were their occupations at the time they entered the ESG.

[14] From the author's copy of the list of graduates between 1950 and 1966, it appears no prominent trade-union leaders were graduates. An interview with Marshal Juarez Távora in Rio de Janeiro, October 8, 1968, confirmed that the university requirement plus the desire for easy, informal seminars about national security probably meant that those whose background did not make for "easy colleagueship" were not invited.

[15] This section is primarily intended to describe the influence of the ESG on the political attitudes of the military prior to the 1964 revolution. It therefore uses the past tense to refer to the ESG during that period. The *Escola Superior de Guerra* is, of course, still very much a part of the education of the Brazilian military.

[16] For the 1963 listing, see *Boletim da Associação dos Diplomados da Escola Superior de Guerra*, No. 100, pp. 4–5.

[17] It contains personal information, such as birthdays and news of social and intellectual meetings of the school, and it prints the best papers of the current ESG students. In 1968 the title of this publication became *Segurança & Desenvolvimento: Revista da Associação dos Diplomados da Escola Superior de Guerra*.

who often used information gathered in their current jobs to write the report.[18] Short courses on ESG doctrine (*Ciclo de Conferencias*) were given throughout the country by alumni with the assistance of the ESG. This greatly increased dissemination of the school's doctrine.[19]

The course itself was a full-time activity for a complete academic year. The core of the course consisted of lectures and seminars that attempted to determine basic goals for Brazil, the obstacles to these goals, and specific policies to achieve them. The final task of the students at the school was to participate in a civil–military team of five or six students in the preparation of a policy paper.

In addition to the lectures given by the permanent civil and military staff, many lectures were given by prominent ministers and technocrats in the government, thus providing some exposure to diverse political views. An essential part of the course was the three or four extended field trips to all parts of Brazil, to see at first hand the problems and projects connected with national development and national security, such as major new hydroelectric projects, new industrial complexes, the nationalized steel industry, major slum housing projects, the regional development agency SUDENE, civic-action programs, and new tactics of counterrevolutionary warfare.

The tradition gradually grew that each class toured the United States as a guest of the U.S. government, visiting major military and industrial complexes. Visits normally included a short meeting with the president of the United States.[20]

THE IDEOLOGY OF THE ESG

The intellectual focus of the ESG as it developed in the mid-fifties and early sixties was the interrelationship of national security

[18] For the 1963 research project and key personnel see *Boletim da Associação dos Diplomados da Escola Superior de Guerra*, no. 101, p. 6.

[19] Most issues of the *Boletim* have information about current *ciclos*. See issue no. 105 (July–August 1964), pp. 67–74.

[20] In the midst of the Cuban missile crisis, President Kennedy talked for a few minutes to the students of the Brazilian ESG. The incident made a deep impression. See Alberto Dines, *et al., O Mundo Depois de Kennedy* (Rio de Janeiro: José Alvaro, 1965), pp. 112–113, and "Palavras Dirigidas de Improviso Pelo Presidente Kennedy à Comitiva da ESG & IME, por Ocasião da Visita à Casa Branca," *Boletim da Associação dos Diplomados da Escola Superior de Guerra*, no. 101, pp. 7–8.

178

and national development.[21] The ESG doctrine strongly emphasized that modern warfare, whether conventional, as in World War II, or revolutionary, as in Indochina, involved the will, unity, and productive capacity of the entire nation. Thus those charged with the formulation and implementation of national security policies could no longer restrict their attention to frontier protection or other conventional uses of the army. National security for the ESG was seen to a great extent as a function of rationally maximizing the output of the economy and minimizing all sources of cleavage and disunity within the country. Consequently great stress was put on the need for strong government and planning. General Golbery, chief theoretician of the ESG and often called its father, stressed that in developing countries, such as Brazil "the planning of national security is an imperative of the hour in which we live . . . for us in the underdeveloped countries . . . planning assumes aspects of another order which puts everything else in relief."[22]

Another key theme was that underdeveloped countries were under great internal pressures not only because of underdevelopment itself but also because of global ideological conflict, which had deep ramifications for the internal security of the country. From the beginning, the ESG was anti-Communist and committed in the cold war. Even before the emphasis in the cold war shifted in the United States from atomic to revolutionary warfare, the ESG became the center of ideological thought concerning counterrevolutionary strategy in Brazil. Since Communism was seen as the enemy, the United States, as the major anti-Communist country, was viewed as a natural ally. In early 1959, General Golbery argued that indirect warfare was a much more realistic threat to Latin America than any direct attack from the exterior:

[21] An insight into the very wide scope of what the ESG considered to be the field of national security can be gained from the special issue of the *Revista Brasileira de Estudos Políticos*, no. 20 (January 1966), devoted to a discussion of *Segurança Nacional* ("national security") by writers closely associated with the school. An attempt to summarize the thought of the ESG was made by the ex-director of the army library, General Umberto Peregrino, in "O Pensamento da Escola Superior de Guerra," in *Cadernos Brasileiros*, no. 38 (November–December 1966), pp. 29–38.

[22] Golbery do Couto e Silva, *Planejamento Estratégico* (Rio de Janeiro: Biblioteca do Exército Editôra, 1955), p. 28. Most of this book had its origin in lectures originally given at the ESG. The book is one of the major sources for the ideology of the ESG.

179

What is certain is that the greater probability today is limited warfare, localized conflict, and above all indirect Communist aggression, which capitalizes on local discontents, the frustrations of misery and hunger, and just nationalist anxieties . . . Latin America now faces threats more real than at any other time, threats which could result in insurrection, outbursts attempting (though not openly) to implant . . . a government favorable to the Communist ideology and constituting a grave and urgent danger to the unity and security of the Americans and the Western world.[23]

In an intellectual formulation of the sort that would later be used to justify the progressive militarization of all phases of society when the military government assumed power in 1964, Golbery argued that when the security threat is great there is an urgent need for strong planning and control of a strategic nature because ". . . the area of politics is permeated . . . by adverse pressures, creating a form of universalization of the factors of security, enlarging the area of strategy [politics of national security] to the point where it almost absorbs all the national activities."[24]

Given this view of the total managerial nature of the task of maintaining national security, the ESG went about the study of all phases of Brazilian political, economic, and social life. The high-level civilian technocrats, the colonels and the low-ranking generals studied inflation, agrarian reform, banking reform, voting systems, transportation, and education, as well as guerrilla warfare and conventional warfare. In many of their studies some of the fundamental aspects of Brazilian social and economic organizations were severely challenged as needing change if Brazil was to grow economically and maintain internal security. Initially these critiques seemed academic, and the influence of the ESG's doctrine was not pervasive within the military in the mid-1950s. But by the early 1960s, as the Brazilian crisis deepened, the ESG's emphasis on the need for a total development strategy to combat internal subversion found an increasingly receptive audience in the military. Much of

[23] Golbery do Couto e Silva, *Geopolítica do Brasil* (Rio de Janeiro: José Olympio, 1967), pp. 198–199 (from a chapter originally written in 1959). This book also is based on ESG lectures. The developments in the Cuban revolution in late 1960 and 1961 increased the ESG fear of the "Communist threat."

[24] Golbery, *Planejamento Estratégico*, pp. 38–39.

its doctrine of internal warfare was incorporated at the General Staff School. For example, in the 1956 curriculum of the ECEME, there were no lectures given on counterguerrilla warfare, internal security, or Communism. Courses in all these subjects increased from 1961 on. By 1968, the curriculum contained 222 hours on internal security, 129 hours on irregular warfare, and only 21 hours on the classical professional topics of territorial defense.[25] Since an officer had to be a graduate of ECEME to become eligible for promotion to the rank of general or for appointment to any of the general staffs, almost all key Brazilian army officers received heavy exposure to the doctrines of internal war. This doctrine was also disseminated in more popularized form in the monthly newsletter *Boletim de Informações*, sent from the General Staff to troop commanders.[26]

The pervasive mood of the policy papers was a desire to perfect the Brazilian polity. Perfect democracy was always considered the ideal, yet political factors in the reform measures were either *ignored*, and only ideal policies discussed, or were treated as structural *obstacles* that had to be removed. Thus the policies suggested, while moderate and technocratic in terms of desired goals, were, in the context of actual Brazilian politics, quite sweeping, and in most cases incapable of being implemented democratically given the balance of political forces.

For example, one lecture complained that political parties were too personalistic and dominated by local issues to give coherent support to national development plans. The ESG lecturer's solution was a new electoral law setting a limit to the number of parties and forcing political figures to represent one party and only that party.[27]

[25] The curricula are on file in the library of ECEME.

[26] Brasil, Ministério da Guerra, Estado Maior do Exército, *Boletim de Informações*. Copies of this are on open file at the army library in Rio de Janeiro. Before October 1961 the tone was that of a very straightforward review of professional topics and routine surveys of international news. From October 1961 on, the tone changed to that much closer to the framework and terminology of the ESG, and most significantly began to deal with the question of the threat to internal security presented by Communism.

[27] David Carneiro, *Organização Política do Brasil*, ESG, Departamento de Estudos, C-47-59, pp. 18–20. (Originally classified lecture at ESG.) This and all subsequent ESG documents that I cite I found in the *Biblioteca Nacional*. Most ESG documents continue to be classified by the Brazilian government.

In an interview with General Golbery in Brasília, September 18, 1967, Golbery commented to the author, "The ESG felt that the political parties

Another common theme of the lectures and studies at the ESG was the need for greater centralization of power. At times this took the form of the reorganization of the borders of the states, both to weaken the power of old oligarchies and to allow greater economic rationality for development plans. But the main thrust of argument was that the executive had to be strengthened to protect the country from subversion. There was little praise for pluralism or participation and mobilization politics, while the cold-war necessity for hierarchy and control was a frequent theme. These arguments became a leitmotif of the military government when it came to power in 1964.

The case for a strong central government for security purposes had actually been stated as early as 1956.

We live in a climate of worldwide war that will decide the destiny of Western civilization.

A decentralized system is fundamentally weak in periods of war, which demand a centralized and hierarchic structure. As total war absorbs all people, institutions, wealth, and human and national resources for the attainment of the objectives, it seems certain that centralization and concentration will increase the efficiency and ability of the political and national power.[28]

Since the need for economic planning and mobilization of resources was seen as necessary for national security in times of great crisis, a central institution was required to perform this function of planning. An ESG lecturer on "economic mobilization" argued that the logical institutions for this purpose were the National Security Council and the General Staff of the armed forces.[29]

---

were unauthoritative and wanted to reduce their numbers." Much of the substance and even the tone of Carneiro's work is later found in the political party statute imposed by the Castello Branco government, which attempted to create a two-party system with a dominant government party. In the election law of 1965, electoral coalitions and alliances were forbidden.

[28] Ildefonso Mascarenhas da Silva, *O Poder Nacional e Seus Tipos de Estructura*, ESG, C-20-56, pp. 32–34. (Originally classified lecture of the ESG.) The government of Castello Branco decreased the power of the legislature and the states, and increased sharply the power of the president and the National Security Council.

[29] Christovão L. Barros Falcão, Capitão-de-mar-e-guerra, *Mobilização no Campo Econômico*, Curso de Mobilização Nacional, ESG, C-03-59, p. 18. (Originally classified lecture of the ESG.) In Brazil, the chief administrative officer and much of the staff of the National Security Council are military

Despite ESG emphasis on "statism," they argued that all possible resources, including private and foreign, should be used to develop Brazil. Leftist nationalists condemned this as *entreguismo* ("giving away"). The ESG countered by calling the left guilty of irrationality and "pseudo nationalism." The ESG desire for efficiency often resulted in their assuming a minority position in regard to nationalization of industries and services. The argument of Juarez Távora, the second commandant of the ESG, in regard to the state-owned coastal freight companies typifies the unemotional, efficiency-oriented approach that characterized the ESG. He argued that the state-owned coastal shipping companies, *Costeira* and *Loíde*, were inefficient. He said *Loíde* needed 12.6 employees per thousand tons of freight, and the other state firm, *Costeira*, needed 38.4 employees per thousand tons of freight. Whereas, he argued, the smaller private firm, *Navegação Mercantil*, needed only 1.3 employees per thousand tons. He maintained that this inefficiency threatened both national security and economic development because it created transportation bottlenecks and it contributed to inflation because it required government subsidies and its prices were too high.[30] Later, as minister of transport in the Castello Branco government, Távora started proceedings to denationalize both *Costeira* and *Loíde*.

THE *Escola Superior de Guerra* AND THE 1964 REVOLUTION

Among members of the ESG there was a growing sentiment in the face of the 1961–1964 crisis that President Goulart was tolerating and implicitly encouraging anarchy and subversion and that Brazil needed a basically new political approach for development and security. The active-duty faculty members of the ESG became an important center of the "defensive conspiracy" against the Goulart government. That the ideology of the ESG was a relevant factor in the revolution of 1964 is borne out by the fact that of the 102 line generals on active duty at the time of the Revolution, those who had attended the ESG were markedly overrepresented

---

men. In the Castello Branco and Costa e Silva governments, a special institution, *Serviço Nacional de Informações* (SNI), was created to oversee the national security aspects for all the ministries. The first director of this office was General Golbery do Couto e Silva.

[30] Marechal Juarez Távora, *Uma Política do Desenvolvimento Para o Brasil* (Rio de Janeiro, Livraria José Olympio Editôra, 1962), p. 41.

among the active plotters against Goulart. Of the generals who had attended the ESG, 60 percent were active plotters, whereas only 15 percent of those who had not attended the ESG were among the active plotters.[31]

The alumni association of the ESG (ADESG) was also active in the campaign of resistance to what it felt was the climate of radicalization, inflation, and anarchy in the Goulart government. It intensified its campaign of indoctrination via conferences held throughout the country.[32]

The very fact that the school was organized to evaluate the development and national security policies of the country tended to create some tension between it and the government of the day, or as General Golbery commented:

> Because the ESG is organized to analyze the country's problems and to think up solutions, it is only natural that if a government is very weak the ESG will be against it. Because the governments of Vargas, Kubitschek—the best of them—and Goulart were weak, the ESG was naturally intellectually against them. We never assumed a position against Quadros.[33]

When asked if the ideas of the ESG could have possibly been implemented at some time without the revolution, he replied that they could, but that the revolution "greatly facilitated" this.[34]

When one examines the prominent men of the Castello Branco government, one sees that in fact a great number of them were

[31] The names of all the line generals and information concerning their attendance at the ESG is contained in Brasil, Ministério da Guerra, *Almanaque do Exército: 1964.*
I asked three of the major participants in the revolution to make a list of those generals they considered active planners and mobilizers in the movement against Goulart. If a general appeared on two of the three lists, I classified him as an active plotter.

[32] In June of 1963, the directorate of the alumni association sent a circular to all its members announcing that the "present directorate, alert to the gravity of the present national situation, judges that it is its duty to give maximum increase to such activities [*ciclos*] for obvious reasons." *Circular no. 10/63, de 7 de Junho de 1963, da Alumni de Escola Superior de Guerra* (ADESG). A description of the range of activities of the São Paulo alumni association from 1961 on is found in "Departmento Regional de São Paulo," *Boletim da Associação dos Diplomados da Escola Superior de Guerra,* no. 107, pp. 4–11.

[33] Interview, Brasília, 1967, September 18.

[34] *Ibid.*

graduates of the ESG, or, even more significantly, were former permanent staff members of the ESG. The president himself, Castello Branco, was director of the Department of Studies of the ESG from April 1956 to November 1958. Marshal Oswaldo Cordeiro de Farias, minister of regional agencies, had been the first commandant of the ESG. The minister of transport, Marshal Juarez Távora, had been the second commandant. The director of the new, very important *Serviço Nacional de Informações* (SNI), General Golbery do Couto e Silva, was known as the "father of the ESG." Both foreign ministers of the government, the civilian Leitão da Cunha and General Juracy Magalhães, were graduates, as well as General Geisel, the chief of the Military Household and the secretary-general of the National Security Council. Many other lesser members of the government might also be listed.[35]

A major actor in the Castello Branco government who was neither a graduate nor on its permanent staff was the powerful minister of planning, Roberto Campos. He, however, had averaged about two lectures a year at the ESG since the mid-1950s, and one of the reasons Castello Branco selected him as minister of planning was because he had heard, and essentially agreed with, Campos' lectures.[36]

The sense of systemic crisis and especially the radicalization of politics between 1961 and 1964 made the counterinsurgency doctrines of the ESG appear to many military men much more relevant and urgent than they had in the period of high growth and relative political peace of 1956 to 1958. The fact that the majority of army officers did not espouse ESG ideas concerning the utility of a strong private sector, or share its distrust of "emotional nationalism" or its perception that the containment of domestic Communism called for aggressive anti-Communist alliances abroad, was glossed over as the military began to close ranks in defense of their institution in the face of what they saw as an immediate security threat. It was only later, after the first military government had been formed, that the differences between the ESG officers in the government and the majority of officers outside the government became an issue.[37]

Yet despite this later widespread military resentment over specific

[35] "Adesgianos no Govêrno," *Boletim da Associação dos Diplomados da Escola Superior de Guerra*, no. 103, pp. 11–15.

[36] Roberto Campos, interview with the author, Rio de Janeiro, September 15, 1967.

[37] See Chap. 11.

ESG policies, the important point not to lose sight of is that many of the doctrines of internal warfare, formulated at the ESG and later institutionalized in the ESG-influenced government of Castello Branco, permeated *all* major military groups in Brazil and were accepted as a basic new fact of political and military life. The central idea formulated at the ESG was that development and security issues are inseparable. Even when differences over specific policies developed between the Castello Branco government and the Costa Silva government, as discussed in a later chapter, almost all military officers agreed that since labor, fiscal, educational, and other problems were intrinsic to the security of the nation, it was legitimate and necessary for military men to concern themselves with these areas. From this basic premise came the steady broadening of military jurisdiction over Brazilian life when the military assumed power in 1964.

By the time of the 1964 revolution, therefore, there existed a body of military officers and civilian technocrats who had had a common schooling on the problems of Brazil and who had evolved a controversial and debatable but reasonably coherent doctrine on how to develop the country. Therefore, after the overthrow of President Goulart in 1964, there was a relatively high level of confidence within the military that they included members with a relevant solution to the problems of Brazil, and who were technically prepared to govern. In addition, the extensive links of the ESG with civilians meant that it was possible to give many of the key posts to civilians who shared the ESG outlook.[38] All of this contributed

[38] A particularly important link between the ESG and civilians was the informal ESG–IPÊS link. IPÊS (*Instituto de Pesquisas e Estudos Sociais*) was an anti-Communist business group that advocated the systematic "progressive capitalist" reform of Brazil's economic and political system as necessary in itself and also for the disarming of the Communist challenge in Brazil. Many of the key civilians at IPÊS had attended the ESG before IPÊS was founded, and later some of the key founding staff members of the ESG, such as General Golbery do Couto e Silva, and General Heitor Almeida Herrera, joined IPÊS. Between 1961 and 1964, IPÊS systematically criticized government reform proposals and offered 23 detailed alternative reform projects of their own. As concrete alternatives, these often went beyond those suggested by the ESG. Later, in Castello Branco's government, many IPÊS projects and personnel were used. This is most striking in the case of the government's agrarian reform law, banking reform, housing program, and workers' job stabilization law. The above assessment is based upon a visit to IPÊS headquarters, examination of their literature, and interviews in Rio de Janeiro with General Herrera (August 29, 1968), Glycon de Paiva

to a belief in their own legitimacy and capacity to rule and is an essential factor in understanding the boundary change in civil–military relations that took place after the overthrow of Goulart. However, the overthrow of Goulart was not a certainty even as late as the first week in March of 1964.

(September 6, 1968), and Paulo Assis Ribeiro (September 9, 1968), all current or former officers of IPÊS.

Chapter 9

The Assumption of Power—
The Revolution of 1964

FACTORS INHIBITING THE MILITARY FROM ASSUMING POWER

In the years leading up to 1964, the increasing economic loads and decreasing belief in the capability and legitimacy of the existing political system weakened some of the major elements inhibiting the military from assuming power. In addition, general pursuit of new political formulae for Brazil resulted in attempts by most sectors to involve the military even more deeply in the process of resolving the crises.

Military officers increasingly felt that their moderating role was destructive of their own unity and integrity as an institution. It would be misleading, however, to imply that these sets of political and economic conditions alone led *inevitably* to the overthrow of President Goulart in 1964 and to the establishment of military government for the first time in the twentieth century.

Three questions involving the actual breakdown and decision to rule by the military need to be explored. First, given the increased pressures on the system, what in fact continued to *inhibit* the military from acting? This involves analysis of several factors. Second, if such a set of factors was operating, what does a step-by-step analysis of the crisis of 1964 reveal about the way in which the removal of Goulart became more than a traditional coup? And last, how did the propensity toward breakdown of the old pattern of civil–military relations become an actual breakdown, so that a new pattern emerged?

There were, in fact, a number of important factors inhibiting the military from assuming power even as late as the beginning of March 1964. Many of the most important civilian governors, who have traditionally played a key role in central power decisions, had a stake in the continuation of the normal functioning of the political system because they were themselves prominent candidates for presidential elections slated for October 1965. Adhemar de Barros of São Paulo, with a state militia of over 30,000 men, was an active candidate of the populist PSP party. Carlos Lacerda, governor of Guanabara, and Magalhães Pinto, governor of Minas Gerais, were not only men with strong state military police forces but also contenders for the nomination of the UDN party. On the left, Presirent Goulart could not, by the terms of the constitution of 1946, succeed himself, and since a relative of the president was also constitutionally forbidden to run for the presidency, Leonel Brizola, former governor of Rio Grande do Sul, was equally denied the opportunity to run. This meant the most powerful governor on the left, Miguel Arraes of Pernambuco, also had a strong vested interest in Goulart remaining in office and elections being held on schedule. Lacerda, Magalhães Pinto, and de Barros all knew of the formulation of a plan to overthrow Goulart in case Goulart attempted a coup to extend his own powers, but none committed himself to this plan until late in March of 1964.

Another factor inhibiting the overthrow of Goulart was that, regardless of the distrust with which he was viewed by many people, he was nonetheless the constitutionally elected president of Brazil. From this fact flowed both the legalistic support acquired from his mere occupancy of this office, and the power to appoint civilians and military officers most loyal to him to positions of importance.

From the military viewpoint, there were also reasons why the emergence of new attitudes, such as institutional fear, declining confidence in civilians, and increased confidence in their own abilities to rule, were nonetheless not sufficient reasons for assuming power. While there were early groups of conspirators who were clearly looking for an excuse to overthrow Goulart, the military as a whole had been badly divided by their abortive attempt to block Goulart from assuming the presidency following the resignation of Quadros in 1961. This fear of splitting the army again acted as a major inhibition to any attempt to overthrow Goulart. General Golbery had said that "1961 was a disaster for the army," that the only way in which the army would attempt to overthrow Goulart was if public opinion clearly favored such a move.[1] Equally important, he argued, was the fact that in 1963 the activists, in planning a revolution, represented only about 10 percent of the higher officer corps, while another 70 to 80 percent were "legalists" or simply nonactivists. While many of this group were becoming

[1] See Chap. 5, n. 52.

189

increasingly apprehensive about the state of Brazil, and especially the question of military discipline and unity, they would nonetheless follow the president in his formal capacity as commander-in-chief of the army. The other 10 to 20 percent of the officer corps were pro-Goulart activists whom Goulart had appointed to most of the key troop commands and administrative posts.[2]

As late as early March of 1964, there was widespread fear that Goulart still had sufficient active support so that an attempt to overthrow him could lead to civil war lasting two or even three months.[3] The most significant military movement against Goulart was what was called the "defensive" coup plan.[4] This plan called for the discussion of measures to be taken by military officers in case Goulart took what the military considered to be illegal steps. The formulation of this conspiracy as *defensive* increased its capacity to recruit support. Nonetheless, as long as Goulart was not taking nonconstitutional steps, there was no loud demand by civilians for the military to intervene. Without this demand, military activists could not get a winning coalition to take an aggressive first step against Goulart.

Given these various sets of inhibiting factors, a strong case could be made that President Goulart could have completed his term of office without being displaced by the military and without the complete breakdown of the political regime.

Why, then, was Goulart actually displaced, and with such relative ease? Clearly, the economic and political crisis had generated, for the military at least, the "chemical reagents" capable of producing a breakdown of the regime. The necessary components for a breakdown existed well before March 13, 1964 but they were not sufficient cause for a change of regime. The reagents had to be brought to critical "temperature" and "pressure" for reaction actually to occur.[5] My point is that the quality of political leadership

[2] *Ibid.*

[3] Numerous military men I talked to mentioned this.

[4] For a discussion of the "defensive coup," see José Stacchini, *Março 64: Mobilização da Audácia* (São Paulo: Companhia Editôra Nacional, 1965), pp. 66–72; and Carlos Castello Branco, "Da Conspiração à Revolução," in *Os Idos de Março*, by Alberto Dines, *et al.* (Rio de Janeiro: José Alvaro, 1964), pp. 277–306.

[5] Chalmers Johnson, *Revolutionary Change* (Boston: Little, Brown & Company, 1966), pp. 90–94, makes a similar distinction between the necessary revolutionary preconditions and final causes of a revolution, which he calls the "accelerator." I prefer not to use this term because it (although

is an important variable and can at times prevent the "necessary revolutionary conditions" from becoming "sufficient conditions."

To analyze, therefore, why the revolution actually occurred, we must discuss the question of political leadership, for despite the many contributing factors at the macro-systemic level, the final causes of the revolution were intimately related to questions of the strategies and tactics that Goulart used in his effort to "re-equilibrate" the political system.

GOULART'S STRATEGIES

In mid-March 1964, Goulart came to a decision to resolve the political crisis by attempting to change the balance of power in his favor. This decision was to alter profoundly the future of Brazilian politics. It is thus legitimate to analyze his action as a strategy, and, since Goulart was deposed a little more than three weeks later, to look for weak points in it. A step-by-step account will show the crisis moving toward resolution.

The final stages of the crisis began on March 13, when a massive rally was held in Rio de Janeiro. The president and his trade union supporters had organized the rally knowingly, in the sense that they considered it the first step toward resolving a crisis. On the morning of the rally, Goulart told an interviewer:

> Today I am going to run all the risks. The most that can happen to me is that I will be deposed. I will not renounce or commit suicide.[6]

The interviewer remarked that the situation in Brazil did not call for either renunciation or suicide. Goulart replied:

> I know. I am only imagining the worst that could happen, following my decision to push reforms and obtain greater powers from Congress. But nothing will happen because my military support [*dispositivo militar*] is excellent. Assis Brasil has guaranteed me that at my command, the army will follow. . . . From here on forward, I am only going to govern with the support of

not the body of Johnson's analysis) implies that we are only concerned with the speeding up of the "inevitable" breakdown.

[6] Quoted in Antonio Callado, "Jango ou o Suicídio sem Sangue," in *Os Idos de Março*, by Alberto Dines, *et al.*, p. 256. The reference to resignation is to the renunciation of President Jânio Quadros in August 1961; the reference to suicide refers to the suicide of President Vargas in August 1954.

the people. And what everyone is going to see today [at the rally] is that the people have changed. They are awakened, they are ready for the grand problems of the country.[7]

Goulart was counting on mobilizing the political power of the masses and demanding reforms by plebiscite or decree, or by pressuring, or even closing, Congress. To do this he implicitly recognized his need for not merely the passive support of the army, but the active, aggressive support of key Goulart-appointed generals. The strategy, to be effective, would have required that federal army troops give protection and backing to the mass demonstrations and strikes Goulart was planning throughout the country. It would also probably have involved key army leaders threatening Congress in order to pass the "basic reforms." If Congress refused, the army would be the key factor in any attempt by Goulart to insist on a national plebiscite for these reforms. Likewise active support of the three service chiefs would be required if Goulart was to attempt to declare a state of siege.[8]

This strong reliance by Goulart on the loyal military activists he had appointed to key positions is consistent with the moderating pattern of civil–military relations until 1964. In this system of civil–military relations, a weak executive ruling a divided country will attempt to use the military to augment his power. One of Goulart's close associates described the president's attitude toward the military as he entered the crisis period:

> Goulart felt he had good relations with the army. . . .
> He wanted to put the military in as many key positions as possible. It was a form of power and had to be used. . . .

[7] *Ibid.*, pp. 256–257. *Dispositivo*, as used in the Goulart period, meant more than "support" (*apoio*). It meant senior officers who were personally loyal and actively committed to implementing the president's policies. The *dispositivo* in theory included all the military officers and troops under the command of these key senior officers.

General Assis Brasil was the chief of the president's Military Household and, as such, one of the president's chief liaison officers with the military.

[8] Since Goulart was overthrown by elements of the military shortly after the March 13 rally that began the deliberate intensification of the crisis, this scenario was never put into effect. Nonetheless, for even the outside observer, the broad outlines of the government's attempt to move the political system toward resolution were clear. The author was in Brazil in this period and wrote an article a week before the revolution entitled, "Brazil: Mend or End," *Economist* (April 4, 1964), p. 31, that reflected this sense of imminent crisis.

192

He felt he had to pressure Congress by mobilizing mass opinion and by use of the military.[9]

As we have seen, this approach is consistent with Goulart's behavior as president in the period 1961 to 1963 in using the military to force an early holding of the plebiscite, to request a state of siege, and to keep opponents in check.[10]

Thus, by mid-March of 1964, when Goulart was planning his strategy of change based on military support, his assumption that he could use the military was not without precedent. However, his tactic of appointing new service chiefs when the old ones did not agree with him—he had had four such chiefs since assuming the presidency—cut him off from accurate feedback about military feeling. Officers closest to him, who urged him forward on his course of increasing pressure on Congress, were more and more out of touch with the bulk of military sentiment.

Moreover, Goulart's strategy of mobilizing the masses by using leftist activists in the country, while expecting to balance the left with the military who would also help push the reforms through, had inherent points of tension and weakness.

The inherent danger in regard to Goulart's military support was that a diffuse, personalist mobilization of the masses, if it were to be successful in pressuring Congress, could go beyond most military officers' tolerance of internal disorder. Also, Goulart's attempts to use the Communist organization ran the risk of diminishing the intensity of support of those officers who endorsed Goulart's reforms on nationalist-left grounds, but who disliked the institutional connection with the Brazilian Communist party.

A major weakness of Goulart's strategy in regard to the left was that the left was too fragmented and too unmobilized to support that strategy; moreover, Goulart himself was unable to lead the left effectively because, in the past, he had made ambiguous turns both to the left and the right. Goulart was not trusted by the major figures of the left. Miguel Arraes, as the major figure on the left eligible for the upcoming presidential elections, feared that Goulart might upset the election schedule. Arraes also knew that Goulart had always attempted to keep him under control by appointing

[9] Interview October 11, 1968, Rio de Janeiro, with Raúl Riff, President Goulart's press secretary, who later had his political rights cancelled by the military government.

[10] See Chap. 4.

strong, anti-Communist generals to command the Fourth Army, based in his state capital of Recife. In addition, Arraes was aware that Goulart had considered deposing both him, the major leftist governor, and Lacerda, the major rightist governor, in 1963 in order to solidify his position. Arraes told various people that he feared that if Goulart executed a coup, Arraes himself would be one of the first to suffer.[11]

The leader of the Communist party, Luís Carlos Prestes, was also deeply ambivalent about Goulart. Prestes wanted to use Goulart to mobilize the country, but he feared that a premature attempt to radicalize the country and eliminate the bourgeoisie from a reform coalition would precipitate a countercoup in which the Communists would be destroyed.[12] Prestes also feared that if Goulart in fact carried off a leftist coup, Goulart might very possibly not keep his promise to make the Communist party legal.[13]

Francisco Julião, the most famous leader of the peasant leagues in the northeast, was hostile to Goulart, whom he accused of trying to turn him into a rural trade-union boss controlled by the Labor Ministry. Julião felt that Goulart had not backed him in his last election campaign.[14]

Brizola, the most volatile member of the left, was constantly charging Goulart with being a bourgeois and an opportunist. Brizola's mouthpiece, *Panfleto*, published in February and March of 1964, often criticized Goulart's policies. In early March, Brizola went so far as to say that he would never stand on the platform

[11] See Fernando Pedreira, *Março 31: Civis e Militares no Processo da Crise Brasileira* (Rio de Janeiro: José Alvaro, 1964), p. 13; also Dines, *Os Idos de Março*, pp. 31, 83.

[12] See Thomas Skidmore, *Politics in Brazil, 1930–1964* (New York: Oxford University Press, 1967), p. 278, and his long bibliographic footnote on p. 414. Since the revolution, the Communist party has published several reevaluations, in which they are critical of the "immature strategy" that precipitated the counterrevolution. Alberto Guerreiro Ramos, an important politician of the left and a distinguished social scientist, authored a prophetic warning before the coup about the dangers of many on the left being more concerned with the "metaphysics," rather than the political realities, of revolution. See *Mito e Verdade da Revolução Brasileira* (Rio de Janeiro: Zahar Editôres, 1963).

[13] Dines, *Os Idos de Março*, p. 30.

[14] See Julião's interview with Antonio Callado, in *Tempo de Arraes: Padres e Comunistas na Revolução Sem Violência* (Rio de Janeiro: José Alvaro, 1965), pp. 59–60.

with Goulart again, because Goulart had so many conservatives in his cabinet.[15]

Finally, with regard to the trade unions, we have already illustrated their basic ambiguity about Goulart by citing their refusal to back his request for the state of siege in September of 1963.

The Goulart strategy of forcing the system in order to bring the crisis to a resolution was successful in that it intensified the crisis. Within nineteen days of the rally on March 13, the Brazilian political system had been fundamentally transformed. The results, however, were the opposite of what Goulart had intended. Let us analyze why.

THE MARCH 13 RALLY AND CIVIL–MILITARY AFTERMATH

The two decisive steps for civil–military relations that precipitated the 1964 revolution were the rally on March 13 and a mutiny of sailors from March 27 to 29.

At the March 13 mass rally, widely televised and broadcast, Goulart launched a campaign for broad structural and political reforms that came to be known as the "basic reforms." He announced he had just signed a land reform decree which declared subject to expropriation all underutilized properties of over twelve hundred acres situated within six miles of federal highways or railways, and lands of seventy acres located within six miles of federal dams or drainage projects. He also nationalized all remaining private oil refineries in Brazil. He announced future plans to enfranchise illiterates, by which means he would almost double the electorate, and to legalize the Communist party.

He demanded that the constitution be reformed because it was obsolete, since it "legalized an unjust and inhuman economic structure." His brother-in-law, Leonel Brizola, went further in saying that Congress had lost "all identification with the people"; he urged the establishment of a "Congress composed of peasants, workers, sergeants, and nationalist officers." Both Brizola and Goulart posed the threat of a plebiscite, using the enlarged electorate to bypass Congress if Congress presented an obstacle to these plans.

Goulart followed up the promise of his rally immediately by presenting his basic reforms to Congress on March 15. He pointedly informed Congress that the three armed services ministers had

[15] Dines, *Os Idos de Março*, p. 19.

195

seen and approved the program. It was announced that a series of mass demonstrations would be held throughout the country. The legally unrecognized high command of labor, the CGT (*Comando Geral dos Trabalhadores*) threatened a general strike if Congress did not approve the constitutional changes by April 20 and also recommended that Goulart declare a unilateral moratorium on the repayment of the foreign debts. May Day loomed as the day of resolution if the political elites remained intransigent.[16]

In terms of strategy and the tactics of political leadership and political survival, what can be said about the effectiveness of Goulart and his allies? Without attempting to discuss the merits of the goals themselves,[17] a good case can be made that Goulart's tactics diminished his support and tended to increase the possibility of a military coup backed by strong civilian opinion.

First, in the euphoric atmosphere that pervaded the left after the March 13 rally, great hope was placed on the mobilization of groups that had previously been marginal to the political process. Goulart launched a major attack on existing holders of power, but he had not first organized sufficient support to make such an attack feasible. As even one of his staff acknowledged, "Goulart wanted to make more reforms than he really had the strength to do. He had no organized support for the big reforms he announced."[18] Almost no effort was made to retain as allies the moderate left and center that had in the past cooperated on some reform issues. A strong case can be made that for Goulart, as well as for a number of other rhetorical nationalists such as Sukarno and Nkrumah, the emotional power of revolutionary symbols and the physical presence of the masses had a debilitating effect on his capacity to make the normal "political survival calculations" of judging actions in terms of strategically located allies gained versus strategically located enemies created. One of Goulart's closest allies in this crisis period later commented that the mass rally had disoriented Goulart's political perceptions:

[16] For the March 13 rally, and immediate aftermath, see the author's "Brazil: Mend or End," p. 31. For a description written by the minister of justice of the Goulart government, see Abelardo Jurema, *Sexta-Feira, 13: Os Última Dias do Govêrno João Goulart* (Rio de Janeiro: Edições O Cruzeiro, 1964), pp. 139–149. Also Dines, *Os Idos de Março*, pp. 195–219, 249–262.

[17] I personally feel that most of the goals were desirable in some form.

[18] Interview with Raúl Riff, Rio de Janeiro, October 11, 1968.

196

Friday, the thirteenth, was the beginning of the president's drive for power. It carried him to a delirium of ephemeral glory . . . [in which] he underestimated his adversaries and overestimated the strength of the masses.[19]

A characteristic example of the almost willful disregard for winning or retaining potential allies was the frequent utterances by major leftist activists that the composition of a future strong reforming government (which the new power of the masses was "certain" to generate shortly) should not include any "bourgeois reformers," such as San Tiago Dantas, the widely respected and influential moderate left politician. Even a newspaper such as *Diário Carioca*, which had strongly supported the programmatic reforms demanded by Goulart, was offended by such tactics.[20]

In addition to losing allies, it is clear that the March 13 rally, by simultaneously raising to the level of crisis numerous fundamental problems, tended to maximize the number of Goulart's opponents among those strategically located in the power structure.[21] Between March 13 and March 15, Goulart's demands for fundamental reforms threatened elements among the landowners, military officers, congressmen, foreign capitalists, anti-Communists and industrialists. The rhetoric of revolution, coupled with the soaring inflation, created increasing fear and insecurity among the middle classes. On many issues these groups were hostile to one another, but the Goulart offensive brought them together and minimized their differences.[22] Many people who were "progovernment" shifted to a position we previously referred to as "proregime but antigovernment." "Antigovernment" conservatives increasingly became "antiregime."

[19] Jurema, *Sexta-Feira, 13*, p. 149.

[20] See their angry editorial, "Frente Ampla ou Frente Estreita?" *Diário Carioca*, March 24, 1964.

[21] For a discussion of the dangers of simultaneously raising numerous problems, see Juan Linz, "The Breakdown of Democratic Regimes" (paper prepared for the Seventh World Congress of Sociology, Varna, Bulgaria, September 14–19, 1970).

[22] Given the widespread feelings that Brazil was in need of fundamental reforms, and the lack of unity among the elites, possibly a more fruitful reform strategy could have been to reform sequentially, attempting to build the biggest possible constituency for each reform, each time reconstituting coalitions for new reforms. For a discussion of this reform strategy, see the last two chapters in Albert Hirschman, *Journeys Toward Progress* (New York: Twentieth Century Fund, 1963); see esp. his "Model 1: Engineering Reform with the Help of the Perspective of Revolution," pp. 277–285.

197

The minister of justice later wrote from exile about this counter-productive aspect of the massive rally for the Goulart government. He acknowledged reluctantly that the March 13 rally "came to be the touchstone of the opposition in combating the government. The rally created the expectation of a crisis, of a 'coup,' raids, riots, mutiny, or general subversion in the country. . . . After March 13, the opposition was galvanized."[23] Indicative of this galvanization of the opposition was the even larger rally of many middle-class people in São Paulo on March 19 to demonstrate against Goulart and in favor of legality.[24] The rhetoric of "resentment politics" gained Goulart a few supporters, but also won him some powerful and strategically located enemies. An example is Brizola's calling General Muricy a "gorilla" to his face on a public platform. General Muricy, a commanding general in the north, was one of the first to go into armed revolt against Goulart. Frequent ridicule of Congress was another tactic that was not conducive to getting Congress to cooperate in passing the basic reforms that the Goulart government needed.

A further and more general example of Brizola's attempts to win marginal additional support at the cost of creating powerful enemies in the center of the political system was his tactic of repeatedly calling for the formation of *grupos de onze* (groups of eleven armed guerrilla revolutionaries). Private appeals might have been just as effective, and would not have created fear among the landowners and middle class, nor have caused some military officers to shift from a position of neutrality to active conspiracy against Goulart.

REACTION TO MARCH 13—THE EFFECTS ON THE MILITARY

Despite the great strains on the Brazilian polity by the end of February of 1964, a number of important factors inhibited the military from attempting to remove Goulart. The most important of these were (1) the fact that Goulart received a reasonable amount of passive support merely by being the constitutionally elected president; (2) the desire by politicians, especially the major governors who were presidential aspirants, to hold elections on schedule; and (3) the fact that the military were still sufficiently

[23] Jurema, *Sexta-Feira, 13*, pp. 144–145.
[24] A detailed study of this counterrally does not yet exist and would be worthwhile.

divided among themselves to be hesitant about initiating a displacement without greatly increased public support. The tactics Goulart and his allies used to promote the basic reforms significantly weakened all these remaining impediments to military action.

Goulart's attack on the constitution as archaic and obsolete during the March 13 rally weakened his own claim, as the constitutional president, to obedience from the military. This point was made a number of times in public statements and newspaper editorials. The *Diário de Notícias* editorialized:

> It is undeniable that subversive forces exist clearly aimed at making an attempt to overthrow the regime and existing institutions. . . . These forces seem to have co-opted the president himself and have placed him for the first time in the forefront of the subversive process of opposition to the law, to the regime and to the constitution.
>
> If the supreme executive authority is opposed to the constitution, condemns the regime, and refuses to obey the laws, he automatically loses the right to be obeyed . . . because this right emanates from the constitution. The armed forces, by article 177 of the constitution, are obliged to "defend the country, and to guarantee the constitutional power, law and order." . . . If the constitution is "useless" . . . how can the president still command the armed forces?[25]

The March 13 rally also generated for the first time a widespread fear that the drive of the Goulart government might result in postponement of national elections, scheduled for October 1965, or a sharp change in the electoral rules (such as making Goulart, or his relative Brizola, eligible). This had an important impact on civilian–military opinion with regard to displacing Goulart. The military had been badly divided in their attempt in 1961 to displace Goulart unilaterally without prior civilian sanction or support. A number of the key conspirators against Goulart decided that any attempt to displace him had to be initiated by the governor of a major state who had the backing of his own state militia.[26] The two most likely

[25] Front page editorial, *Diário de Notícias*, March 23, 1964.

[26] For example, General Mourão Filho, the general who finally initiated the revolution, has written that he would have attempted revolution earlier if he had received a manifesto to the nation from four major governors. See his official account, published as an army order, "Relatório de Revolução Democrática Iniciada Pela 4a. RM E, 4a. DI em 31 de Março de 1964,"

states were São Paulo and Minas Gerais. Both states were governed by men who had helped formulate the defensive coup strategy.[27] The governor of Minas Gerais, in particular, had even made plans to resist a Goulart coup by declaring a state of belligerency, and was willing to use its state militia to attempt to fight the central government.[28] In addition, each state had been strengthening its militias in order to increase its sources of military power.[29]

Nonetheless, as major contenders in the upcoming presidential elections, the two governors had a vested interest in Goulart's remaining in office and elections being held on schedule. However,

---

Comando de 4a. Região Militar, 4a. Divisão de Infantaria e Guarnição de Juiz de Fora (May 9, 1964), p. 1. (Copy in possession of the author.)

[27] In a tape-recorded interview with José Stacchini, of *O Estado de São Paulo*, on March 20, 1965, General Mourão Filho said that in January 1962 Adhemar de Barros sought him out in São Paulo and said that from his conversations with Goulart and Brizola he had become convinced that they would attempt to impose a "syndicalist republic." De Barros asked General Mourão Filho to join with him in preparing a military plan to counter this threat.

[28] See Pedro Gomes, "Minas: Do Diálogo ao 'Front,'" in Dines, *Os Idos de Março*, pp. 73–74. In a signed statement to *O Estado de São Paulo*, made in April 1965, General Guedes, who was the commander of the Fourth Infantry Division located in Minas, between 1962 and 1964, gave his own account: "For a long time Magalhães Pinto and I had a mutual agreement. Minas Gerais would not accept any form of a coup . . . if one was attempted, we would close the frontiers of the state immediately and summon all who were disposed to fight for liberty. We would make these mountains a bulwark from which we would come out sooner or later to reconstruct what had been destroyed." (Copy in possession of the author.)

[29] A signed statement to *O Estado de São Paulo* by Colonel José Canavo Filho, the former commander of the *Força Pública*, the state militia of São Paulo, states that through the clandestine financing by private industry, the state militia received money and technical assistance to make its own anti-tank weapons, hand-grenades, explosives, and some small rockets. He noted that anti-Goulart civilians were arming themselves at a fairly rapid rate. Some attempts were also made to purchase arms from abroad. (Copy in possession of the author.) See also the article about the state militias which mentions the antiguerrilla warfare training of the *Força Pública* before the revolution, and which shows a photograph of the armored-personnel carriers equipped with machine guns, belonging to the São Paulo state militia, "Polícia: Tradição é o seu traço comum," *Visão* (November 5, 1965), pp. 57–58.

In Minas Gerais, the state militia—the *Polícia Militar de Minas Gerais*—expanded from 11,500 men in 1958 to 18,000 in 1964, before the revolution. See Tenente-Colonel Geraldo Tito Silveira, *Crônica da Polícia Militar de Minas* (Belo Horizonte, Imprensa Oficial de Minas Gerais, 1966), pp. 280–298.

when it appeared that Goulart was trying to restructure the political system, an attempt which might preclude their running for the presidency, the two governors began to plot actively against Goulart.

Governor Magalhães Pinto reacted quickly following the March 13 rally. On March 20, he issued a manifesto on national television, saying Minas Gerais would resist any "revolution commandeered from above." The next day he made arrangements with the governor of the neighboring state of Espírito Santo, Governor Lacerda da Aguiar, to use the port of Vitória and railroads to get supplies into Minas in the case of a civil war in which Minas Gerais stood armed against the federal troops of Goulart.[30] Such a war, the governor felt, might last as long as three months. He is reported to have felt that any discussion of the presidential elections was by this time "surrealistic."[31]

The governor of São Paulo, Adhemar de Barros, went on television the night of March 20 to make an impassioned, three-hour-long address condemning the Goulart government for fomenting revolution. He emphasized his willingness to resist by force and said the São Paulo state militia had 30,000 troops, as well as airplanes to transport them. He pointed out that this force was twice as large as the federal army garrisoned in São Paulo, in which there were a number of pro-Goulart generals.[32]

The armed forces were also deeply affected by the meeting of March 13, and their internal divisions over whether they should attempt to displace Goulart began to diminish. The change of position of the governors of Minas Gerais and São Paulo greatly strengthened the military conspirators.

The March 13 rally also resulted in a changed atmosphere in the press. Before March 13, no editorials directly charged the military with the responsibility for resolving the crisis. The rally, however, raised such issues as changing the constitution, holding a constituent assembly, and closing Congress. After March 13, appeals began to be made to the constitutional role of the military to guarantee all three branches of government, the legislative and the

[30] See the extremely interesting chapter by Pedro Gomes on the role of Minas Gerais in the revolution, "Minas: Do Diálogo ao 'Front,' " in Dines, *Os Idos de Março*, pp. 87–89.

[31] *Ibid.*, p. 91.

[32] See the chapter on the role of São Paulo in the revolution by Eurilo Duarte, "32 Mais 32, Igual a 64," in Dines, *Os Idos de Março*, pp. 125–160.

judicial and not just the executive. Editorials requested the military not to give protective backing to government-sponsored threats to order. This loud public response to the rally of March 13 facilitated the role of the conspirators, who were attempting to create a majority within the military ready to remove Goulart from the presidency.

The editorial of *O Jornal*, entitled "Defense of Illegality," appearing two days after the March 13 rally, illustrated the new mood of open condemnation of the military for continuing to obey the "illegal" orders of the president:

> The armed forces say they participated in the illegal and revolutionary rally . . . in obedience to the order of the president!
>
> No one is obliged to accept and obey an abusive order, much less to give protection to those who challenge and break the laws and who agitate in a public square for a Communist revolution.
>
> The Congress is one of the powers of the Republic and the armed forces have a duty to respect it, and defend it against those who attempt to destroy it.
>
> The armed forces did not fulfill this obligation at the rally of March 13.[33]

Another element in the coalition forming against Goulart was the freedom of retired officers to express their feelings against him. Seventy-two retired generals signed a widely circulated manifesto stating that it was the constitutional duty of the military to defend order and obey the president only "within the limits of the law." The manifesto argued that the government had placed itself outside the law in attacking Congress, and concluded, "the armed forces cease to be obliged to preserve and guarantee the government."[34]

Within the military, the development of the crisis was such that, without calling for the overthrow of Goulart, the chief of staff, General Castello Branco, could use the language of the constitution and the traditional rules of the moderating role of the military to alert the army to be prepared to take steps. He sent a classified note to all unit commanders. This was the first such note and was a direct response to the meeting of March 13:

[33] "Defesa da Ilegalidade," *O Jornal*, March 15, 1964.
[34] "Generais: Goulart e Transgressa da Lei," *Diário de Notícias*, March 22, 1964, p. 8.

I understand the intranquillity and questioning of my sub-
ordinates in the days following the meeting of the 13th of this
month. . . .

Two threats are evident, the advent of a constituent congress
as the way to execute the basic reforms and the unleashing of a
greater chain of agitation by the illegal Central Confederation of
Labor. The armed forces have been invoked in support of such
measures.

The national and permanent military institutions are not
properly meant to defend the programs of the government, much
less its propaganda, but to guarantee the constitutional powers
and the functioning and application of the law.

The yearned-for constituent assembly is a violent revolutionary
objective, to be achieved by the violent closing of the present
Congress and the institution of a dictatorship. . . .

There seems to be no other course of action but to guarantee
the law, which does not permit such a grave and illegal movement. . . .

It is necessary therefore to continue to act always within the
"limits of the law," to be ready to defend legality, namely, the
complete functioning of the three constitutional branches and
the application of the law, including that of the electoral process,
and to act against a revolution to establish a dictatorship and a
constituent assembly, against the public calamity which is to be
promoted by the General Confederation of Workers, and against
the perversion of the historic role of the armed forces.[35]

In addition to these specific reactions, there were more general
effects of the March 13 rally on civil–military relations. Implicit
in Goulart's appeal to settle the crisis outside traditional political
channels was the threat of force. Many different groups began to
arm themselves. More important politically, it was widely believed
by key civilian and military officers that the nation was taking to
arms. To this extent, the arena was rapidly becoming one in which
the dominant idiom was one of violence rather than of politics.
Since the military considered themselves to have a monopoly on
the legitimate use of arms, and perceived maintenance of internal
order as one of their primary functions, they began to move to the

[35] Complete text reproduced in Dines, *Os Idos de Março*, pp. 392–393.
Original order is in the *Arquivo do Marechal H. A. Castello Branco*.

center of the arena and assume a dominant position within the political system, thus underlining the relevance of Lasswell and Kaplan's dictum: "The balancing of power is particularly affected by the expectations that prevail about the probable mode by which conflicts will be settled. . . . An arena is *military* when the expectation of violence is high; *civic* when the expectation is low."[36]

The March 13 rally greatly increased expectations of force and preparation for a showdown by the forces of the left and right. On both sides there were multiple movements, with no central organization. Anti-Goulart factions in the military were getting a more receptive hearing for their articulation of the need for preparation for a countercoup, but they were still far from unified over the necessity of backing a coup of their own. For many military men, a coup attempt still spelled civil war, disaster for the country and for the military as an institution.

THE RESOLUTION OF THE CRISIS—THE ENLISTED MEN'S NAVAL MUTINY

It was at this point that there occurred the next decisive step in the crisis of March 1964. Despite the buildup of pressure by the active anti-Goulart civilians and military forces, as late as twelve days after the March 13 rally no "winning coalition" existed to overthrow Goulart. Goulart had a number of strategically located officers who both favored the reform program and were loyal to him. The bulk of the remainder of the officers were legalistic, in the sense of being nonactivists. But arguments expressed in Castello Branco's letter were beginning to make a powerful impression on these men, as they began to ask themselves whether their "legalism" entailed loyalty and obedience to the president, and whether obedience to him was still an obedience "within the limits of the law."

Given this lack of unity among the opposition forces, an attempted revolution by one sector of the military would have risked splitting the military at this time. The active plotters within the military were convinced that Goulart was intent on becoming a dictator. But they felt they must wait until he made such a blatant move that they could mobilize support against him easily.

The probable intention of Goulart's strategy, if it was to be a

[36] Harold D. Lasswell and Abraham Kaplan, *Power and Society: A Framework for Political Inquiry* (New Haven: Yale University Press, 1950), p. 252.

winning strategy, was to build up pressure among the masses for reform, without losing the passive obedience of the legalistic officers and the active support of key military officers, supporters Goulart needed if he were to bypass Congress and rule by decree. Holding these forces together was made especially difficult because to a great extent Goulart was spurred on by the highly emotional and often contradictory forces of the left, which he found difficult to unify and direct. The movement was at an explosive state. There was risk of its getting out of control as an effective tactical instrument. The risk lay in the loss of a delicate balance between the increasingly radical civilians and the increasingly threatened officer corps.[37]

The naval mutiny of March 26 occurred against this background. More than a thousand sailors and marines barricaded themselves in an armory in Rio de Janeiro.[38] The naval minister attempted to quell the mutiny. Goulart, instead of backing the minister, in effect dismissed him and allowed the trade unions to participate in the choice of a new minister in his place.

At the time of the mutiny, Goulart was extremely indecisive about his course of action. The mutiny made him face a decision he did not want to make—to punish the enlisted men for the mutiny and risk losing their active support, or to treat the mutineers lightly and greatly risk increasing fears among those officers who saw leniency as a threat to the principle of military discipline.[39]

In the last moments Goulart vacillated, and according to his chief army aide, General Assis Brasil, he abdicated the decision.

[37] An example of the lack of governmental discretion or control over the left that was endangering this balance was the Ministry of Education's deliberate showing to a militant sailors' organization of the Russian film, *The Battleship Potemkin*, in which the parallel between the role of the sailors in the Russian Revolution and their possible role in Brazil was made in a running commentary. See "Provocações," *O Jornal*, March 24, 1964, p. 4. Two days after the article was published, the sailors rebelled and presented Goulart with an undesired crisis of military discipline.

[38] For a narrative of the mutiny, see Mário Victor, *Cinco Anos Que Abalaram O Brasil*, chap. xxix, "A Sublevação na Marinha," pp. 493–514.

[39] Goulart's minister of justice, Abelardo Jurema, wrote that most of the advice the Goulart government received from civilian activists was to side with the sailors, since Goulart did not have much support to lose among naval officers in any case. See Jurema, *Sexta-Feira, 13*, pp. 151–158. Their arguments overlooked the crucial factor of the intensity of the opposition to Goulart, which was greatly increased, and the fact that other services were also affected since they felt equally threatened by the problem of discipline.

He told the new naval minister: "The problem is yours, Admiral. You have a blank check with which to resolve it. If you wish to punish or expel [the mutineers], the decision is yours." The admiral is reported to have replied, "I intend, President, to grant an amnesty."[40]

Repercussions within the officers corps were profound. The issue of institutional self-preservation by means of control over military discipline was one over which ideologically divided military officers had the highest internal agreement. The naval mutiny caused a shift in position that hurt Goulart among all three major groups within the military—the active plotters against him, the legalist uncommitted officers, and the pro-Goulart officers.[41]

The naval mutiny galvanized the active plotters, both civilian and military, into action against Goulart. The operations order issued on the night of March 31, 1964, by General Guedes, commander of the infantry division that first moved against Goulart in the effort to remove him from the presidency, clearly indicates the way in which Goulart's handling of the mutiny acted as a catalyst in the revolutionary drama. The general's order explained to his division that he and Governor Magalhães Pinto had decided it would be a mistake to move against Goulart without profound provocation. In his opinion, and the governor's, any attempt to displace Goulart before he expressly challenged the law would have given Goulart an air of legality, and would have been counterproductive. "It would have attracted to his side a forceful sector of the armed forces who lack confidence in politics and are committed to legal formalism." It was necessary to assemble a defensive conspiracy, and wait until Goulart stepped beyond the bounds of the law. His slogan, the general explained, was "He who breaks the law first is lost!" What happened in the mutiny, he felt, showed that he was correct. With the naval mutiny the military had "arrived at the moment for action, and had to act quickly lest it be too late."[42]

[40] See the testimony of General Assis Brasil to a military investigating tribunal after the revolution, reprinted in *O Estado de São Paulo*, July 2 and 3, 1964.

[41] The naval mutiny was so obviously counterproductive that two generals who were later purged from the military even argue that it must have been deliberately instigated by right-wing officers. Interview with General Luiz Tavares da Cunha Mello and General Nicolau Fico, Rio de Janeiro, October 10, 1968.

[42] General Bda Carlos Luiz Guedes, *Boletim da Infantaria Divisionária/4 NR 58*, March 31, 1964, p. 2. (Copy in possession of the author.)

Another key general in initiating the offensive against Goulart, General Mourão Filho, also acknowledged the effect of the mutiny on his resolve, and on the resolve of Governor Magalhães Pinto, his chief civilian collaborator: "In face of the grave occurrences in the Navy I traveled . . . to a reunion with Governor Magalhães Pinto and General Guedes, commander of the Fourth Infantry Division, where it was decided that we definitely had to begin the attack as soon as possible."[43]

Among the legalistic officers, who comprised the majority of the military officers and who were reluctant to take a bold step against the constitutionally elected president, Goulart's sanctioning of indiscipline and disorder allowed the question of legalism to be reformulated. Obedience was owed to the president "within the limits of the law." To many officers, the president's actions now seemed to lie outside the law. The military, they felt, had a constitutional obligation to continue in existence as a permanent body to maintain internal order. Many editorials throughout the country now told legalist officers that their obligation, even within the terms of legality, lay with their role in maintaining law, order, and military discipline.[44]

Similar appeals were made to younger military officers by their senior officers. General Moniz de Aragão, who was at this time the leading candidate (and subsequent choice) for the presidency of the Military Club, sent a long letter to the junior officers, spelling out the constitutional duty of the military to maintain law and order, and then listing present threats to law and order. He stopped short of urging the direct overthrow of Goulart. But his letter was clearly aimed at legalist and nonactivist opinion. The letter ended: "Fear of expressing an attitude, or defining a position, is a shame in a soldier."[45]

The impact of the naval mutiny of March 26 upon the strong Goulart supporters was powerful. Juan Linz has noted that the intensity of the belief in the legitimacy of a government is most important for those who participate in a crisis from within the authority structure. Their passive support is not enough; they must

[43] General Div Olympio Mourão Filho, "Relatório de Revolução Democrática Iniciada Pela 4a. RM E 4a. DI em 31 de Março de 1964," May 9, 1964, p. 3. (Copy in possession of the author.)

[44] See Chap. 5.

[45] See "O General Moniz de Aragão Faz Apêlo em Favor de União Militar," *O Estado de São Paulo*, March 27, 1964, p. 4.

feel that the government is so legitimate that it commands their *active* support.[46]

For Goulart, his staff was his *dispositivo militar,* his hand-picked men in key locations throughout the country, who in the past had been his active supporters in crises. Goulart's minister of justice, Abelardo Jurema, described, however, an angry meeting between himself and a military officer, Colonel Lino Teixeira, following the naval mutiny of March 26, which illustrates how seriously the issue of military discipline had weakened active support for Goulart:

> I was eating in a restaurant in the city . . . when I was ap-proached by Colonel Lino Teixeira. He was furious. . . . He did not understand the situation. He passionately declared his feelings of revolt, anger, and surprise, feelings he said that the pro-*Jangistas* [military favorable to Goulart] shared. He stressed that the government had lost substantially all of its military *dispositivo.* . . . He, who only yesterday had been fighting on the side of the president and the reforms, was now ready to fight alongside Carlos Lacerda [a chief plotter against Goulart] to maintain military discipline, which in his view had been irrep-arably wounded.[47]

A member of the General Staff of the army, who did not join the conspiracy against Goulart and who was subsequently purged from the army, commented: "The thing that finally was most im-portant in moving military opinion against him [Goulart] was the 'inversion of hierarchy.' Even strong *Jangistas* broke with him after the mutiny and his speech to the sergeants."[48]

Most of the strong Goulart supporters in the military did not actively join the opposition, but what was crucial was that when the government was actively challenged by the plotters, the intensity of military support for Goulart was not sufficient to prevent Gou-lart's displacement. Not one officer died defending the Goulart government.

A number of interesting questions about Goulart's political style and his fall from power remain for further analysis and research. Why did Goulart overestimate his political strength? I have already mentioned the exhilaration and disorientation he experienced after

[46] Juan Linz, *Breakdown of Democratic Regimes.*
[47] Jurema, *Sexta-Feira, 13,* pp. 162–163.
[48] Interview with General George Rocha, Rio de Janeiro, October 5, 1968.

his crowd speeches. Another clue to the extent of Goulart's estrange-
ment from the political process lies in the nature of his political
advisors. Goulart surrounded himself with men who identified
themselves with him so personally that they were unrepresentative
of the institutions they came from, and uninfluential within them.
General Assis Brasil is a classic example of a military man who
urged Goulart forward to action even though he had himself lost
touch with the military institution he supposedly represented.

A more difficult field of inquiry concerns Goulart's style of politics. Goulart talked of the need for revolution, but in the early
moments of the coup against him, when it was still by no means
certain that he would be overthrown, he personally cautioned his
military commanders to avoid bloodshed. This ambiguity and in-
decisiveness enraged his military supporters.[49]

One other area needs examination—the dimension of political
personality. Goulart had always been the subject of a "whispering
campaign" of innuendo, even among his associates. It was often
hinted he was personally and politically ineffectual. Undoubtedly
his bravado leadership of the masses filled some personal need. The
pattern of confrontation and capitulation in his career suggests that
psychological analysis would be valuable for a fuller understanding
of Goulart's political performance.[50]

THE ASSUMPTION OF POWER BY THE MILITARY

There is a large and growing literature on the revolution of
March 31, 1964, and this chapter does not intend to give a complete narrative of these events.[51] Rather, it focuses on the actual
decision by the military to take over the reins of the government.

[49] Timothy Harding, in his insightful "Revolution Tomorrow: The Failure
of the Left in Brazil," *Studies on the Left*, IV (Fall 1964), pp. 30–54, makes
a forceful case that the explanation behind this kind of ambiguity of purpose
lies in the fact that Goulart owed his political and social power to a system
which the revolution, if it came about, would have to destroy.

[50] A stimulating article indicating the utility of psychological analysis of
political styles and recurrent patterns of behavior is James David Barber's
"The President and His Friends," a paper delivered at the annual meeting
of the American Political Science Association, New York, September 2–6,
1969.

[51] Two bibliographies of the 1964 revolution already exist: Amaury de
Souza, "Março ou Abril? Uma bibliografia comentada sôbre o movimento
político de 1964 no Brasil," *Dados*, I (2° semestre, 1966), pp. 160–175;
and "Bibliografia Sôbre a Revolução de 31 de Março," *Boletim da Biblioteca
da Câmara dos Deputados*, 13:2 (July–December 1964), pp. 499–514. The

When Goulart fled the country on April 1, 1964, it was not immediately apparent to all that there could not be a caretaker civilian government headed by the constitutional successor to the president, the leader of the lower chamber, Ranieri Mazzilli, with presidential elections to be held on schedule in accordance with the rules of the game of the moderating pattern of civil–military relations. Another possibility was a caretaker military government. While a Supreme Military Command was formed on the day of Goulart's flight, the Institutional Act, which definitely signified the new role of the military and a boundary change in the political system, was not issued until April 9. Between these two dates, the significant events were as follows.

April 2 and 3: the president of the United States, with great haste and undisguised warmth, congratulated the victors of the coup, and the State Department opened up AID discussions with the Brazilian government.[52]

April 6: the Brazilian Senate voted for an indirect election by Congress in the near future to choose a president and vice-president to serve out the rest of Goulart's term before the regularly scheduled elections in 1965.

April 7: the military showed congressional leaders the draft of the Institutional Act.

April 9: the Supreme Military Command unilaterally issued the Institutional Act declaring that the revolution had legitimatized itself and granted vast new powers to the military.

April 10: the first of many lists was published cancelling the political rights of individuals.

April 11: Congress ratified the selection of General Castello Branco as president of Brazil. Thus for the first time in the twentieth century, an essentially military government came to power in Brazil.

Clearly widespread fear in the military of the destruction of their own institutional unity, and their desire to purge many actors from the political system, made the return to civilian rule unlikely. In addition, we have seen how the *Escola Superior de Guerra* had

works cited in Chap. 5, n. 1, describe the mechanics of the military movement in great detail.

[52] See Tad Szulc, "Washington Sends 'Warmest' Wishes to Brazil's Leaders," *New York Times*, April 3, 1964, and Max Frankel, "Brazil Chief Picks Aides, Rusk Promises U.S. Help," *New York Times*, April 4, 1964.

formulated development plans and had trained personnel, thus giving the military confidence in their own abilities to rule.

However, while the assumption of power by the military would undoubtedly have occurred even in the absence of civilian support, it is indicative of the state of fear and loss of confidence of much of the salaried classes and business groups, as well as of politicians of the right and the center, that many of them openly requested a temporary military president after the revolution had removed Goulart (although there was little public talk of this beforehand and most would later withdraw their support for a military government).

On April 1, the night after the revolution, the key governors who had supported the military in the overthrow of Goulart met in Rio de Janeiro. They represented all major parties except the PTB.

Governor Carlos Lacerda, who represented the UDN, wrote:

> We counted among us various candidates, declared or about to be declared, for the presidency of the Republic in the elections the military promised the country.
>
> With the exception of two of these governors, who only were convinced later, it was agreed that the head of the revolutionary government should be a military man, in order to guarantee the unity of the armed forces, to avoid eventual usurpation and avoid competition among the politicians in a delicate hour for the country.[53]

Lacerda that night called publicly for an early election of a military man as president, someone who had sufficient authority to rule the country and heal the wounds until presidential elections could be held.[54]

The powerful industrial body in São Paulo, the *Federação e Centro das Indústrias do Estado de São Paulo*, sent a telegram to the Senate, asking for the election of a military officer as president.[55] One of the country's leading newspapers, *O Estado de São Paulo*, ran an editorial arguing that a military president was needed to weed out Communists and because the country needed a man with "no political connection."[56]

[53] Carlos Lacerda, "Análise de Uma Provocação," *Tribuna da Imprensa*, August 26–27, 1967.
[54] Interview printed in the *Jornal do Brasil*, April 2, 1964.
[55] See *O Estado de São Paulo*, April 5, 1964.
[56] See *O Estado de São Paulo* editorial, April 5, 1964.

On April 3, the conservative *Sociedade Rural Brasileira* issued a manifesto essentially requesting a military man as temporary president and calling for political purges. "The revolution has just begun," it announced. On the same day, the militant anti-Communist middle-class women's Catholic group, the *União Carioca Femina* ("Union of Rio Women"), which had been instrumental in organizing the massive anti-Goulart demonstration in São Paulo on March 19, issued its own manifesto, stating that although the first battle in the revolution had been won, the revolution had to be consolidated by eliminating corruption and Communism. They specifically endorsed General Castello Branco for the presidency because he was a general "without political ties."[57]

The assumption of power by the military, however, left many questions unanswered. Which group within the military would assume the reins of leadership? What was their background? Which major socializing experiences were relevant to their attempts to govern? How did the leaders of the revolution compare with the nonactivists and those who opposed it, and what can this tell us about potential sources of consensus and cleavage within the military? What new political problems did the military have to face when it assumed power?

[57] See *O Estado de São Paulo*, April 4, 1964.

PART IV

The Brazilian Military in Power,
1964–1968: A Case Study
of the Political Problems of
Military Government

TRADITIONALLY, many political moralists and analysts have looked at the role of the military in politics from the viewpoint of the threat it presents to democratic processes and national economic development.[1] However, the magnitude of the problems faced by developing nations and the weakness of civilian institutions in coping with these problems have led a revisionist school of writers to emphasize that the organizational and technological features of the military can make it a powerful instrument in the process of political and economic development.[2]

Brazil provided a particularly appropriate test case[3] of the po-

[1] The literature is vast. Some of the more typical writings are: Herbert Spencer, *The Principles of Sociology* (New York: D. Appleton & Company, 1900), II, 568–642, where he argues the systematic opposition of militarism to industrialism; Alexis de Tocqueville, *Democracy in America*, pp. 317–329; Edwin Lieuwen, *Arms and Politics in Latin America* (New York: Frederick A. Praeger, 1960), which sums up the attack on the role of the military in Latin America.

[2] Some of the most influential contributors to this reformulation were Guy Pauker, "Southeast Asia as a Problem Area in the Next Decade," *World Politics*, XI (April 1959), 325–345; Lucian W. Pye, "Armies in the Process of Political Modernization," in *The Role of the Military in Underdeveloped Countries*, ed. John J. Johnson (Princeton: Princeton University Press, 1962), pp. 69–90; and for Latin America, John J. Johnson, *The Military and Society in Latin America* (Stanford, Calif.: Stanford University Press, 1964).

[3] Clearly no "test case" is definitive. Some military governments have met with more success than others. But while almost all military regimes claim to be preparing the way for an eventual return to a stronger, develop-

213

tentialities of military government because so many observers, Brazilian as well as foreign, were initially very optimistic about the chances that the Brazilian military government would use its power to contribute rationally to economic and political development. The United States government in particular, as we have seen, made a major financial and political commitment to the Brazilian military regime.

Part IV is a discussion of the first years of military government in Brazil within this context. It is primarily a study of the new requirements that are made of a military institution when it relinquishes its traditional moderator role for that of executive rule. I do not present in Part IV a "military-power model" for the 1964–1968 period and test hypotheses derived from such a model, as I did in my earlier discussion of the moderating pattern of civil-military relations, because nothing close to what could be called a model was actually established. Rather I have tried to assess the often underestimated or overlooked political problems that a military regime faces before it can achieve some form of reasonable stability and coherence in direction of policy, and generate and institutionalize sources of support besides military force.

In this section, therefore, my major purpose has not been to evaluate in detail the social and political outcome of the policies of the military government since 1964. To make such an evaluation would be a gigantic and important task, but much of the necessary information, such as reliable data on income redistribution, is not yet available.[4] There is no doubt that, despite the high economic growth achieved in Brazil between 1968 and 1970, there has been a general "demobilization" of all mass, change-oriented movements, such as the peasant league, the land-reform and trade-union movements, and the adult literacy movements such as MEB. It appears also that the lower classes have borne the brunt of the fiscal stabilization policy. In addition, political and intellectual repression, including the widespread use of torture, has marked the military

---

mentally oriented government, virtually no military regime has been able to create a functioning political party and to supervise the transition to open, democratic politics. The major exception to this was the creation of the Republican party in Turkey.

[4] Such an evaluation is now being attempted by a group of American and Brazilian scholars, of which the author is a member. The group hopes to publish its conclusions in a book in 1972.

government from the beginning and has increased in the 1968–1970 period.

My main concern in Part IV, however, has been to study the process of military government as it affected the internal organization and purposes of the military institution itself, and to analyze the ability of a military institution to govern. I have used the Brazilian experience of military government between 1964 and 1968 to question and challenge some of the basic assumptions underlying the revisionist interpretations of the military—particularly the assumption that for organizational reasons a military government is less subject to some of the weaknesses most characteristic of civilian governments. The revisionist interpretations of the military as an instrument of development are based more on a series of assumptions about the "unity," "continuity of policy," "monopoly of force," and "stability" of military governments than on actual case studies of military regimes in power.[5] By evaluating these assumptions in the case of one country, I hope to suggest an alternative mode of analysis that will facilitate investigation of other countries.

[5] The actual consequences of military rule are a neglected area of research. Two important attempts to assess the political skills of military governments are Morris Janowitz, *The Military in the Political Development of New Nations* (Chicago: The University of Chicago Press, 1964), and Henry Bienen, ed., *The Military Intervenes: Case Studies in Political Development* (New York: Russell Sage Foundation, 1968).

Chapter 10

The Military in Power: First Political Decisions and Problems

INTRODUCTION

From the coup of April 1, 1964, until the Fifth Institutional Act of December 13, 1968, the Brazilian military found that an internal process had been at work which had broadened their level of involvement and narrowed the base of their support. By December 1968, the military government of tutelary democracy had, in fact, become an open military dictatorship, while the military as an institution had become deeply divided and split. Everything indicated that the military was being carried toward even more authoritarian rule and a deeper involvement in all areas of Brazilian life, and that most of their initial options for extrication from government and phasing out from power were closing off. Why did this happen? What does it illustrate about the political problems of military government? What new political requirements did the military have to cope with that they did not have in the old moderating pattern of civil–military relations?

ORIGINAL MILITARY GOALS

When the military removed President João Goulart from power in April 1964 and assumed it themselves, there was no widely shared plan as to what the major political objectives would be. This was in part deliberate. Before the coup there had been a conscious desire to avoid debate over issues that would have made it more difficult to put together a winning coup coalition.[1] Immediately after the coup, many officers feared that debate might risk military splits and even precipitate a countercoup by the Goulart forces.[2] The major themes heard among the military shortly after

---

[1] This point was made in interviews with several organizers of the coup.
[2] When Goulart left Brazil on April 2, 1964, he claimed he would return to power within a month because the generals would quarrel among themselves. The most feared opponent of the revolution, Brizola, was still in

the coup were therefore vague: the need to control "the Communists," to contain inflation and to implement the minimal political and economic reforms seen as a prerequisite for a return to civilian government some time in the future.

General Castello Branco, chief of the General Staff of the army, was given widespread support by the civilian and military coup leaders in the indirect presidential election in Congress on April 11, 1964. Paradoxically (but predictably) much support for Castello's assumption of the highest *political* office in the land came precisely because of his reputation for being *apolitical*. The military liked his excellent combat record, his academic achievement, and his record of abstention from partisan politics.[3] The civilians found him attractive because of their desire to have a strong apolitical president in charge, who could supervise the return to open elections.

It was also known that Castello Branco had been closely associated with the Superior War College, where development and security problems had been analyzed in a more systematic fashion than elsewhere within the military. When faced with the new challenge of running the nation in the confusion following the coup, the military initially turned to Castello Branco and the officers who had served on the staff of the Superior War College because they appeared to have a set of ideas. However, very few people, not even the president, realized the political implications of attempting to transfer these general ideas into concrete policy.[4]

As president of Brazil, Castello Branco at first pledged himself to hold presidential elections on schedule in 1965. While the question of elections was superficially settled, the military leaders of the

---

Brazil; concerned about a counterattack if they were divided, the generals held a meeting and agreed that unity was the most important factor, and for this reason they would all back one candidate for president. An account of this is found in José Stacchini, *Março 64: Mobilização da Audácia* (São Paulo: Companhia Editôra Nacional, 1965), pp. 128–129.

[3] He was the highly decorated operations officer of the Brazilian Expeditionary Force that fought in Italy in World War II, and he graduated first in his class at two service schools and was a graduate of the General Staff School in France.

[4] This account is based largely on discussions with both civilian and military participants. Various participants have also published their versions. See Carlos Lacerda, "Análise de uma Provocação," *Tribuna da Imprensa*, August 26–27, 1967, p. 1, and Mauro Borges, *O Golpe em Goiás* (Rio de Janeiro: Editôra Civilização Brasileira, 1965), pp. 109–119.

coup clearly also felt that their goals could not be implemented by civilians and that the military would have to provide a major support or prop for reforms, at least from the sidelines.

In the period immediately after the revolution three decisions were taken which were to have far-ranging impact on the nature of the military government. The first was to cancel the political rights of many of the military and political enemies of the coup for a period of ten years by means of an Institutional Act.[5] This decision in essence implied the renunciation of any short-term caretaker or transitional military government, for the military needed to retain sufficient power to enforce this ban.

The second decision was to impose a strict stabilization and development policy.[6] The cabinet felt that no civilian politician would have the will or the power to implement such a policy. They also felt that economic payoffs from the stabilization policy would not be visible for at least five years. As the electoral implications of this became evident, pressure grew to postpone elections. The military began to feel that they could not allow completely free elections until 1970 at the earliest.[7]

Finally, while accepting a large share of the responsibility for the revolution and recognizing the need for institutional support for the revolutionary government, most of the military leaders rejected the idea of government by a single strong man. One reason for this latter decision was the determination to maintain some semblance of democratic legitimacy by obeying the constitutional require-

[5] This First Institutional Act was published in the *Diário Oficial* of April 9, 1964, with a list of 100 names. These lists are still appearing. A good description of the tensions leading up to the issuance of the act is found in the congressional debate of April 9, especially the speech of Juarez Távora reported in the *O Estado de São Paulo*, April 10, 1964, p. 5.

[6] The chief economic architect of the plan was Roberto Campos. It is often erroneously assumed that the military had no economic ideas, and for this reason gave Campos *carte blanche*. A more correct interpretation is that Campos had been a frequent lecturer at the ESG for ten years before the coup; the staff of the ESG liked his ideas and incorporated them into much of the ESG philosophy. The major political thinker of the ESG, General Golbery do Couto e Silva, concurred with this interpretation in an interview in Rio on October 8, 1968. The basic development plan is contained in Brasil, Ministério do Planejamento e Coordenação Econômico, *Programa de Ação Econômica do Govêrno, 1964–1966* (Rio de Janeiro, 1965).

[7] These aspects of economic policy were underscored by the minister of planning in the Castello Branco government, Roberto Campos, in an interview in Rio de Janeiro, September 15, 1967.

ments of a fixed presidential mandate with no second term. In addition, the first military president, Castello Branco, was firmly against any extension of his rule. In the words of one of his closest ministers, Roberto Campos, President Castello Branco "wanted to build institutions. He felt that, in the circumstances, he was of necessity authoritarian, but that it was not necessary to be personalistic. Continuity of ideas and structure was needed, but not of people."[8]

Despite the institutional implications of these decisions and the demands by many of the younger officers that the revolution be pushed further by more purges and more radical restructuring of the political and economic systems, most senior military officers assumed that the military as an institution would be able by 1966 or 1967 to extricate itself slowly from political power.

THE EROSION OF THE CIVIL–MILITARY COALITION OF 1964—ASYMMETRY OF GOALS

One of the forces giving some legitimacy to the military's removal of President Goulart from office had been the support of civilian politicians. Particularly important was the support of the governors of the three most powerful states in the union, Governor Adhemar de Barros of São Paulo, Governor Carlos Lacerda of Guanabara, and Governor Magalhães Pinto of Minas Gerais. All three governors were presidential candidates for elections scheduled in 1964. A major reason for their support of the 1964 coup against Goulart was their fear, as candidates, that Goulart was moving toward a *Peronista* coup that would result in the cessation of normal politics, and elimination, therefore, of their own chances at the presidency.

This type of civilian support for a military coup is, however, largely untranslatable into support for a military government. As it became clear that the military were not going to allow presidential elections for a long time, these governors became some of their most outspoken critics in the period between 1964 and 1966. Indeed, a major loss of civilian support began to occur almost immediately after military officers assumed the reins of government. This was an almost inevitable development owing to the fact

---

[8] Interview with Roberto Campos, *ibid.* The best analysis of the Castello Branco model of government is Cândido Mendes, "Sistema Político e Modelos de Poder no Brasil," *Dados*, no. 1 (2° semestre, 1966), pp. 7–41.

that the goals of the civilians and the military in engineering a coup against Goulart were quite different.

Once in power, the military's own view of the revolutionary but nonpolitical nature of their goals for Brazilian development also led them deliberately to eliminate some of their civilian support. The military leaders felt that part of their legitimacy as a government arose from their revolutionary mission to purge the political system of corruption and subversion. Several of the original civilian supporters of the coup in 1964 were themselves viewed as being part of this "corruption." The presidential candidate for the Social Progressive Party (*Partido Social Progressista*, PSP), for example, was the famous and populist governor of São Paulo, Adhemar de Barros. Though his support had at first been extremely helpful to the military, they came to feel that his association with the revolution deprived it of the legitimacy it had earned as an "anticorruption" force, and that Adhemar's own political base in the powerful state of São Paulo was a threat to the military's desire for national control of the federal political system. In July 1966, the government proscribed his participation in politics for ten years, making him one of the *cassados*.[9] The vastly popular ex-President Kubitschek, who had been instrumental in arranging the support of the Social Democratic Party (*Partido Social Democrático*, PSD) for the selection of Castello Branco in the indirect election, was also *cassado* on charges of corruption.

Likewise, some important support from the left was also refused because the military felt it incompatible with their antisubversion goals. The young governor of Goiás, Mauro Borges Teixeira, was a leader of the nationalist-reformist wing of the Social Democratic Party. His active backing of the military coup and his participation in the selection process of President Castello Branco had added a useful element of reformist support in March and April, 1964. However, the military's excessively broad definition of subversion led them to remove him from his governorship and to take away his political rights by December 1964, despite the fact that he was a former army officer.[10]

[9] For a brief description in English of his career, see his obituary in the *New York Times*, March 14, 1969, p. 41.

[10] Mauro Borges' own account of these events is found in his *O Golpe Em Goiás*, pp. 105–172. As in the case of Adhemar de Barros, an important element of the conflict was the military's desire to reduce the power of the states' political machines.

The purging of civilians continued from 1964 on as the military struggled with the burdens of government and increasingly attempted to control all forms of civilian criticism which it felt presented a threat to military morale and unity. A series of decrees was issued between 1967 and 1969 which made it a punishable offense publicly to discredit the military.[11]

The support of much of the press was lost fairly quickly after the military took over the government. As we saw in Part II, many of the major newspapers, such as the *Correio da Manhã, Jornal do Brasil, Diário de Notícias, O Estado de São Paulo, Tribuna da Imprensa, O Jornal,* and *O Globo,* had accorded very low legitimacy to Goulart's activities as president by late March 1964. They also had accorded a high degree of legitimacy to the military to perform their traditional role of checking the president. However, we also pointed out that none of these papers had explicitly urged the military to assume permanent power themselves. A sharp distinction was made between support for the coup and support for the greatly expanded role of the military in politics that followed the coup. Shortly after the revolution, the *Correio da Manhã* attacked the authoritarian assumption of power by the military, and later the *Tribuna da Imprensa,* as an organ for Carlos Lacerda, echoed his charge that the military had betrayed the revolution by failing to return the government to civilian authority. By December 1968, the military felt it necessary to impose the strongest press censorship in Brazil's history since the semifascist *Estado Nôvo* regime of 1937–1945. The publisher of the *Correio da Manhã* and the editor of the *Jornal do Brasil* were temporarily imprisoned in the aftermath of the Fifth Institutional Act of December 13, 1968.

THE ANTICOUP GROUP AND THE PROBLEM OF EXTRICATION

The political process of a coup is quite different from and much simpler than the political process involved in governing. The new pattern of civil–military relations that emerged after the revolution of 1964 put new and more difficult requirements on the military as an institution.

The moderating pattern of civil–military relations merely called on the military to achieve the minimal level of "crisis consensus"

[11] In March 1969 these laws were increased in severity and private statements against the military also became punishable acts. For the 1969 laws, see the *New York Times,* March 22, 1969.

to allow them to remove a president and hand over power to the most politically legitimate civilian successor. In 1930, for example, Getúlio Vargas, who probably had been defrauded of electoral victory in the election, received power after a broadly based revolution had been launched. As we have seen, almost immediately after the coup of 1945 power was given to the chief justice, in 1954 it was given to the vice-president, and in 1955 to the next in line for constitutional succession, the speaker of the Senate.

In 1964, however, given the widespread belief among military officers that no civilian could solve the crisis, the military were faced, institutionally, with the problem of sustained action for a number of years rather than a number of days, and this in turn required a degree of unity which had not been demanded before. In addition, whereas in the moderating pattern there had been no need to achieve agreement on a program, there would be such a requirement if the military were to stay in power as a purposeful governing force for a number of years.

These two new major requirements—the need for sustained unity and the need for a widely shared program—set up new political problems for the military. Their failure to solve them was largely responsible for the developments that led them to close off their option of withdrawing from government and to move toward increasing authoritarianism and increasing internal disunity.

Once a military regime has made the decision to retain political power it must face the additional problem of what to do with the officers opposing the original coup. There is a tension here between the unity necessary to rule, and the need to maintain a posture that will allow the military to extricate itself eventually from power.

From 1945 to 1964, the military in Brazil had not had to deal with this problem directly because a winning coalition of military officers had to be maintained only for the short time needed to transfer power from one civilian to another. There had been almost no purges of officers opposing the decision to initiate coups. Groups within the military who had opposed the coups were usually transferred away from the centers of power,[12] and their promotions slowed or halted.[13] But officers were not usually removed from the

[12] For example, Nelson Werneck Sodré mentions the transfer of the major left-wing nationalist opposing the 1954 coup in his *História Militar do Brasil* (Rio de Janeiro: Editôra Civilização Brasileira, 1965), pp. 355–357.

[13] For example, in 1955, the staff of the ESG symbolized military resistance

222

service; they remained within it, and if a president of their own political persuasion came into office, they often received rapid promotions.

After the 1964 coup, however, the need for sustained institutional unity, and the need to form a policy that would get strong military backing, led the military away from the traditional attitude of compromise with anticoup activists and toward a purging of these officers as counterrevolutionary threats. On April 11, 1964, 122 officers were formally expelled from the military. Formal expulsions continued throughout the year.[14] In addition, many officers were informally warned that because of their "weak" revolutionary attitude, they would never receive another promotion. This was a deliberate attempt to pressure dissident officers into resigning.

By these means, the antirevolutionary officers were effectively purged from the military. For example, of the 29 officers appointed to the rank of general by Goulart before 1964, only five were listed as being on active duty in the 1968 officers' register.[15] This is clearly largely a politically related attrition-rate, because 17 of the 29 generals who were immediately senior in the promotion lists to the "Goulart" group were still listed in the 1968 register as on active duty. Of these generals still on active duty in 1968, the pre-Goulart generals had received an aggregate of 22 promotions while the Goulart-appointed generals had received an aggregate of only three promotions.[16]

The attempt to solve the question of unity by purging antirevolutionary officers as well as politicians created a new set of problems for the military, and of necessity extended the military's involvement further than they realized at the time.

The majority of the senior military leaders in power between 1964 and 1965 felt that the military would be able to extricate themselves from politics gradually, possibly by allowing a civilian

---

to Kubitschek and Goulart. After the preventive coup of November 11, almost all of the major figures of the ESG were transferred and some of them temporarily arrested. Interview with General Heitor Almeida Herrera in Rio de Janeiro, August 27, 1968. General Almeida was on the ESG staff in 1955. Most of these men received very slow promotions until after the coup of 1964 when they received rapid promotions.

[14] See *Diário Oficial* of April 11 and 14, June 13, September 24 and 28, and October 7 and 8, 1964.

[15] This is based on a study of the dates of promotion as listed in the *Almanaque do Exército*, 1964 and 1968 editions.

[16] *Ibid.*

closely identified with their goals to assume the presidency in 1967, and to phase out completely by 1974, when political rights would be restored to the *cassados* at the end of their ten-year ban.[17] However, the expulsion of a major group of politicians from the political arena, men such as Kubitschek, Arraes, and Brizola, who were viewed by much of the electorate as popular and legitimate participants in the political system, presented a dilemma to the military. On the one hand, if the military withdrew from politics, these politicians could be expected to reenter politics strengthened by their years of political martyrdom and untarnished by the shortcomings of those who had the responsibility for governing. More importantly, the military assumed that these men would be hostile to them. On the other hand, if the military did not accept the inevitable return of these politicians to politics and to positions of power, the military would have to retain power themselves or stay in readiness in the wings to enforce their veto.

In Argentina this tension between the desire to withdraw eventually from politics and the desire to restrict the reentry into politics of major groups of contenders for power has been at the heart of the cycle of military withdrawal and reentry since the overthrow of Perón in 1955. There the military has attempted to return governmental power to civilians, but at the same time to restrict the return of the *Peronistas*. The unresolved tension between these two desires contributed to the reassumption of power by the military in 1962 and 1966.[18]

In Brazil, the problem of extrication was made especially complicated by the purge of military officers. Any general amnesty extended by politicians after a return to liberalization would have presented the threat to the military of the return to the ranks of many of the officers purged in 1964 and after. In many instances, the most vocal advocates of the purges, and the middle-level interrogators on the severe and often arbitrary military investigating committees that meted out revolutionary justice, were only captains

[17] This statement is based on numerous discussions in Brazil with military officers about military extrication strategy. It was clear that they had not systematically considered the question between 1964 and 1966 and had underestimated the problem.

[18] In his discussion of the options facing military regimes, Samuel Huntington similarly refers to this aspect of the Argentine case as the "return and restrict" option. See his *Political Order in Changing Societies* (New Haven: Yale University Press, 1968), pp. 233–234.

and majors, while their victims were senior colonels and junior generals. The possible return of the purged officers in the future presented a built-in institutional obstacle to amnesty.

Largely for these reasons, political amnesty was the greatest fear of the military. For example, in a poll among the São Paulo graduates of the ESG in the period of transition between President Castello Branco and President Costa e Silva, the alumni association was asked what were the areas of most and least success in the revolution, and what types of changes they would like to have implemented by the second government of the revolution. The one point on which there was most agreement was that amnesty was unacceptable.[19] Yet any successful extrication strategy required coming to terms with the political and military forces previously banned. The relative success of the Turkish military in extricating themselves from power between 1961 and 1965 lay precisely in their recognition and treatment of this problem.[20]

Another political problem created by any widespread dismissal of regular army officers is that these resentful and often underemployed specialists in violence (underemployed because of the nontransferability of military skills and/or because civilian employers fear government displeasure) often become available to movements attempting to disrupt or overthrow the military regime.[21] In Brazil, in 1922, for example, there was a purge of *tenentes* from the army: the expelled group formed a body of revolutionary activists engaged in sporadic plotting until, in conjunction with dissatisfied traditional politicians, they led the revolution of 1930. From 1945 to 1964, the military did not undertake a similar purge, but in doing so in 1964, they laid open the possibility of recreating the events of the 1920s. While this has not happened so far (1970)

[19] See "Situação Nacional Configura," *O Estado de São Paulo*, April 30, 1967, p. 6.

[20] Conversation with Professor Ciro E. Zoppo of the University of California at Los Angeles. Interesting analyses of the strategy of Turkish military extrication can also be found in Ergun Özbudun, *The Role of the Military in Recent Turkish Politics*, Occasional Papers in International Affairs, no. 14 (Cambridge: Harvard University, Center for International Affairs, 1966); and Nur Yalman, "Intervention and Extrication: The Officer Corps in the Turkish Crisis," in *The Military Intervenes*, ed. Henry Bienen (New York: Russell Sage Foundation, 1968), pp. 127–144.

[21] Juan Linz develops this theme in "The Breakdown of Democratic Regimes" (paper prepared for the Seventh World Congress of Sociology, Varna, Bulgaria, September 14–19, 1970).

on a large scale in Brazil, there are frequent references to ex-military officers involved in small rural and urban guerrilla groups.

THE NARROWING OF THE MILITARY COUP-LEADERS' COALITION

The banning of civilian or open politics does not abolish the necessity for making political choices. Political decisions and conflict about policies or personal power are simply transferred to the military, and the unity achieved at the time of a coup is sharply challenged. What is clear, indeed, is that military rule is not an effective method of banning the much maligned "divisiveness of politics."

The execution of a military coup before 1964 involved military action for a short time after a winning coalition of civilians and military had been established. In such crisis situations, groups and individuals who did not normally cooperate or share political or developmental perspectives cooperated briefly. The shortness of time and the lack of any need for programmatic action minimized splits and tensions among the coup leaders.

When the military took over the responsibility of governing Brazil in 1964, the alliance brought together at the original time of crisis became subject to strains almost immediately. The process of formulating a policy and establishing a coherent executive group resulted in the relative exclusion from the centers of power of those coup leaders who did not share the basic orientation of the president and his closest advisors. Many of those who actively participated in preparations for the coup or the execution of the revolution, but who were later not included in the inner circles of the government, turned strongly against the government and became damaging and effective critics of military rule. Examples abound.

The first general actually to move troops and start the revolution was General Olympio Mourão Filho. Although he was a revolutionary activist, he was emotionally and intellectually out of tune with the governing elite that emerged after 1964.[22] He did not receive either the command of the politically strategic First Army headquartered in Rio or the presidency of *Petrobrás*. He rapidly

[22] As we shall see, most of this elite had strong roots in the ESG. In an interview with journalists from a large-circulation popular magazine, Mourão Filho said he had declined an opportunity to attend the ESG in 1961 because he disagreed with its ideas. See "Autocrítica de Olympio Mourão Filho," *Manchete*, January 7, 1966, pp. 29–31.

became a critic of President Castello Branco and made overtures to obtain the presidential candidacy of the MDB (*Movimento Democrático Brasileiro*) opposition party. A constant theme of his criticism was that the true revolution of 1964 had been mutilated by subsequent developments.[23] He attacked the provision of the Second Institutional Act which called for the selection of the president by indirect election, and from his privileged position as president of the Supreme Military Court, in a keynote address on the new National Security Law, he urged resistance to the law which "had its roots in the philosophy of national security of the Superior War College." He added, "Either the Brazilian people will react against the Law of National Security or they will become slaves for at least fifty years."[24]

General Amaury Kruel, as commander of the powerful Second Army of São Paulo, had been a reluctant but crucial last-minute adherent to the revolution of 1964. He attempted to become president in the indirect elections of April 1964, and by early 1965 was arguing that the real enemy of Brazil lay within the revolutionary movement itself.[25] He later made political overtures for the presidency and a state governorship, and finally was disciplined for resigning his command without authorization. In 1967, he was elected as an alternate federal deputy of the opposition party.

The commanding officer of the Fourth Army, General Justino Alves Bastos, who dominated the northeast after the revolution and who took pride in calling himself the "hardest" of the hard line officers, later sharply shifted course when the restrictive military-sponsored election laws were used to frustrate his own candidacy for the governorship of Rio Grande do Sul. He called the law a "monstrosity" and attacked the economic austerity program of the regime saying that "the poor people have never been so poor." He was removed from his command of the Third Army in Pôrto Alegre in 1966.[26]

General Pery Constant Bevilaqua, whose strong condemnation

---

[23] "We did not leave Juiz da Fora [the starting point of the revolution] on March 31 to annul, mutilate, or sacrifice the constitution of 1946." See "Mourão Ataca Castello e Preconiza um Plebiscito," *O Estado de São Paulo*, July 26, 1966.

[24] "Mourão vê Morte de Liberdade na Lei de Segurança Nacional," *Jornal do Brasil*, March 16, 1967.

[25] See *Jornal do Brasil*, January 30, 1965.

[26] See various stories describing this incident in the *Jornal do Brasil* of March 19 and 20, 1966.

227

of the sergeants' revolt of September 1963 and of the Goulart government's toleration of sergeant indiscipline had helped prepare the climate for the 1964 revolution, later condemned the regime which he said had turned the country into a "huge barracks." He said the National Security Law was "equivalent to a permanent state of siege and constitutes a threat to the people that they do not merit."[27]

Another activist in the coup was General Poppe de Figueiredo who, though originally a strong nationalist supporter of Kubitschek, turned against Goulart through fear of Communism. He felt insulted at not being offered the command of the Third Army. Later, when he was passed over for promotion, he accused the ruling group within the military of only promoting its own supporters. He resigned from the army saying that he had lost hope that the revolution would ever install in Brazil a nationalist democratic regime.[28]

Even some members of the core group within the government became involved in conflicts over their political ambitions. General Muricy, though he identified intellectually and politically with the Castello Branco government, almost broke with the government at their frustration of his ambitions to run for a governorship.

Other instances could be enumerated, but it is clear that the abolition of open politics by the military had a tendency to turn the competition between ideas and for jobs into an intramilitary conflict. The crisis coalition of 1964 brought together all those who felt the military was threatened, but this coalition was not sustainable as a governing coalition. The key participants in the 1964 revolution who were not included in the inner circle of the government became a national focus for the expression of discontent. This discontent was especially damaging to military unity because the spokesmen had established "revolutionary" credentials. Civilians who disagreed with the government lionized the military dissenters as the "loyal opposition" and attempted to play them off against the government.

In the face of these strains on military government, the success of the strategy of the Castello Branco government became dependent on its ability to win wide acceptance for its ideas within the military as a whole, to control the succession of the next military president, and to maintain military unity.

[27] See "Pery vê País em Sítio Permanente," *Jornal do Brasil*, March 17, 1967, and "Pery: País é Imenso Quartel," *Fôlha de São Paulo*, January 18, 1967.
[28] For various related stories, see *Jornal do Brasil*, December 1, 1965.

Chapter 11

Military Unity and Military Succession:
An Elite Analysis of
the Castello Branco Government

INTRODUCTION

As noted previously, many social scientists believe the military can be an especially effective instrument of development. Their argument rests on various assumptions, especially the assumptions of the monopoly of force and organizational unity. From these, it is argued, flow the strengths and stability of government and the *continuity of policy* that allow the military to implement the necessary but politically difficult development policies.

Prima facie, the military appears to have a "monopoly of force" in most societies. The military organizational structure, its arms and communication equipment, seem to endow it with a "high potential for control." But this image can be very misleading. As Robert Dahl has pointed out, just because there is high potential for control, it cannot be assumed there is actual control.[1] Actual control requires an operational unity which in turn depends upon "an agreement on a key political alternative and some set of specific implementing actions."[2]

Military unity, however, is weakest in regard to such "specific implementing actions" and detailed political and economic development policies, because these normally lie outside the professional domain of the officers, and as such, outside the realm of unquestioning obedience or established military doctrine.

Military unity, on the other hand, is strongest when one of its central principles, such as military discipline, is threatened from the outside. But there are no "rules of the book" in the military for complex political decisions, any more than there are for civilians. Furthermore, by their institutional structure and training, the mili-

[1] See his "A Critique of the Ruling Elite Model," *American Political Science Review*, no. 52 (June 1958), esp. pp. 463–469.
[2] *Ibid.*

tary are not even as well equipped as civilians for the bargaining, persuasion, compromises, and dialogues that are necessary for creating consensus in the absence of a doctrine.

It is logical to expect that in military regimes where the question of succession is involved (as was the case in Brazil from the inception of the revolutionary government of Castello Branco, who rejected one-man rule), continuity of policy, far from being ensured, is often jeopardized when one military government succeeds another. In Part I, I argued that military institutions are open to conflicting political pressures. Therefore, in the absence of a shared doctrine, differences among military officers can influence their political perceptions and policies. These differences may be rooted in their personalities, their regional and socioeconomic backgrounds, their branches of military service, their past political involvements with the resulting allies and enemies, or their major career-experiences, such as belonging to a special wartime unit or setting up an important new school. Such sources of policy conflict are just below the surface in most military regimes. In this chapter we shall examine in detail the policy discontinuity of the Brazilian military regime, giving special emphasis to internal ideological differences.

THE FIRST AND SECOND GOVERNMENTS OF THE REVOLUTION: DISCONTINUITY OF POLICY

The Brazilian military in the period 1963 to 1964 had developed a low level of agreement based on anti-Communism, anticorruption, an opposition to mobilization politics, and a desire for economic growth. This consensus, coupled with the feeling that the military organization was threatened, led to the deposing of João Goulart in 1964. But could the unity of the Brazilian military elite survive implementation of a consistent policy once in government? Was there a consensus, for example, on the following hard questions. Should private foreign capital be used to help overcome investment and technological shortages in Brazil, or should the government lean toward a more nationalist and autarchic policy? How would the low-level agreement on Communism get translated into policy? Did an effective strategy call for the military to become more nationalistic and incorporate the Communists' strongest programmatic points, or did it call for an aggressive anti-Communism that would involve an internationalist foreign policy and alliance with the United States? What should the military government do once in power? Should there be a "tutelary democracy" preparing the way for an eventual return to democratic government, or should the military seize the opportunity to use authoritarian power radically to restructure the political and economic system of the country? Should political purging be minimal or should it be a major means of political control?

The stability of policy in the future was to turn to a large extent upon how the first government of the revolution, headed by President Castello Branco, answered these questions. The acceptance of Branco's policy decisions by the second government of the revolution, under Costa e Silva, depended on the degree to which the major policies and orientations of the first government were shared by the military as a whole. The Castello Branco government of 1964–1967 instituted many new policies.[8] Four characteristics of the government were: (1) an active, anti-Communist foreign policy based on the interdependence of the free world; (2) a preference for a semi-free-enterprise economic system supported and guided by a strong central government; (3) a dislike and distrust of "irrational nationalism" and an emphasis on "realistic and technical" solutions; and (4) an intellectual commitment to democracy that accepted the practical necessity of temporary tutelage.

What were some of the more specific policies that flowed from these general beliefs and attitudes?

The foreign policy of the Castello Branco government was rooted in the cold-war perspective that

in the present context of a bipolar power confrontation with a radical political and ideological divorce between the two respective centers, the preservation of independence presupposes the acceptance of a degree of interdependence, whether in the military, economic, or political fields.

In the Brazilian case, in foreign policy [we] cannot forget that we have made a basic option which stems from cultural and political fidelity to the Western democratic system.

[8] My purpose is not to discuss these policies in detail—which would require another study—but to look at basic attitudes and beliefs lying behind them. A first attempt to describe these policies is Max G. Manwaring's "The Military in Brazilian Politics" (Ph.D. diss., Department of Political Science, University of Illinois, 1968), chap. 8, "Economic and Social Policy of the Revolutionary Government," and chap. 9, "Political Reform and Military Policy."

231

The interests of Brazil coincide, in many cases, in concentric circles with Latin America, the American continent and the Western community.[4]

Given this orientation, the growing trend toward neutralism of the Quadros and Goulart governments was reversed because neutralism was "emotionally immature" and a "flight from international reality."[5] The United States, as a strong anti-Communist force, was seen as an ally, and nationalistic attacks within Brazil on the United States as a threat to this ally. Criticisms of the United States were taken to be virtually equivalent to subversion of Brazilian national security.

These beliefs (classic ESG doctrines) led the Castello Branco government to seek political, economic, and military partnership with the United States. This feeling of shared interests was warmly reciprocated by United States officials and was responsible for the growth of the USAID mission from a mere holding action in the last months of the Goulart government to the largest mission in the world after those in Vietnam and India in the period of Castello Branco. This also explains why Brazil sent the largest foreign contingent to the Dominican Republic in 1965, and led the campaign for the initiation of an inter-American peacekeeping force.[6]

Domestically, in the field of economics the Castello Branco government favored strong and rational planning to strengthen the mixed, free-enterprise system, the elimination of inflation by government control of the cost-push wage spiral, and the elimination of the inflationary demand-pull created by government deficits. The government felt that some nationalized industries operating at a deficit could be handled better by the private sector. *Loide*, the

[4] From a speech by Castello Branco at the Brazilian Foreign Ministry, July 31, 1964, printed in Ministério das Relações Exteriores, *A Política da Revolução Brasileira* (1966), no pagination.

[5] *Ibid.*

[6] The most succinct statement of the foreign and domestic policy of the Castello Branco government is contained in Castello Branco's penultimate address as president, "Segurança e Desenvolvimento," delivered at the ESG and printed verbatim in *Correio da Manhã*, March 14, 1967, p. 14.

A characteristically strong defense of the economic policy and democratic intention of the Brazilian government and of the high level of U.S. aid is given by former U.S. Ambassador Lincoln Gordon to the U.S. Senate Committee on Foreign Relations, *Nomination of Lincoln Gordon to be Assistant Secretary of State for Inter-American Affairs*, 89th Cong., 2nd sess., February 7, 1966.

coastal shipping company, for example, was sold for these reasons.[7] Negotiations were also started to sell the largely nationalized truck manufacturing company, *Fábrica Nacional de Motores*.[8] Foreign private capital was welcomed to help develop Brazil's potential, and the previous prohibition on foreign development of Brazil's huge but unexploited iron-ore deposits was reversed.[9]

Fiscal reforms based on tax procedure were the preferred solution to the problems of creation of government revenue, of redistribution of wealth, and of increased production.[10] The Land Reform Act was typical. The military government's suppression of most of the peasant leagues shored up the position of the large landowners by removing pressures for root-and-branch reform. Nonetheless the Castello Branco government hoped to modernize the agrarian sector by means of tax mechanisms. A carefully executed land-use study was first conducted, and then tax assessment rates were levied, based on maximum rational productivity. The new tax level was designed to force landowners either to be more productive or to sell their lands.[11] In most of these reforms, continuity of policy was essential before the policies could show dividends.[12]

The attack by the government on what it called "pseudonation-

[7] Interview with the former minister of transportation in the Castello Branco government, Marshal Juarez Távora, Rio de Janeiro, October 8, 1968.

[8] The company was sold eventually to Alfa-Romeo of Italy.

[9] Some, but not all, members of the cabinet wanted to allow private and foreign capital a role in the development of oil, traditionally the exclusive domain of the nationalized oil monopoly, *Petrobrás*. Nationalist sentiment in Brazil and in the armed forces was so strong, however, that the government eventually decided not to push the matter but left it an open question for future consideration.

[10] See Brasil, Ministério do Planejamento e Coordenação Econômica, *Programa de Ação Econômica do Govêrno 1964–1966*, 2nd ed., EPEA, no. 1 (May 1965), chap. x.

[11] Interview with Paulo Assis Ribeiro, a major formulator of the Land Reform Act and first president of the government agency in charge of the law, *Instituto Brasileiro de Reforma Agrária*, IBRA, Rio de Janeiro, September 4, 1968.

[12] Much of this analysis of the economic policy is based on interviews with the minister of planning and coordination, Roberto Campos. The development plan is contained in Brasil, *Programa de Ação Econômica do Govêrno 1964–1966*. The Berkeley-USAID team of advisors to the Ministry of Planning from 1964 to 1968 analyze the economic policy in *The Economy of Brazil*, ed. Howard Ellis (Berkeley: University of California Press, 1969).

233

alism" was one of the most pronounced characteristics of the Castello Branco government. Castello Branco argued that to the extent that nationalism

> is manipulated by certain groups to avoid competition and maintain market position; is used to impede the importation of external technology, to maintain mineral resources imprisoned in the soil for which there is no [domestic] exploitation capital, [or] is manipulated by the alienated left to impede the strengthening of the capitalist economic system and the democratic institutions of the west, nationalism comes to be highly negative, not only from the viewpoint of economic development but of national security.[13]

The ministers of the government constantly admonished the people that it was not enough to be *ufanistic* (to have unrealistic confidence or pride) merely because Brazil was rich in resources. Roberto Campos and Castello Branco both argued that resources were worthless unless exploited.

Along with this socially austere and technological approach to problems was the positive dislike of promising or claiming that reforms would yield returns quickly. Even his closest ministers complained that Castello Branco often felt that any dialogue or attempt to win the support of the people for his plans was a form of demagoguery.[14]

A last major characteristic of the Castello Branco government was its intellectual commitment to democracy as a form of government. The government accepted the necessity of a "tutelary democracy" for a time. And though they tended to see political debate as an obstacle rather than an intrinsic part of the process of democracy, nonetheless they believed their goal was an "ideal" democracy.[15] Despite pressure from the hard line officers for greater purges, Castello Branco desired to keep Congress open upon as-

[13] Castello Branco speech, "Segurança e Desenvolvimento."

[14] Although this point was made in interviews by various ex-ministers of the Castello Branco government, their loyalty to Castello Branco is still such that they asked not to be quoted by name.

[15] Based on conversations I had with a number of them and an analysis of their writing, I feel that their concept of democracy was too "ideal." They felt that in a democracy there should be a very high degree of consensus, little political conflict, and an informed citizenry who would be immune to demagogic appeals of politicians.

suming office and to maintain strict limits on the duration of the exceptional powers granted by the First Institutional Act. The commitment to a return to democracy was strong enough that the government planned to hold direct gubernatorial elections in 1965, despite the probable risks to which this would expose the revolution.

An argument often advanced in favor of military regimes is that their political and economic development plans can be systematically implemented over time because of the unity and strength of the military. The widely shared anti-Communist and internal-warfare orientation of the Brazilian army officer corps did, it is true, result in a continuity of a general anti-mobilization political strategy—labor unions were tightly controlled, student movements were suppressed, peasant organizations were repressed, universities and legislative bodies were drastically purged. This strategy was pursued by all three military governments between 1964 and 1970. Nonetheless, when we turn to the area of specific development policies, we find the situation was quite different. Here significant discontinuities existed between successive governments.

The political and economic design of the first military government was significantly altered within two years after the first government left office. These alterations were due partly to internal differences and conflicts within the military. The political engineering strategy of a new constitution, and a revised electoral and party system that the Castello Branco government had constructed to guide the transition back to civilian rule, was largely rendered irrelevant by the military crisis of December 1968, which was resolved only by the issuance of the Fifth Institutional Act, which sharply increased military authoritarian control of the political system.

In economic policy, the Castello Branco government established hundreds of new technically complex fiscal and monetary regulations and guidelines. The policy changes of the second military government, under Costa e Silva, were sufficient to cause Roberto Campos, the economic architect of the first military government, to send a steady stream of acerbic messages to the newspapers decrying them.[16]

[16] Most of these articles appeared in *O Estado de São Paulo* and *O Globo*. The leader of the Berkeley-USAID advisory group to the planning commission of the Brazilian government also complained of policy discontinuities; see Howard S. Ellis, "The Applicability of Certain Theories of

A philosophic difference between the first two military governments concerned attitudes to foreign capital. President Castello Branco and economist Roberto Campos advocated the importation of large quantities of foreign capital in order to stimulate rapid development. The second government, on the other hand, took a less antinationalist position, namely that it was possible and preferable to overcome foreign exchange shortages by increasing exports and that development should be financed by domestic resources. In the crucial area of land reform, the lack of continuity of policy essentially destroyed the careful, if very moderate, Land Reform Statute of 1964. As was discussed previously, the essence of this statute was that large landowners would be forced by high tax assessments either to increase productivity or sell their land. To have succeeded, the policy would have required both time and steady tax collection pressure. The Costa e Silva government took the teeth out of the law by not adjusting delinquent taxes to reflect inflation. The first president of the Agrarian Reform Institute complained that "the agrarian reform in 1968 is semi-paralyzed due to lack of funds and lack of interest."[17]

In place of the active internationalism of the ex-FEB and ESG officers, who as we shall see were the backbone of the Castello Branco government, Costa e Silva appealed to nationalism, and relations with the United States began to experience tension at numerous points. Brazil no longer advocated the inter-American peacekeeping force and became a leading critic of the nuclear test-ban treaty supported by the United States.

Why did this reversal of policies occur? What does it show us about the supposed unity of military government? Are these policy differences associated with specific career-experiences in the officer corps and, if so, were the career experiences of the key members of the Castello Branco government atypical?

CAREER EXPERIENCES OF THE CASTELLO BRANCO OFFICERS

One reason for changes in specific policies was undoubtedly civilian pressure. The Costa e Silva government bought more sup-

---

Economic Development to Brazil," Latin American Center Essay Series, no. 1 (Milwaukee, Wis.: University of Wisconsin Press, December 1968), pp. 5–6.

[17] Interview with Paulo Assis Ribeiro, Rio de Janeiro, September 9, 1968.

port from the landed and coffee elites by not pressing land-reform measures. The president also won some temporary lessening of hostility from the nationalist left by softening the pro-American policies of his predecessor. Nonetheless, a significant number of changes can be accounted for by real differences between the members of the Castello Branco government and that of Costa e Silva, and specifically by the unusual career experiences of the core of officers at the heart of Castello Branco's government. These special career experiences helped shape political attitudes and beliefs that were often quite different from those held by fellow officers, and it was these differences that largely explained the reversals of policy by the succeeding government of Costa e Silva.

To determine the special features, if any, of the group of officers in the first government, I studied the available accounts of the discussions and disputes involved in the formulations of major new policies and interviewed many civilian and military participants.

To determine which officers had most strongly backed or had helped formulate the new policies of 1964, I drew up a list of twenty-five possible candidates for classification as the "core group" of officers in the Castello Branco government. I then submitted a questionnaire designed to determine the core group to two cabinet members whose own membership in this group was beyond dispute. I asked these participant-observers to make their own separate evaluations of the officers they considered the strongest contributors and supporters of the internal and external policies of the Castello Branco government.

Of the 102 active-duty line generals listed in the 1964 officers' register, ten generals were assigned to the core group by both informants.[18] These ten were also found on my own list of twenty-five. After separate consultation with both participant-informants, the names of eight other men who were not active-duty generals at the time of the coup were added. Four of these were retired generals in 1964, and four were colonels (all of whom rapidly advanced to general between 1964 and 1967). The eight officers shared the broad characteristics of the ten generals on active duty in 1964; so in order to heighten comparability with the other generals, I restricted formal analysis to the ten generals forming the core group. These were then compared with the 92 other active-duty generals, giving a total universe for analysis of 102.

[18] Each had three or four names the other did not include.

237

I used various sources of information to collect socioeconomic and career-pattern data for this universe of generals. These were mainly printed or mimeographed materials, some of them of ,a transient variety but all a matter of public record.[19]

From these sources alone I was able to obtain complete data for all 102 generals on about twenty different variables concerning military careers and experiences such as branch of service, schools attended (Brazilian and foreign), dates of all promotions, academic achievements, and place of birth. Fathers' occupations were available in only about 40 percent of the cases.[20]

When the core group of ten generals supporting the Castello Branco government of 1964 was compared with the 92 other generals completing the universe of 102 and with the pro-Goulart subgroup of twenty generals who were purged after the 1964 revolution, several striking differences in their career-patterns and experiences emerged.[21] The variables associated most highly with membership in the core group were: participation on the permanent staff of the Superior War College, attendance at foreign schools, graduation as number one in the class at one of the three major army schools, and membership in the most technically advanced branch of the services of the army. These correlations are summarized in Tables 11.1 and 11.2.

Association in itself, of course, is not causation. The real task of any elite analysis is to determine the possible significance, if any, behind the correlations.[22] We proceed therefore to ask what mean-

[19] Some of the more important of these sources were: annual officers' registers (*Almanaques*), publicly printed each year, containing lists of names, ranks, honors, promotions, and schools of every officer on active duty; the Army Minister's biographical data sheets usually released to the press upon an officer's promotion to general or appointment to a major command; the list, published by the commandant of the Expeditionary Force, of all the participants in the Expeditionary Force to Italy in World War II (checked against the officers' register lists of medals received for participation with this force); newspaper archives of the *Jornal do Brasil* and the *O Estado de São Paulo*, which contained special biographies normally compiled whenever a military officer received a promotion to general or became politically prominent; and, of course, interviews, reinforced by newspaper accounts of political events, to supplement knowledge on the political positions of the officers concerned.

[20] See Chap. 7, n. 36.

[21] Since we are dealing with the entire *universe* of a fair size rather than a *sample*, the question of representativeness does not arise.

[22] A valid criticism of much elite analysis is that it had been weak precise-

ing they had for the exercise and retention of power. What ideas and attitudes, if any, were created by these experiences? Furthermore, if a great number of the ideas of the Castello Branco officers were rooted in atypical career-patterns, rather than in a military-wide sentiment, was it not predictable that, if the military stuck to their decision to limit the length of the presidential term, Castello Branco would have great difficulty in ensuring continuity of his policies and of controlling the succession? This was my working hypothesis.

To determine the significance of a career-experience, such as participation in World War II or membership on the permanent staff of the Superior War College, I conducted interviews and examined relevant archives. It became clear that the four distinctive characteristics and orientations of the Castello Branco government discussed earlier were rooted in the special cluster of these career experiences found to correlate highly with support or membership in the Castello Branco government. The concept of cluster is important, because the experiences were interrelated and mutually reinforcing. Five of the ten generals (50 percent of the core group) had all participated in World War II in FEB, been on the permanent staff of the Superior War College, attended foreign schools, and graduated first in one of the three major army schools. Of the remainder of the universe, only one of the 92 had done all four. The statistical probability of such a difference in proportions occurring by chance are one in a thousand.[23]

SIGNIFICANCE OF CAREER EXPERIENCES

The FEB Experience

The value placed on interdependence in foreign policy, the fear of excessive nationalism, the relatively strong belief that Brazil could profit through a close relationship with the United States, the deep distrust of emotional appeals, the idea that capitalism could create a physically powerful nation, the belief that democracy was a more "civilized" style of politics—these were attitudes that were

---

ly at this step. For a review and critique of the literature, see Dankwart A. Rustow, "The Study of Elites: Who's Who, When, and How," *World Politics*, XVIII (July 1966), 690–717.

[23] This is using the Z test for comparing differences in proportions. For the Z test, see Paul G. Hoel, *Introduction to Mathematical Statistics* (New York: John Wiley & Sons, 1962), pp. 149–150.

TABLE 11.1

CAREER-PATTERN CORRELATES OF CASTELLO BRANCO CORE GROUP COMPARED WITH
ALL OTHER LINE GENERALS ON ACTIVE DUTY, JANUARY 1964

	Member FEB		Attended ESG		Ever Member Permanent Staff ESG		Graduated First in Class		Attended Mil. Sch. Abroad		Attended Mil. Sch. U.S.A.	
	%	N	%	N	%	N	%	N	%	N	%	N
Core Group	60	(10)	90	(10)	70	(10)	100	(10)	100	(10)	80	(10)
All Other Line Generals	29.3	(92)	62.4	(92)	13.1	(84)*	32.6	(92)	23.9	(92)	21.7	(92)

SOURCE: See this Chapter, nn. 19 and 20.

* For 8 of the 92, no information was available for this variable.

TABLE 11.2

CAREER-PATTERN CORRELATES OF CASTELLO BRANCO CORE GROUP COMPARED WITH PRO-GOULART GENERALS PURGED AFTER 1964 REVOLUTION

	Member FEB		Attended ESG		Ever Member Permanent Staff ESG		Graduated First in Class		Attended Mil. Sch. Abroad		Attended Mil. Sch. U.S.A.	
	%	N	%	N	%	N	%	N	%	N	%	N
Castello Branco Core Group	60	(10)	90	(10)	70	(10)	100	(10)	100	(10)	80	(10)
Pro-Goulart Purged Generals	25	(20)	50	(20)	17.6	(17)*	20	(20)	20	(20)	20	(20)

SOURCE: See this Chapter, nn. 19 and 20, and Chapter 7, n. 33.

* For 3 of the 20, no information was available for this variable.

specifically strengthened or largely created by officer participation in the Brazilian Expeditionary Force (FEB) in Italy during World War II.

The FEB was the only ground combat unit from Latin America to participate in the war. The Brazilian division saw heavy action and received the surrender of an entire German division. There is no doubt that this participation with allied troops in combat was a powerful socialization experience for Brazilian officers. Using Karl Mannheim's concept of political generations we can say that the shared, and in many ways upsetting, FEB experience contributed to a "characteristic mode of thought" and behavior, new "integrative attitudes" and "collective strivings."[24] In conversation with these army officers, two themes were often aired. One was that the participation with the United States had favorably impressed the Brazilian contingent with the technical achievements and ability of the United States and the utility of cooperation.[25] Thus the ex-FEB officers tended to be less fearful of cooperation with the United States following World War II. As one prominent general remarked: "In the war, the United States had to give us everything: food, clothes, equipment. After the war, we were less afraid of United States imperialism than other officers because we saw that the United States really helped us without strings attached."[26] Another general made a comment as to why many ex-FEB officers favored extensive U.S. private investment in Brazil:

[24] See his "The Problem of Generations," in *Essays on the Sociology of Knowledge*, ed. Paul Kecskeneti (London: Routledge & Kegan Paul, 1952), pp. 302–312.

The best description of the FEB is in Ten. Cel. Manoel Thomaz Castello Branco, *O Brasil na II Grande Guerra* (Rio de Janeiro: Biblioteca do Exército Editôra, 1960). The FEB commandant has also written an account which lists all the members of the FEB. See Marechal Mascarenhas de Moraes, *A F.E.B. Pelo Seu Comandante* (São Paulo: Instituto Progresso Editorial, 1947).

[25] The FEB members, however, are by no means completely uncritical of the United States. For example, both in their writings and conversations they frequently express their moral and human disgust with the federally sanctioned racism involved in the segregated units of the U.S. military in World War II. An ex-FEB officer has written a book criticizing the haughty attitudes of U.S. commanders and the inferior quality of equipment given to them by the United States. See Marshal Lima Brayner, *A Verdade Sôbre FEB* (Rio de Janeiro: Editôra Civilização Brasileira, 1969).

[26] Interview with General Edson de Figueiredo, commanding general of the Third Infantry Division, Santa Maria, Rio Grande do Sul, September 24, 1968.

The attitude of FEB members was important for opening the country to foreign investment because they feared the United States less . . . the FEB members wanted very rapid development in Brazil.

The FEB was not only important because of going to Italy. Possibly even more important, the FEB members went to the United States and saw at first hand a great democratic industrial power. It was an opening of horizons. I went and it made a great impact; for me it was absolutely apparent that a free enterprise country had been successful in creating a great industrial power.[27]

Another theme that ran through the writings and conversations of ex-FEB participants was the profound dislike of anything that seemed to them to be narrow, unrealistic, emotional nationalism.[28] Castello Branco had been the operations officer of the Brazilian division in Italy. In his archives were numerous notes and handwritten lectures criticizing the "false optimism" and "irrational nationalism" in Brazil. In various places, he commented that participation in World War II made the Brazilian army face up to their inadequacies and overcome them through hard work.[29] When Robert Campos was asked if he felt that the officers who participated in FEB had any special view of Brazilian development, he answered directly:

FEB had a great impact on Castello and others. The contact with logistics in an underdeveloped country made them cool and

[27] Interview with General Golbery do Couto e Silva, Rio de Janeiro, October 8, 1968.

[28] From conversations it was clear that part of what the former FEB members see as their realistic internationalism and concern with fighting Communism abroad comes from their perception in Italy that war physically and morally destroys the country in which it is fought. Therefore they say they are more concerned than those who did not participate in FEB with helping in the fight against Communism abroad so as to avoid that fight in their own country.

[29] In a particularly interesting section of his archives, Castello Branco notes that the first combat performance of the FEB was so poor that the American commanding general asked the Brazilian staff if they felt the Brazilian unit had any offensive capacity. After a bitter and agonizing night of reflection, the answer came that they would have after more hard training. After this realistic and "hard" training, Castello said, the Brazilian troops improved immensely and were equal to the Americans. *Arquivo do Marechal H. A. Castello Branco*, General Staff School (ECEME), Rio de Janeiro.

objective. Castello grasped the difference between verbalization of power and real power. Castello was impressed by the complete failure of Italy and Mussolini, a failure which he considered an example of verbalization not backed by real power.

Campos believed that the FEB experience had had a definite impact on the governing style of those ex-FEB members in government between 1964 and 1967, which set them apart from most of the other military officers.

Castello, Cordeiro de Farias, Mamede, Lyra Tavares all grasped that for the country to be powerful it needed organization, technology, and industry. This sense of reality decreased the propensity to use images and demagoguery as a form of political communication.[30]

It is interesting to note that in a book published by the reservists who had fought in Italy with FEB, the same themes were found: unfavorable comparisons between Brazilian levels of organization and development and those of the United States, the idealization of democracy, and a strong emphasis on the fact that

it is not enough to be brave, to have high political national resources, not enough to have moral reasons. To profit by these resources we must have organization and discipline. We ought to expound in Brazil this idea of organization and discipline in order that the work of utilizing our resources and national possibilities be productive and efficient. By reminding the people of this nation of this idea, we can combat another illusion common in our land, the false patriotism that is content to exalt the grandeur of Brazil but . . . through failure to organize, does not profit by it.

Finally, in the ten months we lived in Italy, we could appreciate in all its implications the tragic condition that a nation is reduced to when it is deprived of its basic liberties and allows an authoritarian regime to govern.[31]

[30] Interview with Roberto Campos, Rio de Janeiro, September 15, 1967. In the FEB preference for actual as opposed to potential power, they mirror Samuel P. Huntington's description of the characteristic military man. "The military man typically . . . wants force in being, not latent force," *The Soldier and the State* (New York: Random House, 1964), p. 67.

[31] Roger de Carvalho Mange, "Alguns Problemas das Pequenas Frações de Infantaria na F.E.B.," in Berta Morais, *et al.*, *Depoimento de Oficiais*

The ESG Experience

Another major experience of the core group of officers in the 1964–1967 government was attendance at the Superior War College, and even more importantly, membership on its permanent teaching and research staff. The six core supporters who participated in the FEB later went on to the War College, and all but one became permanent staff members.

There is a specific link between the FEB and the ESG. The artillery commander of FEB, and its most politically experienced and visible member after the war, was General Cordeiro de Farias.[32] In 1948 he was given the task of preparing a report on the establishment of a war college and in 1950 he became the newly founded war college's first commandant. In his mind, there was a direct relationship between the FEB and the ESG:

> The impact of FEB was such that we came back to Brazil looking for models of government that would work—order, planning, rational financing. We did not find this model in Brazil at this stage, but we decided to seek ways to find the route in the long run. The ESG was one way to this, and the ESG grew out of the FEB experience.[33]

From 1950 until the revolution of 1964, the emerging ideology of the ESG fleshed out and formalized many of the ideas associated with the FEB. As we have seen, these ideas contributed to the military's belief in their own competence to handle questions of national development.[34] The FEB ideal of perfect democracy was maintained as the goal, but the ESG added to it a belief that the central organs of government and planning must be strengthened and made rational.

The most influential school of development ideology in Brazil in the 1950s emphasized nationalism and the public sector.[35] The

---

da Reserva Sôbre a F.E.B. (São Paulo: Instituto Progresso Editorial, 1949), pp. 121–122 and *passim*.

[32] In the Castello Branco government he was the cabinet minister for coordination of regional agencies.

[33] Interviews with Marshal Cordeiro de Farias, Rio de Janeiro, September 16 and 17, 1968.

[34] Chap. 7.

[35] The most famous attempt to formalize a nationalist development doctrine in Brazil was at the *Instituto Superior de Estudos Brasileiros* (ISEB). A good analysis of the *Instituto* and its ideas and disputes is contained in

ESG, however, influenced by its FEB experience, cared more about efficiency and productivity, and argued that because of the scarcity of capital in Brazil, the private sector should be utilized in order to develop Brazil's potential most rapidly.

This favorable view of the role of the private sector is unusual in Brazilian, and more broadly in Latin American, military thinking. In general, the military has poor links with the private sector and tends to favor statism and view the profit motive with distrust and distaste. The favorable impression received by the FEB members of the American economic system as conducive both to military power and national development was a very atypical experience. This openness of the FEB to the private sector was reinforced at the ESG where, as we have seen, over half the students were civilians, many of them associated with large industrial, commercial, or financial enterprises. To my knowledge, this institutionalized relationship between the military and the private sector is unique in Latin America. The fear shared by the military and the private sector of what they felt was the growth of a Communist threat in Brazil from the late 1950s until the 1964 revolution also served to strengthen this relationship.

It is significant that in the great dispute over the establishment of the nationalized oil monopoly, *Petrobrás*, which the majority of the military favored, no prominent member of the ESG permanent staff championed its creation as a monopoly. Indeed the commandant of the ESG at the time, General Juarez Távora, was a prominent spokesman of the policy of allowing private and foreign companies some role in developing oil resources.[36]

With the advent of the cold war and nuclear weapons, the old FEB idea of the usefulness of cooperation with the United States became formalized as the necessity for an "interdependent" foreign policy. Finally, we may note that, in his penultimate address as president, Castello Branco spoke of the ESG as a unique example of "anticipation of ideas," and in fact stated that the school's doc-

---

Frank Bonilla, "A National Ideology for Development: Brazil," in *Expectant Peoples: Nationalism and Development*, ed. K. H. Silvert (New York: Random House, 1963), pp. 232–264. After the military assumed power in 1964, they forcibly closed ISEB.

[36] His position as he publicly expressed it from 1947 to 1954 is contained in his *Petróleo Para O Brasil* (Rio de Janeiro: Livraria José Olympio Editôra, 1955).

trines of national security and development had been incorporated by his government into Brazilian laws, organizations, and constitution.[37]

U.S. School Experience

The other two distinctive features of the core group behind the Castello Branco government had less specific policy implications in themselves, but do reinforce the picture of a distinctive career pattern. While only 33 percent of the generals (excluding the core group) graduated number one in their class, 100 percent of the core group had done so. The intellectualism of the core group was reflected also in their overrepresentation in the technically advanced artillery branch of the army, and their underrepresentation in the two traditional line branches, the infantry and cavalry.

One other feature made the core group distinctive. One hundred percent of the group had attended foreign schools, 80 percent actually going to schools in the United States, whereas only 24 percent of the generals who were not in the core group had attended foreign military schools. Certainly the data do not support the contention that U.S. military training of Latin American officers inculcates apolitical professional values among the officers. *Prima facie*, it could be argued that the dislike of emotional nationalism, as well as the active anti-Communist and openly pro-American stance of the 1964–1967 Castello Branco government was a result of, or was related to, their American training. Certainly it is a major goal of much—some would say all—American-sponsored training to contribute to such attitudes.

In most cases, however, American schooling, rather than creating these beliefs, probably reinforced feelings which, as we have seen, already existed in the FEB officers who went on to found the ESG. Einaudi's study of the Peruvian military similarly suggests the predominance of total career experiences and national situations over any attitudes deriving exclusively from U.S. training by demonstrating that a high percentage of the members of the na-

---

[37] See Castello Branco's speech, "Segurança e Desenvolvimento." In addition to the published sources cited in Chap. 8, the above analysis of the ESG is based on various interviews including those with Marshals Cordeiro de Farias and Juarez Távora, the first two commandants of the school, General Golbery do Couto e Silva, its major political thinker, and Roberto Campos, who was a frequent lecturer and the most influential economic thinker of the ESG.

247

tionalist junta installed in October 1968 (which established relations with the Soviet Union, nationalized a subsidiary of Standard Oil of New Jersey, and discontinued the U.S. military advisory mission) had attended American schools.[38]

It is probably safe to say that many of the top officers in both Peru and Brazil who went to U.S. schools were familiar with the considerable American and French writing on counterrevolutionary warfare and that they developed a desire for the military's mission to include an increasingly active role in the economic and political fields. Thus American and foreign schooling seems to correlate with military managerial *activism* in both cases. This mission or "role-expansion" was an integral part of the deepening involvement of the military in the development process in both Peru and Brazil.[39]

INABILITY TO CONTROL SUCCESSION

There is no doubt that the group of officers supporting Castello Branco's government was atypical of the officers at large in their career experiences and thus in their attitudes to questions of political development. That they knew that their attitudes were not widely shared in the military as a whole is clear from the fact that, at the time of succession, they felt that there was a strong possibility that their policies would be changed. Almost to a man, the officers surrounding Castello Branco urged him to remain in office to ensure survival of his policies. Castello Branco refused, on the grounds that the greatest evil in Brazilian politics was that of *continuismo*.[40] On the other hand, Castello Branco was unable to control the selection of his successor, since none of his choices for the presidency, all officers from the core group or civilians with similar ideas, was acceptable to the officers at large.

Why was Castello Branco unable to control either the selection of his successor or the continuity of his policies? Clearly, the fact that his government's economic liberalism, a philosophy most closely associated with the ESG, was not the ideology of the majority of the civilians or the military officer corps was extremely

[38] Luigi Einaudi, *The Peruvian Military: A Summary Political Analysis*, The RAND Corporation, RM-6048-RC, May 1969.

[39] For an interesting discussion of the concept of "role-expansion," see Moshe Lissak, "Modernization and Role-Expansion of the Military in Developing Countries: A Comparative Analysis," *Comparative Studies in Society and History*, IX (April 1967), 233–255.

[40] Interviews with various members of the government.

important. Many of the officers outside the inner circles of the government were socialized into national politics in the great controversy about the establishment of the national oil monopoly, *Petrobrás*, in the early 1950s. During the debate the majority of officers strongly backed *Petrobrás*, but the ESG was lukewarm about the idea. The Castello Branco officers' ideas on nationalism also represented a minority opinion within the military and were the most intensely hated aspect of the government among civilian nationalists.

One of the basic arguments throughout this work is that the military is a complex, politically heterogeneous institution. Thus any one group, especially a group holding minority views, can only win wide acceptance of its ideas if it engages in effective political persuasion. An "apolitical" style of leadership is unviable in a political institution. Castello Branco's distaste for political persuasion was thus not only a liability in his relations with the civilian public, but also a liability in relation to his fellow officers. It eroded his influence within the military, since he did not present a forceful case for his ideas.

The rejection of his policies was also hastened by the fact that the military felt a collective responsibility for the government. Some of the most unpopular policies, in the view of the civilian nationalists, were those that sprang from the ESG's policy of economic liberalism, such as the granting of the iron-ore concession to United States private foreign capital. Because the military as an institution felt it was incurring increasing political costs by backing Castello Branco's policies, the officers outside the Castello government using "plebiscitary" pressure in effect voted a new look into office in the second government of the revolution, under the leadership of General Costa e Silva.

While rigorous information about the most influential members of the "second government of the revolution" is lacking, it is clear that the following men were near the top in its first year: Costa e Silva himself; his minister of interior, General Albuquerque Lima; commanding general of the politically crucial First Army headquartered in Rio de Janeiro, General Syseno Sarmento; chief of the Military Household and secretary-general of the National Security Council, General Jayme Portella; and the chief of the National Intelligence Service (SNI), General Emilio Garrastazú Medice. These men owed their positions within the second government to

249

the fact that they symbolically and actually represented the opposite of the ideas and career-patterns of the original core group of officers in the 1964–1967 government.

The major opponents within the Brazilian military to the "liberal internationalist" group of officers typified by Castello Branco were originally called the "hard liners" (*linha dura*) by Brazilians. A more accurate term would be the "authoritarian nationalists." This group was not entirely a fixed one, but one whose composition and passions changed according to the political pressures of the day.

The authoritarian nationalists within the military by and large (but not exclusively) were not shaped by the ideas of either the FEB or the policies developed by the permanent staff of the ESG. Whereas the key members of the Castello Branco government had been deeply marked by the FEB experience, only one of the five key officers under Costa e Silva had been in Italy. Whereas the key members of the Castello Branco government all graduated in first place from one of the service schools, only one out of five in Costa e Silva's government did so. Only one of the key officers around Costa e Silva, in addition, had even been on the permanent staff of the ESG. Costa e Silva's officers had few wartime or academic links with the United States. These officers came to power, in fact, as a response to the more nationalist demands of the junior officers and their dissatisfaction with the achievements of the first military government, and to the desire of the military in general to be more "popular." It was the authoritarian nationalists who were the key force behind the near-coups in October 1965 and December 1968, both of which crises were resolved only by a hardening of policies towards civilians by the existing government.[41] In both crises the driving force of the authoritarian nationalists was provided by the mid-level officers who articulated their feelings through troop commands, especially through the *Vila Militar*, the major military base in Rio de Janeiro. The only military school that was a center of authoritarian nationalist feeling was the Junior Officers' School in Rio de Janeiro (*Escola de Apereiçoamento de Oficiais*, EsAO).

Although Costa e Silva's government did not express or put into effect the beliefs of the junior authoritarian nationalists, Costa e Silva emerged as a leader because he was felt to be sympathetic to the somewhat inarticulate but nonetheless powerful sentiments for a more militant, authoritarian government and a less pro-American

[41] See Chap. 12 for discussion of these events.

and more nationalist stance. Given this relationship between the Costa e Silva government and the authoritarian nationalist officers it is interesting to understand the content of some of their beliefs. Because Brazil has been under military rule since 1964, few programmatic statements of the aims and desires of the authoritarian nationalists have been released to the public. However, if one looks at some of the programs they circulated before the revolution of 1964, one realizes how few of their goals have been met by successive military governments, and indeed how fundamentally different were the initial goals of the first government under the liberal internationalists and Castello Branco.

For example, the following is a manifesto entitled "The Ten Commandments of the Law of the People," written by the *Frente Patriotica Civil–Militar*. Prominent figures reputed to be associated with the *Frente* were ex-Naval Minister Sylvio Heck, General José Alberto Bittencourt and the *Estado de São Paulo*'s most prominent columnist, Oliveiros Ferreira. Their goals were stated as follows:

1. Dissolution of Congress in order to restructure the popular democratic base of the country by a new constituent assembly.

2. Confiscation of all fortunes acquired by shady business deals, embezzlement, administrative frauds, or any other illicit means, with the cancelling of the political rights of all involved.

3. Distribution to the peasants of all uncultivated lands with the obligation of immediate cultivation and with direct financial and technical assistance guaranteed.

4. Energetic combating of the high cost of living and inflation by the intervention of the state in the means of production and distribution and the suppression of taxes on the basic necessities of life.

5. Eliminate excessive bureaucracy and unify the social welfare system and guarantee medical and hospital care to all workers, including rural workers.

6. Abolition of all forms of government intervention in trade unions.

7. Preferential concern for the solution to the problems of the north and the northeast and other underdeveloped areas of the country in all national development plans.

8. Defense and development of *Petrobrás* and of the great state industries. Control of the remission of profits abroad and

251

the requirement that profits be reinvested in the development of the country.

9. Extension of free primary, secondary, technical, and higher education by the state for the training of poor students.

10. The pursuit of an independent foreign policy opposed to all forms of totalitarianism and imperialism, respect for the rights of self-determination and condemnation of the monstrous arms-race in accordance with the democratic and Christian principles of Brazil.[42]

The reformist elements of the authoritarian nationalist group, of which the manifesto represented a small and even untypical section, did not come to the fore in the Costa e Silva government itself, nor in later military governments, for numerous reasons. One reason was that as military government wore on, the opposition grew more intense—especially with the rise of urban guerrilla activity—and the tone of authoritarian nationalist feeling grew more harshly repressive and less immediately sensitive to questions of social reform. A second reason may well be that the great size of the industrial sector in Brazil, and the complicated web of interest-group politics, made Brazilian society too developed and complex for military Nasserism even of a Peruvian variety.

As has been mentioned before, Costa e Silva certainly did not represent the authoritarian nationalists within the military, but he did represent a bridge between them and the Castello Branco government's liberal internationalism. His rise to power involved a break with the first government, and the tone of his government ("humanism" as opposed to "austerity," "nationalism" as opposed to "internationalism") emphasized precisely those points deemphasized by the Castello Branco government. The tension between the two governments reflected tensions and disagreements in the officer corps at large. Officers strongly identified with the first government fell into disfavor and openly complained against the policies of the second. Handling of the succession brought about serious discontinuities of policy as well as serious disputes within the military.

[42] The Manifesto was reproduced in José Stacchini, *Março 64: Mobilização da Audácia* (São Paulo: Companhia Editôra Nacional, 1965), pp. 20–22.

Chapter 12

The Military as an Institution Versus the Military as Government

INTRODUCTION

What of the concept of "monopoly of force" and the argument about the "stability of a military government"? Before demonstrating empirically how and why, in the Brazilian case, military rule has been no more stable than civilian government, it is useful first to raise briefly some problems at a more general level.

The theoretical concept of "monopoly of force" is questionable in itself. For example, in Latin America, to assume that the military has a monopoly of force, one must discount the role of the often important police in Bolivia or Colombia, the powerful state militias in a country such as Brazil, and interservice rivalry that has led to shooting in Argentina, Brazil, Venezuela, and Ecuador. Furthermore, if disagreement over the "political alternatives"[1] (i.e., to hold or not to hold elections) or "specific implementing action" is so great that the military splits into opposing camps, then, of course, there is no longer "monopoly," but at best "duopoly" and at worst armed civil war.

Arguments about "unity" and "monopoly of force" lead in turn to the hypothesis that a military government offers "stability." Empirically, there is the obvious but frequently overlooked fact that military governments are often overthrown by the military institution itself. Indeed, a strong general case can be made, on logic alone, for the hypothesis that the military is *more prone* to overthrow a military government than a constitutional civilian government because the disincentives, i.e., the fear and reluctance to overthrow an electorally legitimated government, are decreased. In addition, the incentive to overthrow a military government may

[1] For the argument that there must be a very high level of agreement over "political alternatives" and "specific implementing action" before a potential ruling elite is an actual ruling elite, see Robert Dahl, "A Critique of the Ruling Elite Model," *American Political Science Review*, LII (June 1958), 463–469.

be increased because the military as an institution feels responsible for the performance and success of the government. This added responsibility makes groups within the military more intolerant of slowness in reform, of compromise, or of corruption than they would be in a civilian government, to which they could afford to be more indifferent.

With these ideas in mind, I propose to analyze the manner in which in Brazil the military as an institution has clashed with the military as government in such a way as to create a basic source of instability in the Brazilian military regime.

THE CRISIS OF OCTOBER 1965

As we have seen, differences within the Brazilian military contributed to sharp discontinuity in some key policy areas upon the assumption of office by Costa e Silva in 1967. But tensions within the military were evident well before the succession of 1967. Some army officers, especially those in the middle and lower ranks, were already resentful of the policies of Castello Branco and the harm they might do to military power. Costa e Silva, the war minister, was a symbol of this tension. His post as war minister was due to the fact that he was the senior general among the coup supporters and designated himself war minister at the time of the revolution. He initially opposed the selection of Castello Branco as president.[2] He represented the nonintellectual, non-ESG, hard-line officers, who shared few of the special orientations of the core group surrounding Castello Branco. This second group of officers within the military grew increasingly vocal over time, as civilian support for military government waned and the military as an institution felt increasingly isolated and threatened. The tension was sufficient to initiate the first threat to the Castello Branco government.

Upon assuming power, General Castello Branco had wished to implement some basic political and economic reforms and to preside over a "tutelary democracy" which would prepare for a return to "rational and true democracy" in time. To give the government some national and international legitimacy, Congress was left open and congressional elections were planned to occur on sched-

[2] The most detailed published version of the role of Costa e Silva in the succession decision is found in Mauro Borges, *O Golpe em Goiás* (Rio de Janeiro: Editôra Civilização Brasileira, 1965), pp. 109–119.

ule. While reluctantly postponing direct presidential elections from October 1965 to October 1966, Castello Branco decided to hold elections for state governors on schedule.

This decision was exceedingly unpopular among hard line officers, who feared that widespread antagonism caused by the austerity measures of Castello Branco would result in nonrevolutionary and even antirevolutionary politicians gaining electoral victories which could both preclude the advance of the "real revolution" and present the threat of a return of those purged by the revolution.[3] These fears and pressures caused two election laws to be passed which considerably restricted and "sanitized" the ranks of possible candidates for political office. Nonetheless, on October 3, 1965 candidates associated with the Kubitschek era won in two major state elections. This was interpreted as a defeat for the ideals of the revolutionary movement of 1964. Highlighting this symbolic return to prerevolutionary politics was Kubitschek's own return to Brazil the next day from political exile in France.

While the military government in the person of Castello Branco and the officers surrounding him proclaimed its respect for these victories, the rank and file officers reacted violently. On the night of October 5, the regiments of the strongest garrisons of the *Vila Militar* on the outskirts of Rio were placed on alert by their own commanders. Officers debated what action to take in an atmosphere of hostility and rebellion.[4] The powerful Mechanized-Reconnaissance Regiment had its armor ready to move against Castello Branco. At this point War Minister Costa e Silva appeared, appealed to the younger officers to remain calm, and promised to communicate their grievances to the president. He and Castello Branco spent two and a half hours closeted with the three military ministers before issuing a press statement announcing that the

[3] It is difficult for an Anglo-Saxon audience to comprehend the peculiar mix of emotion and ideas of the leaders of the hard-line younger officers. There was a self-interested element of fear of the return of those they had helped purge. More important, however, were the twin urges to be more *authoritarian*—purge more politicians, disband Congress and political parties, censor the press, cancel all elections—and to be more *radically reformist*—expropriate large landownings, confiscate wealth of profiteering businessmen, and have more nationalistic assertive relations toward foreign capital and the United States.

[4] Numerous details of military movements were printed in the Rio press on October 6–8, but the basic spirit and pattern of events for this account were derived from interviews with military and civilian participants and observers.

revolution would greatly expand its powers.[5] Costa e Silva returned to the *Vila Militar*, and in a passionate address to the younger officers he pledged, "I guarantee to you, my young commanders, that we know where we are going. The present chiefs are as revolutionary as the young revolutionaries. I guarantee you we will not turn back."[6]

In effect, the crisis was one of succession and military unity. The war minister closed the door to any solution of the crisis which would entail keeping Castello Branco in office with strengthened powers, by guaranteeing that Castello Branco was personally against his own continuation as president.[7] When Congress later showed signs of balking at strengthening the powers of the military government, Castello Branco reversed his previous positions and unilaterally issued the Second Institutional Act, which established indirect instead of direct elections for the presidency, abolished the traditional political parties, allowed the Supreme Court to be "packed," and reestablished the government's authority to break the political rights of opponents.[8]

This about-face by President Castello Branco was undoubtedly due to his assessment that he risked a grave military crisis and a probable coup if he refused to respond to military demands. A number of President Castello Branco's former confidants argue that he feared the hard line pressures were leading toward a naked military dictatorship. In these circumstances, Castello Branco felt it would be best to institutionalize a much stronger government, so that his successor could rule in a more authoritarian manner while yet remaining within the confines of law. He therefore set about recreating a new constitution which greatly expanded executive powers.

In the period between 1964 and 1965, the military-backed government of Castello Branco was clearly as subject to ultimatums from the military institution as civilian governments had been in the past. Castello Branco had, in fact, capitulated to the threats

[5] This statement is reprinted in "Fortalecimento da Ação Revolucionária," *Correio da Manhã*, October 7, 1965, p. 5.

[6] The general substance of the atmosphere and events of this meeting are reported in various newspapers. The best account is found in "Costa e Silva Assegura a Posse," *Correio da Manhã*, October 7, 1965, p. 2.

[7] *Ibid.*

[8] The Second Institutional Act was printed in the major Brazilian newspapers on October 28, 1965.

from the military. War Minister Costa e Silva emerged as the mediator between the internationalist intellectual officers of the Castello Branco government and the more authoritarian and nationalist younger hard line officers. There is little doubt that Costa e Silva could have led a coup against Castello Branco. One astute observer remarked that this did not occur because the crisis of 1965 itself resolved the succession problem by making the war minister heir to the presidential office, and the war minister preferred this route to the presidency rather than one via another coup.[9]

The crisis of October 1965, and the results of the succession to power of Costa e Silva in 1967, revealed the deep cleavages within the military. In such circumstances, the assumptions of the "monopoly of force" by the military and the "stability" of military governments conceal more than they reveal.

GROWING CIVILIAN CRITICISM AND ITS IMPACT ON THE MILITARY

The effect of the crisis of October 1965 was that civilian support for the military in government dwindled further. Some of the most respected politicians associated with the Castello Branco regime, such as Minister of Justice Milton Campos, resigned or withdrew from politics, while the elimination of direct elections by the Second Institutional Act destroyed any hopes that civilians would participate effectively in the selection of the next president.

An indication of how far from real civilian desires was the choice of War Minister Costa e Silva as president, through indirect elections, is found in the poll taken at the same time as the indirect election by the *Jornal do Brasil* in Rio de Janeiro. In response to questions asking whom they would vote for in a *direct* election, only 12 percent replied that they would choose Costa e Silva, whereas 71 percent supported Kubitschek or Lacerda, two of the most outspoken critics of the military government.[10]

The austere development policies of Castello Branco's govern-

[9] Interview with one of Brazil's most prominent political columnists, Carlos Castello Branco (no relation of the president), of the *Jornal do Brasil*, in Brasília, September 3, 1967.

[10] See the analysis of opinion-shifts from 1966 to 1967 in the *Jornal do Brasil*, November 15, 1966, part 1, p. 14. Polling methodology is in rather early stages of development in Brazil, so caution is needed. It is important to note, however, that in this period the *Jornal do Brasil* was a generally progovernment newspaper.

ment, coupled with growing authoritarianism, made the military-at-large the recipients of public hostility. Military officers became reluctant to wear their uniforms in public.

A feedback at the institutional level of the unpopularity of the military government was the decline in applications to the military academies.[11] The prestigious *Colégio Militar*, located in Rio de Janeiro (one of the centers of articulate opposition to the military government), had sent an average of 117 cadets to the military academy in each of the years of 1962 and 1963. By 1965 this figure had dropped to 81, and it declined to a low of 47 in 1966.[12] There was simply less competition for military positions than before, and some officers even feared that the intellectual level of cadets might decline.

Public attacks on the military regime by important members of the church deprived the military of many of the symbols of legitimacy in the eyes of the church faithful. A working paper issued by a committee on the National Conference of Brazilian Bishops (CNBB) specifically labeled the ideology of national security a "fascist" doctrine.[13] Many church members charged the Costa e Silva regime with lack of interest in solving basic questions, and priests were arrested increasingly in the latter part of 1968 on grounds of subversion.[14]

Indicative of how bad church–state relations had become by mid-1968 was the incident involving the cardinal of São Paulo, Dom Agnelo Rossi, a leader of the moderate wing of the Brazilian hierarchy and president of the CNBB. Dom Agnelo was subjected to

[11] This was one of the major grievances cited to me in a blistering attack on the "army's" performance in power by a high-ranking air force General Staff officer, Rio de Janeiro, August 9, 1968.

[12] Figures obtained from the files of the military academy (*Academia Militar Agulhas Negras—AMAN*). There are other variables that undoubtedly contributed to the decline; the most important is that military careers became less attractive as the expanding industrial base created much more lucrative employment opportunities.

[13] The text is reprinted in the *Correio da Manhã*, July 21, 1968. This statement was probably to the left of the dominant sentiment of the CNBB. Nonetheless, the church was moving into open conflict with the military regime.

[14] The CNBB in early December issued a number of statements stating that priests who had been punished by the regime for committing crimes against the state had not committed crimes against God or church rule. The crisis is analyzed in "Igreja Rebelde," *Jornal do Brasil*, December 12, 1968 (the day before the Fifth Institutional Act was issued).

such violent criticism for consenting to receive an honorary medal from President Costa e Silva and to celebrate mass for the president on his birthday that at the last minute the cardinal left São Paulo, and the ceremony was cancelled. Military men were enraged at this insult.[15]

THE CRISIS OF DECEMBER 1968

As the frustrations of exercising political power began to affect the government and the military as an institution, Costa e Silva's government began to be subjected to the same pressures as had that of Castello Branco. There was a growing fatigue and frustration at bearing the responsibility of government and a growing desire to return to the former moderator role. Often expressed was the desire for the military to withdraw from politics by inaugurating a civilian president in 1970.

On the other hand, the purges and the ever-present threat of the return of the exiled made such a withdrawal from government difficult. The military was also sensitive to the fact that it had failed to deliver the much-promised economic reforms. There were continual attacks from within the military on President Costa e Silva for "playing the game" of politics with politicians and for betraying the apolitical ideals of the revolution. Since withdrawal from politics was seen as unfeasible, this situation in turn led to a desire to eliminate politics altogether by an even more complete restructuring of the political system by the military. This restructuring was seen as simultaneously *less* political and *more* revolutionary. There was a desire to sweep away political restraints to military achievement of more basic reforms. These conflicting strains led to an increasingly authoritarian attitude among military officers.[16]

In the spring and summer of 1968, student demonstrations against the military dictatorship grew in frequency and intensity.

[15] See the monograph by Luigi Einaudi, Richard Maullin, Alfred Stepan, and Michael Fleet, *Latin American Institutional Development: The Changing Catholic Church* (Santa Monica, Calif., The RAND Corporation, RM-6136-DOS, October 1969) for a more detailed analysis of the sociological and ideological changes within the church and for a discussion of the church–state conflict in Brazil in 1966–1969.

[16] This analysis is based on visits to military bases and schools in Brazil in the period July–October 1968. In this period, I visited military institutions in the states of Rio Grande do Sul, São Paulo, Amazonas, Estado do Rio, and Guanabara. In long informal talks with Brazilian military officers, this picture of the state of military opinion and frustration emerged.

In several large marches through Rio de Janeiro, churchmen and even middle-class office workers joined the students in the streets. In Osasco, an industrial suburb of São Paulo, the first significant workers' strike occurred since the coup of 1964. These events led to growing demands within the military for repressive measures.

The final incident that sent events moving toward a new cycle of military demands and presidential capitulation and to the Fifth Institutional Act of December 13, 1968, was the seemingly trivial attack in Congress on the military by deputy Márcio Moreira Alves, who urged a civilian boycott of the military Independence Day celebrations. Instantly, lower unit-commanders demanded punishment of the deputy. Costa e Silva reluctantly approved the proceedings to remove his political rights, but insisted that ratification of the charges must come from Congress itself.[17]

In this period of crisis, the resentment of the younger officers was expressed in the manifesto issued by the members of the Captain's School in Rio and in constant leaks to the press. The officers complained bitterly that the military *government* was ineffectual and that this reflected badly on the military as an *institution*. They also complained about the decline in the prestige and financial position of the military. They strongly urged that political reasons or civilian criticism should not be allowed to impede the reform they demanded.[18]

Capitalizing on growing frustration in the lower ranks, Interior Minister General Albuquerque Lima argued in a series of speeches to military audiences that there was no going back, that the revolution was irreversible, and that the military was *uniquely* suited to push for even greater reforms because as an institution it had no formal links with economic groups that might resist reform. He claimed the military could and would continue the revolution for 10 or 15 years if necessary.[19]

[17] A running account of the Alves crisis is contained in all the major Brazilian newspapers. The political column in the *Jornal do Brasil* of Carlos Castello Branco covered the crisis with the best "inside dopester" information and behind-the-scenes drama. That the Alves incident was merely a pretext for a new wave of repression was made clear later when President Medice admitted that in his capacity as chief of the Serviço Nacional de Informações (SNI) he had suggested even before the Alves speech that measures similar to the Fifth Institutional Act be implemented.

[18] A discussion of the impact of the manifesto is in "Capitães começam vida política com manifesto da EsAO," *Jornal do Brasil*, December 8, 1968.

[19] See various related stories in the *Jornal do Brasil* from about November

As in October 1965, the crisis of 1968 became one of military unity and presidential succession. Albuquerque Lima emerged rapidly as the leading presidential candidate of the authoritarian nationalists within the military.[20] When Congress refused to revoke the immunity of deputy Alves, the armor of the *Vila Militar* once again threatened to go to the streets, and lower unit commanders served ultimatums on Costa e Silva to take action against Congress. Even though Costa e Silva had insisted that Congress was "untouchable" and any decision they made would have to be respected, he capitulated to military demands as had Castello Branco, and the Fifth Institutional Act was the result. This initiated press censorship, closed Congress indefinitely, and started another round of political purging. Even though the military had created an extremely strong constitution in 1967 as their attempt at institution building, they themselves had violated it by the end of 1968.

The military government of Costa e Silva, it was clear, was as unable to control the military institution as Castello Branco. President Costa e Silva, in explaining in a nationally broadcast television program the reasons behind the Fifth Institutional Act, admitted that even a highly sanitized and controlled Congress was not able to give the military the support it needed in order to govern, because the political base had deserted the revolution. The government, therefore, dependent largely on military support, proceeded to take action even against mild civilian critics, such as Sette Câmara, who had been the revolutionary government's first ambassador to the United Nations, and Alberto Dines, the editor of the *Jornal do Brasil*, who had edited a very sympathetic account of the revolution of 1964, *Os Idos de Março e a Queda em Abril*.

This new wave of authoritarian measures increased the isolation of the military government as many key civilian office holders in the government's political party resigned their positions, and a succession of Supreme Court judges refused the "honor" of becoming president of the Court under such circumstances.[21]

The increasing removal of civilian "buffers" such as Congress and the court made the government even more exposed to the

---

15 until the December 13 crisis, e.g., "Albuquerque Lima defende mais 10 anos de revolução," *Jornal do Brasil*, November 19, 1968.

[20] See "Movimentação sucessória de Albuquerque aflige Govêrno," *Jornal do Brasil*, November 22, 1968.

[21] See the *New York Times*, January 17, 19, and 23, and February 1, 1969.

THE MILITARY IN POWER, 1964–1968

conflicting demands coming from different military groups. The government was dependent on the military but the frustrated and internally divided military only generated new political crises in 1969.

The paramount importance a military institution gives to the maintenance of its own internal unity is sometimes seen as a political asset of military government. In fact it often becomes a characteristic liability. Fearful that criticism might erode its precarious unity, a military government does not easily tolerate the normal level of dissension and debate needed to build or maintain coalitions with civilians. This is an underlying reason why military governments so often become involved in a cycle in which criticism is repressed, so that in turn even sharper criticisms by civilians are provoked, which are then countered by the military with yet further repressions. Military concern for unity and unanimity thus leads to progressive self-isolation.

This repression had reached such heights by 1969 that increasingly well-documented reports began reaching the Vatican and Europe that torture was being widely used at various levels of government in Brazil.[22] Despite attempts by the military either to deny that torture had occurred, or to treat it as individual and unauthorized action by local units, there are indications that torture had in fact become an intrinsic part of the governing process, and that torture or the threat of torture was used to encourage compliance and discourage dissent. Many of the military officers treated student dissenters, critical priests, and hostile journalists, along with urban guerrillas, as all part of the process of subversion by internal warfare. Torture, it seems, became a method of extracting information about the location of urban guerrillas. If this conjecture is correct, then torture had indeed become deeply routinized and institutionalized in Brazil. Given the fact that the rank and file hard line officers had repeatedly imposed their will on military presidents since 1964, the chances of a systematic halt to torture by vigorous presidential action looked bleak even it the president were to take a strong stand against the use of torture.

[22] A disturbing summary of the evidence of torture in Brazil is contained in Ralph Della Cava, "Torture in Brazil," *Commonweal*, XCII (April 24, 1970), 135–141. Also see Phillippe C. Schmitter, "The Persecution of Political and Social Scientists in Brazil," *P.S.*, III (Spring 1970), 123–128.

MILITARY GOVERNMENT IN BRAZIL: AN INTERIM ASSESSMENT

Clearly, the original military plan of government based on a moderate degree of civilian support and complete military unity was almost completely undone by early 1969. The military rulers, despite their long tradition of internal differences over specific policy issues, had nonetheless made consensus within the military the cornerstone of their government in the expectation that their own strength would enable them to weather criticisms for what they felt were tough but necessary policies.

Each cycle of crisis, however, not only revealed dangerous disunities within the military but also narrowed the base of civilian support. Significant gains were achieved in controlling inflation and rationalizing bureaucracies and the tax structure, and in the period 1968 to 1970 the GNP was growing at an impressive rate, possibly over 8 percent a year. However, these gains were countered by social policies which worked against the lower classes: the demobilization of the adult literacy campaigns (such as MEB), of the peasant leagues and the trade unions, the growth of foreign control of the economy, the alienation of civilians, a major "brain drain," the widespread use of torture, and the complete disruption of any semblance of democratic rule. Furthermore, the internal divisions within the military caused serious discontinuities of some of the most important economic and bureaucratic reforms.

Politically, the military government since the Fifth Institutional Act of 1968 appeared to be without a program and without direction. The two major attempts by the military to build new political institutions—the party system and the new constitution—were both victims of the crisis of December 1968. In the aftermath of the Fifth Institutional Act, the military was left even more unclear about its political role than before. The possibility yet remained that a new cycle of crises and capitulations would occur, in which the authoritarian, nationalist officers, who had been the driving force behind the earlier crises, would come to power.

Part of the appeal of authoritarian nationalism for the younger officers was that it offered the possibility of solving two major problems at the same time, namely, the lack of a vigorous program of action and the lack of popular support. Their nationalistic anti-Americanism and their talk of expropriating large landholdings for distribution to the peasants could have the political effect of accruing some left-wing support (in the Peruvian style), and perhaps the support of yet unmobilized peasants. The feelings of the younger officers were strong enough and their frustrations and confusions over the experience of government deep enough to ensure the emergence of new leaders as advocates or brokers of their position, even though the most militant nationalists had been shifted from the centers of power following their indiscipline in December 1968.

On the other hand, the continued crises of discipline within the military created a new caution and conservatism on the part of a growing number of senior officers. Many of them feared that the accession to power of the youthful and more radical nationalist wing of officers could destroy the hierarchy of command, as well as alienate the São Paulo business community, whose cooperation they regarded as necessary for the success of the economic programs of the government.

In the "succession" crisis of September–October 1969 caused by President Costa e Silva's illness, the senior officers were barely able to carry the day and install their candidate in the presidency. After the military's unconstitutional refusal to allow the civilian vice-president to assume the presidency, a bitter conflict developed within the military ranks, which took more than a month and a half to resolve. It involved intense political campaigning among officers, even polling of officer opinion down to the battalion level, and the issuance of numerous manifestos. Ranks were finally closed behind the choice of the senior generals, but only because of the specter of complete military fragmentation. Under these circumstances, the traditional military tendency to resolve conflicts on the basis of seniority prevailed, and General Emilio Garrastazú Medice, formerly chief of national intelligence (SNI) and a four-star general was elected.[23] The possibility still remained, however, that if civilian

[23] No solid account of these events exists. However, it appears that General Emilio Garrastazú Medice was chosen in the "military electoral college" not because he personally was a leader or because he had a program but because (1) he was a four-star general and thus could wield military as well as political authority; (2) he was a close personal and political associate of President Costa e Silva and this softened the image of illegitimate succession; (3) he was not a radical nationalist and was thus acceptable to the São Paulo and international financial community, which had expressed worry lest a Peruvian route be followed if nationalist candidate Lt. Gen. Affonso Albuquerque Lima were to become president; (4) he was not associated with the ESG, which was an anathema to civilian and military na-

political opposition to the military government intensified, and the high economic growth rate of 1968–1970 faltered, the Brazilian military could simultaneously find itself under a growing pressure for an authoritarian nationalist coup at one end of the ideological spectrum and, at the other, for an extrication coup aimed at holding elections and returning power to civilians.

Whatever the future outcome, it is clear that the attraction of military rule—its presumed stability, unity, and fixity of purpose— has been largely illusory. Even more importantly, the difficulties encountered by the highly professional army in Brazil, with its technocratic civilian allies, illustrate that there can be no apolitical solution to the problems of political development.

The experiences of the new pattern of civil–military relations as it has existed since 1964 lead one to ask what might be the conse- quences of a return to the older and traditional moderating pattern. Certainly, as internal divisions within the military proliferate and the alienation of civilian support increases, civilians and military men are beginning to advocate a return to the pre-1964 days. There can probably never be a complete return to the moderating pattern of civil–military relations, since the implicit trust between civilians and military that was an intrinsic part of that pattern has been destroyed. In the future, civilian elites will no longer auto- matically assume that if they encourage the military to overthrow a president, the military will refrain from assuming power them- selves.

Nonetheless, it remains an intriguing idea to many civilians and military officers that the old style of civilian–military relations, in which the military periodically intervened to moderate the political system in times of crisis, should be conducive to peaceful and or- derly political change. In retrospect, however, the consequences of the old moderating pattern were rather different.[24] The constant participation of the military in the resolution of crises may well have had the long-term dysfunctional effect of preventing crises

---

tionalists. Thus, though the image of military rule is frequently one of bold and unified direction, it appears that the intense splits within the military have necessitated a bland compromise figure simply to maintain a minimum of military unity.

[24] See Douglas Chalmers, "Crises and Change in Latin America," *Journal of International Affairs*, XXIII, no. 1 (1969), 76–88, for a useful discussion of the need to analyze the consequences rather than the form of coups and revolutions.

from forcing a change in the political system, thus forestalling the achievement of a new and more stable equilibrium between old and new political groups. It is possible that if power confrontations such as those in 1945 and 1964 had been able to run their course without the threat or possibility of the military intervention, new political groups seeking a voice in politics might have been incorporated into the political system, and traditional groups might have been more willing to come to terms with them as a tactic of political survival. Between 1945 and 1964, the military in Brazil clearly performed a short-term "crisis-limiting" function, but the long-term outcome of their intervention in politics was to leave most of the fundamental conflicts at the heart of the crises unresolved. Samuel Huntington has astutely commented that such guardian-like intervention by the military without assumption of power "has the most debilitating and corrupting effect on the political system. Responsibility and power are divorced."[25] Much of the boundary change in Brazilian civil–military relations is explained by the fact that the middle-level officers rejected parliamentarianism and guardianship and wanted to fuse responsibility and power under military aegis.

[25] Samuel P. Huntington, *Political Order in Changing Societies* (New Haven: Yale University Press, 1968), p. 228.

Conclusion

TO WHAT EXTENT is the Brazilian experience relevant for other
Latin American countries? Are similar patterns of civil–military
relations found elsewhere? Some of the most significant system-
level variables at work in the shift from the moderator model of
civil–military relations to direct military rule are in one degree or
another in existence, or coming into existence, in other Latin
American countries, most notably Peru. These include the great
growth in political demands; the ineffectiveness of parliamentary
forms of government in industrializing an increasingly modernized
society;[1] the growth of military concern with internal security
threats, which the military defines as deriving from an inefficient,
corrupt, and unjust middle- and upper-class parliamentary and social system; the belief that their traditional moderator role of system-maintenance does not contribute to the solution of the problems
of development; and the growth of military confidence that through
their Superior War College they have for the first time a cadre of
specialists and a development program superior to that of the
bankrupt, and therefore illegitimate, politicians. Despite the definite
peculiarities of the Brazilian case, it is possible that cross-national,
system-level changes are taking place in Latin America that will
eventually alter traditional patterns of civil–military relations. Although the Brazilian military to date has been relatively unsuccessful in its new role, the mode of military involvement in Latin
American politics may well shift increasingly from that of system-
maintenance to that of system-transformation.[2] For example, the

---

[1] For a perceptive discussion of the difference between modernization and
industrialization, see David Apter, *The Politics of Modernization* (Chicago:
The University of Chicago Press, 1965), pp. 43–80.

[2] Morris Janowitz, in correspondence with the author in November 1969,
commented that he had not included Latin America in his book, *The Military in the Political Development of New Nations: An Essay in Comparative Analysis* (Chicago: The University of Chicago Press, 1964), not so
much because the Latin American countries were not new nations, but because Latin American military establishments were much less concerned
with directing efforts at system change and modernization than were those

Peruvian military has attempted direct rule in the past, but their current effort at system change is of a much more systematic and thorough order, and is directly related to my analysis of the emergence of new patterns of civil–military relations in Latin America along Brazilian lines. From this perspective, the Peruvian experience will merit very close observation.

Military attempts to rule directly in order to transform the political life of a country and hasten development may or may not be nationalistic in style, but they will probably all be authoritarian. The specific working-out of military attempts at system-transformation will vary with the particular set of circumstances in each country. In Brazil, the military institution's experience of FEB in World War II, their intense anti-Communism after 1963, and their fear that labor unions would infiltrate the sergeant corps, together with the soaring inflation, contributed to a pro-American, pro-foreign-capital, antilabor philosophy in the first government of the military regime. In Peru, many of the same system-level changes occurred, but the circumstances were different. The United States' denial of jets to the Peruvian air force in 1965–1967 and the small alloca-

---

of the new nations. He observed that the system-level changes I had described in Brazil made it a "new nation" in this sense.

It is interesting to note that two of the key supportive attitudes of the moderator model—military acceptance of democratic, parliamentary forms of government as inherently more legitimate in the long run than authoritarian regimes, and military feelings of intellectual and social inferiority toward civilian elites—are for the most part absent in the nations that became independent since World War II. The Russian and Chinese revolutions were powerful models of development in this period and gave authoritarian methods of government an aura of historical legitimacy and necessity. During the period of Latin American independence, in contrast, the political culture was strongly shaped by the American, French, and English models. In Latin America, a small but well-educated civilian political elite had much stronger claims to rule than the poorly educated military. In many of the new post-World War II nations, a highly educated civilian political elite hardly existed. Under colonial rule, modern education was extended not to the political elite but to the military and civil-service bureaucratic elites. Thus, in comparison to Latin America, the military elites of the new nations were not inhibited from assuming governmental control because of feelings of social, intellectual, or educational inferiority vis-à-vis civilians.

India is the most outstanding example of civilian control among the new nations. This was the country with the greatest educational opportunities for the civilian elites, and the history of nearly continuous Congress party elections since the late nineteenth century presents an example of political participation and experience on the part of the civilian elite unmatched in any other developing nation.

tion of funds from the Alliance for Progress represent both military and political sources of anti-Americanism among Peruvian officers. The military campaign in 1965–1966 against a small guerrilla force added to military interest in changing a political system which they associated with developmental failures and the generation of guerrilla violence. The military doctrines developed in the higher war colleges of both Brazil and Peru stressed the nexus of development and security. The absence of a perceived threat to immediate security when the military actually assumed power in Peru in 1968, however, may have contributed to Peruvian emphasis on development. In Brazil, when the military assumed power in 1964, the emphasis was on security. Similarly, the definition of the class enemy was quite different in the two countries. In Brazil, inflation and the link between the sergeants and the trade unions contributed to an antilabor bias. In Peru, the upper-class landowners and urban middle-class politicians were considered the greatest obstruction to long-term development and security because of their lack of national consciousness. The Peruvian land reform act was aimed as much at eliminating upper-class political and economic power as it was at modernizing the agrarian sector.[3]

I argued in Part II of this work that while the officer corps in Brazil is middle class in social composition, the officers see themselves as without a specific class identity, as above class conflicts, and as having the mission of protecting the national good. To the extent that military men in other Latin American countries are beginning to concern themselves with the failure of parliamentary solutions to the problems of development, and seeking to eliminate obstructions to long-term economic development and social stability, they may come to see other groups as hindering such development. From this perspective, even though the evidence from the Brazilian case clearly indicates that the lower classes have benefited the least from military government, the argument that a military government would necessarily tend to repress the emergence of lower groups because of the military's middle-class composition is not completely valid.[4] The military is above all a *situational* elite,

[3] These comments on Peru are based on Luigi Einaudi's ongoing research and his short study, *The Peruvian Military: A Summary Political Analysis* (Santa Monica, Calif.: The RAND Corporation, RM-6048-RC, May 1969).

[4] A widely accepted hypothesis is that the military are able to act as a modernizing force when the question is one of middle-class entry into the political system but become a repressive force concerned with maintaining

269

not a *class* elite. The power and prestige of the Latin American military officers derive from their membership in an institution with power. When such an institutional elite feels that middle- and upper-class life styles and political practices impede development by contributing to internal disruption or guerrilla activity which could threaten military power, it is very possible that in their own self-interest the military could take aggressive action against those aspects of middle- and upper-class life which threatened their institutional position. We see this in the Peruvian military's stand on land reform.

If one were to speculate about potential military policy in Latin America in those countries where the military come to power, a more useful framework than that provided by the class analysis, which sees the military restricted in their economic policies because of their allegiance to middle-class values, is to recognize that the military often view their own power as unrelated to the outcome of economic class conflicts. This self-image implies that a wide range of possible positions on economic issues is available to a military regime. The same military institution could shift from far left to far right, and back again, in regard to economic policy.

In political matters, however, the range of the military governments that may emerge in the future will probably be much more limited. In regard to participation, the desire of military radicals for control would tend to conflict with free democratic electoral campaigns, but would be congruent with a military populist plebiscitary style of politics. As regards mobilization, military radicals' preference for order and unity would make them resistant to the proliferation of autonomous lower-class, mass-action groups, but favorably disposed to mass parades. A natural military style might

the status quo when the question revolves around lower-class demands. The compelling formulation of this argument is found in Samuel Huntington, *Political Order in Changing Societies* (New Haven: Yale University Press, 1968), pp. 220–226. His Latin American data are drawn largely from Martin Needler's interesting article, "Political Development and Military Intervention in Latin America," *American Political Science Review*, LX (September 1966), 616–626. Another variant of this argument is contained in José Nun, "The Middle-Class Military Coup," in *The Politics of Conformity in Latin America*, ed. Claudio Véliz (New York: Oxford University Press, 1967), pp. 66–118.

therefore be a populist variant of nationalist socialism, or, to use the phrase of the thirties, fascism.[5]

It is too early to estimate how successful military attempts at system-transformation will be. In Part IV of this book, I indicated some of the grave political difficulties that face military government, difficulties that are frequently overlooked. Furthermore, in comparison to new nations, Latin America has a much greater degree of urbanization and industrialization, and much more powerful social groups—such as labor, the intellectuals, the industrialists, and the middle-class interest groups. This makes military control and transformation of the social system a much more politically complicated task than military rule of a less developed social structure. These same conditions make military "radicalism" much more improbable in Brazil than in Peru.

Because military rule is unable to solve the political problems of development, it is likely that the military will attempt to retreat to a modified form of the moderator role. However, as I have already indicated, a return to the earlier pattern of civil–military relations is made much more difficult by the experience of military rule, and by the fact that this rule itself reflected system-level changes no longer supportive of a moderator role.

[5] In our recurrent dialogues, my colleague, Richard Maullin, has insistently underscored the political importance for Latin America today of those political movements, often associated with military leaders, which manipulate the symbols of social grievance and of nationality and culture in an essentially populist manner. For an earlier formulation, see our joint *Latin American Security Issues* (The RAND Corporation P–4109, April 1969), by L. Einaudi, R. Maullin, and A. Stepan, particularly pp. 15–16.

Appendix

Researching a Semiclosed Institution—A Note on Sources and Field Techniques

Many scholars have voiced the opinion that research into contemporary civil–military relations in Latin America is made virtually impossible by the scarcity of sources. It is true that systematic survey work is normally ruled out and unlimited access to military files is usually not obtainable, but in fact such access is unavailable in most countries of the world. Nonetheless, the subject of civil–military relations is too central to politics to be ignored by political and social scientists. There is, moreover, far more material and information available to scholars than is commonly realized.

Since so much of what is important in civil–military relations has to do with civilian and national politics, much useful information is gained by beginning with the general literature available in libraries. A wealth of material relevant to modern civil–military relations in Brazil is obtainable at the *Biblioteca Nacional*, Rio de Janeiro. In addition to its collection of military and civilian memoirs, essays and books, it has complete sets of Brazilian laws, congressional debates, newspapers, and magazines going back to the nineteenth century.

At the *Congressional Library* in Brasília one can obtain a more complete breakdown on congressional material, as well as expert guidance. A note of introduction from a Brazilian congressman is often useful.

For information on the Brazilian army, the most valuable library is the *Biblioteca do Exército*, located in the General Staff headquarters of the army in Rio de Janeiro. The library is open to the general public five days a week, has open stacks and a Dewey decimal system of classification. In the stacks are found nearly complete sets of all the army periodicals, such as *A Defesa Nacional, Revista Militar Brasileira, Revista de Intendência Do Exército Brasileira, Boletim do Exército*, and the *Boletim de Informações*. An analysis of the contents of these journals illustrates the changing ideology and concerns of the Brazilian military in various periods. Much valuable work remains to be done on this data alone.

The library also contains the publications of the army-related social organizations, such as the *Revista do Clube Militar*, as well as the only publicly available series of the Superior War College alumni association's *Segurança e Desenvolvimento* (pre-1968 title, *Boletim da As-*

273

sociação dos Diplomados da Escola Superior de Guerra). This bulletin is useful for insights into the ideology of the Superior War College and its change over time. It contains some working papers from the Superior War College itself, as well as lists of all graduates, both civilian and military.

The army officer annual register, the *Almanaque do Exército*, going back to the late nineteenth century, is also available at the library in a complete series. The modern *Almanaque* contains the names and ranks of all officers on active duty, as well as such information as all promotions, foreign and national schools attended, branch of service, and medals received. It is an excellent source for studying the evolution of the size and structure of the officer corps of the army. The *Almanaque* can also be used to determine information on rates of promotion under different governments, and career-pattern correlates of known members of winning or losing coups or major supporters of particular governments.

The navy and the air force also have their own libraries in their Rio headquarters, though these are somewhat smaller, less systematically arranged, and while accessible to scholars, are not as geared to the researcher as the army library.

Budgets for the federal and state governments are on open stack in the library of the *Ministério da Fazenda* in Rio de Janeiro. These contain data on army, navy, and air force budgets as well as those of the state militias.

Among archives available to the researcher on civil–military relations in Brazil, newspaper archives are a very valuable source of information. The best and the most accessible is that of the *O Estado de São Paulo* in the city of São Paulo. Upon request, the librarian of the archive will give the researcher a file of clippings on almost any topic that has been well reported in the press. The archive also contains biographical files on most military leaders, including official army press releases as well as newspaper clippings.

The archive of the *Jornal do Brasil* is similar in organization, but it is only open to the researcher by permission of the publisher. A letter from the researcher's institution to the publisher is recommended. The special utility of the archive is that it contains the newspaper's own unpublished background data and notes from interviews with key figures in the Brazilian military and politics.

The archive of the important military club, the *Clube Militar*, in Rio de Janeiro is open to certified scholars by special permission only. In my own case, permission to examine the archive was granted by the acting vice-president of the club. The archive contains nearly complete election records of the club's politically important biennial elections, with total votes received and the names of the entire slate of candidates. Less completely available are the minutes of the extraordinary sessions of the club, such as the debate within the club demanding the resignation of President Vargas in August 1954.

A new archive that should be of great interest to scholars is that of the ex-President Castello Branco, located in the library of the army General Staff School (ECEME) in Rio de Janeiro. Procedures for access have not yet been established. I received permission from the commandant of ECEME and was the first foreign scholar to use this archive. The archive is made up of roughly 80 files (pastas), almost all of which contain material covering the period from Castello Branco's service as operations officer in the Brazilian division in Italy in World War II until his assumption of the presidency in April 1964. Among other things, the files contain lecture notes for the General Staff School and the Superior War College, his command diary while commander of the Third Army in Recife, recommendations for reform of the army, reflections on Brazil's participation in World War II, and political speeches delivered to army audiences before the civil–military crises of 1955 and 1964. Some of this material has appeared in *Marechal Castello Branco, Seu Pensamento Militar, 1946–1964,* ed., Colonel Francisco Ruas Santos (Rio de Janeiro: Imprensa do Exército, 1968). However, this collection emphasizes Castello's military thought, and some of the most revealing political material is either not presented or has been deleted.

For more historical data on the Brazilian army, there is the *Arquivo do Exército,* located at army headquarters in Rio de Janeiro and normally accessible to qualified scholars with letters of introduction from their institutions. A useful guide to archives and sources for the late nineteenth century is June E. Hahner's "Bibliographical Note" in her *Brazilian Civilian–Military Relations, 1889–1898,* Latin American Studies Program Dissertation Studies, no. 2 (Ithaca, New York: Cornell University, 1967) pp. 268–315.

The businessmen's pressure group *Instituto de Pesquisas e Estudos Sociais* (IPÊS), which played a key role in the 1964 revolution and the 1964–1967 government, has a small library-archive in its Rio de Janeiro headquarters where its publications are on file.

Shortly after the revolution of 1964, Júlio de Mesquita Filho, owner of the powerful *O Estado de São Paulo,* and a key mobilizer of support for the revolution, asked other activists to give their own account of its origin and preparation, so that the historical record would be intact. Some responded with typed manuscripts, others were interviewed on tape by José Stacchini, a senior reporter for the newspaper. About one-third of this material has been produced in a book by Stacchini, *Março 64: Mobilização da Audácia* (São Paulo: Companhia Editôra Nacional,

1965). The rest of the personal statements, plus some military operations orders and other documents, are now in the small personal archive of José Stacchini, who can be reached through the *O Estado de São Paulo.*

To turn finally to interviews and specialized sources of information, I have been writing and thinking about Brazil since March of 1964, and since then have informally discussed Brazilian politics with congressmen, journalists, students, professors, and judges. Much of my feeling for Brazilian politics comes from these pleasurable conversations. For the present work, because of the political sensitivity of the subject, I carried out no formal interviewing until I had researched the libraries and archives for six months. When I began to interview military officers, I relied exclusively upon personal introductions by mutual friends. If the interview went well, the officer concerned would often arrange further introductions to his colleagues, or if he was a commanding officer, he would arrange for his staff to give me a tour and answer my general questions. In this way I informally talked to over 200 officers and formally interviewed over 60 officers. In a number of these interviews and talks, the individual concerned gave me permission to quote, and these names appear in the footnotes to the chapters. From these interviews came invitations to visit several military installations and schools. I had long talks with two former commandants of the *Escola Superior de Guerra* and many of the staff of the Brazilian Military Academy (*Academia Militar das Agulhas Negras,* AMAN) and the General Staff School (*Escola de Commando e Estado Maior do Exército,* ECEME).

Through an introduction from the commandant of the army General Staff School, I met the commandant of the Brazilian Military Academy. The commandant, who was familiar with Morris Janowitz' *The Professional Soldier,* arranged for me to gather similar information on the social and economic background of the military cadets at the school from the files of the academy.

In all I visited military installations in Guanabara, São Paulo, Rio Grande do Sul, Estado do Rio de Janeiro and Amazonas.

Selected Bibliography

1. Relevant General Works on Civil–Military Relations, Research Approaches, and Methodology

A. Books and Monographs

Almond, G., and Coleman, J., eds. *The Politics of the Developing Areas.* Princeton: Princeton University Press, 1960.

Almond, G., and Powell, G. B. *Comparative Politics: A Developmental Approach.* Boston: Little, Brown & Company, 1966.

Almond, G. A., and Verba, S. *The Civic Culture.* Princeton: Princeton University Press, 1963.

Apter, D. *The Politics of Modernization.* Chicago: University of Chicago Press, 1965.

Barber, W. F., and Ronning, C. N. *Internal Security and Military Power: Counterinsurgency and Civic Action in Latin America.* Columbus, Ohio: Ohio State University Press, 1966.

Bienen, H., ed. *The Military Intervenes: Case Studies of Political Development.* New York: Russell Sage Foundation, 1968.

Bragulat, Julio Busquets. *El Militar de Carrera en España.* Barcelona: Ediciones Ariel, 1967.

Brill, W. *Military Intervention in Bolivia: The Overthrow of Paz Estenssoro and the MNR.* Political Studies Series, no. 3. Washington, D.C.: Institute for the Comparative Study of Political Systems, 1967.

Caballero, Ricardo. *Yrigoyen: La conspiración civil y militar del 4 de febrero de 1905.* Buenos Aires: Editorial Raigal, 1951.

Coward, H. Roberts. *Military Technology in Developing Countries.* Cambridge, Mass.: Center for International Studies, M.I.T., 1964.

Deutsch, K. *The Nerves of Government; Models of Political Communication and Control.* New York: The Free Press of Glencoe, 1963.

Easton, D. *A Systems Analysis of Political Life.* New York: John Wiley & Sons, 1965.

Einaudi, Luigi. *The Peruvian Military: A Summary Political Analysis.* Santa Monica, Calif.: The RAND Corporation, RM-6048-RC, May 1969.

————. *The Peruvian Military.* (In preparation.)

Finer, S. *The Man on Horseback: The Role of the Military in Politics.* New York: Praeger, 1962.

277

Gilmore, R. *Caudillism and Militarism in Venezuela, 1810–1910*. Athens: Ohio University Press, 1964.

Girardet, Raoul, ed. *La Crise Militaire Française, 1945–1962: Aspects sociologiques et idéologiques*. Paris: Librairie Armand Colin, 1964.

Gutteridge, William. *Armed Forces in New States*. London: Oxford University Press, 1962.

————. *Military Institutions and Power in the New States*. London: Pall Mall Press, 1964.

Halpern, Manfred. *The Politics of Social Change in the Middle East and North Africa*. Princeton: Princeton University Press, 1963.

Hammond, Paul. *Organizing for Defense: The American Military Establishment in the Twentieth Century*. Princeton: Princeton University Press, 1961.

Hamon, L., ed. *Le Role Extra-Militaire De l'Armée Dans Le Tiers Monde*. Paris: Presses Universitaires de France, 1966.

Huntington, Samuel P., ed. *Changing Patterns of Military Politics*. New York: The Free Press of Glencoe, 1962.

————. *Political Order In Changing Societies*. New Haven: Yale University Press, 1968.

————. *The Soldier and the State*. Cambridge, Mass.: Harvard University Press, 1957.

Hurewitz, J. C. *Middle East Politics: The Military Dimension*. New York: Praeger, 1969.

Imaz, J. *Los que Mandan*. Buenos Aires: Editorial Universitaria de Buenos Aires, 1964.

Janda, K. *Data Processing: Applications to Political Research*. Evanston, Ill.: Northwestern University Press, 1965.

Janowitz, M. *The Military in the Political Development of New Nations; An Essay in Comparative Analysis*. Chicago: University of Chicago Press, 1964.

————, ed. *The New Military: Changing Patterns of Organization*. New York: Russell Sage Foundation, 1964.

————. *The Professional Soldier, A Social and Political Portrait*. Glencoe, Ill.: The Free Press of Glencoe, 1960.

Joffe, E. *Party and Army: Professionalism and Political Control in the Chinese Officer Corps, 1949–1964*. Harvard East Asian Monographs, no. 19. Cambridge, Mass.: Harvard University, 1965.

Johnson, Chalmers. *Revolutionary Change*. Boston: Little, Brown & Co., 1966.

Johnson, J. J. *The Military and Society in Latin America*. Stanford, Calif.: Stanford University Press, 1964.

————, ed. *The Role of the Military in Underdeveloped Countries*. Princeton: Princeton University Press, 1962.

Kolkowicz, R. *The Soviet Military and the Communist Party*. Princeton: Princeton University Press, 1967.

Lang, K. *Sociology of the Military. A Selected and Annotated Bibliography*. Issued by the Inter-University Seminar on Armed Forces and Society, 1969.

Lasswell, H., and Kaplan, A. *Power and Society; A Framework for Political Inquiry*. New Haven: Yale University Press, 1950.

Lasswell, H., and Lerner, D., eds. *World Revolutionary Elites; Studies in Coercive Ideological Movements*. Cambridge, Mass.: The M.I.T. Press, 1965.

Lieuwen, E. *Arms and Politics in Latin America*. New York: Praeger, 1960.

——. *Generals vs. Presidents, Neo-Militarism in Latin America*. New York: Praeger, 1964.

Mannheim, K. *Ideology and Utopia*. New York: Harcourt, Brace & World, 1966.

Mosca, Gaetano. *The Ruling Class*. New York: McGraw-Hill, 1939.

Needler, M. *Political Development in Latin America*. New York: Random House, 1968.

North, L. *Civil–Military Relations in Argentina, Chile and Peru*. Berkeley: Institute of International Studies, University of California, 1966.

North, R.; Holsti, O.; Zaninovich, M.; and Zinnes, D. *Content Analysis; A Handbook with Applications for the Study of International Crisis*. Evanston, Ill.: Northwestern University Press, 1963.

Özbudun, Ergun. *The Role of the Military in Recent Turkish Politics*. Occasional Papers in International Affairs, no. 14. Cambridge: Harvard University, Center for International Affairs, November 1966.

Payne, S. *Politics and the Military in Modern Spain*. Stanford, Calif.: Stanford University Press, 1967.

Pool, I., ed. *Trends in Content Analysis; Papers*. Urbana, Ill.: University of Illinois Press, 1959.

Potash, R. *The Army and Politics in Argentina, 1928–1945*. Stanford, Calif.: Stanford University Press, 1969.

Pye, L. *Aspects of Political Development*. Boston: Little, Brown & Co., 1966.

Russett, Bruce M., *et al. World Handbook of Political and Social Indicators*. New Haven: Yale University Press, 1964.

Rustow, D. *A World of Nations*. Washington, D.C.: The Brookings Institution, 1967.

Schelling, T. *The Strategy of Conflict*. New York: Oxford University Press, 1963.

Spencer, H. *The Principles of Sociology*. 3 vols. New York: D. Appleton & Company, 1889–1905.

Tocqueville, A. de. Vol. II. *Democracy in America.* New York: Schocken Books, 1961.

Vallenilla Lanz, L. *Cesarismo democrático. Estudios sobre las bases sociológicas de la constitución efectiva de Venezuela.* 3rd ed. Caracas: Garrido, 1952.

Van Doorn, J., ed. *Armed Forces and Society. Sociological Essays.* The Hague: Mouton, 1968.

Vatikiotis, P. *The Egyptian Army in Politics: Pattern for New Nations?* Bloomington, Ind.: Indiana University Press, 1961.

Véliz, C., ed. *Obstacles to Change in Latin America.* London: Oxford University Press, 1965.

————, ed. *The Politics of Conformity in Latin America.* London: Oxford University Press, 1967.

Villanueva, V. *El Militarismo en el Peru.* Lima: Empresa Gráfica, T. Scheuch, 1962.

————. *¿Nueva Mentalidad Militar en el Peru?* Lima: Editorial Juan Mejia Baca, 1969.

Von Vorys, K. *Political Development in Pakistan.* Princeton: Princeton University Press, 1965.

Weber, M. *The Theory of Social and Economic Organization.* New York: The Free Press of Glencoe, 1964.

Wirth, J. D. *The Politics of Brazilian Development.* Stanford, Calif.: Stanford University Press, 1970.

Zeitlin, M. *Revolutionary Politics and the Cuban Working Class.* Princeton: Princeton University Press, 1967.

B. *Articles and Manuscripts*

Cantón, Darío. "Notas sobre las Fuerzas Armadas Argentinas," Documento de trabajo, no. 27, Instituto Torcuato Di Tella, Centro de Investigaciones Sociales, Buenos Aires, June 1967.

Chalmers, D. "Crises and Change in Latin America," *Journal of International Affairs,* XXIII, no. 1 (1969), 76–88.

————. "Parties and Society in Latin America." Paper delivered at the 1968 annual meeting of the American Political Science Association, September 2–7, 1968, Washington, D.C.

Coleman, J., and Price, B. "The Role of the Military in Sub-Saharan Africa," in Johnson, J., ed., *The Role of the Military in Underdeveloped Countries.* Princeton: Princeton University Press, 1962.

Dahl, R. "A Critique of the Ruling Elite Model," *American Political Science Review,* LII (June 1958), 463–469.

Davies, J. "Political Stability and Instability: Some Manifestations and Causes," *Journal of Conflict Resolution,* XIII (March 1969), 1–17.

————. "Toward A Theory of Revolution," *American Sociological Review*, XXVII (February 1962), 5–19.

Deutsch, K. "Social Mobilization and Political Development," *American Political Science Review*, LV (September 1961), 493–514.

Feit, E. "Military Coups and Political Development: Some Lessons from Ghana and Nigeria," *World Politics*, XX (January 1968), 179–193.

Felix, D. "An Alternative View of the 'Monetarist–Structuralist' Controversy," in Hirschman, A., ed., *Latin American Issues*. New York: Twentieth Century Fund, 1961, 81–93.

Fossum, E. "Factors Influencing the Occurrence of Military Coups d'Etat in Latin America," *Journal of Peace Research*, III (Fall 1967), 228–251.

Francis, M. "Military Aid to Latin America in the United States Congress," *Journal of Inter-American Studies*, VI (July 1964), 389–401.

Geertz, C. "The Integrative Revolution: Primordial Sentiments and Civil Politics in the New States," in Geertz, C., ed., *Old Societies and New States: The Quest for Modernity in Asia and Africa*. New York: The Free Press of Glencoe, 1963, 105–157.

Girardet, R. "Civil and Military Power in the Fourth Republic," in Huntington, S., ed., *Changing Patterns of Military Politics*. New York: The Free Press of Glencoe, 1962.

Goldwert, M. "The Rise of Modern Militarism in Argentina," *Hispanic American Historical Review*, XLVIII (May 1968), 189–205.

Gutteridge, W. "Military Elites in Ghana and Nigeria," *African Forum*, II (Summer 1966).

Horowitz, I. "The Military Elites," in Lipsit, S., and Solari, A., *Elites in Latin America*. New York: Oxford University Press, 1967, 146–189.

Huntington, S. "Civilian Control of the Military: A Theoretical Statement," in Eulau, H., Eldersveld, S., and Janowitz, M., eds., *Political Behavior: A Reader in Theory and Research*. Glencoe: The Free Press of Glencoe, 1956, 380–385.

Kim, C. "The South Korean Military Coup of May, 1961: Its Causes and the Social Characteristics of Its Leaders," in Van Doorn, J., ed., *Armed Forces and Society: Sociological Essays*. The Hague: Mouton, 1968, 298–316.

Klein, H. "David Toro and the Establishment of 'Military Socialism' in Bolivia," *Hispanic American Historical Review*, XLV (February 1965), 25–52.

————. "Germán Busch and the Era of 'Military Socialism' in Bolivia," *Hispanic American Historical Review*, XLVII (May 1967), 166–184.

281

Lang, K. "Bureaucracy in Crisis: A Role-Analysis of German Generals Under Hitler," master's diss., Department of Sociology, University of Chicago, 1952.

————. "Military Sociology: A Trend Report and Bibliography," *Current Sociology*, XIII (1965), 1–53.

Lasswell, H. "The Garrison State and Specialists on Violence," *American Journal of Sociology*, XLVI (January 1941), 455–468.

————. "The Garrison State Hypothesis Today," in Huntington, S., ed., *Changing Patterns of Military Politics*. New York: The Free Press of Glencoe, 1962, 51–70.

Lerner, D., and Richardson, R. "Swords and Ploughshares: The Turkish Army as a Modernizing Force," *World Politics*, XIII (October 1960), 19–44.

Linz, J. "An Authoritarian Regime: Spain," in Allardt, E., and Littunen, Y., eds., *Cleavages, Ideologies and Party Systems*. Helsinki: Transactions of the Westermarck Society, 1964, 291–342.

————. "The Breakdown of Democratic Regimes." Paper prepared for the Seventh World Congress of Sociology, Varna, Bulgaria, September 14–19, 1970.

————. "The Party System of Spain: Past and Future," in Lipset, S., and Rokkan, S., eds., *Party Systems and Voter Alignments: Cross-National Perspectives*. New York: The Free Press, 1967, 197–282.

Lissak, M. "Modernization and Role-Expansion of the Military in Developing Countries: A Comparative Analysis," *Comparative Studies in Society and History*, IX (April 1967), 233–255.

Loftus, J. *Latin American Defense Expenditures, 1938–1965*. Santa Monica, Calif.: The RAND Corporation, RM-5310-PR/ISA, January 1968.

McAlister, L. "The Military," in Johnson, J., ed., *Continuity and Change in Latin America*. Stanford, Calif.: Stanford University Press, 1964, 136–160.

————. "Recent Research and Writings on the Role of the Military in Latin America," *Latin American Research Review*, II (Fall 1966), 5–36.

Needler, M. "Political Development and Military Intervention in Latin America," *American Political Science Review*, LX (September 1966), 616–626.

Nun, J. "A Latin American Phenomenon: The Middle Class Military Coup," *Trends in Social Science Research in Latin American Studies*. Berkeley, Calif.: University of California, Institute of International Studies, 1965, 55–99.

————. "The Middle-Class Military Coup," in Véliz, C., ed., *The*

Politics of Conformity in Latin America. London: Oxford University Press, 1967, 66–118.

Parsons, T. "Some Reflections on the Place of Force in Social Process," in Eckstein, H., ed., *Internal War, Problems and Approaches*. New York: The Free Press of Glencoe, 1964, 33–70.

Pauker, G. "Southeast Asia as a Problem Area in the Next Decade," *World Politics*, XI (April 1959), 325–345.

———. "The Military in Indonesia," in Johnson, J., ed., *The Role of the Military in Underdeveloped Countries*. Princeton: Princeton University Press, 1962, 185–230.

———. *The Indonesian Doctrine of Territorial Warfare and Territorial Management*. Santa Monica, Calif.: The RAND Corporation, RM-3312-PR, November 1963.

Putnam, R. "Toward Explaining Military Intervention in Latin American Politics," *World Politics*, XX (October 1967), 83–110.

Rapoport, D. "Coup d'Etat: The View of the Men Firing Pistols," in Friedrich, C., ed., *Revolution*. New York: Atherton Press, 1966, 53–74.

———. "The Political Dimensions of Military Usurpation," *Political Science Quarterly*, LXXXIII (December 1968), 551–573.

Rustow, D. "The Army and the Founding of the Turkish Republic," *World Politics*, XI (July 1959), 513–552.

———. "The Military: Turkey," in Ward, R., and Rustow, D., eds., *Political Modernization in Japan and Turkey*. Princeton: Princeton University Press, 352–388.

———. "The Study of Elites: Who's Who, When, and How," *World Politics*, XVIII (July 1966), 690–717.

Sayeed, K. "The Capabilities of Pakistan's Political System," *Asian Survey*, VII (February, 1967), 102–110.

Searing, D. "The Comparative Study of Elite Socialization," *Comparative Political Studies*, I (January 1969), 471–500.

Siekman, P. "When Executives Turned Revolutionaries," *Fortune* (September 1964), 147–149, 210, 214, 221.

Silvert, K., and Germani, G. "Politics, Social Structure and Military Intervention in Latin America," *European Journal of Sociology*, II (1961), 62–81.

Sklar, R. "Contradictions in the Nigerian Political System," *Journal of Modern African Studies*, III (August 1965).

Snow, P. "The Class Basis of Argentine Political Parties," *American Political Science Review*, LXIII (March 1969), 163–167.

Stepan, A. "Discussion: The Middle Classes in Latin America," *New Politics*, IV (Spring 1965), 87–90.

Stepan, A. "Political Development Theory: The Latin American Experience," *Journal of International Affairs*, xx (1966), 223–234.

———. "The Military's Role in Latin American Political Systems: A Review Article," *Review of Politics*, xxvii (October 1965), 564–568.

Wiatr, Jerzy. "Expert and Politician—The Divergent Aspects of the Social Role of the Army Man," *Polish Sociological Bulletin*, no. 1 (1964), 44–53.

2. WORKS RELEVANT TO THE PROBLEM OF CIVIL–MILITARY REI.ATIONS: BRAZIL

A. Books

Almeida, (General) Gil de. *Homens e Factos de Uma Revolução.* Rio de Janeiro: Calvino Filho, 1934.

Almeida, José Américo de. *Ocasos de Sangue.* Rio de Janeiro: Livraria José Olympio, 1954.

Alves, Márcio Moreira. *Torturas e Torturados.* Rio de Janeiro: Idade Nova, 1966.

Andrade, Euclides, and Camara, Hely F. da. *A Fôrça Publica de São Paulo: Esbôço Histórico: 1831–1931.* São Paulo: Sociedade Impressora Paulista, 1931.

Araripe, (General) Tristão de Alencar. *Tasso Fragoso: Um Pouco de História do Nosso Exército.* Rio de Janeiro: Biblioteca do Exército, 1960.

Baer, W. *Industrialization and Economic Development in Brazil.* Homewood, Ill.: Richard D. Irwin, 1965.

Barbosa, Ruy. *Commentários à Constituição Federal Brasileira.* São Paulo: Saraiva & Cia, 1932, i.

———. *Contra o Militarismo: Companha Eleitoral de 1909 a 1910.* Rio de Janeiro: J. Ribeiro do Santos, n.d.

Bastos, (General) Joaquim Justino Alves. *Encontro com o Tempo.* Pôrto Alegre: Editôra Globo, 1965.

Bello, José Maria. *A History of Modern Brazil, 1889–1964.* Trans. J. L. Taylor. Stanford, Calif.: Stanford University Press, 1966.

Bemis, G. *From Crisis to Revolution: Monthly Case Studies.* Los Angeles, International Public Administration Center, School of Public Administration, University of Southern California, 1964.

Borges, Mauro. *O Golpe em Goiás.* Rio de Janeiro: Editôra Civilização Brasileira, 1965.

Brayner, (Marshal) Lima. *A Verdade Sôbre FEB.* Rio de Janeiro: Editôra Civilização Brasileira, 1969.

Burns, E. B. *Nationalism in Brazil; A Historical Survey.* New York: Praeger, 1968.

284

Café Filho, João. *Do Sindicato ao Catete: Memórias Políticas e Confissões Humanas.* 2 vols. Rio de Janeiro: Livraria José Olympio, 1966.

Callado, Antônio. *Tempo de Arraes: Padres e Comunistas na Revolução Sem Violência.* Rio de Janeiro: José Alvaro, 1964.

Calogeras, João Pandiá. *A History of Brazil.* Trans. and ed., Percy Alvin Martin. New York: Russell & Russell, 1963.

Campos, Roberto de Oliveira. *Do Outro Lado da Cêrca.* Rio de Janeiro: APEC Editôra, 1967.

————. *A Moeda, O Govêrno e o Tempo.* Rio de Janeiro: APEC Editôra, 1964.

Caó, José. *Dutra.* São Paulo: Instituto Progresso Editorial, 1949.

Carli, Gileno dé. *JQ, Brasília e a Grande Crise.* Rio de Janeiro: Irmãos Pongetti Editôres, 1961.

Carneiro, Glauco. *História das Revoluções Brasileiras.* 2 vols. Rio de Janeiro: Edições O Cruzeiro, 1965.

Carone, E. *Revoluções do Brasil Contemporâneo, 1922–1938.* São Paulo: Coleção Buriti, 1965.

Carvalho, Estevão Leitão de. *Dever Militar e Política Partidaria.* São Paulo: Companhia Editôra Nacional, 1959.

Castello Branco, (Lt. Col.) Manoel Thomaz. *O Brasil na II Grande Guerra.* Rio de Janeiro: Biblioteca do Exército, 1960.

Cavalcanti, T., and Dubnic, R., eds., *Comportamento Eleitoral no Brasil.* Rio de Janeiro: Fundação Getúlio Vargas, 1964.

Costa, (Major) Joffre Gomes da. *Marechal Henrique Lott.* Rio de Janeiro: no publisher, 1960.

Coutinho, Lourival. *O General Góes Depõe.* Rio de Janeiro: Livraria Editôra Coelho Branco, 1955.

Daland, R. *Brazilian Planning: Development Politics and Administration.* Chapel Hill, N.C.: The University of North Carolina Press, 1967.

Dines, Alberto, *et al. Os Idos de Março: E a Queda em Abril.* Rio de Janeiro: José Alvaro, 1964.

————. *O Mundo Depois de Kennedy.* Rio de Janeiro: José Alvaro, 1965.

Dória, Seixas. *Eu, Réu Sem Crime.* 2nd ed. Rio de Janeiro: Editôra Equador, 1964.

Duarte, José. *A Constituição Brasileira de 1946: Exegese dos Textos a Luz dos Trabalhos da Assembléia Constituinte.* Vol. 3. Rio de Janeiro: Imprensa Nacional, 1947.

Dulles, J.W.F. *Vargas of Brazil: A Political Biography.* Austin, Tex.: University of Texas Press, 1967.

Dulles, J.W.F. *Unrest in Brazil: Political Military Crises, 1955–1964.* Austin, Tex.: University of Texas Press, 1970.

Ellis, H. *The Applicability of Certain Theories of Economic Development to Brazil.* Latin American Center Essay no. 1. Milwaukee, Wis.: University of Wisconsin Press, December 1968.

————, ed. *The Economy of Brazil.* Berkeley, Calif.: University of California Press, 1969.

Faust, J. *A Revolução Devora Seus Presidentes.* Rio de Janeiro: Editôra Saga, 1965.

Ferreira, Oliveiros. *As Fôrças Armadas e o Desafio da Revolução.* Rio de Janeiro: Edições GRD, 1964.

Figueiredo, Euclydes. *Contribução para a História da Revolução Constitucionalista de 1932.* São Paulo: Livraria Martins, 1954.

Franco, Virgílio A. de Mello. *Outubro, 1930.* 4th ed. Rio de Janeiro: Schmidt-Editôr, 1931.

Furtado, Celso. *Dialética do Desenvolvimento.* Rio de Janeiro: Editôra Fundo de Cultura, 1964.

Golbery, (General) do Couto e Silva. *Geopolítica do Brasil.* Rio de Janeiro: Livraria José Olympio, 1967.

————. *Planejamento Estratégico.* Rio de Janeiro: Biblioteca do Exército, 1955.

Guerreiro Ramos, Alberto. *A Crise do Poder no Brasil.* Rio de Janeiro: Zahar Editôres, 1961.

————. *Mito e Verdade da Revolução Brasileira.* Rio de Janeiro: Zahar Editôres, 1963.

Gusmão, Paulo Dourado de. *Manual de Direito Constitucional.* Rio de Janeiro: Livraria Freitas Bastos, 1957.

Hahner, J. *Brazilian Civilian–Military Relations, 1889–1898.* Latin American Studies Program Dissertation Series, no. 2. Ithaca, N.Y.: Cornell University, 1966.

Ianni, Octavio, *et al. Política e Revolução Social no Brasil.* Rio de Janeiro: Editôra Civilização Brasileira, 1965.

Jaguaribe, Hélio. *Desenvolvimento Econômico e Desenvolvimento Político.* Rio de Janeiro: Editôra Fundo de Cultura, 1962.

Jurema, Abelardo. *Sexta-feira, 13: Os Últimos Dias do Govêrno João Goulart.* Rio de Janeiro: Edições O Cruzeiro, 1964.

Leff, N. *Economic Policy-Making and Development in Brazil, 1947–1964.* New York: John Wiley & Sons, 1968.

Luz, Carlos. *Em Defesa da Constituição.* Rio de Janeiro: Organização Simões, 1956.

Malvasio, (Captain) Luiz Sebastião. *História da Fôrça Pública.* São Paulo: Fôrça Pública do Estado de São Paulo, 1967.

Mascarenhas, (Marshal) J. B. de Moraes. *A F.E.B. Pelo Seu Comandante.* São Paulo: Instituto Progresso Editorial, 1947.

Morais, Berta, *et al. Depoimento de Oficiais da Reserva Sôbre a F.E.B.* São Paulo: Instituto Progresso Editorial, 1949.

Nabuco, Carolina. *A Vida de Virgílio de Melo Franco.* Rio de Janeiro: Livraria José Olympio, 1962.

Ouro Prêto, Visconde de. *Advento da Ditadura Militar no Brasil.* Paris: F. Pichon, 1891.

Pedreira, Fernando. *Março 31: Civis e Militares no Processo da Crise Brasileira.* Rio de Janeiro: José Alvaro, 1964.

Peixoto, Alzira Vargas do. *Getúlio Vargas, Meu Pai.* Pôrto Alegre: Editôra Globo, 1960.

Peregrino, Umberto. *História e Projeção das Instituições Culturais do Exército.* Rio de Janeiro: Livraria José Olympio, 1967.

Pereira, Osny Duarte. *Quem Faz as Leis no Brasil?* Cadernos do povo brasileiro, vol. 3. Rio de Janeiro: Editôra Civilização Brasileira, 1962.

Quem é Quem no Brasil. Vols. 4 and 7. São Paulo: Sociedade Brasileira de Expansão Comercial, 1955 and 1963.

Rabello, Manoel Henrique da Cunha. *Guia de Legislação Militar.* 2nd ed. Rio de Janeiro: Irmaõs Di Giorgio & Cia, 1948.

Rocha Netto, Bento Munhoz da. *Radiografia de Novembro.* Rio de Janeiro: Editôra Civilização Brasileira, 1961.

Rodrigues, José Honório. *Conciliação e Reforma no Brasil; Um desafio histórico-cultural.* Rio de Janeiro: Editôra Civilização Brasileira, 1965.

Santos, Francisco Ruas. *Coleção Bibliográfica Militar.* Rio de Janeiro: Biblioteca do Exército, 1960.

———. *Fontes para a História da FEB.* Rio de Janeiro: Biblioteca do Exército, 1958.

———. *Marechal Castello Branco, Seu Pensamento Militar.* Rio de Janeiro: Imprensa do Exército, 1968.

Seabra Fagundes, M. *As Fôrças Armadas na Constituição.* Rio de Janeiro: Biblioteca do Exército, 1955.

Silva, Hélio. *1922: Sangue na Areia de Copacabana.* Vol. I, O Ciclo de Vargas. Rio de Janeiro: Editôra Civilização Brasileira, 1964.

Silveira, J. *As Duas Guerras da FEB.* Rio de Janeiro: Editôra Idade Nova, 1965.

Skidmore, T. *Politics in Brazil, 1930–1964; An Experiment in Democracy.* New York: Oxford University Press, 1967.

Sodré, Nelson W. *História Militar do Brasil.* Rio de Janeiro: Editôra Civilização Brasileira, 1965.

———. *Memórias de um Soldado.* Rio de Janeiro: Editôra Civilização Brasileira, 1967.

Stacchini, José. *Março 64: Mobilização da Audácia.* São Paulo: Companhia Editôra Nacional, 1965.

Tavares, (General) A. de Lyra. *The Brazilian Army.* Guanabara, Brazil: EGGCF, 1967.

Távora, (General) Juarez. *Petróleo para o Brasil.* Rio de Janeiro: Livraria José Olympio, 1955.

————. *Uma Política de Desenvolvimento para o Brasil.* Rio de Janeiro: Livraria José Olympio, 1962.

Tito Silveira, (Colonel) Geraldo. *Crônica da Polícia Militar de Minas.* Belo Horizonte: Imprensa Oficial do Estado de Minas Gerais, 1966.

Vargas, Getúlio. Vol. 5. *A Nova Política do Brasil.* Rio de Janeiro: Livraria José Olympio, 1938.

Victor, Mário. *Cinco Anos Que Abalaram O Brasil (de Jânio Quadros ao Marechal Castelo Branco).* Rio de Janeiro: Editôra Civilização Brasileira, 1965.

Wagley, Charles. *An Introduction to Brazil,* New York: Columbia University Press, 1963.

B. Articles and Manuscripts

Alexander, R. "Brazilian Tenentismo," *Hispanic American Historical Review,* XXXVI (May 1956), 229–242.

Bermudez, (Major) Washington. "O Espírito da Revolução e sua Contribuição para uma Renovação da Mentalidade Nacional," *A Defesa Nacional,* no. 596 (July–August 1964), 11–18.

Boehrer, G. "O Partido Republicano, O Exército e a Revolução de 1889," in his *Da Monarquia À República.* Rio de Janeiro: Ministério da Educação e Cultura, Serviço de Documentação, 1954, 275–286.

Bonilla, F. "A National Ideology for Development: Brazil," in Silvert, K., ed., *Expectant Peoples: Nationalism and Development.* New York: Random House, 1963, 232–264.

"Bibliografia Sôbre a Revolução de 31 de Março," *Boletim da Biblioteca da Camara dos Deputados,* XIII, no. 2 (July–December, 1964), 499–514.

Carneiro, D. "Organização Política do Brasil," Departmento de Estudos, Escola Superior de Guerra. C-47-59.

Carneiro, G. "A Guerra de 'Sorbonne,' " *O Cruzeiro,* Ano XXXII, no. 39 (June 24, 1967), 16–21.

Carvalho, (Captain) Luiz Paulo Macedo. "O Papel Social do Oficial." *A Defesa Nacional,* no. 597 (September–October 1964), 81–84.

Carvalho, (Lt. Col.) Ferdinando de. "A Guerra Revolucionária Comunista no Brasil," *A Defesa Nacional,* no. 597 (September–October 1964), 31–48.

288

Carvalho, Murilo. "On the Belief System of the Brazilian Military." MS, March 1968. On file at the International Data Library and Reference Service, Survey Research Center, University of California at Berkeley.

Castello Branco, (General) Humberto de Alencar. "Ação Educativa Contra Guerra Revolucionária" (Lecture given to the army General Staff School [ECEME], December 9, 1963). In folder 8, Castello Branco archive, Escola de Comando e Estado Maior do Exército, Rio de Janeiro.

————. "A Esao na Atualidade Militar," *Revista De Aeronautica*, Ano VI, no. 24 (January–February 1964), 4–8.

————. "O Dever do Militar en Face da Luta Ideológica," *Revista De Aeronautica*, Ano VI, no. 23 (November–December 1963), 29–32.

————. "Os Meios Militares na Recuperação Moral do País." Lecture given to the Escola Superior de Guerra, September 19, 1955. In Castello Branco archive, Escola de Comando e Estado Maior do Exército, Rio de Janeiro.

Da Silva, Ildefonso Mascarenhas. "O Poder Nacional e Seus Tipos de Estrutura." Escola Superior de Guerra, C-20-56, 32–34.

Della Cava, Ralph. "Torture in Brazil," *Commonweal*, XCII (April 24, 1970), 129, 135–141.

Díaz-Alejandro, Carlos F. "Some Aspects of the Brazilian Experience with Foreign Aid." Center Discussion Paper No. 77. New Haven: Yale University, Economic Growth Center, October 1969.

Falcão, (Capitão-de-Mar-e-Guerra) Christovão L. Barros. "Mobilização no Campo Econômico." Curso de Mobilização Nacional. Escola Superior de Guerra, C-03-59.

Francis, Paulo. "Tempos de Goulart," *Revista Civilização Brasileira*, I (May 1966), 75–91.

Freyre, Gilberto. "Fôrças Armadas e Outras Fôrças," *A Defesa Nacional*, LII (January/February 1966), 7–22.

Furtado, Celso. "Obstáculos Políticos ao Crescimento Econômico no Brasil," *Revista Civilização Brasileira*, Ano I, no. 1 (March 1965), 129–145.

Gasper Gomes, Lúcia Maria. "Cronologia do Govêrno Castelo Branco," *Dados*, no. 2/3 (1967), 112–132.

————. "Cronologia do 1° ano do Govêrno Costa e Silva," *Dados*, no. 4 (1968), 199–220.

Hahner, J. "The Paulistas' Rise to Power: A Civilian Group Ends Military Rule," *Hispanic American Historical Review*, XLVII (May 1967), 149–165.

Harding, T. "Revolution Tomorrow: The Failure of the Left in Brazil," *Studies on the Left*, IV (Fall 1964), 30–54.

289

Hutchinson, B. "The Social Grading of Occupations in Brazil," *British Journal of Sociology* (June 1957), 176–189.

Iglesias, José. "Report from Brazil: What the Left is Saying," *New York Times Magazine*, December 7, 1969.

Jaguaribe, Hélio. "A Renúncia do Presidente Quadros e a Crise Política Brasileira," *Revista Brasileira de Ciências Sociais*, I (November 1961), 272–311.

Leff, N. "Export Stagnation and Autarkic Development in Brazil, 1947–1962," *Quarterly Journal of Economics*, LXXXI (May 1967), 286–301.

———. "Import Constraints and Development: Causes of Recent Decline of Brazilian Economic Growth," *Review of Economics and Statistics*, XLIX (November 1967), 494–501.

Love, J. "Rio Grande do Sul as a Source of Political Instability in Brazil's Old Republic, 1909–1932," Ph.D. diss., Department of History, Columbia University, 1967.

Magessi, (Marshal) Augusto C. "Considerações Sôbre o Sindicalismo," *Revista de Intendência do Exército Brasileiro*, no. 132 (November–December 1963), 56–61.

Mange, Roger de Carvalho. "Alguns Problemas das Pequenas Frações de Infantaria na F.E.B.," in Morais, B., *et al., Depoimento de Oficiais da Reserva Sôbre a F.E.B.* São Paulo: Instituto Progresso Editorial, 1949, 103–122.

Manwaring, M. "The Military in Brazilian Politics," Ph.D. diss., Political Science Department, University of Illinois, 1968.

Mourão Filho, Olympio. "Autocrítica de Olympio Mourão Filho." *Manchete* (January 7, 1967), 29–31.

———. "Relatório de Revolução Democrática Iniciada Pela 4a. RM E 4a. DI em 31 de Março de 1964." *Comando de 4a. Região Militar, 4a. Divisão de Infantaria e Guarnição de Juiz de Fora* (May 9, 1964).

Meira Matos, (Colonel) Carlos de. "O Pensamento Revolucionário Brasileiro," in *A Revolução de 31 de Março, 2° Aniversário*. Rio de Janeiro: Biblioteca do Exército, 1966, 128–142.

Mendes, Cândido. "O Govêrno Castelo Branco: Paradigma e Prognose," *Dados*, no. 2/3 (1967), 63–111.

———. "Sistema Político e Modelos de Poder no Brasil," *Dados*, no. 1 (1966), 7–41.

"O Ensino na Aman," *Revista Agulhas Negras* (1965), 7.

"Os Militares," *Cadernos Brasileiros*, no. 38 (November–December 1966). Special issue devoted to role of military in the political system.

Moura, Ricardo. "A Renda Nacional e Sua Distribuição." Curso Superior de Guerra, Escola Superior de Guerra, C1-70-58.

Muricy, (General) Antonio Carlos. *Os Motivos da Revolução Demo-crática Brasileira: Palestras Pronunciadas na Televisão Canal 2, nos Dias 19 e 25 de Maio de 1964.* Recife: Imprensa Oficial, n.d.

Nunn, F. "Civil–Military Relations in Chile, 1891–1938," Ph.D. diss., University of New Mexico, 1963.

Pearson, N. "Small Farmer and Rural Worker Pressure Groups in Brazil," Ph.D. diss., University of Florida, 1965.

Peregrino, (General) Umberto. "O Pensamento da Escola Superior de Guerra," *Cadernos Brasileiros*, no. 38 (November–December 1966), 29–38.

Peterson, P. "Brazilian Political Parties: Formation, Organization, Leadership, 1945–1959," Ph.D. diss., University of Michigan, 1962.

Poppino, R. "The Military in Brazilian Politics: Tradition and Innovation." Davis: University of California, May 1965. Mimeographed.

Quadros, Jânio and Franco, Afonso Arinos de Mello. "O Porquê da Renúncia," *Realidade* (November 1967), 27–34.

Reis, (Colonel) Everaldo de Oliveira. "O Problema da Falta de Sub-alternos," *A Defesa Nacional*, no. 608 (July–August 1966), 99–102.

Revista Brasileira de Estudos Políticos, no. 21 (July 1966). Special issue devoted to articles on national security doctrine by writers close to the Escola Superior de Guerra.

Reynolds, R. "Brazil's Overseas Military Operations," *Military Review*, XLVI (November 1966), 85–91.

Rowe, J. "Revolution or Counterrevolution in Brazil," *American Universities Field Staff Reports Service*, East Coast South America Series, XI, nos. 4 and 5, 1964.

––––––. "The 'Revolution' and the 'System': Notes on Brazilian Politics," *American Universities Field Staff Reports Service*, East Coast South America Series, XII, nos. 3–5, 1966.

Saunders, J. "A Revolution of Agreement Among Friends: The End of the Vargas Era," *Hispanic American Historical Review*, XLIV (May 1964), 197–213.

Schmitter, Phillipe C. "The Persecution of Political and Social Scientists in Brazil," *P.S.*, III (Spring 1970), 123–128.

Schneider, R. "Election Analysis," in Daugherty, C., Rowe, J., and Schneider, R. *Brazil Election Factbook: Number 2, September 1965.* Washington: Institute for the Comparative Study of Political Systems, 1965, 53–71.

Simmons, C. "Deodoro da Fonseca, Fate's Dictator," *Journal of Inter-American Studies*, V (January 1963), 45–52.

––––––. "The Rise of the Brazilian Military Class, 1870–1890." *Mid-America*, XXXIX (October 1957), 227–238.

Souza, Amaury de. "Março ou Abril? Uma Bibliografia Comentada

Sôbre o Movimento Político de 1964 no Brasil," *Dados*, no. 1 (2° semestre, 1966), 160–175.

Souza Sampaio, Nelson de. "As Doutrinas Políticas Contemporâneas e Suas Relações con a Segurança Nacional," Escola Superior de Guerra, C-11-56.

Stein, S. "The Historiography of Brazil, 1808–1889," *Hispanic American Historical Review*, XL (May 1960), 234–278.

Stepan, A. "The Continuing Problem of Brazilian Integration: The Monarchical and Republican Periods," in Pike, F., ed., *Latin American History: Select Problems; Identity, Integration, and Nationhood*. New York: Harcourt, Brace & World, 1969, 259–296.

Tavares, (General) Aurélio de Lyra. "A Pesquisa Social e A Segurança da Democracia," Recife: Imprensa Universitária, Instituto Joaquim Nabuco de Pesquisas, 1965.

Tavares, María Conceição, *et al.* "The Growth and Decline of Import Substitution in Brazil," *Economic Bulletin for Latin America*, IX (March 1964), 1–59.

Távora, Juarez. "Escola Superior de Guerra," *A Defesa Nacional*, XLI (February 1954), 111–120.

Tiller, A. "The Igniting Spark—Brazil, 1930," *Hispanic American Historical Review*, XLV (August 1965), 384–392.

Tuthill, J. "Economic and Political Aspects of Development in Brazil and U.S. Aid," *Journal of Inter-American Studies*, XI (April 1969), 186–208.

Vianna, (Captain of Corveta) José Augusto Didier Barbosa, "Vencimentos dos Militares," *Boletim do Clube Naval*, no. 176 (4° trimestre, 1963), 121–134.

Vidal, (Colonel) Germano Seidl. "Ação Cívica das Fôrças Armadas," *A Defesa Nacional*, no. 613 (May–June 1967), 41–54.

Wirth, J. "Tenentismo in the Brazilian Revolution of 1930," *Hispanic American Historical Review*, XLIV (May 1964), 161–179.

Young, J. "Military Aspects of the 1930 Brazilian Revolution," *Hispanic American Historial Review*, XLIV (May 1964), 180–196.

3. PUBLIC DOCUMENTS

Estados Unidos do Brasil, Coleção Das Leis.

———. *Diário Oficial.*

———. Congresso Nacional, Câmara dos Deputados, *Diário do Congresso.*

———. ———. *Annais de Constituinte de 1891.*

———. ———. *Diário da Assembléia, 1946.*

———. Inquérito Policial Militar N° 709. *O Comunismo no Brasil.* 4 vols. Rio de Janeiro: Biblioteca do Exército, 1966–1967.

————. Instituto Brasileiro de Geografia e Estatística, *Anuário Estatístico do Brasil* (annual).

————. Ministério de Aeronautica, *Almanaque dos Oficiais da Aeronautica* (annual).

————. Ministério do Exército, *Almanaque do Exército* (annual).

————. ————. *Boletim do Exército* (daily).

————. ————. *A Ação do Exército no Programa do Govêrno.* General A. de Lyra Tavares. Rio de Janeiro: Imprensa do Exército, 1968.

————. ————. *Efetivos do Exército: Exposição do Ministro do Exército ao Senado Federal.* Rio de Janeiro: Imprensa do Exército, 1968.

————. ————. *Estatuto do Clube Militar.* Rio de Janeiro: Imprensa do Exército, 1968.

————. ————. *Instruções para o Concurso de Admissão e Matrícula na Escola Preparatória de Campinas.* São Paulo, 1968.

————. ————. *O Orçamento do Ministério do Exército.* Rio de Janeiro: Imprensa do Exército, 1968.

————. ————. *Operações Em Localidade Contra Fôrças Irregulares.* Rio de Janeiro: EGGCF, 1967.

————. Ministério da Guerra. *O Exército e o Êxodo Rural.* Coronel Hygino de Barros Lemos. Rio de Janeiro: Biblioteca do Exército, 1959.

————. Ministério do Exército, *Fator de Integração Nacional.* Coronel Octávio Costa. Rio de Janeiro: Imprensa do Exército, 1967.

————. ————. *Manual de Campanha, Guerra Psicológica.* 1st ed. Rio de Janeiro: Estabelecimento General Gustavo Cordeiro de Farias, 1966.

————. ————. *Manual de Campanha, Polícia, Distúrbios Civis e Calamidades Públicas.* Rio de Janeiro: Estabelecimento General Gustavo Cordeiro de Farias, 1967.

————. ————. *Plano Geral de Convocação para o Serviço Militar en 1961.*

————. ————. *Os Caminhos da Integração Nacional.* Rio de Janeiro: Gráficos Block. 1967.

————. ————. *O Seu Exército.* Rio de Janeiro: Gráficos Block, n.d.

————. ————. *O Serviço Militar como Elemento de Uma Política de Valorização do Homen Brasileiro.* General Aurélio de Lyra Tavares. Rio de Janeiro: Imprensa do Exército, 1968.

————. ————. *1930–1940. A República dos Estados Unidos do Brasil e o Exército Brasileiro.* Rio de Janeiro: Livraria José Olympio, 1941.

Estados Unidos do Brasil, Ministério do Exército. Academia Militar das Agulhas Negras. *Aula Inaugural Ano Letivo de 1968, Novas Dimensões da Profissão Militar, 1968.*

———. ———. ———. *Concurso de Admissão, 'Questões Propostas.'* January 1966.

———. ———. ———. *Direito Constitucional.* 1966.

———. ———. ———. *Formando Oficiais para o Exército do Brasil.* n.d. (1967 or 1968).

———. ———. ———. *Instruções para o Concurso de Admissão e Matricula,* n.d. (1967 or 1968).

———. ———. ———. *Perfis de Chefia Militar, 1968.*

———. ———. Estado-Maior do Exército, *Boletim de Informações* (usually issued monthly).

———. Ministério da Marinha, *Almanaque* (annual).

———. Ministério do Planejamento e Coordenação Econômica. *Programa de Ação Econômica do Govêrno: 1964–1966.* 2nd ed. Documentos EPEA, no. 1, May 1965.

———. ———. *Consolidação Orçamentária do Govêrno Federal, 1965.* June 1965.

———. ———. *Balanço Orçamentário Consolidado do Govêrno Federal, 1964.* September 1964.

———. Ministério das Relações Exteriores. *A Política Exterior da Revolução Brasileira.* Rio de Janeiro, 1966.

———. ———. Discurso de Embaixador, Juracy Magalhães em Washington, 16 de Fevereiro de 1965. *Textos e Declarações sôbre Política Externa: Primeiro Aniversário de Revolução de 31 de Março de 1964.* 1965.

———. Secretaria de Imprensa. Humberto de Alencar Castello Branco, *Discursos 1964.*

———. ———. ———. *Discursos 1965.*

———. ———. ———. *Discursos 1966.*

International Monetary Fund. *IMF International Financial Statistics, Annual Supplement to 1967/1968.*

U. S. Congress. Senate. Committee on Foreign Relations. *Hearing Before the Committee on Foreign Relations on the Nomination of Lincoln Gordon to be Assistant Secretary for Inter-American Affairs.* 89th Congress, 2nd sess., February 7, 1966.

U. S. Department of the Army. *U. S. Army Area Handbook for Brazil,* Maday, B. C., *et al.* Washington, D.C., U.S. Government Printing Office, 1964.

———. United States Information Agency. *Latin American Attitudes Toward Social Reform.* R-212-65. Publicly released January 17, 1969.

United Nations. *Demographic Yearbook, 1966.*
————. *Economic Bulletin for Latin America.* "Fifteen Years of Economic Policy in Brazil," IX, no. 2 (November 1964).
————. UNESCO. *Statistical Yearbook.*

4. PERIODICALS

A Defesa Nacional
Air University Library Index to Military Periodicals (U.S.A.)
Agulhas Negras (official yearbook of military academy)
Army (U.S.A.)
Army Information Digest (U.S.A.)
Boletim da Associação Dos Diplomados da Escola Superior de Guerra
Boletim do Clube Naval
Cadernos Brasileiros
Cadernos do Nosso Tempo
Conjuntura Econômica
Dados
Ipês: Boletim Mensal
Manchete
Military Review (U.S.A.)
O Cruzeiro
Revista Brasileira de Estudos Políticos
Revista Civilização Brasileira
Revista de Aeronautica
Revista de Intendência do Exército Brasileiro
Revista do Clube Militar
Revista Militar Brasileira

5. NEWSPAPERS

A Tarde (Salvador)
Correio da Manhã (Rio)
Correio do Povo (Pôrto Alegre)
Diário Carioca (Rio) [stopped publishing, 1965]
Diário de Notícias (Rio)
Diário de Pernambuco (Recife)
Estado de Minas (Belo Horizonte)
Jornal do Brasil (Rio)
O Estado de São Paulo (São Paulo)
O Globo (Rio)
O Jornal (Rio)
Tribuna da Imprensa (Rio)
Última Hora (Rio and São Paulo)

Index

Academia Militar das Agulhas Negras, AMAN, 30-33, 36, 36, 50, 258; entrance exam and requirements, 32, 34, 37, 41-42; occupations of fathers of entering cadets, 32-33, 41-42

Ação Popular (student activists), 156

ADESG (ESG alumni group), 184

Agrarian Reform Institute, 236

air force, 26-27, 102, 106, 107, 119, 160, 161, 162. *See also* comparison of army, navy, and air force in Brazil

Albuquerque Lima, General Affonso Augusto de, 249, 260, 261, 264

Alessandri, President Arturo, 71

Alliance for Progress, 156, 269

ally relationship between U.S. and Brazil, 128, 129; Brazilian graduates of U.S. military academies, 130-131, 173, 239-241, 247-248, 250; fought together in World War II, 128, 242; Joint Brazil–United States Defense Commission, 129; U.S. advisory mission to ESG, 129-130. *See also* U.S. policies toward Brazil and Latin America

Almeida, General Reynaldo Mello de, 51

Almeida Herrera, General Heitor, 186, 223

Almond, Gabriel A., 135, 136, 137, 140

Alves, Márcio Moreira, 260

AMAN. *See Academia Militar das Agulhas Negras*, AMAN

amnesty for military coup leaders, 224-225

antimilitary school of analysis, 7-8, 10

apolitical military, 71, 73, 79, 210-212, 217

Aragão, General Moniz de, 207

Aranha, Oswaldo, 88

Aranha Plan (1953–1954), 144

Argentina, 27, 46-47, 62, 71, 73, 174, 224, 253

Arinos, Alfonso, 92

aristocratic model of civil–military relations, 10, 13, 14, 57-58, 59, 60, 61, 63

army, 102, 106, 107; structure of, 13-16, 17-19, 28-29, 37-40, 55. *See also* Comparison of Army, Navy, and Air Force in Brazil, Military institutional characteristics

army headquarters in Rio. *See Vila Militar*

Arraes, Miguel, 189, 192, 194

A Tarde, 100-101

authoritarianism, 18, 87, 232, 256, 258; clashes with middle class, 48; declining viability, 88, 222; growing isolation, 44; under military rule, 232, 249-252, 256, 258, 259. *See also Estado Nôvo*, military government

Baer, Werner, 142

Barbosa, Ruy, 77-78

Barcelona, 39

Barros, Adhemar de, 188, 200, 201, 219, 220

Bastos, General Justino Alves, 227

Batista, Fulgencio, 52

Bello, José Maria, 82

Bernardes, Arthur, 82

Bevilacqua, General Pery Constant, 118, 163, 227

Biafra civil war, 11

birthplace of army cadets, 37-40, 230

Bittencourt, General José Alberto, 251

Bolivia, 23, 253

boundaries on military coups before 1964, 115-121, 152, 168; distinction between intervention and rule, 115-116, 120-121, 168; low confidence in ruling ability of military, 120, 172, 186; low legitimacy of military to rule, 120, 172, 221-222; military confidence in civilian rule, 115-120, 168, 169, 172, 222; no purges of military after coup, 119-120, 222; perceived military working within constitution, 115, 118, 119, 120; traditional

297

boundaries *(cont.)*
restrictions on intervention, 115-
118, 120, 168, 169
Branco, General Castello, 94-95,
229-266; and Goulart regime, 157,
201, 204, 210; belief in civilian
rule, 120-121, 172, 231, 234-235,
254; friendships in U.S., 128;
government, 156, 164, 182, 183,
218, 219, 220, 225, 226, 228;
leader in 1964, 121; U.S. help
in 1964, 124
Brazil, General Assis, 191, 192,
205, 206, 209
Brasília, 162, 163
Brazilian Army Academy. *See
Academia Militar das Agulhas
Negras*, AMAN
Brazilian Communist Party, 193, 194
Brazilian Expeditionary Force in
Italy (FEB), 87, 117, 128, 174,
175, 217, 242, 250; and ESG,
245-247. *See also* elite analysis of
core group of officers of Branco
Brazilian military as agent of
national integration argument, 12-13,
20, 42-43. *See also* nation-building
potential of Brazilian army
Brazilian Military Academy. *See
Academia Militar das Agulhas
Negras*, AMAN
Brazilian Military regime. *See*
military government
Brazilian monarchy of 1822–1889,
25, 66, 76
Brazilian Naval Academy. *See
Escola Naval*
Brizola, Leonel: and Bevilacqua,
163; and Goulart, 19, 69, 194,
195, 216, 224; and sergeants,
160-162; denial of political rights,
170, 189; *grupos de onze*, 148, 156,
198; role in 1961 succession crisis,
19
Bulgaria, 136
bureaucratic norms in military, 48-51,
55, 81. *See also* military
institutional characteristics
Busch, Colonel Germán, 173

Cadets; high schools they attended,
41, 258; recruitment of, 41-42, 258;
self-assessment of economic status,
36-37; shortage of, 40-41, 258;
with military background, 40-41.
See also socioeconomic status of
officers

Café Filho, President João, 103, 117
Câmara, Sette, 261
Campos, Francisco, 88
Campos, Milton, 257
Campos, Roberto, 185, 218, 219,
233, 234, 235, 243, 244
Canavo Filho, Colonel José, 200
Canby, Steven, 50
Cárdenas, General Lázaro, 173
career soldiers in Brazil, 14, 42-44, 50
caretaker role of military, 56
Carneiro, Glauco, 85, 182
Carvalho, Murilo, 44
Casa Militar, 94
Cassados, 220
Castro, Fidel, 52, 73, 126, 156, 173
Catete, 104
Celebes, 12
censorship of newspapers, 100, 221, 261
Central Confederation of Labor, 203
Centro de Altos Estudios Militares
(CAEM), 174, 175
CGT (*Comando Geral dos Trabalhadores*), 196
Chile, 24, 25, 49, 55, 71, 74, 79, 144
China, 52
Church, 153, 212, 258-259, 260, 262
civilian anarchy, 22
civilian groups that solicit military
support, 67-79, 154, 188, 190;
antiregime civilians, 67, 72-73,
79, 80, 197; groups seeking
support of enlisted ranks, 159, 160-
161; proregime civilians, 67, 73-79,
80-81, 197; the government,
67-72, 79, 81, 192-193
civilian image of military, 42, 43-44,
80, 85, 219-221
civilian response to political
environment 1961–1964, 169-170.
See also crisis of 1961–1964
Civilian sanction for military
intervention, 93, 97, 98-99, 189;
nature of demands on military,
102-104, 105-107; sanction given,
86-92, 95, 96, 102-104, 108;
sanction withheld, 92-93, 96, 105,
106-107. *See also* editorials in
newspapers (1945–1964)
civil liberties, 48, 79
Civil–military relations. *See* models
of civil–military relations, moderator
pattern of civil–military relations
civil war in Brazil, threat of,
18-19. *See also* military coups
during 1945–1964

298

Clube Militar. See Military Club in
Rio de Janeiro
Colégio Militar, 258
Colombia, 253
combat experience of Latin
American armies, 51
communication channels between
civilians and the military,
94-95, 157, 176
Communist model of civil–military
relations, 57, 58-60
Communist rebellion in 1935, 73
comparison of army, navy, and
air force in Brazil, 26-27, 50, 230
comparison of classes in Brazil,
34-35, 48
comparison of U.S. and Brazilian
armies, 27-28, 49-51
conflict between political and military
leaders, 11, 12, 18-19, 57
Congress in Brazil, 74-75, 144;
demands of sergeants, 161, 162;
during military regime, 210, 251,
254, 256, 260, 261; Goulart's
demands, 91, 104, 151, 191, 193,
195-196; important to careers of
political leaders, 74-75; military
pressure on, 69-70, 74; party
fragmentation, 144-145; reforms,
74, 104, 144, 151, 161; support
from military, 201-202; Vargas
crisis 1945, 89-90. *See also*
president of Brazil
constitutions of Brazil, 73; constituent
assemblies, 75, 76-78; constitution
questioned by Goulart, 147, 199,
207; *dentro dos limites da leí*
clause, 76-77; *Estado Nôvo*
authoritarian constitution, 1937,
76; imperial constitution, 1824,
76; military links with drafters of
constitutions, 76-77; of Castello
Branco, 256, 261, 263; of 1891,
1934, and 1946, 75, 76-78, 91,
227; provisions for military in,
75-79, 102, 104, 105, 201-202,
207. *See also* political leadership
strategies and tactics in 1964
Correio da Manhã, 90, 100, 101,
105, 221, 258; backed Goulart
in 1961, 105, 107; nonideological,
101, 114; urged inauguration of
Kubitschek, 106; 1964 coup, 105,
107, 150, 221
Correio do Povo, 100-101
Costa, Coronel Octávio, 13

Costa e Silva, Arthur da. *See* Silva,
Arthur da Costa e
Costa Filho, Odylo, 100
Costeira, 183
counterinsurgency, 27, 173, 248.
See also civil war in Brazil, U.S.
policies toward Brazil and Latin
America
coups, 56, 64, 65, 79-80; against
a president-elect, 92, 105, 106-108;
civilian arming during coups,
148-149, 150; civil–military coup
coalition, 93-94, 96-97, 106-108,
115, 157, 176, 188, 190, 204, 219-
221, 226; debate essential to coup,
86, 87, 88, 96, 101-102, 117,
147-150; economic and political
strains add to breakdown, 132,
133; hypotheses of civil–military
relations, 80, 99; internal weakness
of regime, 132-133, 190; military's
self-interest in coup, 98, 105, 116;
newspaper and radio role, 90, 91,
94, 99; nonmilitary aspects of, 56,
148-149, 150; problem of avoiding
anarchy, 90-91; relate to constitution,
79, 100; successful military coups,
85, 86, 99, 109, 114; unsuccessful
coups, 85, 92, 99, 105, 106-107,
109, 114. *See also* legitimacy,
military coups 1945–1964, "Old
Republic," 1894–1930
crisis of 1961–1964, 153, 154, 163,
172, 188; and the ESG, 180, 183-187;
altered officer's self-image of
ruling ability and legitimacy, 172,
186; blame placed on labor unions,
141-142, 155, 163, 164; civilians
prepared for civil war, 148-149,
150, 200, 203; military agreed on
certain issues, 230; movement to
right, 154, 163-164; radical changes
were necessary in all systems,
154, 168; some wanted military
rule, 169-170, 211. *See also*
economic and political changes in
Brazil in 1961–1964
Cuba, 52, 60, 154, 155, 178
culture in which moderator model
develops, 62-64, 67
Cunha, Leitão da, 185

Dahl, Robert, 229, 253
Daland, Robert, 144, 161
Dantas–Furtado Plan, 1963, 144, 148
Dantas, San Tiago, 197
Davies, James C., 48

defensive coup plan, 1964, 190, 200
democratic Caesarism, 22
Denmark, 136
Denys, General Odílio, 119
Diário Carioca, 90, 100, 101, 197;
    nonideological, 101, 114; 1945
    coup, 102
Diário de Notícias, 100, 101, 107;
    nonideological, 101, 114; no support
    for military in 1967, 107; 1954
    coup, 103; 1964 coup, 104, 199, 221
Diário de Pernambuco, 150
dictatorships, 172-173, 216, 259, 260
Dines, Alberto, 100, 178, 261
dispositivo militar, 191-192, 208
divisions in army, 27-28
Documento LEEX, 1964, 141-142,
    157
Dominican Republic, 25, 232
drafting of men, 15-17
Dulles, John W. F., 87
Dutra, General Eurico, 117, 176

ECEME. *See Escola de Comando e
    Estado Maior do Exército*
economic and political changes in
    Brazil, 1961–1964, 132, 134-135,
    172, 188; balance of payments,
    142, 143-144, 196; decreasing
    extractive capability, 135, 138-143;
    high urbanization, 136, 149;
    inability of government to deal
    with demands, 132, 134, 135,
    143-147, 152; increased electorate,
    138; increased government
    expenditure, 139-140; increased
    mobilization of armed forces, 148;
    increasing demands on government,
    135-138, 143; inflation, 132,
    137, 140-141, 143-144; politicization
    of military, 132, 154-155;
    population growth, 136, 149;
    rapid social mobilization, 134,
    135-138; reinforcement by U.S.
    policy, 132, 143; slowing economy,
    132, 135, 136, 139-140, 141, 142;
    tax receipts declined, 139-140;
    withdrawal of commitment to
    government, 135, 143, 147-152
Ecuador, 253
editorials in newspapers, 1945–1964,
    99-108, 110-113, 150, 201; debate
    before coups, 101-102; tone of
    debate, 102, 150; 1964 differed
    from other coups, 150. *See also*
    measure of legitimacy, newspapers
    in Brazil

education in Brazil, 34, 35-37, 40,
    252. *See also* socioeconomic status
    of officers
education level in Brazilian army,
    15-17, 32, 34, 158
effect of Cuban revolution on
    civilian left, 155-156, 157
Egypt, 53
Einaudi, Luigi, 30, 51, 79, 128, 247,
    259, 269, 271
Eisenhower, Dwight D., 51
elections in Brazil, 81-85, 88, 102,
    138, 151, 188, 195; election in
    1965, 188-189, 198-199, 200, 210,
    211, 217-218, 254, 255; election
    laws set up under military regime,
    227, 255, 256, 257
elite analysis of core group of
    Branco's officers 237-248, 254;
    career patterns of core group,
    236, 238-239, 247; ESG experience,
    239-241, 245-247; FEB experience,
    239-244; significance of analysis,
    239-248; U.S. school experience,
    239-241, 247-248. *See also* policy
    in Branco's government
elites' political behavior, 42-51,
    52-53
El Salvador, 24, 25
EsAO. *See Escola de Aperfeiçoamento
    de Oficiais*
*Escola de Aperfeiçoamento de
    Oficiais* (EsAO), 50
*Escola de Comando e Estado Maior
    do Exército* (ECEME), 30-31,
    50-51, 95, 181, 243
Escola de Sargentos das Armas, 159
Escola Naval, 16
Escola Superior de Guerra (ESG),
    44, 51, 94, 120, 129, 130, 155,
    176-178, 180, 182, 225, 236, 264,
    267; anti-Communist, 179,
    185, 186, 231-232; belief in private
    sector, 246, 248; civilian
    participation, 175-176, 177, 186,
    246; ESG–FEB, 245-247; ESG–IPÊS,
    186; formation of, 129, 174-178;
    functions of, 175, 176, 178, 184;
    graduates of, 177, 184, 211;
    important staff members, 184-185,
    218, 239, 240-241, 245-247, 250;
    interrelationship of security and
    development doctrine, 178-183,
    184, 186, 217, 227; officers
    opinions of, 185, 245-247, 264;
    national security doctrine, 178-180,
    184-186; policies suggested by ESG,

181, 184, 217, 218, 245; role of
ESG in military government, 186,
210-211, 217, 223, 226, 236,
239, 240-241, 245-247, 248;
strong central government, 182, 184
Escuela Nacional de Guerra, 174
ESG. *See Escola Superior de Guerra*
Espírito, Santo, 201
Estado de Minas, 100-101
Estado Novo, 68, 87-89, 100, 221
Events of March 1964, 188,
189, 190; all components for
breakdown existed, 188-190;
civilians and military expected
violence, 200, 203-204; March
13 rally, 191-192, 195-204;
naval mutiny, March 26, 204-209

Fábrica Nacional de Motores, 233
factor analysis for military, 21, 28
factors affecting upper-class
representation in army, 40
Factors which inhibited military
rule until 1964, 188-190; election
slated for 1965, 188-189, 198,
199, 200; fear of civil war, 204;
military divided on Goulart,
189, 192, 198-199, 204
Farias, General Oswaldo Cordeiro
de, 97-98, 174, 244, 245, 247;
and ESG, 185; and 1961 crisis, 19;
resignation of Vargas, 117;
tenentes revolt, 82, 98, 117;
U.S. National War College, 175;
1950 military club election, 44
Fascist (*Integralista*) uprising, 73, 87
FEB. *See* Brazilian Expeditionary
Force in Italy
federal army, 18-19; local base of
national army, 13-15, 18-19, 27-28
Ferreira, Oliveiros, 149, 170, 251
Fico, General Nicolau, 162, 206
Fifth Army, 142
Fifth Institutional Act, 1968,
216, 260, 261, 263
Figueiredo, Euclides, 19
Figueiredo, General Edson de, 242
Figueiredo, General Poppe de, 228
Figueiredo, Wilson, 100
Finer, S. E., 14
First Army, 27, 39-40, 70, 249
First Institutional Act, 123, 168,
210, 218, 235
Fleet, Michael, 153, 259
Fôlha de Minas, 100
Fonseca, Deodoro da, 76, 77

Fôrça Expedicionária Brasileira.
See Brazilian Expeditionary Force
in Italy
Fôrça Pública. See São Paulo
state militia
Fourth Army, 227
France, 40, 136, 217
Frente Patriótica Civil–Militar,
170, 251

Garrastazú Medice, General Emilio.
See Medice, General Emilio
Garrastazú
Geisel, General Ernesto, 185
General Confederation of Workers,
203
General Labor Command (CGT), 163
General Staff School, army. *See*
Escola de Comando e Estado
Maior do Exército
Germany, 61, 87, 136
Ghana, 15, 22
Girardet, Raoul, 173
goals of Brazilian military, 42-43
Góes Monteiro, General, 77, 87, 95
Goiás, 220
Golbery do Couto e Silva, General:
and ESG, 185, 186, 218, 247; and
FEB, 243; and revolution of 1964,
97, 189; interest in revolutionary
warfare, 130, 131, 156, 159, 179,
180, 181-183
Gomes, Brigadier Eduardo, 117
Gorden, Lincoln, 124-126, 143
Goulart, João, 68, 86, 92, 93, 101;
and ESG, 184, 186; assumption
of presidency, 19, 45, 69, 96, 101,
105, 107-108, 160; attempt to
bypass norms, 55, 70-71, 104;
denial of political rights, 170;
overthrown in 1964, 28, 45, 47, 69,
91-92, 97-98, 104-105, 108, 124,
125, 169, 188, 189, 216, 221;
plebiscite, 69-70, 151, 192; use of
military in crisis, 69-70, 71; U.S.
involvement in overthrow, 124-125,
131, 143
Goulart's regime, 1961–1964, 157,
183, 223, 228, 230; and sergeants,
165; end of, 28, 45, 47, 69, 91-92, 97,
98, 104-105, 108, 124, 125, 188-212;
military promotion system, 155,
165-167; rally of March 13, 1964,
191-192, 195-204
Goulart's strategies and tactics in
1964, 191, 209; and Congress, 104,
191, 193, 195-196, 201, 205; and

Goulart's strategies (*cont.*)
supporters, 93, 105, 107-108, 165-168, 190, 192-193, 196, 197, 198-201, 204, 205, 207-208, 209, 223; and the constitution, 195, 196, 199, 201; and use of the left-wing activists, 193-194, 195, 205; effect of tactics, 196-204; mobilizing the masses, 191-193, 195, 196, 197, 198, 201, 203, 205; needed army support, 192-193, 196; overestimated political strength, 196-197, 208; plebiscite issue, 69-70, 151, 192, 193, 195; pushed reforms, 191-193, 195-196, 205; rally of March 13, 191-192, 195-204
Great Britain, 74, 136
Grupos de onze, 148, 156
Guanabara, 38, 39, 71
Guanabara State Militia, 17
Guatemala, 49-50, 73
Guedes, General Carlos Luiz, 157, 158, 200, 206, 207
Gutteridge, William F., 15, 22

Halpern, Manfred, 41
Harding, Timothy, 209
Harvey, Colonel William W., 175
Heck, Sylvio, 251
Hitler, Adolf, 167
Honduras, 79
Huntington, Samuel, 58-60, 61, 62
Hypotheses of civil–military relations, 80, 99; hypothesis of success of coups and legitimacy of executive and military, 80, 84, 85, 101, 108, 109-115; hypothesis of military intervention and cohesion in political strata, 80, 81, 83-84

Ibáñez, Colonel Carlos, 173
ideological development during 1961–1964, 147-150, 151-152, 155, 170-171, 188, 209, 210-212, 231, 234-235
ideology in military institution, 56, 106; agreement on self-preservation, 206, 236, 261, 262, 264; corporate consciousness of military, 41, 42, 50; diversity of ideology, 157, 188; effect of naval mutiny, 206, 207, 208; effect of 1961 coup attempt, 189; ideology of ESG, 177-183; issues which have divided officers, 131; military seldom united group, 27-28, 29, 41, 44-45, 67, 76-77, 81, 82, 92; moderator to director

role, 134, 207, 210, 214, 221; sustained unity in military rule, 222-224, 226, 228, 229-230, 236, 261, 262, 264; unity affected by internal diversity, 67, 131, 156, 160, 189, 235-236, 253-254, 262; unity hurt by external pressures, 67, 92, 257-259, 260, 262, 263; unity important in crisis, 45, 81, 97, 217, 221. *See also* institutional fears within military, 1961–1964
illiteracy in Brazil, 34-36. *See also* education in Brazil
Imaz, José Luis de, 30
imbalance in Brazilian army, 13; educational, 15-17, 34, 35-36; occupational, 31-33; regional, 13-15, 17, 37-40
importance of military institution to middle class, 45-48
India, 136, 268
Indochina, 179
Indonesia, 12, 120, 174
Industrial College of the Armed Forces, 175
industrialized areas of Brazil, 37-39
industry in Brazil, 37-39, 40, 42, 258
instability in government, 22, 23, 68, 86, 89, 91-92, 253
institutional fears within military 1961–1964, 141, 153-171, 188, 189, 204; and Goulart, 155, 165-168, 190, 206, 208; breakdown of hierarchy, 155, 158, 165, 168, 182, 208; destruction by some group, 155, 156, 157, 164; due to politicization of military, 154-155, 165; effect on sons of military officers, 167-168; fears prevented return to civilian rule in 1964, 210; hostility to mobilization policies, 154, 156, 163, 164, 182; political use of promotion structure, 155, 165-167; radical left and Communist subversion, 155-156, 157-158; replacement by popular militia, 155, 157, 158, 164; sergeant activism, 158, 161-162, 163, 164; that civilian rule was inadequate, 155, 168, 222; trade-union movement, 155, 161, 164; weakened military discipline, 154-155, 157, 163, 165, 190, 206, 208
Instituto Brasileiro de Acão Democrática (IBAD), 154

moderator pattern *(cont.)*
countries, 79, 267-269, 270. *See
also* boundaries to military coups
before 1964, ideological development
during 1961-1964

moderator role of military, 74, 75,
79, 85-93, 134, 154, 221, 259,
265-266; as stated in constitution,
75-78, 102-105, 201-202, 203;
given by civilians, 73-79, 80, 154,
192-193; rejection 1964, 162, 166,
188, 207, 259; right to refuse to
obey the president, 74-79, 102,
105, 201-202, 204, 206, 207;
self-limiting, 115-120, 172. *See also*
institutional fears within military
1961-1964, moderator pattern of
civil-military relations

Monteiro, General Góes. *See* Góes
Monteiro, General

Monteiro, Silvestre Pericles de Góis,
77

Morel, Edmar, 124

Mosca, Gaetano, 58

Mourão Filho, General Olímpio,
199, 200, 207, 226

Movimento de Educacão de Base,
153, 214

Muricy, General Antônio Carlos da
Silva, 198, 228

Mussolini, Benito, 244

Napoleonic French Revolution, 55

Nasser, Colonel, 53

National Conference of Brazilian
Bishops (CNBB), 258

National Intelligence Service (SNI),
249

National Security Council, 94,
169, 174, 249

National Security Laws, 227-228

National Steel Company, 94

nation-building potential of Brazilian
army, 15-17, 20, 42-43, 63; affected
by regionalism problem, 13-15,
17-19, 27-28, 72

naval mutiny, 1964, 98, 105, 204-209

navy in Brazil, 26-27, 102, 106,
107, 119, 161, 162. *See also*
comparison of army, navy and air
force in Brazil

newspapers in Brazil, 18-19, 100-101,
262; as communication channels,
90-91, 94, 96, 99-115; ideology of
papers, 101-104, 114; periods of
censorship of, 100, 221, 261

Nigeria, 10-11, 15, 22, 120

North, R. C., 52

Northeast region. *See* SUDENE

Nun, José, 30, 45-46

O Estado de São Paulo, 101, 113,
115-116, 169, 200, 211, 221, 235;
conservative, 101; demanded
intervention in 1954, 103; foe of
Vargas, 103; under government
control until 1945, 103; urged coup
of 1955, 106

Obino, General Cesar, 174

Odría, Manuel, 155

officers in military, 11, 26, 28, 29,
31-32, 40-41, 49-50. *See also*
elite analysis of core group of
Branco's officers, socioeconomic
status of officers

officers with military background, 32,
33, 34, 39-42, 167-168

O Globo, 101, 113, 235; conservative,
101; restrictions on military in
1954, 116; 1964 coup, 104-105,
116, 221

O Jornal, 101; nonideological, 101,
114; urged inauguration of
Kubitschek, 107; 1945 coup, 102;
1964 coup, 202, 221

"Old Republic," 18-19, 81; election
of 1910, 81-84; coup of 1930,
72, 82, 123, 150, 225; first
constitution of, 77-78; military
involvement, 71, 81-84; splits in
participant political strata,
81-82, 83

Onitsha, 11

"operation presence," 27-28

Osasco, 28

Paiva, Glycon de, 154, 185

Pakistan, 12, 41

Paraguay, 27

Paris, 100

Parsons, Talcott, 51

Partido Republicano, 83. *See also*
"Old Republic"

Patton, General, 51

Pauker, Guy, 9, 12, 174, 213

Paulistas, 19

Paz Estenssoro, Victor, 23

peasant leagues, 137-138, 147, 153,
156, 214, 233, 235, 251, 263, 270

Peçanha, Nilo, 82

Pellacani, Dante, 170

Pena, Afonso, 81

Peralva, Oswaldo, 100

Pérez Jiménez, General, 155

Selected RAND Books

Arrow, Kenneth J., and Marvin Hoffenberg. A TIME SERIES ANALYSIS OF INTERINDUSTRY DEMANDS. North-Holland Publishing Company, Amsterdam, Holland, 1959.

Bellman, Richard E. DYNAMIC PROGRAMMING. Princeton University Press, Princeton, New Jersey, 1957.

Brodie, Bernard. STRATEGY IN THE MISSILE AGE. Princeton University Press, Princeton, New Jersey, 1959.

Dantzig, George B. LINEAR PROGRAMMING AND EXTENSIONS. Princeton University Press, Princeton, New Jersey, 1963.

Dole, Stephen H. HABITABLE PLANETS FOR MAN. (Reprint), American Elsevier Publishing Company, New York, 1970.

Dorfman, Robert, Paul A. Samuelson, and Robert M. Solow. LINEAR PROGRAMMING AND ECONOMIC ANALYSIS. McGraw-Hill Book Company, Inc., New York, 1958.

Downs, Anthony. INSIDE BUREAUCRACY. Little, Brown and Company, Boston, Massachusetts, 1967.

Fisher, Gene H. COST CONSIDERATIONS IN SYSTEMS ANALYSIS. American Elsevier Publishing Company, New York, 1970.

George, Alexander L. PROPAGANDA ANALYSIS: A STUDY OF INFERENCES MADE FROM NAZI PROPAGANDA IN WORLD WAR II. Row, Peterson and Company, Evanston, Illinois, 1959.

Goldhamer, Herbert, and Andrew W. Marshall. PSYCHOSIS AND CIVILIZATION. The Free Press, Glencoe, Illinois, 1953.

Gurtov, Melvin. SOUTHEAST ASIA TOMORROW: PROBLEMS AND PROSPECTS FOR U.S. POLICY. Johns Hopkins Press, Baltimore, Maryland, 1970.

Halpern, Manfred. THE POLITICS OF SOCIAL CHANGE IN THE MIDDLE EAST AND NORTH AFRICA. Princeton University Press, Princeton, New Jersey, 1963.

Hearle, Edward F. R., and Raymond J. Mason. A DATA PROCESSING SYSTEM FOR STATE AND LOCAL GOVERNMENTS. Prentice-Hall, Inc., Englewood Cliffs, New Jersey, 1963.

Hitch, Charles J., and Roland McKean. THE ECONOMICS OF DEFENSE IN THE NUCLEAR AGE. Harvard University Press, Cambridge, Massachusetts, 1960.

Johnson, John J. (ed.). THE ROLE OF THE MILITARY IN UN-DERDEVELOPED COUNTRIES. Princeton University Press, Princeton, New Jersey, 1962.

Johnstone, William C. BURMA'S FOREIGN POLICY: A STUDY IN NEUTRALISM. Harvard University Press, Cambridge, Massachusetts, 1963.

Kolkowicz, Roman. THE SOVIET MILITARY AND THE COMMUNIST PARTY. Princeton University Press, Princeton, New Jersey, 1967.

Leites, Nathan. ON THE GAME OF POLITICS IN FRANCE. Stanford University Press, Stanford, California, 1959.

Leites, Nathan, and Charles Wolf, Jr. REBELLION AND AUTHORITY. Markham Publishing Company, Chicago, Illinois, 1970.

McKean, Roland N. EFFICIENCY IN GOVERNMENT THROUGH SYSTEMS ANALYSIS: WITH EMPHASIS ON WATER RESOURCE DEVELOPMENT. John Wiley & Sons, 1958.

McKinsey, J.C.C. INTRODUCTION TO THE THEORY OF GAMES. McGraw-Hill Book Company, Inc., New York, 1952.

Mead, Margaret. SOVIET ATTITUDES TOWARD AUTHORITY: AN INTERDISCIPLINARY APPROACH TO PROBLEMS OF SOVIET CHARACTER. McGraw-Hill Book Company, Inc., New York, 1951.

Meyer, John R., Martin Wohl, and John F. Kain. THE URBAN TRANSPORTATION PROBLEM. Harvard University Press, Cambridge, Massachusetts, 1965.

Nelson, Richard R., Merton J. Peck, and Edward J. Kalachek. TECHNOLOGY ECONOMIC GROWTH AND PUBLIC POLICY. The Brookings Institution, Washington, D.C., 1967.

Nelson, Richard R., T. Paul Schultz, and Robert L. Slighton. STRUCTURAL CHANGE IN A DEVELOPING ECONOMY. Princeton University Press, Princeton, New Jersey, 1971.

Pascal, Anthony. THINKING ABOUT CITIES: NEW PERSPECTIVES ON URBAN PROBLEMS. Dickenson Publishing Company, Belmont, California, 1970.

Quade, Edward S., and Walter I. Boucher. SYSTEMS ANALYSIS AND POLICY PLANNING: APPLICATIONS IN DEFENSE. American Elsevier Publishing Company, New York, 1968.

Rosen, George. DEMOCRACY AND ECONOMIC CHANGE IN INDIA. University of California Press, Berkeley and Los Angeles, California, 1966.

Sharpe, William F. THE ECONOMICS OF COMPUTERS. Columbia University Press, New York, 1969.

312

Smith, Bruce L., and Chitra M. Smith. INTERNATIONAL COMMU-
NICATION AND POLITICAL OPINION: A GUIDE TO THE
LITERATURE. Princeton University Press, Princeton, New Jersey,
1956.

The RAND Corporation. A MILLION RANDOM DIGITS WITH
100,000 NORMAL DEVIATES. The Free Press, Glencoe, Illinois,
1955.

Williams, J. D. THE COMPLEAT STRATEGYST: BEING A PRIM-
ER ON THE THEORY OF GAMES OF STRATEGY. McGraw-
Hill Book Company, Inc., New York, 1954.

Wolf, Charles, Jr. FOREIGN AID: THEORY AND PRACTICE IN
SOUTHERN ASIA. Princeton University Press, Princeton, New
Jersey, 1960.